Pillars of Prosperity

FREE MARKETS, HONEST MONEY, PRIVATE PROPERTY

Pillars of Prosperity

FREE MARKETS, HONEST MONEY, PRIVATE PROPERTY

RON PAUL

PREFACE BY ROBERT P. MURPHY
FOREWORD BY LLEWELLYN H. ROCKWELL, JR.

Ludwig
von Mises
Institute

AUBURN, ALABAMA

Copyright 2008 © by the Ludwig von Mises Institute

ISBN: 978-1-933550-24-4

Contents

Preface

Ron Paul is an amazing individual. Not only has he been the most consistent voice for liberty in the U.S. Congress in our time — perhaps in *all* time — but he is also surprisingly well versed in economic theory. Indeed, if I were to dissect one of his speeches or articles, I would have to treat him as I would a fellow economist, not as "a politician."

On top of all that, Ron Paul is a successful OB-GYN, who delivered over 4,000 babies during his career. This is why I'm so amazed at his nuanced understanding of economics. Let me put it this way: Ron Paul knows a lot more about current account deficits than I do about giving a sonogram.

We economists talk a lot about the division of labor, and moreover we *libertarians* often invoke the concept to stir everyone to action. Sure, it's important for the great thinkers like Ludwig von Mises and Murray Rothbard to come up with the grand ideas, but it's also crucial for parents to teach their kids the virtue in hard work, and for crotchety old men to write nasty Letters to the Editor whenever the city council is considering a hike in property taxes.

Now in the division of labor in the battle of ideas, is there a place for someone in the U.S. *Congress*?! I have to admit I wouldn't have thought so had you asked me five years ago. But even the purest of libertarians can't deny that the Ron Paul movement is exciting, and is bringing the message of liberty to people who otherwise wouldn't have heard it.

The present collection seeks to give the reader a solid understanding of Ron Paul's views on various economic issues. The core
of the book concerns Dr. Paul's strong support for honest money.
(It was, after all, Nixon's closing of the gold window that
prompted Dr. Paul to run for office in the first place.) There are
also entire sections on trade, international organizations such as
the IMF and WTO, and a section outlining Dr. Paul's attempts to
protect Social Security from the big spenders in D.C. The collection
also includes a selection of specific tax cuts Dr. Paul has suggested,
which shows that — despite his nickname of "Dr. No" — Ron Paul is
a real congressman, who brings real bills to the floor for consideration.

Most of the selections are straight testimony from Dr. Paul,
though a few transcripts of actual floor debate have been included
to give the reader a feel for the deliberative body of which Paul is
a member. There are numerous exchanges between Ron Paul and
Alan Greenspan, as well as an encounter with George Soros that
somehow turns to drug legalization. And perhaps the most surreal
event is the duel between Ron Paul and Nancy Pelosi (over the
constitutionality of the Export-Import Bank).

Besides the eloquence and wisdom of his remarks, the reader
will also be struck by Ron Paul's *consistency* over the decades. This
makes perfect sense for someone who actually holds principles
and makes speeches accordingly. But as we all know, this is rare
indeed for a politician. As an experiment, I had toyed with the idea
of combing through, say, Charles Rangel's Congressional testimony in five-year increments, to see if he were as consistent (in his
own way) as Ron Paul. I quickly abandoned the plan, however,
when I realized it would involve reading Charles Rangel's Congressional testimony in five-year increments.

Unfortunately, the consistency of the speeches contained in this
book is also somewhat depressing. For example, now it's down-
right cute that Ron Paul (in 1982) was aghast that the federal debt
had topped $1.1 trillion. It would be one thing if no one saw our
current financial mess coming, but plenty of people — especially
Ron Paul — did.

On the other hand, we can take this as a sign of hope. The
details are always shifting, but the basic problem remains the
same: Too much government interference with markets in general,

and money in particular. And the solution is the same: A truly free market in which the citizens' property rights are respected by their so-called public servants.

Robert P. Murphy
Adjunct Scholar
Ludwig von Mises Institute
September 30, 2007

Foreword

Congressman Ron Paul has been working for decades to bring economics to the forefront of political life. In doing so, he has raised topics that nearly everyone else in public life wants buried.

But isn't economics a dull topic, interesting only to Wall Street traders and government bureaucrats? Isn't it just about math and graphs?

Not in Ron Paul's view. He has an intensity of passion for the discipline of economics that follows up on what Ludwig von Mises believed. Economics is the pith of material life. It is the core body of knowledge that seeks an explanation for all material phenomena as they are affected by human choice. Economics is as unavoidable in politics as gravity is in the natural world. It is a ubiquitous reality whether we speak about it openly or not.

Therefore everyone should be interested in economics. The choice we make about our economic system will determine whether we rise or fall as a people, whether our families will thrive or die, and whether the future itself has a future.

The cause-and-effect relationship between bad policy and bad economic outcomes, however, is not always obvious. We need teachers and public intellectuals to point out the connections between the money supply and inflation, between regulations and slow growth, between protectionism and lowered living standards, between public ownership and the decline of innovation.

The relationship is most clearly spelled out in the Austrian tradition represented by Carl Menger, Eugen von Böhm-Bawerk, Ludwig von Mises, F.A. Hayek, Henry Hazlitt, Hans Sennholz, and Murray Rothbard, for here we have a body of economic logic that refines and improves classical doctrines to permit us to understand cause and effect in economic life. Dr. Paul has read these authors in detail, and learned from them. He has gone further, in a pioneering way, to apply them to political life. In so doing, he has earned for himself a high place in the annals of history.

There are easier roads to political success than using every opportunity to speak on economic issues. Why did he choose this path? Not merely to spread knowledge for its own sake. He believes that public awareness and knowledge is the key to establishing and keeping freedom, which is the basis of civilization itself. Without a deep and abiding love of freedom in all spheres of life, the government can ravage the human population. But for a people who love liberty, no power is strong enough to finally take away the right to pursue happiness.

Others who came before Dr. Paul in this respect are people like Cobden and Bright in England, Frédéric Bastiat in France, and Thomas Jefferson in America. All of them spoke the great unspeakable truth that there are forces operating in the world more powerful than the whims of the political class. Every effort at centralized planning, and every attempt to legislate political dreams, bumps up against economic law. Economics is the great brick wall, a thousand feet thick, that limits the maniacal dreams, benevolent or malevolent, of the political imagination. We ignore these economic forces at our peril.

In Dr. Paul's view, if we seriously paid attention to the teaching of economics, and the population understood those truths, the central bank would be closed, the bureaucracies would be shut down, taxes would be repealed, spending programs would be abolished, and regulations would be stripped from the books—for all these efforts to manage society not only fail to achieve their stated objectives; they also reduce our living standard and artificially restrict the scope of freedom in our lives.

So there is a reason why politicians ignore the problem of economics, and why they prefer to characterize it as a narrow field dominated by number crunchers who care only tangentially about issues that impact the rest of society. Instead, officials speak vagaries about leading the country into the future and meeting human needs because this sort of language empowers the political class.

I have no doubt that the contents of this book will make even some of his supporters uncomfortable. The right imagines that it supports free enterprise, but even in the area of trade and money? Even to the point at which the state is denied permission to undertake tasks such as imposing sanctions on unfriendly foreign regimes? The left might like his antiwar positions, but what if giving up war mongering also requires rethinking the merit of the redistributionist welfare state?

Dr. Paul writes that freedom is all of a piece. You can't pick and choose. Moreover, it is impossible to speak of the future or of human needs without trusting economic freedom and disempowering the state to intervene in every area of life. Without sound money, there is no protection for savings and property, nor capital accumulation, nor long-term investment, nor entrepreneurship, nor social advance. Without the right to own and control property, we have no real say over our lives. Without the freedom to make contracts, to take risks, and to live in whatever peaceful way we choose, there is no hope for the future.

A state strong enough to redistribute wealth at a whim will not hesitate to wage war, impose sanctions, take away privacy, and violate core human rights. A state strong enough to wage war will not think twice about redistributing wealth and running a cradle-to-grave welfare state. These are truths that the right and left need to deal with. Nor are half-way measures a permanent fix. Real Social Security reform returns the financial responsibility for old age to the institutions of a voluntary society. Real reform in foreign policy means eliminating all restrictions on trade.

We have to consider the courage it takes to speak this way in times when the common belief is that the government can and should do all things. Ron Paul dares to ask us to rethink the way the world works, to have confidence in the ability of society — meaning the millions of individuals of which it is constituted — to manage itself. He is uncompromising not because he is inflexible or unthoughtful, but because he has vision and faith to see the unseen benefits of freedom and to ask us to do the same.

In this volume are collected the wise statements from the nation's leading teacher of free-market economic principles. One is struck by his consistency and willingness to state the truth, even when it is unpopular to do so. He is right to believe that the most important step in this struggle is to state the truth, openly and without fear.

In many ways, these speeches and essays amount to a chronicle of incredible failure: for the state has failed in a million ways to protect and defend our material well-being, and its very attempt has come at great cost.

But it is also a chronicle of hope that if we are willing to listen and learn, we can choose a different future for ourselves, one that removes responsibility for economic well-being from the government and gives it back to those to whom it belongs: the people in their capacity as living, choosing, creative human beings. Now that is leadership, properly construed.

Llewellyn H. Rockwell, Jr.
Ludwig von Mises Institute
December 2007

PART ONE

The Economics
of a Free Society

These selections lay out my views of the proper role of government, namely that it should serve only to protect the life and property of its citizens. I respect the Constitution not because of a nostalgic attachment to an anachronistic document, but because the Founders knew the danger in allowing government to overstep its legitimate functions. It is unfortunate that many Americans today don't understand the Founders' wisdom in framing our government on the principles of federalism and republicanism – as opposed to "democracy." A free society can only work when its members agree that there are certain things left to the discretion of individuals – no matter what a temporary majority might think. In practice this means the government must respect private property and the rule of law, or what is also called free market capitalism.

Current Political Philosophies' Errors to Result in Political and Economic Crisis

Congressional Record – U.S. House of Representatives
September 20, 1984

Mr. Speaker, I have a deep concern for the direction in which our country is going. I have expressed this concern by pointing out the political and economic contradictions that surround us and have suggested that these contradictions merely are manifestations of philosophic errors made by our intellectual leaders.

Although the country currently is more or less in a euphoric mood, I am convinced the errors we are making today will eventually result in a severe political and economic crisis.

I don't believe anyone precisely knows the future, yet we all make projections as to our expectations. It's impossible to know exact events and their timing but trends are known to us and certain policies do have specific consequences. Economically definable laws do exist and cannot be repealed. For what it's worth, I would like to make a few comments about what we can expect if our current beliefs about governmentment's role are not changed. The odds of a significant change in attitude occurring in Washington in the near future are utterly remote. Repealing the welfare-warfare state may be popular with a growing number of frustrated American citizens, but that attitude is not yet reflected in Washington. The constituency for the monolithic state is alive and well in the U.S. Congress. When disagreement exists in areas such as welfare versus warfare, the poor versus the rich, labor versus business, compromise is always reached and both sides receive an increase in funding. This is a policy of utter folly and is tragically locked in place.

Government is literally out of control. Spending, taxes, regulations, monetary inflation, invasion of our privacy, welfarism to both the rich and the poor, military spending, and foreign adventurism around the world will one day precipitate a crisis that will truly test our will to live in a free society. If government were not so much out of control, would not the most conservative President of the last 50 years be able to do something about the runaway deficits? The deficits have tragically only gotten very much worse under Reagan. All the problems we face, high interest rates, inflation, deficits, vicious business cycles with accelerating unemployment are serious problems indeed, but the real threat under the conditions to come will be the potential loss of our personal liberty. Without liberty, prosperity is lost and equality of poverty prevails.

We have a cancer in the land—the malignant growth of big government—and we can ignore it, treating only the symptoms, hoping they are not reliable signs that a horrible disease has struck our nation. But if we do, we are treating our problems as some foolishly deny the early signs of cancer, by taking aspirin and hoping the pain to be only that of inconvenience and that the symptoms will go away in the morning. Instead, the pain gets worse requiring more and more narcotics to numb the pain. Magic cures are sought and tried. Although big government is the disease, attempts to solve all the problems by making government even bigger and more intrusive in our lives are continually tried. This will soon end. We cannot forever ignore the root causes. It's highly unlikely that we'll reach the 1990s without a convulsion of our economic or political system.

Although nothing goes up or down in a straight line, we can be sure the long term will bring us ever-increasing interest rates— higher with each cycle and over 20 percent before this cycle completes itself in 1986 or 1987. Without the introduction of a commodity money, one with quality—as well as limitation on its quantity—we will never see the return of long-term fixed low interest rates. The reform will come eventually, if we're to continue to have even a relatively free society. I just hope we don't wait too long.

Price inflation, although difficult to predict on a month-to-month or even year-to-year basis, will reach unbelievable heights in this decade. Currency destruction, through the insatiable desire to create massive new fiat monetary units, eventually brings higher prices. Wage and price controls will return regardless of whether a Republican or a Democrat occupies the White House. Free market rhetoric will do nothing to protect us from the pressure the administration will receive to "do something," even if it's the wrong thing. Nixonian Keynesianism will continue to dominate, and abusive people-control in the form of wage, price, currency and credit controls will return, more vicious than ever before.

There will come a day that the world financiers will rush from dollars just as they have recently rushed into dollars, causing even worse chaos in the international financial markets. Without a stable monetary unit, the speculation will continue and worsen. Overreaction is now becoming more commonplace, but this is a predictable consequence of a world gone mad with fiat currencies, debt creation, and overspending.

Massive debt liquidation will come. The early stages have already started. It will occur with old-fashioned defaults, threats of deflation, and further currency destruction through monetary inflation and liquidation of debt with a depreciating dollar. Whether or not the liquidating debt collapse will be dominated by deflation or inflation of the money supply is yet to be determined since that will depend on government actions and many market forces. An inflationary collapse is a more likely scenario — knowing the special interests, the Congress, the administration, and the central bankers' unwillingness to face up to the reality of cutting spending, balancing the budget, and curtailing the supply of money. So in spite of all the tough talk, we can expect the Fed to accommodate and reverse any trend toward deflation.

Without a significant change in attitude by the American people and Congress as to the purpose of government, the choices are horrible; an inflationary collapse or a deflationary one. The form and timing of the collapse is yet to be determined; the event itself is certain. This crisis will come, as others have, because we refuse to face up to reality and live within our means.

The people's insatiable appetite for the goods of life without providing a commensurate amount of work and effort needed to produce them (while demanding that politicians deliver the loot) guarantees the process will continue. But a penalty will have to be paid. That penalty—a major banking, currency, economic, and political crisis—will hit this nation and the western world, most likely before the 1990s.

The economic hardship, of which we had a taste in 1981 and 1982, will be much worse. That in itself is bad enough news, but historically, when a nation debauches its currency international trade breaks down—today 40 percent of international trade is carried out through barter—protectionist sentiments rise—as they have in Congress already—eliciting hostile feelings with our friends. Free trade alliances break down, breeding strong feelings of nationalism—all conditions that traditionally lead to war; a likely scenario for the 1990s, unless our economic policies and attitudes regarding government are quickly changed.

Many who concede we are moving in this direction of war, carelessly believe that the lack of military spending is the problem and insist on new massive military spending as the solution. This only serves the inflationists, the internationalists, the banking elite, and industrialists who benefit from the massive manufacture of military weapons. It ignores the important fact that most military conflicts throughout history have been the consequence of economic events. Economic events, when combined with a foreign policy void of wisdom and fraught with folly, sets the stage for needless war.

Conservatives are quick to correctly point out that guns don't cause crime, criminals do, but fail to see that weapons, or the lack of massive weapons, don't cause war, politicians' bad policies do. This is a good reason why the current conservative administration should have stopped subsidizing trade and foreign assistance to the Soviet bloc nations and to Red China, which includes nuclear and military technology, instead of increasing it. This is sheer madness.

Massive military spending to stop the spread of communism, which our own taxpayers are also required to finance, contributes to the economic problem of deficits, inflation, and high interest rates. In addition it justifies, in the political world of compromise, increased domestic spending, higher deficits, accelerating inflation and higher interest rates—all compounding the economic problems that started the trouble in the first place.

Depression and war are the needless consequences of politicians' folly. They are prevented by limiting government power, not by expanding it. Today, campaign rhetoric is frequently heard about balanced budgets and reducing the size of the government; witness the success of conservatives in 1980; yet nothing ever happens. The spending, the regulations, the taxing, and the deficits continue. Time is running short, the frustration running high. Hiding from reality won't help; kidding ourselves won't do. The sooner we admit, "you can't get blood from a turnip," the better off we'll be.

Solution

What is the solution?

Most importantly, a new attitude about the role of government is necessary if we expect to solve our problems. As long as we, as a nation, accept the notion that government is the ultimate provider and world policeman, implementing the elusive concept of liberty will be impossible. The degree to which governments are permitted to exert force over the people determines the extent to which individuals retain their liberty as well as the chances for peace and prosperity. Historically, governments have always initiated force against the people with disastrous results. America is the best example of what can happen if that force is restrained, thus maximizing individual freedom and prosperity. Yet today, that wonderful experiment is all but abandoned. We must once again clearly reject the idea that government force and threat of force can be carelessly administered.

Voluntary contracts must be permitted. The trend toward government dominance, interference, and altering of voluntary contracts is prevalent and a most dangerous sign. Responsibility to care for one's self is necessary for a free society to function, and trust that individuals will look out for their own self-interest, even if imperfectly, is required and should be achieved through contractual arrangements. Government interference in voluntary agreements between two parties must be strictly prohibited. Enforcement of those contracts in event of a violation invites the government's participation in settlement of the dispute. This limited involvement of government in voluntary contracts is necessary in a free society.

The strict limitation of government power imposed by the Constitution must be respected. We must accept the principle that government's function is not to regulate and plan the economy, protect us from ourselves, arbitrarily attempt to make us better people, or police the world by interfering in the internal affairs of other nations. Its proper function in a free society is to protect liberty and provide for a common defense. When that proper role is assumed, our problems will vanish.

To bring about real changes, we first need to recognize that the politician, *per se,* is a lot less important than he appears. He is basically a puppet of public opinion that reflects the prevailing ideas of the intellectual and thought leaders. John Maynard Keynes, in one of his more lucid moments, said:

> Practical men who believe themselves to be quite exempt from any intellectual influence, are usually the slaves of some defunct economist. Madmen in authority, who hear voices in the air, are distilling their frenzy from some academic scribbler of a few years back.

Media opinion is critical in establishing popular views just as that same media may support or destroy certain political careers. Having accepted the philosophy of economic interventionism and political pragmatism, our society grants political knighthood to the highly paid lobbyists who represent the powerful special interests. But we must remember the lobbyists are the result, not the cause, of our problems. The politician is the puppet of the opinion makers.

Political success is the single goal that drives participants in our political system. No invitations to participants are sent to men of principle, upholders of equal rights, and defenders of the Constitution. Determined political aspirations under today's circumstances are key to achieving a successful political career—the career being an end in itself. We must be aware that this system of politics is not conducive to bringing about changes necessary to solve our problems. The legislative and political intrigues that control the system for the benefit of the special interests must one day come to an end if personal liberty is to be restored.

The resort to power to control people and the economy must be rejected. Also violence to bring changes beneficial to liberty serves no purpose (unless exerted in true defense under reprehensible conditions). The illicit use of power, even with noble intentions, has created history's dung heap of human misery. True change will come through persuasive intellectual influence. If the people refuse to listen, mere recording of significant movements in history will be the limited result of the effort. Yet, not making the effort to persuade the thought leaders to accept freedom and total nonviolence of the state, guarantees that the perpetuation of organized force—the tyranny of the state—will flourish and the suffering will continue for all of us.

Ideas do count; all government action is a result of ideas. It's incorrect to suggest that freedom ideas must be rejected because they are idealistic—the planned economy is also a result of an idea. It's only a choice between good and bad ideas. The job of the true believer in liberty is to convince the majority of our leaders that freedom ideas are superior to the ideas of government coercion. Never can we relax by hoping that the good intentions of the big government proponents will protect us from the evils of government power that intimidate us all. All politicians, from total statists—Marxists and Fascists—to average conservatives and liberals of today's Congress, devoutly promise that all their actions are based on good intentions. But it doesn't matter: Bad ideas regarding the nature and role of government breed bad results and suffering occurs nevertheless. Twisted logic, Machiavellian justifications, excuse making, and short-run benefits can never justify the removal of one iota of liberty from any one person if we intend to live in a free society.

Once the role of government is agreed upon, and government initiation of force is rejected as a legitimate function, the consequences will quickly occur—all positive.

Individuals will reclaim their moral and natural right to their lives and liberty as granted to them by the Creator. The state will be put in its proper place as the protector of equal rights, not the usurper. That in itself should be enough reason to institute a system of limited government, but the benefits go far beyond the moral justification of true liberty. Prosperity will abound and the chance for war will be greatly reduced.

If this is done, the welfare-warfare state is repealed and spending by the federal government reduced by 80 percent. Special interest politicians will not be served and will vanish. Lobbyists will become mere petitioners for liberty. The budget will be immediately balanced and the debt repaid. No more wealth will be transferred to the poor, the rich, the foreigner, the bankers, or arms manufacturers. Military spending will once again be used for defense and not for the domination of an unofficial American empire.

Money will be honest, the unit precisely defined, and its integrity guaranteed by government or by voluntary contracts. Counterfeiting privileges of the Fed will be abolished and relegated to notorious underground figures. Honest money will allow credit to be freely created in the market and not by the privileged banking cartel, yet controlled by the integrity of the market and the convertibility of the dollar. The economic benefits of low-long-term fixed interest rates will be welcomed by all, since credit can then fuel true long-term economic growth.

This scenario sounds utopian, yet it's more practical than the ill effects of the planned society financed by fiat money and debt creation. It's difficult to understand the persistence in following the impractical ideas of runaway government coercion.

The philosophy of the free market, sound money, private property ownership, and equal rights, offers the only real "compromise" to the impasse existing in Washington where only token attempts are made to cut the deficit. A truly practical approach to this dilemma can be immediately implemented. I suggest six points:

First, instead of debating forever over whether or not the cuts should be made in domestic welfare or military spending, the answer is simple: Cut both, and quit arguing—that is, if anyone is serious about his declared hostility toward massive deficits.

Second, all votes on spending should be tradeoffs. Welfare to the poor versus welfare to the rich; domestic aid versus foreign aid; aid to friends versus aid to Communists; water projects in the United States versus water projects in Africa; subsidized loans for steel plants in the United States versus those in South America. Sure, many projects will still exist inconsistent with a truly free market but these projects would only be financed by dropping expenditures elsewhere.

Third, centralized planning fails everywhere else so we can expect it to fail with centralized control over bank credit. Sound money, and breaking up the credit/bank cartel, will solve the problem of high interest rates and long-term financing.

Fourth, talks with the Soviets need not stop—only be redirected. But all subsidies to all Communists must end. We can discuss ways to enhance free trade and voluntary cultural exchanges. True friendly unsubsidized relations with even the apparent enemy go a long way toward reducing the chances of war. A nonaggressive purely defensive foreign policy which would prompt troop and missile withdrawals from Europe and elsewhere would be actions much stronger than all the political rhetoric heard surrounding disarmament conferences.

Fifth, equal rights must be guaranteed and enforced regardless of circumstances of race, color, or creed. Equal rights cannot, however, be defined vaguely to include demands on another's life or property. The goal of freedom must surpass our obsession with material wealth and its forced redistribution.

Sixth, prosperity with freedom for the individual is the only humanitarian system ever offered that prevented mass starvation and suffering. Refusal to accept the free market based on a natural rights philosophy is the most impractical thing we can do. A system that provides sound money, low interest rates, the removal of the bankers' monopoly over credit, and peace and prosperity will restore trust in the politicians, the money, the future, and in ourselves.

More government cannot possibly offer the solution to the problems we face. Big government is the cause; freedom is the answer. ∎

Challenge to America:
A Current Assessment of Our Republic

Congressional Record – U.S. House of Representatives
February 7, 2001

The beginning of the 21st century lends itself to a reassessment of our history and gives us an opportunity to redirect our country's future course if deemed prudent.

The main question before the new Congress and the administration is: Are we to have gridlock or cooperation? Today we refer
to cooperation as *bipartisanship*. Some argue that bipartisanship is
absolutely necessary for the American *democracy* to survive. The
media never mention a concern for the survival of the Republic.
But there are those who argue that left-wing interventionism
should give no ground to right-wing interventionism — that too
much is at stake.

The media are demanding the Bush administration and the
Republican Congress immediately yield to those insisting on
higher taxes and more federal government intervention for the
sake of *national unity*, because our government is neatly split
between two concise philosophic views. But if one looks closely,
one is more likely to find only a variation of a single system of
authoritarianism, in contrast to the rarely mentioned constitutional, nonauthoritarian approach to government.

The big debate between the two factions in Washington boils
down to nothing more than a contest over power and political
cronyism, rather than any deep philosophic differences.

The feared gridlock anticipated for the 107th Congress will dif-
fer little from the other legislative battles in recent previous Congresses. Yes, there will be heated arguments regarding the size of
budgets, local vs. federal control, and private vs. government
solutions. But a serious debate over the precise role for government is unlikely to occur. I do not expect any serious challenge to
the 20th century consensus of both major parties — that the federal
government has a significant responsibility to deal with education,
health care, retirement programs, or managing the distribution of
the welfare state benefits. Both parties are in general agreement on
monetary management, environmental protection, safety, and
risks both natural and man-made. Both participate in telling others
around the world how they must adopt a *democratic process* similar
to ours, as we police our worldwide financial interests.

We can expect most of the media-directed propaganda to be
designed to speed up and broaden the role of the federal government in our lives and the economy. Unfortunately, the token opposition will not present a principled challenge to big government,
only an argument that we must move more slowly and make an
effort to allow greater local decision-making. Without presenting a

specific philosophic alternative to authoritarian intervention from the left, the opposition concedes that the principle of government involvement *per se* is proper, practical, and constitutional.

The cliché *Third Way* has been used to define the so-called compromise between the conventional wisdom of the conservative and liberal firebrands. This nice-sounding compromise refers not only to the noisy rhetoric we hear in the U.S. Congress but also in Britain, Germany, and other nations as well. The question, though, remains: Is there really anything new being offered? The demand for bipartisanship is nothing more than a continuation of the *Third Way* movement of the last several decades.

The effort always is to soften the image of the authoritarians who see a need to run the economy and regulate people's lives, while pretending not to give up any of the advantages of the free market or the supposed benefits that come from a compassionate-welfare or socialist government. It's nothing more than political *have-your-cake-and-eat-it-too* deception. Many insecure and wanting citizens cling to the notion that they can be taken care of through government benevolence without sacrificing the free market and personal liberty. Those who anxiously await next month's government check prefer not to deal with the question of how goods and services are produced and under what political circumstances they are most efficiently provided. Sadly, whether personal freedom is sacrificed in the process is a serious concern for only a small number of Americans.

The *Third Way*, a bipartisan compromise that sounds less confrontational and circumvents the issue of individual liberty, free markets, and production is an alluring, but dangerous, alternative. The harsh reality is that it is difficult to sell the principles of liberty to those who are dependent on government programs. And this includes both the poor beneficiaries as well as the self-serving wealthy elites who know how to benefit from government policies. The authoritarian demagogues are always anxious to play on the needs of people made dependent by a defective political system of government intervention while perpetuating their own power. Anything that can help the people to avoid facing the reality of the shortcomings of the welfare/warfare state is welcomed. Thus our system is destined to perpetuate itself until the immutable laws of economics bring it to a halt at the expense of liberty and prosperity.

Third Way compromise, or bipartisan cooperation, can never reconcile the differences between those who produce and those who live off others. It will only make it worse. Theft is theft, and forced redistribution of wealth is just that. The *Third Way*, though, can deceive and perpetuate an unworkable system when both major factions endorse the principle.

In the last session of the Congress, the Majority Party, with bipartisan agreement, increased the Labor, Health and Human Services, and Education appropriations by 26 percent over the previous year, nine times the rate of inflation. The Education Department alone received $44 billion, nearly double Clinton's first educational budget of 1993. The Labor, HHS, and Education appropriation was $34 billion more than the Republican budget had authorized.

Already the spirit of bipartisanship has prompted the new president to request another $10 billion, along with many more mandates on public schools. This is a far cry from the clear constitutional mandate that neither the Congress nor the federal courts have any authority to be involved in public education.

The argument that this bipartisan approach is a reasonable compromise between the total free-market or local-government approach and that of a huge activist centralized government approach may appeal to some, but it is fraught with great danger. Big government clearly wins; limited government and the free market lose. Any talk of a *Third Way* is nothing more than propaganda for big government. It's no compromise at all. The principle of federal government control is fully endorsed by both sides, and the argument that the *Third Way* might slow the growth of big government falls flat. Actually, with bipartisan cooperation, government growth may well accelerate.

How true bipartisanship works in Washington is best illustrated by the way a number of former Members of Congress make a living after leaving office. They find it quite convenient to associate with other former Members of the opposing party and start a lobbying firm. What might have appeared to be contentious differences when in office are easily put aside to lobby their respected party Members. Essentially no philosophic difference of importance exists — it's only a matter of degree and favors sought, since both parties must be won over. The differences they might have had while they were voting Members of Congress existed only for the purpose of appealing to their different constituencies, not serious differences of opinion as to what the role of government ought to be. This is the reality of bipartisanship. Sadly our system handsomely rewards those who lobby well and in a bipartisan fashion. Congressional service too often is a training ground or a farm system for the ultimate government service: lobbying Congress for the benefit of powerful and wealthy special interests.

It should be clearly evident, however, that all the campaign finance reforms and lobbying controls conceivable will not help the situation. Limiting the right to petition Congress or restricting people's right to spend their own money will always fail and is not morally acceptable and misses the point. As long as government has so much to offer, public officials will be tempted to accept the generous offers of support from special interests. Those who can benefit have too much at stake not to be in the business of influencing government. Eliminating the power of government to pass out favors is the only real solution. Short of that, the only other reasonable solution must come by Members' refusal to be influenced by the pressure that special-interest money can exert. This requires moral restraint by our leaders. Since this has not happened, special-interest favoritism has continued to grow.

The bipartisanship of the last 50 years has allowed our government to gain control over half of the income of most Americans. Being enslaved half the time is hardly a good compromise. But supporters of the political *status quo* point out that, in spite of the loss of personal freedom, the country continues to thrive in many ways.

But there are some serious questions that we as a people must answer:

- Is this prosperity real?
- Will it be long-lasting?
- What is the cost in economic terms?
- Have we sacrificed our liberties for government security?

- Have we undermined the very system that has allowed productive effort to provide a high standard of living for so many?
- Has this system in recent years excluded some from the benefits that Wall Street and others have enjoyed?
- Has it led to needless and dangerous U.S. intervention overseas and created problems that we are not yet fully aware of?
- Is it morally permissible in a country that professes to respect individual liberty to routinely give handouts to the poor, and provide benefits to the privileged and rich by stealing the fruits of labor from hard-working Americans?

As we move into the next Congress, some worry that gridlock will make it impossible to get needed legislation passed. This seems highly unlikely. If big government supporters found ways to enlarge the government in the past, the current evenly split Congress will hardly impede this trend and may even accelerate it. With a recession on the horizon, both sides will be more eager than ever to cooperate on expanding federal spending to *stimulate the economy*, whether the fictitious budget surplus shrinks or not.

In this frantic effort to take care of the economy, promote education, save Social Security, and provide for the medical needs of all Americans, no serious discussion will take place on the political conditions required for a free people to thrive. If not, all efforts to patch the current system together will be at the expense of personal liberty, private property, and sound money.

If we are truly taking a more dangerous course, the biggest question is: How long will it be before a major political-economic crisis engulfs our land? That, of course, is not known, and certainly not necessary if we as a people and especially the Congress understand the nature of the crisis and do something to prevent the crisis from undermining our liberties. We should, instead, encourage prosperity by avoiding any international conflict that threatens our safety or wastefully consumes our needed resources.

Congressional leaders have a responsibility to work together for the good of the country. But working together to promote a giant interventionist state dangerous to us all is far different from working together to preserve constitutionally protected liberties.

Many argue that the *compromise* of bipartisanship is needed to get even a little of what the limited-government advocates want. But this is a fallacious argument. More freedom can never be gained by giving up freedom, no matter the rationale.

If liberals want $46 billion for the Department of Education and conservatives argue for $42 billion, a compromise of $44 billion is a total victory for the advocates of federal government control of public education. "Saving" $2 billion means nothing in the scheme of things, especially since the case for the constitutional position of zero funding was never entertained. When the budget and government controls are expanding each year, a token cut in the proposed increase means nothing, and those who claim it to be a legitimate victory do great harm to the cause of liberty by condoning the process. Instead of it being a *Third Way* alternative to the two sides arguing over minor details on how to use government force, the three options instead are philosophically the same. A true alternative must be offered if the growth of the state is to be contained. *Third Way* bipartisanship is not the answer.

However, if in the future, the constitutionalists argue for zero funding for the Education Department, and the liberals argue to increase it to $50 billion, and finally $25 billion is accepted as the compromise, progress will have been made.

But this is not what is being talked about in D.C. when an effort is made to find a *Third Way*. Both sides are talking about expanding government, and neither side questions the legitimacy of the particular program involved. Unless the moral and constitutional debate changes, there can be no hope that the trend toward bigger government with a sustained attack on personal liberty will be reversed. It must become a moral and constitutional issue.

Budgetary tokenism hides the real issue. Even if someone claims to have just saved the taxpayers a couple billion dollars, the deception does great harm in the long run by failure to emphasize the importance of the Constitution and the moral principles of liberty. It instead helps to deceive the people into believing something productive is being done. But it's really worse than that, because neither party makes an effort to cut the budget. The American people must prepare themselves for ever-more spending and taxes.

A different approach is needed if we want to protect the freedoms of all Americans, to perpetuate prosperity, and to avoid a major military confrontation. All three options in reality represent only a variation of the one based on authoritarian and interventionist principles.

Nothing should be taken for granted, neither our liberties nor our material well being. Understanding the nature of a free society and favorably deciding on its merit are required before true reform can be expected. If, however, satisfaction and complacency with the current trend toward bigger and more centralized government remain the dominant view, those who love liberty more than promised security must be prepared for an unpleasant future. And those alternative plans will surely vary from one another. Tragically for some it will contribute to the violence that will surely come when promises of government security are not forthcoming. We can expect further violations of civil liberties by a government determined to maintain order when difficult economic and political conditions develop.

But none of this need occur if the principles that underpin our Republic, as designed by the Founders, can be resurrected and re-instituted. Current problems that we now confront are government-created and can be much more easily dealt with when government is limited to its proper role of protecting liberty, instead of promoting a welfare-fascist state.

There are reasons to be optimistic that the principles of the Republic, the free market, and respect for private property can be restored. However, there remains good reason as well to be concerned that we must confront the serious political and economic firestorm seen on the horizon before that happens.

My concerns are threefold: the health of the economy, the potential for war, and the coming social discord. If our problems are ignored, they will further undermine the civil liberties of all Americans. The next decade will be a great challenge to all Americans.

The Economy

The booming economy of the last six years has come to an end. The only question remaining is how bad the slump will be.

Although many economists expressed surprise at the sudden and serious shift in sentiment, others have been warning of its inevitability. Boom times built on central-bank credit creation *always* end in recession or depression. But central planners, being extremely optimistic, hope that *this time* it will be different; that a new era has arrived.

For several years, we've heard the endless nostrum of a technology and productivity-driven new paradigm that would make the excesses of the 1990s permanent and real. Arguments that productivity increases made the grand prosperity of the last six years possible were accepted as conventional wisdom, although sound free-market analysts warned otherwise. We are now witnessing an economic downturn that will, in all likelihood, be quite serious. If our economic planners pursue the wrong course, they will surely make it much worse and prolong the recovery.

Although computer technology has been quite beneficial to the economy, in some ways these benefits have been misleading by hiding the ill effects of central-bank manipulation of interest rates and by causing many to believe that the usual business-cycle correction could be averted. Instead, delaying a correction that is destined to come only contributes to greater distortions in the economy, thus requiring an even greater adjustment.

It seems obvious that we are dealing with a financial bubble now deflating. Certainly, most observers recognize that the NASDAQ was grossly overpriced. The question remains, though, as to what is needed for the entire economy to reach equilibrium and allow sound growth to resume.

Western leaders for most of the 20th century have come to accept a type of central planning they believe is not burdened by the shortcomings of true socialist-type central planning. Instead of outright government ownership of the means of production, the economy was to be fine-tuned by fixing interest rates (Fed Funds Rates), subsidizing credit (Government Sponsored Enterprises), stimulating sluggish segments of the economy (Farming and the Weapons Industry), aiding the sick (Medicaid and Medicare), federally managing education (Department of Education), and many other welfare schemes.

The majority of Americans have not yet accepted the harsh reality that this less-threatening, friendlier type of economic planning is minimally more efficient than that of the socialist planners with their five-year economic plans. We must face the fact that the business cycle, with its recurring recessions, wage controls, wealth transfers, and social discord are still with us and will get worse unless there is a fundamental change in economic and monetary policy. Regardless of the type, central economic planning is a dangerous notion.

In an economic downturn, a large majority of our political leaders believe that the ill effects of recession can be greatly minimized by monetary and fiscal policy. Although cutting taxes is always beneficial, spending one's way out of a recession is no panacea. Even if some help is gained by cutting taxes or temporary relief given by an increase in government spending, they distract from the real cause of the downturn: previously pursued faulty monetary policy. The consequences of interest-rate manipulation in a recession—along with tax and spending changes—are unpredictable and do not always produce the same results each time they're used. This is why interest rates of less than 1 percent and massive spending programs have not revitalized Japan's economy or her stock market. We may well be witnessing the beginning of a major worldwide economic downturn, making even more unpredictable the consequence of conventional Western-style central bank tinkering.

There's good reason to believe the Congress and the American people ought to be concerned and start preparing for a slump that could play havoc with our federal budget and the value of the American dollar. Certainly the Congress has a profound responsibility in this area. If we ignore the problems, or continue to endorse the economic myths of past generations, our prosperity will be threatened. But our liberties could be lost, as well, if expanding the government's role in the economy is pursued as the only solution to the crisis.

It's important to understand how we got ourselves into this mess. The blind faith that wealth and capital can be created by the central bank's creating money and credit out of thin air, using government debt as its collateral, along with fixing short-term interest rates, is a myth that must one day be dispelled. All the hopes of productivity increases in a dreamed-about new-era economy cannot repeal eternal economic laws.

The big shift in sentiment of the past several months has come with a loss of confidence in the status of the new paradigm. If we're not careful, the likely weakening of the U.S. dollar could lead to a loss of confidence in America and all her institutions. U.S. political and economic power has propped up the world economy for years. Trust in the dollar has given us license to borrow and spend way beyond our means. But just because world conditions have allowed us greater leverage to borrow and inflate the currency than otherwise might have been permitted, the economic limitations of such a policy still exist. This trust, however, did allow for a greater financial bubble to develop and dislocations to last longer, compared to similar excesses in less powerful nations.

There is one remnant of the Bretton Woods gold-exchange standard that has aided U.S. dominance over the past 30 years. Gold was once the reserve all central banks held to back up their currencies. After World War II, the world central banks were satisfied to hold dollars, still considered to be as *good as gold* since internationally the dollar could still be exchanged for gold at $35 an ounce. When the system broke down in 1971, and we defaulted on our promises to pay in gold, chaos broke out. By default the dollar maintained its status as the reserve currency of the world.

This is true, even to this day. The dollar still represents approximately 77 percent of all world central-bank reserves. This means that the United States has license to steal. We print the money and spend it overseas, while world trust continues because of our dominant economic and military power. This results in a current account and trade deficit so large that almost all economists agree that it cannot last. The longer and more extensive the distortions in the international market, the greater will be the crisis when the market dictates a correction. And that's what we're starting to see.

When the recession hits full force, even the extraordinary power and influence of Alan Greenspan and the Federal Reserve, along with all the other central banks of the world, won't be able to stop the powerful natural economic forces that demand equilibrium. Liquidation of unreasonable debt and the elimination of the over-capacity built into the system and a return to trustworthy money and trustworthy government will be necessary. Quite an undertaking!

Instead of looking at the real cost and actual reasons for the recent good years, politicians and many Americans have been all too eager to accept the new-found wealth as permanent and deserved, as part of a grand new era. Even with a national debt that continued to grow, all the talk in D.C. was about how to handle the magnificent budget surpluses.

Since 1998, when it was announced that we had a budgetary surplus to deal with, the national debt has nevertheless grown by more than $230 billion, albeit at a rate less than in the early 1990s, but certainly a sum that should not be ignored. But the really big borrowing has been what the U.S. as a whole has borrowed from foreigners to pay for the huge deficit we have in our current account. We are now by far the largest foreign debtor in the world and in all of history.

This convenient arrangement has allowed us to live beyond our means and, according to long-understood economic laws, must end. A declining dollar confirms that our ability to painlessly borrow huge sums will no longer be cheap or wise.

During the past 30 years in the post-Bretton Woods era, worldwide sentiment has permitted us to inflate our money supply and get others to accept the dollar as if it were as good as gold. This convenient arrangement has discouraged savings, which are now at an historic low. Savings in a capitalist economy are crucial for furnishing capital and establishing market interest rates. With negative savings and with the Fed fixing rates by creating credit out of thin air and calling it capital, we have abandoned a necessary part of free-market capitalism, without which a smooth and growing economy is unsustainable.

No one should be surprised when recessions hit or bewildered as to their cause or danger. The greater surprise should be the endurance of an economy fine-tuned by a manipulative central bank and a compulsively interventionist Congress. But the full payment for all past economic sins may now be required. Let's hope we can keep the pain and suffering to a minimum.

The most recent new era of the 1990s appeared to be an answer to all politicians' dreams: a good economy, low unemployment, minimal price inflation, a skyrocketing stock market, with capital gains tax revenues flooding the Treasury, thus providing money to accommodate every special-interest demand. But it was too good to be true. It was based on an inflated currency and massive corporate, personal, and government borrowing. A recession was inevitable to pay for the extravagance that many knew was an inherent part of the new era, understanding that abundance without a commensurate amount of work was not achievable.

The mantra now is for the Fed to quickly lower short-term interest rates to stimulate the economy and alleviate a liquidity crisis. This policy may stimulate a boom and may help in a mild downturn, but it doesn't always work in a bad recession. It actually could do great harm since it could weaken the dollar, which in turn would allow market forces instead to push long-term interest rates higher. Deliberately lowering interest rates isn't even necessary for the dollar to drop, since our policy has led to a current-account deficit of a magnitude that demands the dollar eventually readjust and weaken.

A slumping stock market will also cause the dollar to decline and interest rates to rise. Federal Reserve Board central planning through interest-rate control is not a panacea. It is instead the culprit that produces the business cycle. Government and Fed officials have been reassuring the public that no structural problem exists, citing no inflation and a gold price that reassures the world that the dollar is indeed still king.

The Fed can create excess credit, but it can't control where it goes as it circulates throughout the economy; nor can it dictate value either. Claiming that a subdued government-rigged CPI and PPI proves that no inflation exists is pure nonsense. It is well established that, under certain circumstances, new credit inflation can find its way into the stock or real estate market, as it did in the 1920s, while consumer prices remain relatively stable. This does not negate the distortion inherent in a system charged with artificially low interest rates. Instead it allows the distortion to last longer and become more serious, leading to a bigger correction.

If gold prices reflected the true extent of the inflated dollar, confidence in the dollar specifically and in paper more generally would be undermined. It is a high priority of the Fed and all central banks of the world for this not to happen. Revealing to the public the fraud associated with all paper money would cause loss of credibility of all central banks. This knowledge would jeopardize the central banks' ability to perform the role of lender of last resort and to finance/monetize government debt. It is for this reason that the price of gold in their eyes must be held in check.

From 1945 to 1971, the United States literally dumped nearly 500 million ounces of gold at $35 an ounce in an effort to do the same thing by continuing the policy of printing money at will, with the hopes that there would be no consequences to the value of the dollar. That all ended in 1971 when the markets overwhelmed the world central banks.

A similar effort continues today, with central banks selling and loaning gold to keep the price in check. It's working and does convey false confidence, but it can't last. Most Americans are wise to the government's statistics regarding prices and the "no-inflation" rhetoric. Everyone is aware that the prices of oil, gasoline, natural gas, medical care, repairs, houses, and entertainment have all been rapidly rising. The artificially low gold price has aided the government's charade, but it has also allowed a bigger bubble to develop. This policy cannot continue. Economic law dictates a correction that most Americans will find distasteful and painful. Duration and severity of the liquidation phase of the business cycle can be limited by proper responses, but it cannot be avoided and could be made worse if the wrong course is chosen.

Recent deterioration of the junk-bond market indicates how serious the situation is. Junk bonds are now paying 9 percent to 10 percent more than short-term government securities. The quality of business loans is suffering, while more and more corporate bonds are qualifying for junk status. The Fed tries to reassure us by attempting to stimulate the economy with low short-term Fed fund rates at the same time interest rates for businesses and consumers are rising. There comes a time when Fed policy is ineffective, much to everyone's chagrin.

Micromanaging an economy effectively for a long period of time, even with the power a central bank wields, is an impossible task. The good times are ephemeral and eventually must be paid for by contraction and renewed real savings.

There is much more to inflation than rising prices. Inflation is defined as the increase in the supply of money and credit. Obsessively sticking to the rising prices definition conveniently ignores placing the blame on the responsible party — the Federal Reserve. The last thing central banks or the politicians, who need a backup for all their spending mischief, want is for the government to lose its power to create money out of thin air, which serves political and privileged financial interests.

When the people are forced to think only about rising prices, government-doctored price indices can dampen concerns for inflation. Blame then can be laid at the doorstep of corporate profiteers, price gougers, labor unions, oil sheikhs, or greedy doctors. But it is never placed at the feet of highly paid athletes or entertainers. It would be economically incorrect to do so, but it's political correctness that doesn't allow some groups to be vilified.

Much else related to artificially low interest rates goes unnoticed. An overpriced stock market, overcapacity in certain industries, excesses in real-estate markets, artificially high bond prices, general malinvestments, excessive debt, and speculation all result from the generous and artificial credit the Federal Reserve pumps into the financial system. These distortions are every bit, if not more, harmful than rising prices. As the economy soars from the stimulus effect of low interest rates, growth and distortions compound themselves. In a slump the reverse is true, and the pain and suffering is magnified as the adjustment back to reality occurs.

The extra credit in the 1990s has found its way especially into the housing market like never before. GSEs, in particular Freddie Mac and Fannie Mae, have gobbled up huge sums to finance a booming housing market. GSE securities enjoy implicit government guarantees, which have allowed for a generous discount on most housing loans. They have also been the vehicles used by consumers to refinance and borrow against their home equity to use these funds for other purposes, such as investing in the stock market. This has further undermined savings by using the equity that builds with price inflation that homeowners enjoy when money is debased. In addition, the Federal Reserve now buys and holds GSE securities as collateral in their monetary operations. These securities are then literally used as collateral for printing Federal Reserve notes; this is a dangerous precedent.

If monetary inflation merely raised prices, and all prices and labor costs moved up at the same rate, and it did not cause disequilibrium in the market, it would be of little consequence. But inflation is far more than rising prices. Creating money out of thin air is morally equivalent to counterfeiting. It's fraud and theft, because it steals purchasing power from the savers and those on fixed incomes. That in itself should compel all nations to prohibit it, as did the authors of our Constitution.

Inflation is socially disruptive in that the management of fiat money—as all today's currencies are—causes great hardships. Unemployment is a direct consequence of the constantly recurring recessions. Persistent rising costs impoverish many as the standard of living of unfortunate groups erodes. Because the pain and suffering that comes from monetary debasement is never evenly distributed, certain segments of society can actually benefit.

In the 1990s, Wall Streeters thrived, while some low-income, nonwelfare, nonhomeowners suffered with rising costs for fuel, rent, repairs, and medical care. Generally one should expect the middle class to suffer and to literally be wiped out in a severe inflation. When this happens, as it did in many countries throughout the 20th century, social and political conflicts become paramount when finger pointing becomes commonplace by those who suffer looking for scapegoats. Almost always the hostility is inaccurately directed.

There is a greater threat from the monetary mischief than just the economic harm it does. The threat to liberty resulting when economic strife hits and finger-pointing increases should concern us most. We should never be complacent about monetary policy.

We must reassess the responsibility Congress has in maintaining a sound monetary system. In the 19th century, the constitutionality of a central bank was questioned and challenged. Not until 1913 were the advocates of a strong federalist system able to foist a powerful central bank on us, while destroying the gold standard. This banking system, which now serves as the financial arm of Congress, has chosen to pursue massive welfare spending and a foreign policy that has caused us to be at war for much of the 20th century.

Without the central bank creating money out of thin air, our welfare state and worldwide imperialism would have been impossible to finance. Attempts at economic fine-tuning by monetary authorities would have been impossible without a powerful central bank. Propping up the stock market as it falters would be impossible as well.

But the day will come when we will have no choice but to question the current system. Yes, the Fed does help to finance the welfare state. Yes, the Fed does come to the rescue when funds are needed to fight wars and for us to pay the cost of maintaining our empire. Yes, the Fed is able to stimulate the economy and help create what appear to be good times. But it's all built on an illusion. Wealth cannot come from a printing press. Empires crumble and a price is eventually paid for arrogance toward others. And booms inevitably turn into busts.

Talk of a new era the past five years has had many, including Greenspan, believing that *this time* it really would be different. And it may indeed be different this time. The correction could be an especially big one, since the Fed-driven distortion of the past 10 years, plus the lingering distortions of previous decades have been massive. The correction could be big enough to challenge all our institutions, the entire welfare state, Social Security, foreign intervention, and our national defense. This will only happen if the dollar is knocked off its pedestal. No one knows if that is going to happen sooner or later. But when it does, our constitutional system of government will be challenged to the core.

Ultimately the solution will require a recommitment to the principles of liberty, including a belief in sound money — when money once again will be something of value rather than pieces of paper or mere blips from a Federal Reserve computer. In spite of the grand technological revolution, we are still having trouble with a few simple basic tasks — counting votes or keeping the lights on or understanding the sinister nature of paper money.

Potential for War

Foreign military interventionism, a policy the U.S. has followed for over 100 years, encourages war and undermines peace. Even with the good intentions of many who support this policy, it serves the interests of powerful commercial entities. Perpetual conflicts stimulate military spending. Minimal and small wars too often get out of control and cause more tragedy than originally anticipated. Small wars like the Persian Gulf War are more easily tolerated, but the foolishness of an out-of-control war like Vietnam is met with resistance from a justifiably aroused nation. But both types of conflicts result from the same flawed foreign policy of foreign interventionism. Both types of conflicts can be prevented.

National security is usually cited to justify our foreign involvement, but this excuse distracts from the real reason we venture so far from home. Influential commercial interests dictate policy of when and where we go. Persian Gulf oil obviously got more attention than genocide in Rwanda. If one were truly concerned about our security and enhancing peace, one would always opt for a less militarist policy. It's not a coincidence that U.S. territory and U.S. citizens are the most vulnerable in the world to terrorist attacks. Escalation of the war on terrorism and not understanding its cause is a dangerous temptation.

Not only does foreign interventionism undermine chances for peace and prosperity, it undermines personal liberty. War and preparing for war must always be undertaken at someone's expense. Someone must pay the bills with higher taxes, and someone has to be available to pay with their lives. It's never the political and industrial leaders who promote the policy who pay. They are the ones who reap the benefits, while at the same time arguing for the policy they claim is designed to protect freedom and prosperity for the very ones being victimized.

Many reasons given for our willingness to police the world sound reasonable: We need to protect *our* oil. We need to stop cocaine production in Colombia. We need to bring peace to the Middle East. We need to punish our adversaries. We must respond because we are the sole superpower and it's our responsibility to maintain world order. It's our moral obligation to settle disputes. We must follow up on our dollar diplomacy after sending foreign aid throughout the world. In the old days it was: we need to stop the spread of Communism. The excuses are endless!

But it's rarely mentioned that the lobbyists and proponents of foreign intervention are the weapons manufacturers, the oil companies, and the recipients of huge contracts for building infrastructures in whatever far corner of the earth we send our troops. Financial interests have a lot at stake, and it's important for them that the United States maintains its empire. Not infrequently, ethnic groups will influence foreign policy for reasons other than preserving our security. This type of political pressure can at times be substantial and emotional.

We often try to please too many, and by doing so support both sides of conflicts that have raged for centuries. In the end, our efforts can end up unifying our adversaries while alienating our friends.

Over the past 50 years, Congress has allowed our presidents to usurp the prerogatives the Constitution explicitly gave only to the Congress. The term *foreign policy* is never mentioned in the Constitution and it was never intended to be monopolized by the president. Going to war was to be strictly a legislative function, not an executive one.

Operating foreign policy by Executive Orders and invoking unratified treaties is a slap in the face to the rule of law and our republican form of government. But that's currently being done.

U.S. policy over the past 50 years has led to endless illegal military interventions, from Korea to our ongoing war with Iraq and military occupations in the Balkans. Many Americans have died and many others have been wounded or injured or have been forgotten. Numerous innocent victims living in foreign lands have died, as well, from the bombing and blockades we have imposed. They have been people with whom we have had no fight but who were trapped between the bad policy of their own leaders and our eagerness to demonstrate our prowess to the world. Over 500,000 Iraqi children have reportedly died as a consequence of our bombing and denying food and medicine by our embargo.

For over 50 years, there has been a precise move toward one-world government at the expense of our own sovereignty. Our presidents claim that authority to wage war can come from the United Nations or NATO resolutions, in contradiction of our Constitution and everything our Founding Fathers believed. U.S. troops are now required to serve under foreign commanders and wear UN insignias. Refusal to do so prompts a court martial.

The past President, before leaving office, signed the 1998 UN Rome Treaty, indicating our willingness to establish an International Criminal Court. This gives the UN authority to enforce global laws against Americans if ratified by the Senate. Even without ratification, we have gotten to the point where treaties of this sort can be imposed on nonparticipating nations. Presidents have, by Executive Order, been willing to follow unratified treaties in the past. This is a very dangerous precedent.

We already accept the WTO and its international trade court. Trade wars are fought with this court's supervision, and we are only too ready to rewrite our tax laws as the WTO dictates. The only portion of the major tax bill at the end of the last Congress to be rushed through for the President's signature was the Foreign Sales Corporation changes dictated to us by the WTO.

For years the U.S. has accepted the international financial and currency management of the IMF — another arm of one-world government.

The World Bank serves as the distributor of international welfare, of which the U.S. taxpayer is the biggest donor. This organization helps carry out a policy of taking money from poor Americans and giving it to rich foreign leaders, with kickbacks to some of our international corporations. Support for the World Bank, the IMF, the WTO, and the International Criminal Court always comes from the elites and almost never from the common man.

These programs run by the international institutions are supposed to help the poor, but they never do. It's all a charade, and if left unchecked, they will bankrupt us and encourage more world government mischief.

It's the responsibility of Congress to curtail this trend by reestablishing the principles of the U.S. Constitution and our national sovereignty. It's time for the United States to give up its membership in all these international organizations.

Our foreign policy has led to an incestuous relationship between our military and Hollywood. In December, Secretary of Defense William S. Cohen used $295,000 of taxpayer money to host a party in Los Angeles for Hollywood bigwigs. Pentagon spokesman Kenneth Bacon said it was well worth it. The purpose was to thank the movie industry for *putting the military in a good light*. A similar relationship has been reported with TV stations licensed by the U.S. government. They have been willing to accept suggestions from the government to place political messages in their programming. This is a dangerous trend, mixing government and the media. Now here's where real separation is needed!

Our policy should change for several reasons. It's wrong for our foreign policy to serve any special interest, whether it's for financial benefits, ethnic pressures, or some contrived moral imperative. Too often the policy leads to an unintended consequence, and more people are killed and more property damaged than was intended. Controlling world events is never easy. It's better to avoid the chance of one bad decision leading to another. The best way to do that is to follow the advice of the Founders and avoid *all* entangling alliances and pursue a policy designed solely to protect U.S. national security interests.

The two areas in the world that currently present the greatest danger to the United States are Colombia and the Middle East. For decades, we have been engulfed in the ancient wars of the Middle East by subsidizing and supporting both sides. This policy is destined to fail. We are in great danger of becoming involved in a vicious war for oil, as well as being drawn into a religious war that will not end in our lifetime. The potential for war in this region is great, and the next one could make the Persian Gulf War look small. Only a reassessment of our entire policy will keep us from being involved in a needless and dangerous war in this region.

It will be difficult to separate any involvement in the Balkans from a major conflict that breaks out in the Middle East. It's impossible for us to maintain a policy that both supports Israel and provides security for Western-leaning secular Arab leaders, while at the same time taunting the Islamic fundamentalists. Push will come to shove, and when that happens in the midst of an economic crisis, our resources will be stretched beyond the limit. This must be prevented.

Our involvement in Colombia could easily escalate into a regional war. For over 100 years, we have been involved in the affairs of Central America, but the recent escalation of our presence in Colombia is inviting trouble for us.

Although the justification for our enhanced presence is the War on Drugs, protecting U.S. oil interests and selling helicopters are the real reasons for last years' $1.3 billion emergency funding. Already neighboring countries have expressed concern about our presence in Colombia. The U.S. policymakers gave their usual response by promising more money and support to the neighboring countries that feel threatened.

Venezuela, rich in oil, is quite nervous about our enhanced presence in the region. Their foreign minister stated that if any of our ships enter the Gulf of Venezuela they will be *expelled*. This statement was prompted by an overly aggressive U.S. Coast Guard vessel's intrusion into Venezuelan territorial waters on a drug expedition. I know of no one who believes this expanded and insane drug war will do anything to dampen drug usage in the United States. Yet it will cost us plenty. Too bad our political leaders cannot take a hint. The war effort in Colombia is small now, but under current conditions it will surely escalate. This is a 30-year-old civil war being fought in the jungles of South America. We are unwelcome by many, and we ought to have enough sense to stay out of it. Recently new policy has led to the spraying of herbicides to destroy the coca fields. It's already been reported that the legal crops in nearby fields have been destroyed as well. This is no way to win friends around the world.

There are many other areas of the world where we ought to take a second look, and then come home. Instead of bullying the European Union for wanting to have their own rapid deployment force, we should praise them and bring our troops home. World War II has been over for 55 years.

It's time we look at Korea and ask why we have to broker, with the use of American dollars and American soldiers, the final settlement between North and South Korea.

Taiwan and China are now trading and investing in each other's country. Travel restrictions have been recently liberalized. It's time for us to let the two of them settle their border dispute.

We continue to support Turkey with dollars and weapons. We once supported Iraq with the same. Now we permit Turkey, armed with American weapons, to kill Kurds in Iraq, while we bomb the Iraqis if they do the same. It makes no sense.

Selling weapons to both factions of almost all the major conflicts of the past 50 years reveals that our involvement is more about selling weapons than spreading the message of freedom. That message can never be delivered through force to others over their objection. Only a policy of peace, friendship, trade, and our setting a good example can inspire others to look to what once was the American tradition of liberty and justice for all. Entangling alliances won't do it. It's time for Congress and the American people to wake up.

Social Discord

The political system of interventionism always leads to social discord. Interventionism is based on relative rights, majoritarianism, and disrespect for the Constitution. Degenerating moral standards of the people encourages and feeds on this system of special-interest favoritism, all of which contribute to the friction.

Thomas Jefferson was worried that future generations might squander the liberties the American Revolution secured. Writing about future generations, Jefferson wondered if: "in the enjoyment of plenty, they would lose the memory of freedom." He believed: "Material abundance without character is the path to destruction."

The challenge to America today is clearly evident. We lack character, and we also suffer from a loss of respect, understanding, and faith in the liberty that offers so much. The American Republic has been transformed and only a remnant remains. It appears that in the midst of plenty, we have forgotten about freedom.

We have just gone through a roaring decade with many Americans enjoying prosperity beyond their wildest dreams. Because this wealth was not always earned and instead resulted from borrowing, speculation, and inflation, the correction that's to come will contribute to the social discord already inherent in a system of government interventionism. If, indeed, the economy enters a severe recession, which is highly possible, it will compound the problems characteristic of a system that encourages government supervision over all that we do.

Conflicts between classes, races, ethnic groups, and even generations are already apparent. This is a consequence of pitting workers and producers against moochers and the special-interest rich. Divvying up half of the GDP through a process of confiscatory taxation invites trouble. It is more easily tolerated when wealth abounds; but when the economy slips, quiescent resentment quickly turns to noisy confrontation. Those who feel slighted become more demanding at the same time resources are diminished.

But the system of government we have become accustomed to has, for decades, taken over responsibilities that were never intended to be the prerogative of the federal government under the Constitution. Although mostly well intended, the efforts at social engineering have caused significant damage to our constitutional Republic and have resulted in cynicism toward all politicians. Our presidents are now elected by less than 20 percent of those old enough to vote. Government is perceived to be in the business of passing out favors rather than protecting individual liberty. The majority of the people are made up of independents and nonvoters.

The most dramatic change in 20th century social attitudes was the acceptance of abortion. This resulted from a change in personal morality that then led to legalization nationally through the courts and only occurred by perverting our constitutional system of government. The federal courts should never have been involved, but the Congress compounded the problem by using taxpayer funds to perform abortions both here and overseas. Confrontation between the pro-life and the pro-abortion forces is far from over. If government were used only to preserve life, rather than act as an accomplice in the taking of life, this conflict would not be nearly so rancorous.

Once a society and a system of laws deny the importance of life, privacy and personal choice are difficult to protect. Since abortions have become commonplace, it has been easier to move the issue of active euthanasia to center stage. As government budgets become more compromised, economic arguments will surely be used to justify reasonable savings by not wasting vital resources on the elderly.

Issues like abortion and euthanasia don't disappear in a free society but are handled quite differently. Instead of condoning or paying for such acts, the state is responsible for protecting life, rather than participating in taking it. This is quite a different role for government than we currently have.

We can expect the pro-life and pro-abortion and euthanasia groups to become more vocal and confrontational in time, as long as government is used to commit acts that a large number of people find abhorrent. Partial-birth abortion dramatizes the issue at hand and clearly demonstrates how close we are to legalizing infanticide. This problem should be dealt with by the states and without the federal courts or U.S. Congress involvement.

The ill-conceived drug war of the past 30 years has caused great harm to our society. It has undermined privacy and challenged the constitutional rights of all our citizens. The accelerated attack on drug usage since the early 1970s has not resulted in any material benefit. Over $300 billion has been spent on this war, and we are all less free and poorer because of it. Civil liberties are sacrificed in all wars, both domestic and foreign. It's clear that, even if it were a legitimate function for government to curtail drug usage, eliminating bad habits through government regulation is not achievable. Like so much else that government tries to do, the harm done is not always evenly distributed. Some groups suffer more than others, further compounding the problem by causing dissension and distrust.

Anthony Lewis of the *New York Times* reported last year: "The 480,000 men and women now in U.S. prisons on drug charges are 100,000 more than all prisoners in the European Union, where the population is 100 million more than ours."

There are ten times the number of prisoners for drug offenses than there were in 1980, and 80 percent of the drug arrests are for nonviolent possession. In spite of all the money spent and energy wasted, drug usage continues at a record pace. Someday we must wake up and realize the federal drug war is a farce. It has failed and we must change our approach.

As bad as drug addiction is and the harm it causes, it is miniscule compared to the dollar cost, the loss of liberty, and social conflict that results from our ill-advised drug war.

Mandatory drug sentencing laws have done a great deal of harm by limiting the discretion that judges could use in sentencing victims in the drug war. Congress should repeal or change these laws, just as we found it beneficial to modify seizure and forfeiture laws two years ago.

The drug laws, I'm sure, were never meant to be discriminatory, yet they are. In Massachusetts, 82.9 percent of the drug offenders are minorities, but they make up only 9 percent of the state population. The fact that crack-cocaine users are more likely to land in prison than powder-cocaine users, and with harsher sentences, discriminates against black Americans. A wealthy suburbanite caught using drugs is much less likely to end up in prison than someone from the inner city. This inequity adds to the conflict between races and between the poor and the police. And it's unnecessary.

There are no documented benefits from the drug war. Even if a reduction in drug usage could have been achieved, the cost in dollars and loss of liberty would never have justified it. But we don't have that to deal with, since drug usage continues to get worse; in addition we have all the problems associated with the drug war.

The effort to diminish the use of drugs and to improve the personal habits of some of our citizens has been the excuse to undermine our freedoms. Ironically we spend hundreds of billions of dollars waging this dangerous war on drugs while government educational policies promote a huge and dangerous over-usage of Ritalin.

Seizure and forfeiture laws, clearly in violation of the Constitution, have served as a terrible incentive for many police departments to raise money for law-enforcement projects outside the normal budgeting process. Nationalizing the police force for various reasons is a trend that should frighten all Americans. The drug war has been the most important factor in this trend.

Medicinal use of illegal drugs, in particular marijuana, has been prohibited and greater human suffering has resulted. Imprisoning a person who is dying from cancer and AIDS for using his own self-cultivated marijuana is absolutely bizarre and cruel.

All addiction—alcohol and illegal drugs—should be seen as a medical problem, not a legal one. Improving behavior, just for the sake of changing unpopular habits, never works. It should never be the responsibility of government to do so. When government attempts to do this, the government and its police force become the criminals. When someone under the influence of drugs, alcohol (also a drug), or even from a lack of sleep causes injury to another, local law-enforcement officials have a responsibility. This is a far cry from the Justice Department using army tanks to bomb the Davidians because federal agents claimed an amphetamine lab was possibly on the premises.

An interventionist government, by its nature, uses any excuse to know what the people are doing. Drug laws are used to enhance the IRS agent's ability to collect every dime owed the government. These laws are used to pressure Congress to spend more dollars for foreign military operations in places such as Colombia. Artificially high drug prices allow government to clandestinely participate in the drug trade to raise funds to fight the secret controversial wars with off-budget funding. Both our friends and foes depend on the drug war at times for revenue to pursue their causes, which frequently are the same as ours.

The sooner we wake up to this seriously flawed approach to fighting drug usage the better.

The notion that the federal government has an obligation to protect us from ourselves drives the drug war. But this idea also drives the do-gooders in Washington to involve themselves in every aspect of our lives. American citizens cannot move without being constantly reminded by consumer advocates, environmentalists, safety experts, and bureaucratic busybodies what they can or cannot do.

Once government becomes our protector, there are no limits. Federal regulations dictate the amount of water in our commodes and the size and shape of our washing machines. Complicated USDA regulations dictate the size of the holes in Swiss cheese. We cannot even turn off our automobile airbags when they present a danger to a child without federal permission. Riding in a car without a seat belt may be unwise, but should it be a federal crime? Why not make us all wear rib pads and football helmets? That would reduce serious injury and save many dollars for the government health system.

Regulations on holistic medicine, natural remedies, herbs, and vitamins are now commonplace and continue to grow. Who gave the government the right to make these personal decisions for us? Are the people really so ignorant that only politicians and bureaucrats can make these delicate decisions for them?

Today if a drug shows promise for treating a serious illness, and both patient and doctor would like to try it on an experimental basis, permission can be given only by the FDA—and only after much begging and pleading. Permission frequently is not granted, even if the dying patient is pleading to take the risk. The government is not anxious to give up any of its power to make these decisions. People in government think that's what they are supposed to do *for the good of the people*.

Free choice is what freedom is all about. And it means freedom to take risks as well. As a physician deeply concerned about the health of all Americans, I am convinced that the government encroachment into health-care choices has been very detrimental.

There are many areas where the federal government has gotten involved when it shouldn't have, and created more problems than it solved. There is no evidence that the federal government has improved education or medicine, in spite of the massive funding and mandates of the last 40 years. Yet all we hear is a call for increased spending and more mandates. How bad it will get before we reject the big-government approach is anybody's guess.

Welfarism and government interventionism are failed systems and always lead to ever-more intrusive government. The issue of privacy is paramount. Most Americans and Members of Congress recognize the need to protect everyone's privacy. But the loss of privacy is merely the symptom of an authoritarian government. Effort can and should be made, even under today's circumstances, to impede the government's invasion of privacy.

We must realize that our privacy and our liberty will always be threatened as long as we instruct our government to manage a welfare state and to operate foreign policy as if we are the world's policemen.

If the trends we have witnessed over the past 70 years are not reversed, our economic and political system will soon be transposed into a fascist system. The further along we go in that direction, the more difficult it becomes to reverse the tide without undue suffering. This cannot be done unless respect for the rule of law is restored. That means all public officials must live up to their promise to follow the written contract between the people and the government: the U.S. Constitution.

For far too long, we have accepted the idea that government can and should take care of us. But that is not what a free society is all about. When government gives us something, it does two bad things. First it takes it from someone else; second, it causes dependency on government. A wealthy country can do this for long periods of time, but eventually the process collapses. Freedom is always sacrificed and eventually the victims rebel. As needs grow, the producers are unable or unwilling to provide the goods the government demands. Wealth then hides or escapes, going underground or overseas, prompting even more government intrusion to stop the exodus from the system. This only compounds the problem.

Endless demands and economic corrections that come with the territory will always produce deficits. An accommodating central bank then is forced to steal wealth through the inflation tax by merely printing money and creating credit out of thin air. Even though these policies may work for a while, eventually they will fail. As wealth is diminished, recovery becomes more difficult in an economy operating with a fluctuating fiat currency and a marketplace overly burdened with regulation, taxes, and inflation.

The time to correct these mistakes is prior to the bad times, before tempers flare. Congress needs to consider a new economic and foreign policy.

Conclusion

Why should any of us be concerned about the future, especially if prosperity is all around us? America has been truly blessed. We are involved in no major military conflict. We remain one of the freest nations on earth. Current economic conditions have allowed for low unemployment and a strong dollar, with cheap purchases from overseas further helping to keep price inflation in check. Violent crimes have been reduced and civil disorder, such as we saw in the 1960s, is absent.

But we have good reason to be concerned for our future. Prosperity can persist, even after the principles of a sound market economy have been undermined, but only for a limited period of time.

Our economic, military, and political power, second to none, has perpetuated a system of government no longer dependent on the principles that brought our Republic to greatness. Private-property rights, sound money, and self-reliance have been eroded, and they have been replaced with welfarism, paper money, and collective management of property. The new system condones special-interest cronyism and rejects individualism, profits, and voluntary contracts.

Concern for the future is real, because it's unreasonable to believe that the prosperity and relative tranquility can be maintained with the current system. Not being concerned means that one must be content with the *status quo* and that current conditions can be maintained with no negative consequences. That, I maintain, is a dream.

There is growing concern about our future by more and more Americans. They are especially concerned about the moral conditions expressed in our movies, music, and television programs. Less concern is expressed regarding the political and economic system. A nation's moral foundation inevitably reflects the type of government and, in turn, affects the entire economic and political system.

In some ways I am pleasantly surprised by the concern expressed about America's future, considering the prosperity we enjoy. Many Americans sense a serious problem in general, without specifically understanding the economic and political ramifications.

Inflation, the erosion of the dollar, is always worse than the government admits. It may be that more Americans are suffering than is generally admitted. Government intrusion in our lives is commonplace. Some unemployed aren't even counted. Lower-middle-class citizens have not enjoyed an increase in the standard of living many others have. The fluctuation in the stock market may have undermined confidence.

Most Americans still believe everyone has a right to a *free* education, but they don't connect this concept to the evidence: that getting a good education is difficult; that drugs are rampant in public schools; that safety in public schools is a serious problem; and that the cost is amazing for a system of education if one wants a real education.

The quality of medical care is slipping, and the benefits provided by government are seen by more and more people to not really be benefits at all. This trend does not make America feel more confident about the future of health care.

Let there be no doubt, many Americans are concerned about their future, even though many still argue that the problem is only that government has not done enough.

I have expressed concern that our policies are prone to lead to war, economic weakness, and social discord. Understanding the cause of these problems is crucial to finding a solution. If we opt for more government benevolence and meddling in our lives, along with more military adventurism, we have to expect an even greater attack on the civil liberties of all Americans, both rich and poor.

America continues to be a great country, and we remain prosperous. We have a system of freedom and opportunities that motivate many in the world to risk their lives trying to get here.

The question remains: can we afford to be lax in the defense of liberty at this juncture in our history? I don't think so.

The problems are not complex, and even the big ones can be easily handled if we pursue the right course. Prosperity and peace can be continued, but not with the current system that permeates Washington. To blindly hope our freedom will remain intact, without any renewed effort in its defense, or to expect that the good times will automatically continue, places our political system in great danger.

Basic morality, free markets, sound money, living within the rule of law, and adhering to the fundamental precepts that made the American Republic great are what we need. And it's worth the effort. ∎

Has Capitalism Failed?

Congressional Record — U.S. House of Representatives
July 9, 2002

It is now commonplace and politically correct to blame what is referred to as *the excesses of capitalism* for the economic problems we face, and especially for the Wall Street fraud that dominates the business news. Politicians are having a field day with demagoguing the issue while, of course, failing to address the fraud and deceit found in the budgetary shenanigans of the federal government— for which they are directly responsible. Instead, it gives the Keynesian crowd that runs the show a chance to attack free markets and ignore the issue of sound money.

So once again we hear the chant: *"Capitalism has failed; we need more government controls over the entire financial market."* No one asks why the billions that have been spent and thousands of pages of regulations that have been written since the last major attack on capitalism in the 1930s didn't prevent the fraud and deception of Enron, WorldCom, and Global Crossings. That failure surely couldn't have come from a dearth of regulations.

What is distinctively absent is any mention that all financial bubbles are saturated with excesses in hype, speculation, debt, greed, fraud, gross errors in investment judgment, carelessness on the part of analysts and investors, huge paper profits, conviction that a new era economy has arrived and, above all else, pie-in-the-sky expectations.

When the bubble is inflating, there are no complaints. When it bursts, the blame game begins. This is especially true in the age of victimization, and is done on a grand scale. It quickly becomes a philosophic, partisan, class, generational, and even a racial issue. While avoiding the real cause, all the finger pointing makes it difficult to resolve the crisis and further undermines the principles upon which freedom and prosperity rest.

Nixon was right—once—when he declared "We're all Keynesians now." All of Washington is in sync in declaring that too much capitalism has brought us to where we are today. The only decision now before the central planners in Washington is whose special interests will continue to benefit from the coming pretense at reform. The various special interests will be lobbying heavily like the Wall Street investors, the corporations, the military-industrial complex, the banks, the workers, the unions, the farmers, the politicians, and everybody else.

But what is not discussed is the actual cause and perpetration of the excesses now unraveling at a frantic pace. This same response occurred in the 1930s in the United States as our policymakers responded to the very similar excesses that developed and collapsed in 1929. Because of the failure to understand the problem then, the depression was prolonged. These mistakes allowed our current problems to develop to a much greater degree. Consider the failure to come to grips with the cause of the 1980s bubble, as Japan's economy continues to linger at no-growth and recession level, with their stock market at approximately one-fourth of its peak 13 years ago. If we're not careful—and so far we've not been—we will make the same errors that will prevent the correction needed before economic growth can be resumed.

In the 1930s, it was quite popular to condemn the greed of capitalism, the gold standard, lack of regulation, and a lack government insurance on bank deposits for the disaster. Businessmen became the scapegoat. Changes were made as a result, and the welfare/warfare state was institutionalized. Easy credit became the holy grail of monetary policy, especially under Alan Greenspan, "the ultimate Maestro." Today, despite the presumed protection from these government programs built into the system, we find ourselves in a bigger mess than ever before. The bubble is bigger, the boom lasted longer, and the gold price has been deliberately undermined as an economic signal. Monetary inflation continues at a rate never seen before in a frantic effort to prop up stock prices and continue the housing bubble, while avoiding the consequences that inevitably come from easy credit. This is all done because we are unwilling to acknowledge that current policy is only setting the stage for a huge drop in the value of the dollar. Everyone fears it, but no one wants to deal with it.

Ignorance, as well as disapproval for the natural restraints placed on market excesses that capitalism and sound markets impose, cause our present leaders to reject capitalism and blame it for all the problems we face. If this fallacy is not corrected and capitalism is even further undermined, the prosperity that the free market generates will be destroyed.

Corruption and fraud in the accounting practices of many companies are coming to light. There are those who would have us believe this is an integral part of free-market capitalism. If we did have free-market capitalism, there would be no guarantees that some fraud wouldn't occur. When it did, it would then be dealt with by local law-enforcement authority and not by the politicians in Congress, who had their chance to "prevent" such problems but chose instead to politicize the issue, while using the opportunity to promote more Keynesian useless regulations.

Capitalism should not be condemned, since we haven't had capitalism. A system of capitalism presumes sound money, not fiat money manipulated by a central bank. Capitalism cherishes voluntary contracts and interest rates that are determined by savings, not credit creation by a central bank. It's not capitalism when the system is plagued with incomprehensible rules regarding mergers, acquisitions, and stock sales, along with wage controls, price controls, protectionism, corporate subsidies, international management of trade, complex and punishing corporate taxes, privileged government contracts to the military-industrial complex, and a foreign policy controlled by corporate interests and overseas investments. Add to this centralized federal mismanagement of farming, education, medicine, insurance, banking and welfare. This is not capitalism!

To condemn free-market capitalism because of anything going on today makes no sense. There is no evidence that capitalism exists today. We are deeply involved in an interventionist-planned economy that allows major benefits to accrue to the politically connected of both political spectrums. One may condemn the fraud and the current system, but it must be called by its proper names — Keynesian inflationism, interventionism, and corporatism.

What is not discussed is that the current crop of bankruptcies reveals that the blatant distortions and lies emanating from years of speculative orgy were predictable.

First, Congress should be investigating the federal government's fraud and deception in accounting, especially in reporting future obligations such as Social Security, and how the monetary system destroys wealth. Those problems are bigger than anything in the corporate world and are the responsibility of Congress. Besides, it's the standard set by the government and the monetary system it operates that are major contributing causes to all that's wrong on Wall Street today. Where fraud does exist, it's a state rather than a federal matter, and state authorities can enforce these laws without any help from Congress.

Second, we do know why financial bubbles occur, and we know from history that they are routinely associated with speculation, excessive debt, wild promises, greed, lying, and cheating. These problems were described by quite a few observers as the problems were developing throughout the '90s, but the warnings were ignored for one reason. Everybody was making a killing and no one cared, and those who were reminded of history were reassured by the Fed Chairman that "this time" a new economic era had arrived and not to worry. Productivity increases, it was said, could explain it all.

But now we know that's just not so. Speculative bubbles and all that we've been witnessing are a consequence of huge amounts of easy credit, created out of thin air by the Federal Reserve. We've had essentially no savings, which is one of the most significant driving forces in capitalism. The illusion created by low interest rates perpetuates the bubble and all the bad stuff that goes along with it. And that's not a fault of capitalism. We are dealing with a system of inflationism and interventionism that always produces a bubble economy that must end badly.

So far the assessment made by the administration, Congress, and the Fed bodes badly for our economic future. All they offer is more of the same, which can't possibly help. All it will do is drive us closer to national bankruptcy, a sharply lower dollar, and a lower standard of living for most Americans, as well as less freedom for everyone.

This is a bad scenario that need not happen. But preserving our system is impossible if the critics are allowed to blame capitalism and sound monetary policy is rejected. More spending, more debt, more easy credit, more distortion of interest rates, more regulations on everything, and more foreign meddling will soon force us into the very uncomfortable position of deciding the fate of our entire political system.

If we were to choose freedom and capitalism, we would restore our dollar to a commodity or a gold standard. Federal spending would be reduced, income taxes would be lowered, and no taxes would be levied upon savings, dividends, and capital gains. Regulations would be reduced, special-interest subsidies would be stopped, and no protectionist measures would be permitted. Our foreign policy would change, and we would bring our troops home.

We cannot depend on government to restore trust to the markets; only trustworthy people can do that. Actually, the lack of trust in Wall Street executives is healthy because it's deserved and prompts caution. The same lack of trust in politicians, the budgetary process, and the monetary system would serve as a healthy incentive for the reform in government we need.

Markets regulate better than governments can. Depending on government regulations to protect us significantly contributes to the bubble mentality.

These moves would produce the climate for releasing the creative energy necessary to simply serve consumers, which is what capitalism is all about. The system that inevitably breeds the corporate-government cronyism that created our current ongoing disaster would end.

Capitalism didn't give us this crisis of confidence now existing in the corporate world. The lack of free markets and sound money did. Congress does have a role to play, but it's not proactive. Congress's job is to get out of the way. ■

PART TWO

Mises and Austrian Economics: A Personal View

> [U]nder the predominance of interventionist ideas, a political career is open only to men who identify themselves with the interests of a pressure group. . . . Service to the short-run interests of a pressure group is not conducive to the development of those qualities which make a great statesman. Statesmanship is invariably long-run policy; pressure groups do not bother about the long-run.[1]

I decided to run for Congress because of the disaster of wage and price controls imposed by the Nixon administration in 1971. When the stock market responded euphorically to the imposition of these controls and the closing of the gold window, and the U.S. Chamber of Commerce and many other big business groups gave enthusiastic support, I decided that someone in politics had to condemn the controls, and offer the alternative that could explain the

---

Originally published in 1984 by the Ludwig von Mises Institute.

[1]Ludwig von Mises, *Human Action*, Scholar's Edition (Auburn, Ala.: Ludwig von Mises Institute, 1998), p. 866.

past and give hope for the future: the Austrian economists' defense of the free market. At the time I was convinced, like Ludwig von Mises, that no one could succeed in politics without serving the special interests of some politically powerful pressure group.

Although I was eventually elected, in terms of a *conventional* political career with real Washington impact, he was absolutely right. I have not developed legislative influence with the leadership of the Congress or the administration. Monies are deliberately deleted from routine water works bills for my district because I do not condone the system, nor vote for any of the appropriations.

My influence, such as it is, comes only by educating others about the rightness of the free market. The majority of the voters in my district have approved, as have those familiar with free-market economics. And voters in other districts, encouraged by my speaking out for freedom and sound money, influence *their* representatives in the direction of a free market. My influence comes through education, not the usual techniques of a politician. But the more usual politicians in Congress will hardly solve our problems. Americans need a better understanding of Austrian economics. Only then will politicians become more statesmanlike.

My introduction to Austrian economics came when I was studying medicine at Duke University and came across a copy of Hayek's *The Road to Serfdom*.[2] After devouring this, I was determined to read whatever I could find on what I thought was this new school of economic thought—especially the work of Mises. Although the works were magnificent, and clarified many issues for me, it was more of a revelation to find intellectuals who could confirm what I "already knew"—that the free market is superior to a centrally planned economy. I did not know *how* a free market accomplished its work, and so the study of economics showed me this, and how to build a case for it. But, like many people, I did not need to be convinced of the merits of individual freedom—for me that came naturally.

---

[2]Friedrich A. Hayek, *The Road to Serfdom* (Chicago: Univesity of Chicago Press, 1944).

For as long as I can remember, I wanted to be free from government coercion in any form. All my natural instincts toward freedom were inevitably challenged by the established school system, the media, and the government. These systems tried to cast doubt on my conviction that only an unhampered market is consonant with individual liberty. Although reassured that intellectual giants like Mises agreed with a *laissez-faire* system, I was frustrated by knowing what was right, while watching a disaster developing for our economy. The better I came to understand how the market worked, the more I saw the need to implement these ideas through political action.

Political action aimed at change can, of course, take various forms. In 1776, in America, it was a war for independence from British oppression. In 1917, in Russia, violence was used to strengthen oppression.

Fortunately, it is possible to accomplish the proper sort of change through education, persuasion, and the democratic process. Our rights of free speech, assembly, religion, petition, and privacy remain essentially intact. Before our rights are lost, we must work to change the policies of 70 years of government interventionism. And the longer we wait the harder it will be.

Because of my interest in individual liberty and the free market, I became closely associated over the years with friends and students of Mises, those who knew the greatness of Mises from a long-term personal friendship with him. My contact, however, was always through his writings, except on one occasion. In 1971, during a busy day in my medical office, I took a long lunch to drive 60 miles to the University of Houston to hear one of the last formal lectures Mises gave—this one on socialism. Although 90 at the time, he was most impressive, and his presentation inspired me to more study of Austrian economics.

My subsequent meetings and friendship with the late Leonard Read and his Foundation for Economic Education also inspired me to work harder for a society unhampered by government intrusion into our personal and economic lives. My knowledge has been encouraged and bolstered through the extraordinary work of the Mises Institute, with its many publications and conferences, and its inspiring work among students choosing academic careers.

My friendships with two important students of Mises, Hans Sennholz and Murray Rothbard, were especially helpful in getting firsthand explanations of how the market functions. They helped me to refine my answers to the continual barrage of statist legislation that dominates the U.S. Congress. Their personal assistance was invaluable to me in my educational and political endeavors.

Such friendships are valuable, but the reassurance that sound thinkers were on my side was inspirational. It gave me the confidence I needed to intellectually defend my political and economic positions on the campaign trail and on the House floor.

Mises's Character and Its Influence

My association with the Austrian School of economic thought has been invaluable to me, but so have the personal testimonials as to the character of Mises. He never yielded to any temptation to soften his stand to be more acceptable to the conventional economic community, which proved him to be a man of strong will and character. If he had softened his stands, his recognition during his lifetime would have been enhanced. But his goal was economic truth, not a prestigious academic position and superficial acclaim. His determination and consistency were buoyed by the confidence that he was right, and that rectitude was all that mattered. Mises was always a gentleman, kind and considerate of all, and I have tried to emulate him. When the world of economists and politicians is going mad, it is difficult to respond with quiet and deliberate discussion. Yet this response served him well and enhanced his ability to teach. In due time, his quiet voice and those of his students will be heard, despite the shouting and demagoguery that afflicts Washington, D.C.

When exasperated with the current state of affairs, we must remember Mises's admonishment: "No one should expect that any logical argument or any experience could shake the almost religious fervor of those who believe in salvation through spending and credit expansion."[3]

---

[3]Ludwig von Mises, "Stones into Bread: The Keynesian Miracle," *Planning for Freedom* (South Holland, Ill.: Libertarian Press, 1974), p. 63.

But we must also remember that it is the acceptance of economic interventionism that breeds this disease of demagoguery that plagues the thinking and speech of the politicians.

After coming to believe in themselves as planners and decision-makers for consumers, businesspeople, and working people, the politicians soon can arrogantly rationalize any position for *any* reason. It wouldn't be as bad if they knew they were demagogues—at least this would be honest. But this arrogance becomes a way of life, and the tool to achieve their next "important and necessary" intervention.

It is only with full assurance gained from Austrian economics, and the example of Mises's character, that I am able to tolerate the daily circus of Congress.

Economic knowledge is not nearly as scarce in Washington as one might suspect from a superficial observation of Congress. Other Congressmen frequently express sound judgments to me privately regarding deficits and runaway expenditures. What they lack is the *will* to resist the pressure groups. As desperately as we need a better economic understanding, even more we need Mises's trait of gentlemanly firmness on issues of principle. Character is more necessary than eloquence in economic theory.

Jacques Rueff described well this quality of Mises's:

> With an indefatigable enthusiasm, and with courage and faith undaunted, he has never ceased to denounce the fallacious reasons and untruths offered to justify most of our new institutions. . . . No consideration whatever can divert him in the least from the straight steep path where his cold reason guides him. In the irrationalism of our era he has remained a person of pure reason.[4]

Murray Rothbard in *The Essential Ludwig von Mises* writes that Mises:

---

[4]Jacques Rueff, "The Intransigence of Ludwig von Mises," in *On Freedom and Free Enterprise*, Mary Sennholz, ed. (Princeton, N.J.: D. Van Nostrand, 1956), p. 15.

reacted to the darkening economic world around him
with a lifetime of high courage and personal integrity.
Never would Ludwig von Mises bend to the winds of
change that he saw to the unfortunate and disastrous;
neither changes in political economy nor in the discipline
of economics could bring him to swerve a single iota
from pursuing and propounding the truth as he saw it.[5]

The Subjective Theory of Value

The study of Austrian economics has helped me in many ways
to understand what happens in our economy, and the excuses of
the establishment economists as to why we're not achieving the
paradise that politicians promised if only their legislation were
passed. It is time, of course, for them to do some serious explaining, since after 70 years of intervention, conditions have gotten
worse, and we face an international banking crisis unprecedented
in all of history.

Of all the important contributions of the Austrian School, the
subjective theory of value has proven most helpful to me in understanding why things aren't as the interventionists say they ought
to be. According to the soothsayers, there's always an easy excuse.
In Russia, it's always the weather. In the interventionist United
States, it's "timing," "the technicians," "the residuals of capitalism," "tax policy," "too little spending," "assistance to the wrong
special interest," etc. The excuses are endless.

Except for a few other Members, no one in Congress has ever
heard of the subjective theory of value (or the labor theory of
value, for that matter), and none really care. Yet I believe it is crucial for them to understand the theory if true reform is to be
achieved. Since little thought has been given to the fundamentals,
smatterings of the labor theory of value still motivate many in
Congress to promote legislation that will secure a "fair" return for
the working man. The explanation of how individuals, acting

---

[5]Murray Rothbard, *The Essential Ludwig von Mises* (Auburn, Ala.: Ludwig
von Mises Institute, 1983), p. 25.

freely in the market, determine values and prices of specific goods, dispels the myths spread by both the Keynesians and the monetarists. Keynesians blame the Arabs for the inflation; the monetarists, limiting their thoughts to quantity of money as the sole determinant of prices, raise more questions than they answer. It has only been through a basic understanding of how price is determined subjectively that I have not yielded to the "plausible" arguments of the planners who are able to dwell on partial truths and short-term consequences. When viewed from an Austrian viewpoint, "stagflation" is hardly the mystery it was proclaimed to be in the recession of 1974 to 1976.

There are some who have heard of the subjective theory of value but are hesitant to accept it because they prefer "objectivity" to "subjectivity." Yet if consumers subjectively set prices and values by affecting supply and demand (and thus sales), this is an important *objective* finding. Just because we can measure monetary aggregates, or hours spent producing a product, we decide these objective facts can be used to determine value. Yet it is really not the way prices are determined, so these facts are not *objectively useful* for this purpose. Those who would use these "objective" facts for calculating future "price levels" are quick to *reject* the objectivity of certain economic laws that are glaringly apparent, e.g., government planning leads to chaos; printing money creates no new wealth; fiat money cannot replace commodity money without force and fraud, etc. They thus reject subjectivity where it is important—in understanding how individual prices are set—and ignore objective economic laws so that their schemes of planning can be pursued. This is a mechanism of both convenience and ignorance. It allows planners in Washington to persistently defy all economic laws so the politicians can pursue preconceived and erroneous notions of what is best for everyone.

Once they accept the idea that prices are an "objective" consequence of certain previous events—money supply, oil boycotts, wage settlements, or farm policy—they naturally feel that prices can be altered easily. Legislation to establish wage, price, credit, dividend, and profit controls have been introduced in the House and conceivably could be passed if conditions "warrant" it. Although free-market pricing is crucial for sending necessary messages to entrepreneurs and consumers, its origin is totally misunderstood in Washington, so it is no wonder our economy remains threatened.

If there is no general understanding of the essentials of a free pricing structure, the market economy will always be threatened. And without a free pricing structure, the market cannot function. To understand how prices are determined, one must understand the subjective theory of value.

The Importance of Money

Today, it's hard to believe that it was a major breakthrough in economics for Mises to show logically that under socialism prices cannot be established and economic calculation is impossible. Is it any wonder that socialist nations, without subsidies from a capitalist nation, are unable to feed themselves? This is why the threat of communism would be greatly reduced if only we could stop our elected officials from bailing these countries out. Only force enables a system to survive without a free-market pricing mechanism.

Against a background in free-market economics, the disastrous effects of wage and price controls are never a surprise. In spite of both recent and ancient failures of wage and price controls, they — as well as credit controls, currency controls, and an attack on hard assets — will be used to our great economic detriment, because the political pressures to continue the tremendous deficits are so strong in Washington and, inevitably, the dollar will be destroyed.

Since we cannot predict the future because we cannot know the subjective decisions of millions of consumers and producers, we cannot know exactly when this will come about. Yet we can be certain, from history, that the politicians will continue to destroy our money, and that they will put off for as long as possible the consequences that must follow.

Mises writes that eventually we must make a choice:

> Men must choose between the market economy and socialism. The state can preserve the market economy in protecting life, health, and private property against violent or fraudulent aggression; or it can itself control the conduct of all production activities. Some agency must determine what should be produced. If it is not

the consumers by means of demand and supply on the
market, it must be the government by compulsion.[6]

Understanding money is the key to restoring a sound economy.
Since entering politics, I have spent more time on the money issue
than any other. Austrian economics, and especially Mises's writings, have been especially helpful to me. Mises's explanation of
how money originated in the market as a useful commodity convinced me that money once again must be returned to the market
as a commodity.

Politicians inevitably destroy money when they gain control of
it, and attempt to make it a mere product of the State, completely
separate from any commodity sought by the consumer. Mises
understood how the money issue became as much a political issue
as an economic one. His insights helped me to oppose both liberal
and conservative excuses for deficits. Both factions, regardless of
rhetoric, depend on a fiat money system and inflation. These hide
the exactions necessary to continue government financing while
serving the special interests who get the new money before the
depreciation is recognized by the general public.

My support for legalizing competition in currencies has obviously been influenced by the Misesian explanation of money. This
is one area where we can even get the monetarists to agree. Mises
explains that money—like any commodity—has a marginal utility,
and its value is set subjectively. This has helped me refute the pure
quantity theory of money as presented by the Chicago School.
Money as a commodity must have a *quality* to it, and consumers
must trust the money for it to function—something increasingly
absent today. Once this is understood, there is no mystery as to
why the bond market acts as it does, and why interest rates are
"too high," as the monetarists and Keynesians have proclaimed.

The most common misunderstanding in Washington regarding
money is the conviction that economic growth depends on money
growth. Ricardo mentioned this, but it was Mises who emphasized
and clarified this point—duplication of money units bestows no

---

[6]Ludwig von Mises, *Planned Chaos* (Irvington-on-Hudson, N.Y.: Foundation for Economic Education, 1947), p. 34.

social benefit. If it did, we'd have a hard time explaining why economic growth did so poorly in the 1970s when the Federal Reserve Board nearly tripled the money supply (M3). Yet today, the vast majority of the bureaucrats and politicians believe that without money growth, economic growth cannot occur. They see money as separate from taxing, spending, and regulatory policies; without an understanding of value, pricing, and money quality, it is virtually impossible to explain to them that prices can easily adjust downward if a free market requires it. The prevailing opinion is that falling prices are synonymous with depression—an obviously erroneous idea. Those who believe this do not understand the nature of capital—that it comes from productive effort and savings. They believe capital is something you get when the Fed increases the money supply.

In *A Critique of Interventionism,* Mises wrote:

> By its very nature, a government decree that "it be" cannot create anything that has not been created before. Only the naive inflationists could believe that government could enrich mankind through fiat money. Government cannot create anything; its orders cannot even evict anything from the world of reality, but they can evict him from the world of the permissible. Government cannot make man richer, but it can make him poorer.[7]

In applying the concept of the marginal utility of money, Mises superbly explains the befuddlement expressed by the conventional economist about government's velocity statistics. The propensity of consumers to hold cash or to spend explains why sometimes prices go up more slowly than some say they "should," and why they go up more rapidly than they "should" at the end of a currency destruction, in spite of the slowing of new money creation. Only Austrian economics can adequately explain these economic occurrences.

---

[7]Ludwig von Mises, *A Critique of Interventionism* (New Rochelle, N.Y.: Arlington House, 1977), p. 23.

In 1913, Mises published *The Theory of Money and Credit*.[8] In this masterpiece he gave us all we would have needed to avoid the financial calamities of the 20th century and possibly even the wars fought with the weapon of inflation. Tragically, the U.S. took another course; with Colonel House advising President Wilson, we established a powerful central bank and introduced the destructive graduated income tax, all in that same year. The subsequent cost in human suffering and loss of freedom has been immeasurable.

Several Special Points

The clear explanation provided by Mises of the nature of money and inflation has served me well in defending a hard money system. Understanding the subjective theory of value has been most helpful to me personally in understanding all the contradictions pressed by the establishment economists, but it does not lend itself to popular expression on the House floor. In contrast, the truth about money and inflation, and how inflation benefits the politicians and special interests, and serves as a hidden tax, is much easier to present in ordinary language.

Understanding the concept of "time preference" in explaining and defending profits and interest is not practical in general debate, but it is useful in providing the information to show that the liberal welfarists and socialists are absurd in their contentions that working people are injured by a free-market economy.

In a similar way, Mises's refutation of the Marxian theory of the inevitability of class struggle is beneficial for reassurance but not useful practically, since those who are in charge in Congress neither understand nor care to understand something they would consider esoteric. Nevertheless, it is important for a defender of capitalism to understand the Austrian explanation that capitalism ends class struggle, builds a huge middle class, and raises the standard of living of everyone. The specific choices of consumers become key in a free market—which can exist only in a nation that has a high regard for individual liberty. Although the politicians in Washington refuse to think in these terms, the fact is that positive change will only come when our intellectual leaders accept the

---

[8]Ludwig von Mises, *The Theory of Money and Credit* (New Haven, Conn.: Yale University Press, 1953).

importance of concepts like time preference, the nature of class conflicts, and subjective valuations. When the Austrian view becomes commonly accepted, capitalism will result from a political order that holds individual liberty in high esteem.

The Business Cycle

There are some in the U.S. Congress who are knowledgeable and enthusiastic about socialism, and who fight for it as tenaciously as I fight for the free market. But their numbers are few. For the most part, the Members are well-intentioned, ostensibly pragmatic do-gooders—"pragmatic" enough to latch on to the interventionism most beneficial to their particular political needs and to provide an intellectual defense. Whether Keynesians, supply-siders, or monetarists, there is always an explanation for deficits, taxes, central banks, fiat money, inflation, and all flavors of interventionism. Yet the bulk of the Members remain well-intentioned, but, by their compromises, seriously misled. Actually, compromise becomes a "beneficial philosophy" in itself. If one does not compromise, he becomes "rigid," "sterile," "impractical," "egotistical," "ideological," and "ineffectual." Politics becomes the art of compromise. Yet with closer scrutiny, it's easily seen that it is the compromisers who are rigid, sterile, impractical, ideological, and egotistical in their defense of the very dangerous system of interventionism and inflation.

It is rare in Washington for anyone to be accused of deliberately hurting the poor. No one deliberately creates unemployment. No one likes high interest rates, rising prices, or a falling standard of living. They all claim they know how to prevent suffering brought on by the business cycle—yet nearly all accept the proposition that the cycle comes out of uncontrolled capitalism. Since only a handful ever studied Mises's superb explanation of how government monetary policy creates the cycle, only foolish, political solutions are offered. Even monetarism offers no help, since commodity money is condemned and the subjective theory of value rejected.

It's tragic to watch, day after day, the flow of statist solutions from both parties in Washington while knowing the answers are readily available if our current leaders would only open their eyes, reject demagogues, and restore order with a sound monetary system and a free-market economy.

I found Rothbard's and Sennholz's Austrian explanation of the Great Depression truly eye-opening. Convinced of the cause of the Depression both from the theoretical (Mises) and the more practical (Rothbard and Sennholz) viewpoint, I became more determined than ever to work for a sound monetary system—without a central bank or political (paper) money. All people concerned with the suffering and degradation of unemployment should study the Austrian explanation of how distorted interest rates, malinvestment, skewed economic calculation, and preferential treatment for favored business and government constituencies, cause the crime of the business cycle.

Politicians are easily misled and conveniently tempted by the boom phase of the cycle. As Mises points out:

> [t]hus it conclusively proved that the slump, whose appearance the inflationists attributed to an insufficiency of the supply of money, is on the contrary the necessary outcome of attempts to remove such an alleged scarcity of money through credit expansion. . . . This demonstration could appeal to statesmen intent on promoting the enduring well-being of their nation. It could not influence demagogues who care for nothing but success in the impending election campaign and are not in the least troubled about what will happen the day after tomorrow.[9]

Obviously one cannot deal in politics without being aware of human nature and how interventionism attracts demagogues. Refuting the demagogues who prate about their great skills during the boom, and shout louder and louder for statism as the busts get more severe with each cycle, seems an overwhelming task. It is easy to see that many economic "recoveries" are nothing but more of the same—spending and inflating our way into a new cycle,

---

[9]Ludwig von Mises, "Lord Keynes and Say's Law," *Planning for Freedom* (South Holland, Ill.: Libertarian Press, 1974), p. 68.

hoping for yet another boom, which may or may not materialize. Eventually, the deceitful trick of inflation will fail to create "prosperity." When that time comes, due to the sustained period of inflation that we have endured, we can expect a serious political and economic crisis for Western civilization. The incantations of supply-sidism, monetarism, or Keynesianism will not suffice, and the fascist and socialist voices of oppression will grow louder and more influential.

International Politics

My main motivation in entering politics was to contribute something toward establishing a free society. This desire, combined with the Austrian arguments for the efficient functioning of the market economy, has served me well. The particular interest that has occupied my time and interest has been the issue of money and inflation.

It is impossible to concentrate on money and inflation and ignore foreign affairs, however. The two are intertwined. The fact that economic interventionism leads to a lowering of our standard of living is bad enough, but its breeding of excessive nationalism, protectionism, economic isolationism, militarism, and war should prompt us all to fear for the fate of freedom and even civilization itself. Mises's prediction that the U.S. type of interventionism will lead to a German type of national socialism appears to be accurate. In *Human Action* Mises states:

> An essential point in the social philosophy of interventionism is the existence of an inexhaustible fund which can be squeezed forever. The whole doctrine of interventionism collapses when this fountain is drained off. The Santa Claus principle liquidates itself.[10]

Evidence of his prediction is all around us today. We can only hope that we can turn things around before his prediction that it leads to a German-type fascism comes true.

---

[10]Mises, *Human Action*, p. 854.

The nonliberals who admit to the failure of their brand of interventionism now plot schemes for "reindustrialization" — a euphemism for fascism (government "partnership" with business). Banking Regulation Number One and the Defense Production Act, already on the books, allow under emergency conditions for an economic despot to take charge almost immediately. In a panic, it will not take much to topple us over. Since Americans dislike outright government ownership we will have the deception of private ownership in combination with government's authoritarian control over the economy. And some businessmen, under this system, will always hope to secure greater profits at the expense of innocent (and unknown) victims.

In *Human Action*, Mises points out:

> Aggressive nationalism is the necessary derivative of the policies of interventionism and national planning. While laissez faire eliminates the causes of international conflict, government interference with business and socialism create conflicts for which no peaceful solution can be found. While under free trade and freedom of migration no individual is concerned about the territorial size of his country, under the protective measures of economic nationalism nearly every citizen has a substantial interest in these territorial issues. The enlargement of the territory subject to the sovereignty of his own government means material improvement for him or at least relief from restrictions which a foreign government has imposed upon his well-being. What has transformed the limited war between royal armies into total war, the clash between peoples, is not technicalities of military art, but the substitution of the welfare state for the laissez-faire state.[11]

And again on page 828, he reiterates:

> Interventionism generates economic nationalism, and economic nationalism generates bellicosity. If men and commodities are prevented from crossing the borderlines, why should not the armies try to pave the way for

---

[11]Ibid., p. 819.

them? . . . The root of the evil is not the construction of
new, or dreadful weapons. It is the spirit of conquest.

As Mises shows, the "spirit of conquest" is the problem, not the
weapons themselves. For this reason, he places no confidence
whatever in treaties and conferences, which to him were all
bureaucratic nonsense.

International tensions are building as never before, with the
war on terrorism fueling more terrorism, which provides more
rationale for the war. The magnitude of these tensions is even
greater than in the 1930s. International debt is deeper; the degree
of worldwide inflation is more ominous.

Gold has been "discredited" by all governments. The engines of
inflation throughout the world are running at full throttle, struggling to keep the debt pyramid from collapsing. True capital
formation diminishes yearly. Military build-ups continue at
unprecedented rates. Western governments continue to finance
ruthless regimes, loaning more than $100 billion. As foreign mili-
tary capability is enhanced by our financing, we hear urgent
requests from both Democrats and Republicans to increase our
military expenditures massively. We never question our subsidies
to our "allies and friends" through massive military and economic
aid. We tear down Texas's Gulf Coast airbases, and send AWACs
aircraft to Europe and the Mideast, leaving our coastlines vulnerable. All of Japan's defense needs are paid for by the American taxpayer and the savings are passed on to their car companies and
other exporters. American car and steel industries then ask for
more protectionism through quotas and tariffs.

All this insanity, of course, is financed through massive taxation and inflation borne by our taxpayers. Without fiat money,
these wild schemes would be impossible. And, more inflation and
more planning only makes things worse. We are now in the midst
of compensating for the problems we have created with trade barriers, devaluations, floating exchange rates, bank bailouts, and
Third World and foreign government bailouts. The only answer
given to the deteriorating conditions is to either spend more on
bombs or sign worthless treaties with untrustworthy governments, and yet there is clearly another option.

No one wants to consider seriously sound money and free
trade as an alternative. Central banking and fiat money bring us

the business cycle and unemployment. They also give us international crises and war. To achieve peace and prosperity, we must accept the ideas of the free market and honest money.

Natural Rights

Ludwig von Mises was the greatest economist of all time. But he never convinced me that it

> is metaphysical nonsense to link together the "slippery" and vague notion of liberty and the unchangeable absolute laws of cosmic order. Thus the fundamental idea of liberalism [that all men are created equal and endowed by their creator with certain unalienable rights] is unmasked as a fallacy. . . . There is no room left in the framework of an experimental observation of natural phenomena for such a concept of natural rights.[12]

Mises also wrote:

> The Utilitarians do not combat arbitrary government and privileges because they are against natural law but because they are detrimental to prosperity. They recommend equality under the civil law not because men are equal but because such a policy is beneficial to the commonweal. In rejecting the illusory notions of natural law and human equality modern biology only repeated what the utilitarian champions of liberalism and democracy long before had taught in a much more persuasive way. It is obvious that no biological doctrine can invalidate what utilitarian philosophy says about the social utility of democratic government, private property, freedom and the equality under the law.[13]

Though Mises states that the "idea of natural law is quite arbitrary," I might suggest that so are the *interpretations* of utility. Inflation is very "useful" to those in power. Only a concept of natural rights can condemn the "perceived" utility of interventionism. In an effort to refute those who cautioned about policy consequences

---

[12]Ibid., p. 174.
[13]Ibid., p. 175.

"in the long run," Keynes relied upon utilitarianism by replying that "in the long run, we are all dead." Every argument I have ever heard on the House floor is presented as utilitarian and—for the *pressure groups* represented—the proposals certainly are "utilitarian." These arguments are never based on the moral principles of people's natural right to run their own lives. Santa Claus wins the "utilitarian" argument until it's too late to do anything about it.

The interventionist's reliance on the appeal of Santa Claus, "utilitarianism," and an ostensibly high-minded concern for the downtrodden can only be countered by a more truly utilitarian defense of the free market *and* the concept of natural rights—which allows the noninterventionists to take the true moral high ground. In the absence of a natural rights argument, a moral vacuum exists, into which the socialists rush, winning every time. They have won throughout the 20th century, while the concept of God-given rights has been almost obliterated. Austerity for the benefit of the next generation won't get enough votes in a democratic political system. Combine it with a moral argument for natural rights, and the chances of success are greatly enhanced.

Mises's rejection of natural rights allowed him to be "utilitarian" on the conscription issue:

> The essential task of government is defense of the social system not only against domestic gangsters but also against external foes. He who in our age opposes armaments and conscription is, perhaps unbeknown to himself, an abettor of those aiming at the enslavement of all.[14]

Conscription challenges the idea of the truly free society. But ironically, an in-depth study of the draft reveals that it is *not* practical or efficient but eminently dangerous. The utilitarian argument for conscription is an "arbitrary" argument. A natural rights philosophy is not arbitrary on the issue of the draft, which is especially dangerous in an age when economic interventionism has set the stage for war. Conscription under these conditions provides the *actors*.

---

[14]Ludwig von Mises, *Human Action*, 3rd rev. ed. (Chicago: Henry Regnery, 1966), p. 282.

Yes, interventionism leads to militant nationalism and economic isolationism. The wars that usually follow foolish economic policy depend on a fiat monetary system for financing *and* on conscription for the participants. A truly defensive war by a free society must be fought with volunteers. Only by combining a free-market economy based on a natural rights philosophy can we expect to minimize the likelihood of war.

Summary

Austrian economics has provided me with the intellectual ammunition to support my natural tendency to say "no" to all forms of government intervention. Mises provides an inspiration to stick to principle and to argue quietly and confidently in favor of the superiority of a decentralized, consumer-oriented market, in contrast to a bureaucratic centrally planned economy.

Mises is clear about the responsibility we all have in establishing a free society. He concludes *Socialism* with this advice:

> Everyone carries a part of society on his shoulders; no one is relieved of his share of responsibility by others. And no one can find a safe way out for himself if society is sweeping towards destruction. Therefore everyone, in his own interests, must thrust himself vigorously into the intellectual battle. None can stand aside with unconcern; the interests of everyone hang on the result. Whether he chooses or not, every man is drawn into the great historical struggle, the decisive battle into which our epoch has plunged us.[15]

And in *Human Action* he states:

> There is no means by which anyone can evade his personal responsibility. Whoever neglects to examine to the best of his abilities all the problems involved voluntarily surrenders his birthright to a self-appointed elite of supermen. In such vital matters blind reliance upon

---

[15]Ludwig von Mises, *Socialism* (New Haven, Conn.: Yale University Press, 1951), p. 151.

"experts" and uncritical acceptance of popular catch-
words and prejudices is tantamount to the abandon-
ment of self-determination and to yielding to other people's domination. As conditions are today, nothing can
be more important to every intelligent man than economics. His own fate and that of his progeny is at
stake.[16]

I'm convinced, as was Mises, that the solutions to the crisis we
face must be positive (which is just one reason I am so pleased by
the establishment of the Ludwig von Mises Institute). He stated in
The Anti-Capitalistic Mentality that the "anti-movement" has "no
chance whatever to succeed" and that "what alone can prevent the
civilized nations of western Europe, America and Australia from
being enslaved by the barbarism of Moscow is open and unre-
stricted support of *laissez-faire* capitalism."[17]

Without Austrian economics, I would not have had my political career. The strongest motivating force in my political activities
is to live free since I was born free. Liberty is my first goal. The free
market is the only result that can be expected from a free society. I
do not accept individual freedom *because* the market is efficient.
Even if the free market were less "efficient" than central planning,
I would still prefer my personal freedom to coercion. Fortunately,
I don't need to make a choice. Austrian economics upholds the
market's efficiency, and that reinforces my overwhelming desire
and right to be free.

If no adequate intellectual explanation existed as to the efficiency of the free market, no political activism of any sort would
be possible for any pro-freedom person. Our position would only
be a theoretical pipe dream.

I see no conflict however between a utilitarian defense of the
market economy and the argument for a free market as a *consequence* of a moral commitment to natural God-given rights, for
there is no conflict. The economist's approval of the market for

---

[16]Mises, *Human Action*, Scholar's Edition, pp. 874–75.
[17]Ludwig von Mises, *The Anti-Capitalistic Mentality* (South Holland, Ill.:
Libertarian Press, 1972), p. 112.

purely utilitarian reasons actually becomes a more "objective" analysis if *not* approached from a natural rights standpoint. But when combined with a natural-rights philosophy, it is even *more* powerful. No choice must be made. The utilitarian argument does not exclude the belief that life and liberty originate with the Creator. When they are added together they become doubly important.

When one argues for the free market on utilitarian grounds, one starts with particular actions by the individual. In starting with a natural rights argument the "a priori" becomes "the gift of life and liberty" as natural or God-given.

The utilitarians may be neutral or antagonistic regarding the origins of life and liberty, but this in no way weakens their explanation of the technical advantages of a free economic system. However, those who accept a natural rights philosophy have no choice whatsoever but to accept *laissez-faire* capitalism.

Mises's utilitarian defense of the market opens political careers for those who believe in liberty, courage, and even dares one who truly believes in the system to present it in political terms.

Mises in *Human Action* says:

> The flowering of human society depends on two factors: the intellectual power of outstanding men to conceive sound social and economic theories, and the ability of these or other men to make these ideologies palatable to the majority.[18]

Ludwig von Mises certainly provided sound economic and social theories. I hope that my modest success in politics may encourage others to try it, and help prove Mises "wrong," showing that a political career *is* open to men and women who do not identify themselves with the interests of a pressure group, but with the liberty of all. ∎

---

[18]Mises, *Human Action*, Scholar's Edition, p. 860.

PART THREE

Reforming Social Security

Everyone concedes that Social Security needs to be reformed or it will soon be insolvent. However, what analysts often omit is that the so-called "trust fund" consists of IOUs from the government. Right now when the federal government takes in more money from Social Security withholding than it pays out to current beneficiaries, it still spends the difference, and "sells" a government bond into the Social Security trust fund. All this smoke-and-mirrors doesn't evade the fact that the government has made trillions of dollars of promises that it can't keep. In this section I outline some of my proposals to restore sanity to Social Security.

Senior Citizens' Freedom to Work Act of 1999

Congressional Record – U.S. House of Representatives
March 1, 2000

Mr. Speaker, I am pleased to offer my support to the Senior Citizens' Freedom to Work Act (H.R. 5), which repeals the Social Security "earnings limitations." During a time when an increasing number of senior citizens are able to enjoy productive lives well past retirement age and businesses are in desperate need of experienced workers, it makes no sense to punish seniors for working. Yet the federal government does just that by deducting a portion of seniors' monthly Social Security check should they continue to work and earn income above an arbitrary government-set level.

When the government takes money every month from people's paychecks for the Social Security Trust Fund, it promises retirees that the money will be there for them when they retire. The government should keep that promise and not reduce benefits simply because a senior chooses to work.

Furthermore, Mr. Speaker, by providing a disincentive to remaining in the workforce, the earnings limitation deprives the American economy of the benefits of senior citizens who wish to continue working but are discouraged from doing so by fear of losing part of their Social Security benefits. The federal government should not discourage any citizen from seeking or holding productive employment.

The underlying issue of the earnings limitation goes back to the fact that money from the trust fund is routinely spent for things other than paying pensions to beneficiaries. This is why the first bill I introduced in the 106th Congress was the Social Security Preservation Act (H.R. 219), which forbids Congress from spending Social Security funds on anything other than paying Social Security pensions.

In conclusion, Mr. Speaker, I wish to reiterate my strong support for the Senior Citizens' Freedom to Work Act. Repealing the "earnings limitation" will help ensure that America's seniors can continue to enjoy fulfilling and productive lives in their "golden years." I also urge my colleagues to protect the integrity of the Social Security Trust Fund by cosponsoring the Social Security Preservation Act (H.R. 219). ■

Social Security Tax Relief Act

Congressional Record – U.S. House of Representatives
September 6, 2000

Mr. Speaker, I am pleased to rise in support of the Social Security Tax Relief Act (H.R. 4865). By repealing the 1993 tax increase on Social Security benefits, Congress will take a good first step toward eliminating one of the most unfair taxes imposed on seniors: the tax on Social Security benefits.

Eliminating the 1993 tax on Social Security benefits has long been one of my goals in Congress. In fact, I introduced legislation to repeal this tax increase in 1997, and I am pleased to see Congress acting on this issue. I would remind my colleagues that the justification for increasing this tax in 1993 was to reduce the budget deficit. Now, President Clinton, who first proposed the tax increase, and most members of Congress say the deficit is gone. So, by the President's own reasoning, there is no need to keep this tax hike in place.

Because Social Security benefits are financed with tax dollars, taxing these benefits is yet another incidence of "double taxation."

Furthermore, "taxing" benefits paid by the government is merely an accounting trick, a "shell game" which allows members of Congress to reduce benefits by subterfuge. This allows Congress to continue using the Social Security trust fund as a means of financing other government programs and mask the true size of the federal deficit.

Mr. Speaker, the Social Security Tax Relief Act, combined with our action earlier this year to repeal the earnings limitation, goes a long way toward reducing the burden imposed by the federal government on senior citizens. However, I hope my colleagues will not stop at repealing the 1993 tax increase, but will work to repeal all taxes on Social Security benefits. I am cosponsoring legislation to achieve this goal, H.R. 761.

Congress should also act on my Social Security Preservation Act (H.R. 219), which ensures that all money in the Social Security Trust Fund is spent solely on Social Security. When the government takes money for the Social Security Trust Fund, it promises the American people that the money will be there for them when they retire. Congress has a moral obligation to keep that promise.

In conclusion, Mr. Speaker, I urge my colleagues to help free senior citizens from oppressive taxation by supporting the Social Security Benefits Tax Relief Act (H.R. 4865). I also urge my colleagues to join me in working to repeal all taxes on Social Security benefits and ensuring that monies from the Social Security trust fund are used solely for Social Security and not wasted on frivolous government programs. ∎

Social Security Preservation Act
Congressional Record – U.S. House of Representatives
January 8, 2003

Mr. Speaker, I rise to protect the integrity of the Social Security trust fund by introducing the Social Security Preservation Act. The Social Security Preservation Act is a rather simple bill which states that all monies raised by the Social Security trust fund will be spent in payments to beneficiaries, with excess receipts invested in interest-bearing certificates of deposit. This will help keep Social Security trust fund monies from being diverted to other programs, as well as allow the fund to grow by providing for investment in interest-bearing instruments.

The Social Security Preservation Act ensures that the government will keep its promises to America's seniors that taxes collected for Social Security will be used for Social Security. When the government taxes Americans to fund Social Security, it promises the American people that the money will be there for them when they retire. Congress has a moral obligation to keep that promise.

The return of massive federal deficits, and the accompanying pressure for massive new raids on the trust fund, make it more important than ever that Congress protect the trust fund from big spending, pork-barrel politics. I call upon all my colleagues, regardless of which proposal for long-term Social Security reform they support, to stand up for America's seniors by cosponsoring the Social Security Preservation Act. ■

Social Security for American Citizens Only!

Congressional Record – U.S. House of Representatives
January 30, 2003

Mr. Speaker, today I introduce the Social Security for American Citizens Only Act. This act forbids the federal government from providing Social Security benefits to noncitizens. It also ends the practice of totalization. Totalization is where the Social Security Administration takes into account the number of years an individual worked abroad, and thus was not paying payroll taxes, in determining that individual's eligibility for Social Security benefits!

Hard as it may be to believe, the United States government already provides Social Security benefits to citizens of 17 other countries. Under current law, citizens of those countries covered by these agreements may have an easier time getting Social Security benefits than public school teachers or policemen!

Obviously, this program provides a threat to the already fragile Social Security system, and the threat is looming larger. Just before Christmas, the press reported on a pending deal between the United States and the government of Mexico, which would make hundreds of thousands of Mexican citizens eligible for U.S. Social Security benefits. Totalization is the centerpiece of this proposal, so even if a Mexican citizen did not work in the United States long enough to qualify for Social Security, the number of years worked in Mexico would be added to bring up the total and thus make the Mexican worker eligible for cash transfers from the United States.

Mr. Speaker, press reports also indicate that thousands of foreigners who would qualify for U.S. Social Security benefits actually came to the United States and worked here illegally. That's right: The federal government may actually allow someone who came to the United States illegally, worked less than the required number of years to qualify for Social Security, and then returned to Mexico for the rest of his working years, to collect full U.S. Social

Security benefits while living in Mexico. That is an insult to the millions of Americans who pay their entire working lives into the system and now face the possibility that there may be nothing left when it is their turn to retire.

The proposed agreement is nothing more than a financial reward to those who have willingly and knowingly violated our own immigration laws. Talk about an incentive for illegal immigration! How many more would break the law to come to this country if promised U.S. government paychecks for life? Is creating a global welfare state on the back of the American taxpayer a good idea? The program also establishes a very disturbing precedent of U.S. foreign aid to individual citizens rather than to states.

Estimates of what this deal with the Mexican government would cost top one billion dollars per year. Supporters of the Social Security to Mexico deal may attempt to downplay the effect the agreement would have on the system, but actions speak louder than words: According to several press reports, the State Department and the Social Security Administration are already negotiating to build a new building in Mexico City to handle the expected rush of applicants for this new program!

As the system braces for a steep increase in those who will be drawing from the Social Security trust fund, it makes no sense to expand it into a global welfare system. Social Security was designed to provide support for retired American citizens who worked in the United States. We should be shoring up the system for those Americans who have paid in for decades, not expanding it to cover foreigners who have not.

It is long past time for Congress to stand up to the internationalist bureaucrats and start looking out for the American worker. I therefore call upon my colleagues to stop the use of the Social Security trust fund as yet another vehicle for foreign aid by cosponsoring the Social Security for American Citizens Only Act. ■

PART FOUR

Giving Money Back
to the Taxpayers

These selections are some of my attempts over the years to return income back to its rightful owners. Many of my colleagues in Congress share my goals to provide assistance to education, health care, and volunteering. But unfortunately they don't understand the crucial difference between giving people a tax credit, versus giving them a government subsidy. But of course there's all the difference in the world between letting Paul keep more of his paycheck, versus robbing Peter to give a subsidy to Paul. Another point I stress is that if the federal government would simply respect the limits set forth in the Constitution, we could easily abolish the income tax and IRS forever.

The Agriculture Education Freedom Act

Congressional Record – U.S. House of Representatives
February 16, 2000

Mr. Speaker, I rise to introduce the Agriculture Education Freedom Act. This bill addresses a great injustice being perpetrated by the federal government on those youngsters who participate in programs such as 4-H or the Future Farmers of America. Under current tax law, children are forced to pay federal income tax when they sell livestock they have raised as part of an agricultural education program. Think of this for a moment. These kids are trying to better themselves, earn some money, save some money, and what does Congress do? We pick on these kids by taxing them.

It is truly amazing that with all the hand-wringing in this Congress over the alleged need to further restrict liberty and grow the size of government "for the children" we would continue to tax young people who are trying to lead responsible lives and prepare for the future. Even if the serious social problems today's youth face could be solved by new federal bureaucracies and programs, it is still unfair to pick on those kids who are trying to do the right thing.

These children are not even old enough to vote, yet we are forcing them to pay taxes! What ever happened to no taxation without representation? No wonder young people are so cynical about government!

It is time we stopped taxing youngsters who are trying to earn money to go to college by selling livestock they have raised through their participation in programs such as 4-H or Future Farmers of America. Therefore I call on my colleagues to join me in supporting the Agriculture Education Freedom Act. ∎

The Family Health Tax Cut Act

Congressional Record — U.S. House of Representatives
June 30, 2000

Mr. Speaker, today I attempted to help working Americans provide for their children's health care needs by introducing the Family Health Tax Cut Act. The Family Health Tax Cut Act provides parents with a tax credit of up to $500 for health care expenses of dependent children. Parents caring for a child with a disability, terminal disease, cancer, or any other health condition requiring specialized care would receive a tax credit of up to $3,000 to help cover their child's health care expenses. The tax credit would be available to all citizens regardless of whether or not they itemize their deductions.

The tax credits provided in this bill will be especially helpful to those Americans whose employers cannot afford to provide their employees health insurance. These workers must struggle to meet the medical bills of themselves and their families. This burden is especially heavy on parents whose children have a medical condition, such as cancer or a physical disability, which requires long-term or specialized health care.

As an OB-GYN who has had the privilege of delivering more than four thousand babies, I know how important it is that parents have the resources to provide adequate health care for their children. The inability of many working Americans to provide health care for their children is rooted in one of the great inequities of the tax code: Congress's failure to allow individuals the same ability to deduct health care costs that it grants to businesses. As a direct result of Congress's refusal to provide individuals with health care related tax credits, parents whose employers do not provide health insurance have to struggle to provide health care for their children. Many of these parents work in low-income jobs; oftentimes their only recourse to health care is the local emergency room.

Sometimes parents are forced to delay seeking care for their children until minor health concerns that could have been easily treated become serious problems requiring expensive treatment! If these parents had access to the type of tax credits provided in the Family Health Tax Cut Act they would be better able to provide care for their children and our nation's already overcrowded emergency room facilities would be relieved of the burden of having to provide routine care for people who otherwise cannot afford any other alternative.

According to research on the effects of this bill done by my staff and legislative counsel, the benefit of these tax credits would begin to be felt by joint filers with incomes slightly above $18,000 a year or single income filers with incomes slightly above $15,000 per year. Clearly this bill will be of the most benefit to low-income Americans balancing the demands of taxation with the needs of their children.

Under the Family Health Tax Cut Act, a struggling single mother with an asthmatic child would at last be able to provide for her child's needs, while a working-class family will not have to worry about how they will pay the bills if one of their children requires lengthy hospitalization or some other form of specialized care.

Mr. Speaker, this Congress has a moral responsibility to provide low-income parents struggling to care for a sick child tax relief in order to help them better meet their child's medical expenses. I would ask any of my colleagues who would say that we cannot enact the Family Tax Cut Act because it would cause the government to lose too much revenue, who is more deserving of this money, Congress or the working-class parents of a sick child?

The Family Health Tax Cut Act takes a major step toward helping working Americans meet their health care needs by providing them with generous health care related tax cuts and tax credits. I urge my colleagues to support the pro-family, pro-health care tax cuts contained in the Family Health Tax Cut Act. ∎

The Public Safety Tax Cut Act

Congressional Record – U.S. House of Representatives
June 25, 2002

Mr. Speaker, I am pleased to introduce the Public Safety Tax Cut Act. This legislation will achieve two important public policy goals. First, it will effectively overturn a ruling of the Internal Revenue Service which has declared as taxable income the waiving of fees by local governments who provide service for public safety volunteers.

Many local governments use volunteer firefighters and auxiliary police either in place of, or as a supplement to, their public safety professionals. Often as an incentive to would-be volunteers, the local entities waive all or a portion of the fees typically charged for city services such as the provision of drinking water, sewer charges, or debris pick up.

Local entities make these decisions for the purpose of encouraging folks to volunteer, and seldom do these benefits come anywhere near the level of a true compensation for the many hours of training and service required of the volunteers. This, of course, does not even mention the fact that these volunteers very possibly could be called into a situation where they have to put their lives on the line.

Rather than encouraging this type of volunteerism, which is so crucial, particularly to America's rural communities, the IRS has decided that the provision of the benefits described above amounts to taxable income. Not only does this adversely affect the financial position of the volunteer by imposing new taxes upon him or her, it has in fact led local entities to stop providing these benefits, thus taking away a key tool they have used to recruit volunteers. That is why the IRS ruling in this instance has a substantial negative impact on the spirit of American volunteerism. How far could this go? For example, would consistent application mean that a local Salvation Army volunteer must be taxed for the value of a complimentary ticket to that organization's annual county dinner? This is obviously bad policy.

This legislation would rectify the situation by specifically exempting these types of benefits from federal taxation.

Next, this legislation would also provide paid professional police and fire officers with a $1,000 per year tax credit. These professional public safety officers put their lives on the line each and every day, and I think we all agree that there is no way to properly compensate them for the fabulous services they provide. In America we have a tradition of local, as opposed to federal, law enforcement and public safety provision. So, while it is not the role of our federal government to increase the salaries of local officers, it certainly is within our authority to increase their take-home pay by reducing the amount of money that we take from their pockets via federal taxation, and that is something this bill specifically does as well.

President George Bush has called on Americans to volunteer their time and energy to enhance public safety. Shouldn't Congress do its part by reducing taxes that discourage public safety volunteerism? Shouldn't Congress also show its appreciation to police officers and fire fighters by reducing their taxes? I believe the answer to both of these questions is a resounding "Yes," and therefore I am proud to introduce the Public Safety Tax Cut Act. I request that my fellow Members join in support of this key legislation. ∎

End the Income Tax — Pass the Liberty Amendment

Congressional Record – U.S. House of Representatives
January 30, 2003

Mr. Speaker, I am pleased to introduce the Liberty Amendment, which repeals the 16th Amendment, thus paving the way for real change in the way government collects and spends the people's hard-earned money. The Liberty Amendment also explicitly forbids the federal government from performing any action not explicitly authorized by the United States Constitution.

The 16th Amendment gives the federal government a direct claim on the lives of American citizens by enabling Congress to levy a direct income tax on individuals. Until the passage of the 16th Amendment, the Supreme Court had consistently held that Congress had no power to impose an income tax.

Income taxes are responsible for the transformation of the federal government from one of limited powers into a vast leviathan whose tentacles reach into almost every aspect of American life. Thanks to the income tax, today the federal government routinely invades our privacy, and penalizes our every endeavor.

The Founding Fathers realized that "the power to tax is the power to destroy," which is why they did not give the federal government the power to impose an income tax. Needless to say, the Founders would be horrified to know that Americans today give more than a third of their income to the federal government.

Income taxes not only diminish liberty, they retard economic growth by discouraging work and production. Our current tax system also forces Americans to waste valuable time and money on compliance with an ever-more complex tax code. The increased interest in flat-tax and national sales tax proposals, as well as the increasing number of small businesses that question the Internal Revenue Service's (IRS) "withholding" system provides further proof that America is tired of the labyrinthine tax code. Americans are also increasingly fed up with an IRS that continues to ride roughshod over their civil liberties, despite recent "pro-taxpayer" reforms.

Mr. Speaker, America survived and prospered for 140 years without an income tax, and with a federal government that generally adhered to strictly constitutional functions, operating with modest excise revenues. The income tax opened the door to the era (and errors) of Big government. I hope my colleagues will help close that door by cosponsoring the Liberty Amendment. ∎

Teacher Tax Cut Act

Congressional Record – U.S. House of Representatives
February 11, 2003

Mr. Speaker, I am pleased to introduce two pieces of legislation that raise the pay of teachers and other educators by cutting their taxes. I am sure that all my colleagues agree that it is long past time to begin treating those who have dedicated their lives to educating America's children with the respect they deserve. Compared to other professionals, educators are under-appreciated and under-paid. This must change if America is to have the finest education system in the world!

Quality education is impossible without quality teaching. If we continue to undervalue educators, it will become harder to attract, and keep, good people in the education profession. While educators' pay is primarily a local issue, Congress can, and should, help raise educators' take home pay by reducing educators' taxes.

This is why I am introducing the Teachers Tax Cut Act. This legislation provides every teacher in America with a $1,000 tax credit. I am also introducing the Professional Educators Tax Relief Act, which extends the $1,000 tax credit to counselors, librarians, and all school personnel involved in any aspect of the K–12 academic program.

The Teacher Tax Cut Act and the Professional Educators Tax Relief Act increase the salaries of teachers and other education professionals without raising federal expenditures. By raising the take-home pay of professional educators, these bills encourage highly qualified people to enter, and remain in, education. These bills also let America's professional educators know that the American people and the Congress respect their work.

I hope all my colleagues join me in supporting our nation's teachers and other professional educators by cosponsoring the Teacher Tax Cut Act and the Professional Educators Tax Relief Act. ∎

The Family Education Freedom Act

Congressional Record – U.S. House of Representatives
February 11, 2003

Mr. Speaker, I rise today to introduce the Family Education Freedom Act, a bill to empower millions of working and middle-class Americans to choose a nonpublic education for their children, as well as making it easier for parents to actively participate in improving public schools. The Family Education Freedom Act accomplishes its goals by allowing American parents a tax credit of up to $3,000 for the expenses incurred in sending their child to private, public, parochial, other religious school, or for home schooling their children.

The Family Education Freedom Act returns the fundamental principle of a truly free economy to America's education system: what the great economist Ludwig von Mises called "consumer sovereignty." Consumer sovereignty simply means consumers decide who succeeds or fails in the market. Businesses that best satisfy consumer demand will be the most successful. Consumer sovereignty is the means by which the free market maximizes human happiness.

Currently, consumers are less than sovereign in the education market. Funding decisions are increasingly controlled by the federal government. Because "he who pays the piper calls the tune," public, and even private schools, are paying greater attention to the dictates of federal "educrats" while ignoring the wishes of the parents to an ever-greater degree. As such, the lack of consumer sovereignty in education is destroying parental control of education and replacing it with state control. Loss of control is a key reason why so many of America's parents express dissatisfaction with the educational system.

According to a study by The Polling Company, over 70 percent of all Americans support education tax credits! This is just one of numerous studies and public opinion polls showing that Americans want Congress to get the federal bureaucracy out of the schoolroom and give parents more control over their children's education.

Today, Congress can fulfill the wishes of the American people for greater control over their children's education by simply allowing parents to keep more of their hard-earned money to spend on education rather than force them to send it to Washington to support education programs reflective only of the values and priorities of Congress and the federal bureaucracy.

The $3,000 tax credit will make a better education affordable for millions of parents. Mr. Speaker, many parents who would choose to send their children to private, religious, or parochial schools are unable to afford the tuition, in large part because of the enormous tax burden imposed on the American family by Washington.

The Family Education Freedom Act also benefits parents who choose to send their children to public schools. Parents of children in public schools may use this credit to help improve their local schools by helping finance the purchase of educational tools such as computers or to ensure their local schools can offer enriching extracurricular activities such as music programs. Parents of public school students may also wish to use the credit to pay for special services, such as tutoring, for their children.

Increasing parental control of education is superior to funneling more federal tax dollars, followed by greater federal control, into the schools. According to a Manhattan Institute study of the effects of state policies promoting parental control over education, a minimal increase in parental control boosts students' average SAT verbal score by 21 points and students' SAT math score by 22 points! The Manhattan Institute study also found that increasing parental control of education is the best way to improve student performance on the National Assessment of Education Progress (NAEP) tests.

Clearly, enactment of the Family Education Freedom Act is the best thing this Congress could do to improve public education. Furthermore, a greater reliance on parental expenditures rather than government tax dollars will help make the public schools into true community schools that reflect the wishes of parents and the interests of the students.

The Family Education Freedom Act will also aid those parents who choose to educate their children at home. Home schooling has become an increasingly popular, and successful, method of educating children. Home schooled children outperform their public school peers by 30 to 37 percentile points across all subjects on nationally standardized achievement exams. Home schooling parents spend thousands of dollars annually, in addition to the wages forgone by the spouse who forgoes outside employment, in order to educate their children in the loving environment of the home.

Ultimately, Mr. Speaker, this bill is about freedom. Parental control of child rearing, especially education, is one of the bulwarks of liberty. No nation can remain free when the state has greater influence over the knowledge and values transmitted to children than the family.

By moving to restore the primacy of parents to education, the Family Education Freedom Act will not only improve America's education, it will restore a parent's right to choose how best to educate one's own child, a fundamental freedom that has been eroded by the increase in federal education expenditures and the corresponding decrease in the ability of parents to provide for their children's education out of their own pockets. I call on all my colleagues to join me in allowing parents to devote more of their resources to their children's education and less to feed the wasteful Washington bureaucracy by supporting the Family Education Freedom Act. ∎

The False Tax Cut Debate

Congressional Record – U.S. House of Representatives
May 6, 2003

The current tax cut debate is more about politics than serious economics. Both sides use demagoguery but don't propose significant tax cuts. The benefits that could come from the current tax cut proposal unfortunately are quite small and not immediate.

Some say tax cuts raise revenues by increasing economic activity, thus providing Congress with even more money to spend. Others say lowering taxes simply lowers revenues and increases deficits.

Some say we must target tax cuts to the poor and middle class so they will spend the money. Others say tax cuts should be targeted to the rich so they can invest and create jobs.

We must accept that it's hard to give tax cuts to people who don't pay taxes. But, we could, if we wanted, cut payroll taxes for lower income workers.

The truth is, government officials can't know what consumers and investors will do if they get a tax cut. Plugging tax cut data into a computer and expecting an accurate projection of the economic outcome is about as reliable as asking Congress to project government surpluses.

Two important points are purposely ignored:

1. The money people earn is their own and they have a moral right to keep as much of it as possible. It is not Congress's money to spend.

2. Government spending is the problem! Taking a big chunk of the people's earnings out of the economy, whether through taxes or borrowing, is always harmful.

Taxation is more honest and direct, and the harm is less hidden. Borrowing, especially since the Federal Reserve creates credit out of thin air to loan to big spenders in Congress, is more deceitful. It hides the effects and delays the consequences. But over the long term this method of financing is much more dangerous.

The process by which the Fed monetizes debt and accommodates Congress contributes to, if not causes, most of our problems.

This process of government financing:

1. Generates the business cycle and thus increases unemployment;

2. Destroys the value of the dollar and thus causes price inflation;

3. Encourages deficits by reducing restraints on congressional spending;

4. Encourages an increase in the current account deficit (the dollar being the reserve currency) and causes huge foreign indebtedness;

5. Reflects a philosophy of instant gratification that says, "Live for the pleasures of today and have future generations pay the bills."

Two points to remember:

1. Whether or not people can keep what they earn is first a moral issue and second an economic issue. Tax cuts should never be referred to as a "cost to government." Tax cuts should be much bigger and come much sooner for everyone.

2. The real issue is total spending by government, yet this issue is ignored or politicized by both sides of the aisle in Congress.

The political discussion about whether to cut taxes avoids the real issues and instead degenerates into charges of class and party warfare, with both sides lusting for power.

Of course the real issue for the ages, namely "What is the proper role for government in a constitutional republic?" is totally ignored. And yet the bigger question is: "Are the American people determined they still wish to have a constitutional republic?"

Police Security Protection Act

Congressional Record — U.S. House of Representatives
August 1, 2007

Mr. Speaker, I am pleased to help America's law enforcement officers by introducing the Police Security Protection Act. This legislation provides police officers a tax credit for the purchase of armored vests.

Professional law enforcement officers put their lives on the line each and every day. Reducing the tax liability of law enforcement officers so they can afford armored vests is one of the best ways Congress can help and encourage these brave men and women. After all, an armored vest could literally make the difference between life or death for a police officer. I hope my colleagues will join me in helping our nation's law enforcement officers by cosponsoring the Police Security Protection Act. ■

PART FIVE

Money and Banking:
Gold versus Fiat

These selections show my overriding concern throughout my political career for sound money. Only an honest dollar backed up by gold can provide a solid foundation for sustainable economic growth. As theory and history show, politicians can't be trusted with the printing press. Inflating the currency not only causes prices to rise, but the Fed's manipulation of interest rates leads to the boom-bust cycle in the economy.

To Provide for Amendment of the Bretton Woods Agreement Act, and for Other Purposes

Hearing before the Subcommittee on International Finance
of the Committee on Banking, Housing and Urban Affairs
Congressional Record – U.S. House of Representatives
August 27, 1976

In the Banking Committee I was the one who voted against this bill. It was a 24-to-1 vote.

By the time it got to the floor, ten members of the Banking Committee voted against this bill. So I think this goes to show that there were some reconsiderations and second thoughts on this bill.

It was stated in our committee that these were some technical changes in the Bretton Woods Agreement.

This is the size of it, and I would like to emphasize this. This is more than technical.

The Senate statement in one of the introductions I read said that they were fundamental changes, and I would have to agree with that, that these are fundamental changes, that we are going through fundamental changes in the International Monetary Fund.

I feel as though a vote for this bill is a vote for inflation, especially on an international level.

I do not agree with the sale of the gold. I do not think that is the proper way to handle this.

I think what they are doing also with the profits from this gold, funds that they get, they are using them to give to the Third World nations is truly foreign aid and should be under control of the Congress and not through some international body.

I believe in international monetary issues, we find a good bit of ignorance floating about.

I think there are several reasons for this. It is boring to many people. They do not involve themselves in the issues. And it is also a nonpolitical issue. You don't gain votes by talking about IMF back in your district.

So for this reason people do not interest themselves in a political sense and there is disinterest in subjects such as this.

We have had statements made in the past on monetary policy that disturb me. I think they reflect the disinterest they have.

At one meeting Kennedy walked into, he said, "Tell me again; how does the Federal Reserve System finance our debt." He was confused about exactly how the financing worked.

Mr. Johnson one time said that, "We will see that there are so many silver half-dollars in circulation that nobody will hold them," not understanding that bad money drives out good money. So he produced more half-dollars in one year than had been minted in approximately 100 years. Yet the silver half-dollars disappeared. He could not defy the laws of economics.

I understand on one of the Watergate tapes Mr. Nixon said, "Don't bother me with devaluation. Just take care of it. Do what you have to do." To him it was unimportant.

But I do believe that this is a general problem. There is a good bit of economic ignorance that floats around.

After the Smithsonian agreement, which was in 1971—it was heralded by the President, "The greatest monetary agreement in the history of the world." It lasted a little over a year.

People are heralding this as a fundamental basic good change. I don't think it will be any better than the changes made in the Smithsonian agreement.

This bill, in essence, ratifies floating, phasing out the gold, increases quotas, and establishes a new powerful executive council.

I think the phasing out of the gold problem is a continual harassment and continual hostility toward sound money, honest money, commodity money, and I disagree with this.

The opposite of honest commodity money is inflation, inflation either at a local governmental/national level or on a scale such as we are talking about later in the IMF.

The sales of gold, I consider illegal. This was backed up by a statement from the Library of Congress; they use the scarce currency clause to sell this gold. If anybody knows anything about dollars these days they are not too scarce so they are really stretching the point about the scarce currency clause.

And the method they are using in selling the gold, by first giving it to the Treasury for $42, then the Treasury resells it to the Fund at $42 and the Fund sells it at market price using the profit for foreign aid. They have disrupted the market so much that the price of gold has been driven down to such a degree that what it is trying to accomplish it is not doing because they are not having near the funds they once thought they would accumulate for these foreign aid projects.

I think what they don't want is the discipline and integrity of an honest money system. This is the reason that they must go and be on record and be registered saying that we do not want to have anything to do with gold and restraints and disciplines.

On the subject of quotas; I disagree that it is a transfer of assets. If the American taxpayer wants those $2 billion, he cannot get them back. It is only under very special circumstances that we can benefit once that $2 billion gets into the fund. I think it should be in the budget.

I know Mr. Proxmire has always been concerned about budgetary matters and watches fiscal policy and I would hope he would agree it must be put into the budget because I think it is dereliction of our duty if we do not.

It was in the budget up until 1969 and it should be put back. The Executive Council bothers me. You mentioned your concern about getting information and materials from the IMF. Let me tell you, when this goes into effect, the information is going to go in one direction. It is going to go from us to the IMF.

Mr. Simon stated the amendment

> provides broad new authority for the IMF to oversee the compliance of each member with its obligation. This authority for fund surveillance gives the fund the tactic

of applying a global perspective to action of those members that cause adjustments or other problems for other nations.

Members are obliged to provide the fund with information necessary for surveillance of these exchange rate policies.

The other thing that is very important here, it isn't only the deficit countries they want to control and tell them what to do with their fiscal and monetary policies, it is the surplus countries.

If we ever went back in this country to sound monetary policy and sound fiscal policy, and had a sound dollar and did not inflate, we could become a surplus country again. Even if we kept our house in order under these arrangements, they will have the right to come in and supervise our fiscal policy so that they can take the benefits we have had in this country from good monetary policy and export them to somebody such as England or Italy that may be needing some help due to an inflationary policy.

This act also ratifies floating. We have been floating since 1973, officially. We do not need an IMF to float. The float evidently is necessary as a market adjustment for different nations inflating at different rates. We cannot go back to arbitrarily fixed rates.

The only way you could get a fixed rate is if you related each individual currency to some relatively fixed commodity such as silver and gold. So you cannot arbitrarily set fixed rates but try to supervise floating rates and set up a lot of rules and regulations and then you have England inflating at a certain rate and us at another rate. It's doomed to failure.

The devaluation that everybody heralded as a tremendous help to us a couple years ago has not really helped. Devaluation in this way is a temporary device that helps just for a short time. Right now, if you look in the papers in the *Wall Street Journal*, it shows our deficit in our balance of trade was up over $800 million last month.

Just because you lowered the cost of exports, the cost of imports go up. It also increases demands because your prices went down temporarily. With the increase in demands and increase in the cost of your imports, you go back to the need for higher prices in your country and then a need and incentive to inflate the currency again.

Switzerland hasn't belonged to the IMF. They have a relatively sound currency. They do not have inflation. They do not have this kind of problem. To think that a system, an international system can work on floating is like arguing for 50 currencies in this country.

If we can realize that, the benefit of the sound currency or one currency that we can relate to in 50 States, then we can realize why we need one currency of soundness throughout the world. The problem here is a moral problem as well as an economic problem.

The problem is that of inflation. The unwillingness of nations to pay for what they are spending. We inflate because we have a deficit, $75 billion, $80 billion a year because we pass out to people things that they want and we don't have the guts and the courage to tax them if that is what truly is necessary.

So, what do we do, we increase the monetary supply and that is inflation. Now, we are planning to condone it and do it on an international scale. I am convinced it will not work. Within a few years we will know that I don't think there is any doubt that we cannot defy the laws of economics.

Sound money has always been the rallying point, 5,000 years of history has proven that. Even though we have gotten away with this for a good many years, even though we arbitrarily kept the dollar related to gold at $35 an ounce, it was because we were so wealthy that we got away with it. Eventually the system fell apart and now we are in worse shape than we have ever been.

We do not have a store of wealth like we had before. We have an economy that is very shaky. Nobody is sure that we will completely get out of this recession that we have just gotten over. How can we support an unsound dollar and unsound currency and an international monetary scheme that we are working on here now, I say that we have serious considerations for what is going on and it is our obligation and duty as Representatives in this nation to study it closely. ■

Inflation — The Overriding Concern of All Americans

Congressional Record — U.S. House of Representatives
February 15, 1979

Mr. Speaker, today the overriding concern of all Americans is the inflation with which they have been forced to live. In recent years concern about inflation has been transformed into fear. If we, as their representatives, do not do something quickly to stop this destructive process, this fear will turn to panic.

Not one Member of this House publicly endorses inflation as a proper economic policy. We all denounce the evil that it brings, and yet the inflation continues at an unprecedented rate.

If all our colleagues are well intended, as I sincerely believe, why are we so unsuccessful in providing an economy with falling or stable prices?

I would like to suggest to you and to my colleagues that perhaps the conventional definition of inflation is incorrect. If it could be shown that our basic assumption about the cause of inflation is wrong, it would help us to understand why the concerted efforts of Republicans, Democrats, liberals, and conservatives, have failed so miserably in the past ten years, in accomplishing anything whatsoever in restraining the destructive forces of inflation. ∎

Curtailing the Discretionary Powers of the Federal Reserve

Congressional Record – U.S. House of Representatives
March 15, 1979

Mr. Speaker, while I applaud the committee's recognition of the fact that "reducing inflation will require persistent, measured, monetary and fiscal restraint," I believe that the committee is still looking at the Federal Reserve through rose-colored glasses. Throughout its 65-year history, the Federal Reserve has pursued a policy of deliberate inflation and manipulation of the money supply, a policy which has caused numerous recessions, massive unemployment, double-digit price inflation, international exchange crises, and the largest and longest depression in our national history. The committee does note that the Federal Reserve had promised moderation and consistency in monetary policy before, but that it has been either "unwilling or unable" to keep its promise. I concur with the committee's view of the importance and necessity of the Federal Reserve keeping its promises on monetary policy, but I am skeptical nonetheless. We need only look at the record of the Federal Reserve, which I have briefly recapitulated above, in order to understand my skepticism. The only permanent and practical solution to the problem of inflation – the only way to implement the Federal Reserve's and this committee's goal of persistent monetary restraint – is to decouple money and politics altogether, removing control over the money supply from any governmental or quasi-governmental institution. The deregulation of money, not simply a slowing in the growth of the money supply, must be our goal. The committee is looking in the right direction, but it has not yet seen the correct destination.

There seems to be a growing consensus among economists that the American people will suffer through another government-caused recession later this year or early next year. The committee takes note of this view and expresses its concern. What it does not seem to realize, however, is that the persistent policy of monetary inflation pursued by the Federal Reserve makes these recessions inevitable. The timing of the next recession may be a matter of guessing; the fact of the next recession is not. In view of this fact, it is not enough to express concern and then declare that the Federal Reserve's monetary growth targets are appropriate. They are not. If we intend to pursue a genuine anti-inflationary policy, it is not appropriate to endorse a growth in the money supply. Nor is it appropriate for the committee to endorse even greater inflation should "measurements reveal that the Federal Reserve's target ranges for the growth of the other monetary and credit aggregates are not being met."

The committee is correct in demanding monetary restraint from the Federal Reserve; the problem is that it does not demand enough restraint and allows the Federal Reserve to exercise entirely too much discretion in its control of the money supply. This, of course, is not to argue for congressional control of the money supply, but it is to argue that discretionary and arbitrary control over the money supply by any governmental agency must be abolished. If any responsibility is granted to the government with respect to money, it should be to insure that the value of the money is maintained, not systematically destroyed through a policy of deliberate inflation. In medicine there is a term for diseases caused by physicians: iatrogenic. Inflation might` correctly be called politico-genic, for it is caused by the politicians (including the officers of the Federal Reserve) who for 65 years have declared that they intend to cure inflation.

One hopes that the Federal Reserve abides by its promise to decrease the rate of monetary growth; it definitely should keep its word. But its past record is not encouraging, and the committee should consider legislation to curtail the Federal Reserve's discretionary powers and to begin the process of depoliticizing money altogether. Fiat money, with which we have been forced to live, requires extensive control and management at all times, with the hope of not disrupting the functioning of the economy too greatly. As the failure of the money managers becomes more and more apparent, other programs will be declared "necessary" and "required" by those same managers: price and wage controls, rationing, import controls, capital market controls, and so on. All these programs will be imposed on the people at the sacrifice of personal freedom and the destruction of a market economy, should our present policies of monetary management continue. Sound, honest money needs no managers. The integrity of our leaders should ensure money of real value. If this were so, inflation would disappear and our economy could be put on the road to recovery. ■

Print 3 Million and Take 1 Million for Yourself

Congressional Record – U.S. House of Representatives
May 31, 1979

Mr. Speaker, David Ottaway, in writing about Idi Amin's economic atrocities, discussed with a salesman for a British banknote firm who personally negotiated a contract with the former dictator of Uganda for printing up 2 million Ugandan shillings worth of 100 shilling notes. "At the close of their conversation," said Mr. Ottaway, the salesman "gingerly asked how he was to be paid."

"Print 3 million and take 1 million for yourself," Amin angrily retorted.

Inflation, the expansion of the money supply, helped destroy Uganda's economy, along with other forms of government regulation and interference. Amin doubled the money supply in his last two years as dictator, flooding the country with paper money. Prices naturally skyrocketed.

Idi Amin is no longer oppressing the people of Uganda, but his monetary policies live on, in more moderate form, at the U.S. Federal Reserve Board.

We will never have stable prices until we stop flooding our country with paper dollars, and solving—or trying to solve—our problems by printing more money. It will not work for us, any more than it did for Idi Amin. ■

Gold Prices Soar; Dollar Declines

Congressional Record – U.S. House of Representatives
September 28, 1979

Mr. Speaker, gold prices continue to soar – or rather, the dollar continues to decline in value. In terms of gold, the dollar has now been devalued by 92 percent since 1971. It is not coincidental that 1971 was the last time the dollar had an official relationship with gold, until Nixon closed the gold window and ushered in the first official devaluation of the dollar since the Depression.

What are the currency trading and gold panic telling us? We are now witnessing the remonetization of gold, in disregard of the official U.S. government position concerning the precious metal. The surge in gold prices is the world's vote of no confidence in paper currencies and the governments that promote fiat monetary policies.

People, as they have throughout history, want and demand money with intrinsic value. Governments are always resorting to inflation to fulfill the desires of special interest groups for something for nothing, but the majority will eventually insist on a return to commodity money – gold or silver.

Some try to brush off the skyrocketing price of gold as irrational panic. Panic there is, but it is neither irrational nor led by the uninformed. It is a logical reaction to the discovery that paper money is ultimately worthless.

The decision of millions of people in their attempt to protect themselves from the onslaught of inflation means they no longer trust the politicians nor the politicians' money.

The panic will end when we shut off the printing presses and make our dollar redeemable in gold once more. ∎

Government Should Stop Destroying Value of the Dollar

Congressional Record – U.S. House of Representatives
July 20, 1979

Mr. Speaker, in 1964, you could buy a suit of clothes for $35: 1 ounce of gold. Today, you can buy a very nice suit for 1 ounce of gold: $300.

Prices have not gone up in terms of real values. And the hours of labor it takes to earn enough Federal Reserve notes to buy a good suit are not significantly different from 15 years ago.

Dollar prices have zoomed, however, because the government has increased the supply of money and credit. This is inflation.

Just last week, M2 went up $4.5 billion. In the past three months, it has risen at an annual rate of 11.7 percent.

Is this Chairman Miller's parting gift to the American people as head of the Federal Reserve System?

Now he is going to the Treasury Department, to manage all of our financial affairs.

We will never have stable prices, until the government—Congress, President, Treasury, and Federal Reserve—ceases the policies of increasing money and credit that are destroying the value of every dollar that belongs to the American people. ∎

Increased Money Supply Cause of Inflation

Congressional Record — U.S. House of Representatives
November 16, 1979

Mr. Speaker, interest rates are a hot subject in Washington these days, and no wonder. The record-high prime rate of 13 1/4 percent and discount rate of 11 percent have made even the most unsophisticated realize that something is drastically wrong.

But just what these high rates actually mean seems to be a mystery to those in charge in this city. This tells me something about why a solution to inflation has been so elusive.

The *New York Times* two days ago complained bitterly about the "tight" monetary policy of our new Fed Chairman, and charged that he has "a leaden foot on the monetary brakes."

In the Senate Banking Committee yesterday Chairman Volcker was praised for his tight monetary policy, and his use of high interest rates to fight inflation.

Recently in this Chamber a member of the House Banking Committee condemned high interest rates as the cause of inflation, insinuating that a lowering of these rates would go a long way toward solving the problem.

The truth is that the money supply, as measured by the monetary base, has increased during the last month at the astounding rate of 15.1 percent. We are inflating — increasing the supply of money and credit — at a record rate, and this is why interest rates are also at record rates.

Until we realize that rising interest rates and prices are caused by inflation, and not the other way around, our patchwork financial and monetary policies will only continue to add to our problems, instead of solving them. ■

The Recent Strength of the Dollar and Inflation

Congressional Record – U.S. House of Representatives
October 17, 1979

Mr. Speaker, in the last several days we have read a lot in the newspapers about the strong dollar that we have had since the Federal Reserve took action last week to raise the interest rates.

I would like to suggest that these high interest rates and what the Fed has done are only a result of inflation and really will not do a whole lot to solve the problem of inflation unless the Fed continues with a very long and determined effort to curb the increase in the money supply. The strength of the dollar as reported in recent days is very much a deception to us because it is not telling us a whole lot.

We have to decide this: What are we talking about, and in terms of what? In terms of other currencies, it is true we can get more Japanese yen today than we could a week or two ago. But the American housewife who has to go to the grocery store does not understand this because her dollar is still very weak and buys as little or less today than it did one month ago.

So it is only a deception to think that we have a stronger dollar as a result of the recent Fed action. This is only reflecting the fact that other countries are inflating as well. In the traditional sense, as in days gone by when we measured the strength of the dollar in terms of gold, we find that the dollar is very, very weak.

In recession and in bad economic times prices drop. In terms of gold, prices today are at historic lows. Ten years ago one ounce of gold bought 100 gallons of gasoline, today it will buy nearly 400 gallons.

Until we in the Congress realize our problem is the depreciating American dollar and not the high prices that are merely the consequence of our spendthrift ways, we will never solve the problems of inflation that is eating away at the earnings and savings of every American citizen. ∎

Inflation is Caused by Government

Congressional Record – U.S. House of Representatives
November 16, 1979

Mr. Speaker, a recent survey of the people of the 22nd district of Texas revealed that their overwhelming concern is inflation. And with good reason.

Will prices ever stop rising? The government admits to 13 percent inflation, but every homemaker knows that the real rate is much higher.

The politicians try to blame inflation on labor unions, businessmen, Arabs, and consumers, but only the federal government can cause inflation, and only it is responsible.

When the federal government spends money it does not have — some $30 to $50 billion this fiscal year alone — and pays the bills by creating new dollars out of thin air, the value of each existing dollar must fall. Even worse, off-budget and other hidden expenditures have added $99 billion to the national debt, which is also financed with inflation.

At the Bureau of Engraving and Printing in Washington, D.C., giant printing presses run 24 hours a day, 7 days a week, 365 days a year, printing up new paper money. The government also creates new money in the banking system, by a complicated process called monetizing the debt. What this all amounts to is inflation.

The can of peas that you buy today isn't more valuable than the can you bought a year ago. But your money is worth less. This is what causes prices to go up. High prices are a consequence of inflation, not its cause.

Business Does Not Cause Inflation

Some argue that greedy businessmen are the cause of inflation. Are businessmen today more "greedy" than they were in the 1950s and early 1960s, when prices rose much more slowly? If greed can cause prices to rise 13 percent, why not 130 percent or

1,300 percent? If businessmen tried it, they would go out of business. The reason is that nobody would pay $10 for a can of peas with the number of dollars in circulation today. But if that number continues to increase, peas may be $10 per can in the near future. Competition tends to keep the price as low as possible.

Union Workers Do Not Cause Inflation

Others say that greedy union workers demand wages that cause businesses to raise their prices, and this is what brings about inflation. But in all inflationary periods, unionized workers—like all working people—fall behind the rising cost of living. How can it be fair for government to hold raises to 7 percent when inflation is at least twice that? If unions are so greedy, and have this power, why do they not push up wages 100 percent instead of 10 percent?

If a company allowed this, it would have to pass on the increased costs to the consumers in much higher prices. But this wouldn't be possible, because again you wouldn't pay $10 for a can of peas. In fact, for working people to stay even with the cost of living—given our inflation and tax system—they would have to get raises of 18 percent or 20 percent a year. No union is getting these kinds of increases.

Any person who works for a living deserves to be paid in a currency that maintains its value and not have part of his pay stolen by loss of purchasing power.

Consumers Do Not Cause Inflation

A few years ago, the government ran an expensive advertising campaign blaming inflation on consumers for being too greedy. TV commercials—produced at your expense—showed snorting people with the heads of pigs, asking for more and more.

People have always wanted a better life for themselves and their families, and only government—constantly grasping for more money and power from the people—could condemn this as wrong.

Are people today more "greedy" than in the past? To ask the question is to answer it. Human nature is not different today than it was 1,000 years ago.

But people can spend only so much without ending up in bankruptcy.

Arabs Do Not Cause Inflation

The government blames inflation on the Arabs. Oil is getting more and more expensive, and the Arabs do want every dollar they can get.

But if the money supply were not increasing, and we had to spend more on foreign oil, we would have less to spend on everything else, which would mean less demand and lower prices for nonpetroleum-related products. The overall cost of living would not increase.

We import about half our oil. Switzerland, West Germany, and Japan—with much lower inflation rates—import all their oil. If OPEC caused inflation, they would be in worse shape than we are. But they aren't because their governments inflate less.

Printing Paper Dollars will Not Help

Just since 1970, we have seen the U.S. money supply more than double. This has meant more paper dollars in circulation, but not, of course, more wealth. This is the reason prices go up.

Inflation Is a Tax

Since the federal government uses inflation—the creation of new money—to pay its bills, we can look on it as a tax, a tax we all pay in higher prices.

But inflation is an exceedingly unfair and regressive tax. Not all sectors of the economy suffer equally. In fact, some benefit, since inflation results in a transfer of wealth from savers and workers to speculators, bureaucrats, and the special interests favored by government.

Inflation also breeds mistrust. Its economic effects are so destructive, because it leads—as it has in our country—to rising prices and rising unemployment.

It misdirects the economy and prevents accurate assessment of future business conditions, thus contributing to bankruptcies of cities and corporations, like New York City, Cleveland, and Chrysler.

At first, inflation does "stimulate" the economy, in the same way a dose of heroin stimulates a drug addict. It feels great for a while, but there is a price to be paid.

Eventually, the economic conditions created by inflation lead to social discontent and anger, as classes, races, and regions are set against one another. Everybody grows irritable and uncertain about the future, as they find it harder and harder to make ends meet.

Plans become difficult to make, and everyone directs his efforts toward day-to-day survival, rather than the long-term efforts that build an economy and a society.

Inflation is Theft

People who worked hard and saved, the retired, and others on fixed incomes, are robbed, just as surely as if an armed criminal mugged them on the street. The very people who should be rewarded for their effort in caring for themselves are the ones hurt the most.

Morally, inflation is not different from the private counterfeiter printing up notes in his basement, and buying goods and services with them. Everyone sees this as stealing—fraudulently exchanging something worthless for something valuable. And this is exactly what the government does through inflation. If a private counterfeiter were never caught, his counterfeiting would "stimulate" the economy as much as the government's.

Inflation is Not a Modern Invention

Long before big business, labor unions, and OPEC, there was inflation. Governments well realize that people will pay only so much in outright taxes (inflation usually starts when taxes reach 25 percent), and the later Roman emperors, for example, routinely diluted their silver and gold coins by adding more and more cheap alloys. This expanded the money supply and enabled them to pay for more welfare programs—for a time. But prices rose dramatically, and the resultant economic distortions helped lead to the breakdown of the empire and the coming of the Dark Ages.

During our Revolutionary War, the Continental Congress printed $240 million of paper money to pay the government's expenses. Prices rose, and by the time we had won, a paper dollar was worth 2 cents in silver or gold money, leading to the saying, "Not worth a Continental."

During the Civil War, both the North and South inflated. Prices doubled in Washington, D.C., from 1861 to 1865, thanks, to the $400 million worth of paper greenbacks. After the war, it took three paper dollars to buy one gold dollar.

The South went on even more of an inflationary binge, so the region was not only devastated militarily, it was also wiped out economically. It was generations before the South recovered.

Falling Prices are Normal in a Free-Market Economy

During the 19th century in America, except in times of war, prices fell. In fact, this is the normal condition in a free market economy. Some of the modern economists claim that without inflation we cannot have economic growth. But this is just not true. Wages, in the 19th century, bought more and more each year, as economic growth and industrialization continued at the greatest pace in the history of mankind.

It is only government that gives us what today seems normal — constantly rising prices. Constantly rising prices are not a "fact of life," they are an act of government. This inflation undermines growth, so we are all much less well off than would otherwise have been the case; without constant printing of billions of paper dollars.

Price and Wage Controls Do Not Stop Inflation

Price and wage controls, which have been tried for more than 4,000 years by inflating governments, have always failed, because they attack a symptom of inflation, not its cause.

Controls make as much sense as a doctor dipping a thermometer in ice water to cure a fever.

In fact, controls cause shortages, black markets, and rationing, as the government continues to pump out paper money.

Price and wage controls — or even guidelines — are like sealing the hole on a pressure cooker while keeping the burner on high. Something has to give. The only way to lower the inflationary pressure is by turning off the monetary heat.

What if the Texas State government, as a "solution" to rising housing prices, told everyone that he couldn't sell his house for more than it would have brought in 1969.

Would this make housing cheaper, or would it kill the housing market, making houses unavailable for buyers and violating the constitutional rights of sellers? The answer is obvious. A few house sales would take place, but in secret on the black market. Law-abiding Texans would be turned into criminals.

Sound Money is the Answer to Inflation

The Founding Fathers, after their experience with inflation during the Revolution, said that real money was gold or silver.

A dollar was about 1/20th of an ounce of gold. But we have had so much inflation that today's dollar—which is only a piece of paper backed by nothing—is worth less than 1/400th of an ounce of gold.

To end inflation, we need to stop deficit spending and have a dollar that is tied to a specific commodity, like gold or silver.

The government has now brought on a recession deliberately, in an attempt to lower prices. It may do so for a time, but at what a cost in human suffering.

It also, in an absurd attempt to "stop inflation," dumps the gold that once backed our dollar in hopes that it will lower the price of gold and somehow miraculously lower all other prices. All it accomplishes is the loss of our gold to Arabs and European banks, and the inflation rages on.

We can have strong economic growth, more jobs and prosperity, and an end to rising prices only with a sound dollar that can't be inflated.

Let us pull the plug on the printing presses, stop the destruction of our money and our country through inflation, and encourage the healthy economic growth we need. ∎

Debasement

Congressional Record – U.S. House of Representatives
December 12, 1979

Mr. Speaker, the inflation debate rages on. Everyone's against inflation, but that does not do much good unless we can agree on its cause. Those most responsible for it would have us believe there are multiple causes, ranging from consumer greed to Arab oil prices, business profits to union demands. Their insistence on using consumer price levels instead of the value of the currency is the principal source of confusion.

We fail to use one particular word often enough in describing the inflation fraud. That word is debasement. It is to the debasement of the dollar that we should direct our attention, not to the price levels that merely reflect the debasement.

Webster defines debase as:

> loss of soundness, purity, and integrity through forces that break down, pollute, or destroy; to reduce from a high quality, purity, worth, and value to a lower one; to corrupt, to debauch; moral deterioration by evil influence.

A more descriptive explanation of what we have done to our money could not be given.

To debase the currency is to inflate it. To inflate the currency is to distend, swell, and expand the money supply, and thereby destroy its value. To destroy the currency is to undermine and attack freedom. Without a sound and honest money, a free society cannot long exist.

Only one instrumentality is capable of swelling the money supply, and that is the federal government. It is on Congress, the Executive, and the Federal Reserve that the blame for inflation must rest, not on consumers, union members, businessmen, or Arabs.

Walter Wriston, chairman of Citicorp, gave a recent speech in which he compared the drive to control prices and wages with government attempts to suppress the media because politicians do not like the bad news being reported. Rising prices report the bad news of inflation. The answer is not to cut the messenger's head off, and destroy the free market with price and wage controls, but to blame the party responsible for the bad news. To quote Pogo, "the enemy is us." It is Congress that bears the responsibility, under the Constitution, for protecting the soundness of the dollar, and it is Congress which has abandoned that responsibility, with consequences that may be terrifying for the cause of freedom. ■

Congressional Inflation

Congressional Record – U.S. House of Representatives
March 6, 1980

Mr. Speaker, in 1954, a small can of frozen orange juice cost 12 cents. A pound of hamburger was 37 cents. The best sirloin steak was 75 cents a pound.

Since then as we all know, congressionally caused inflation has driven working and middle-class Americans to the wall.

Congress tries to blame unions, businessmen, Arabs, and even consumers themselves for inflation, but only Congress – working through the Federal Reserve System – is responsible.

Inflation is the expansion of the supply of money and credit. This expansion depreciates the value of each existing dollar. For many years, Congress has gotten away with inflation, which it used to pay for deficits and to stimulate the economy. This inflation has stolen hundreds of billions of dollars from orphans and widows, from the aged and the poor, from the thrifty and hard working.

Congress is guilty of this crime, and Congress must be reformed. We need many new faces here next year, if we are to have a chance of preventing disaster for our country. I predict the people will clean this House. It needs a thorough cleaning. ∎

Gold versus Paper

Congressional Record – U.S. House of Representatives
July 1, 1980

Mr. Speaker, governments for thousands of years abused their power and held the people in check with various forms of inflation. Originally, inflation was accomplished by coin clipping, but today the theft through monetary destruction is a highly sophisticated procedure involving the politicians, the bureaucrats, and the Federal Reserve System — our present-day central bank. All inflation involves the rejection of commodity money and acceptance of the arbitrary expansion of money and/or credit by government officials. The conflict is between gold and paper, honest money and dishonest money. The power hungry have insisted on paper and the people have demanded honest money such as gold.

It is disturbing to see so many present-day experts call unbacked currency modern and scientific and label gold archaic or mystical. As long ago as 2000 B.C., the Hammurabic code mandated wage and price controls in an unsuccessful attempt to control inflation. The failure of the Roman Emperor Diocletian in A.D. 301 to stop inflation with wage and price controls is another well-known example of the failure of an unsound currency. The past 200 years also reveal the serious harm brought on by wage and price controls which hide the real cause of inflation. Our most recent example is the imposition of controls by Nixon in 1971. I am convinced if we do not look at the fundamental nature of money itself, all other attempts to thwart our impending economic crisis will fail. I recall first reading about the dangers of inflation in the 1950s. There were economists even then predicting serious consequences from the inflationary programs that were growing by leaps and bounds. But the consequence about which of these predictions never seemed to materialize. Even though the exact timing of our crisis is not known, it is becoming apparent to more people every day that the day of reckoning is coming, that prolonged inflation has consequences, and that a nation living beyond its means suffers penalties; these are accepted by almost everyone.

Balanced Budgets

Today there is a clamor for a balanced budget. Already, we have 30 states demanding a constitutional convention to compel the Congress to stop spending more than it takes in. Since the chief reason for inflation is the printing of money and the creation of credit to pay for federal deficits, this restriction would be a big step in the right direction. It's also healthy because it would mean the people themselves would be speaking out and going around the Congress to implement a constitutional change for the first time. If four more States request the convention, we can place this restraint on the politicians into the Constitution.

I have two reservations, however, regarding this amendment. First, I do not believe that instructing the politicians to balance the budget through a constitutional amendment will accomplish all that is hoped. The amendments proposed have a clause in them saying that in a time of emergency, by a vote of three-fourths of the Congress, the requirement to balance the budget can be suspended. All it would take is an increased rate of unemployment and the Congress would succumb to the temptation to inflate. The prevailing economic understanding in the Congress, the administration, and the Federal Reserve is that the only correction available to them is to stimulate the economy with deficits, and the spending of more and more new money. I am convinced this will happen with or without an amendment that provides for a balanced budget.

With our economic downturn, the deficits will probably top the $100 billion per year mark in a vain effort to hold off the impending collapse. Government programs will be coming out our ears and the rhetoric about a balanced budget will soon be forgotten.

My other reservation is this: Even if by some miracle Congress should balance the budget, the Federal Reserve can inflate without deficits. The Federal Reserve has the means whereby it can do pretty much what it wants, with or without a balanced budget. For this reason, we need a more fundamental change in the nature of our money.

The monetary unit cannot remain as it is today, a tool of the rich, the powerful, the politicians, the central bankers, and the international corporations. For the middle class to survive and the poor to gain an opportunity to improve their lot, a sound currency is a must. Destructive wealth redistribution through inflation should not be tolerated any longer. Although eventually all economic classes will suffer with economic upheaval and loss of political freedom, up to a point certain groups do benefit at the expense of others. Many a businessman has expressed his acceptance and approval of the inflationary process to me since it affords him a chance to accumulate more material wealth. The unscrupulous businessman, banker, politician, or union leader who encourages inflation for personal gain is guilty of committing the serious crime of theft, and must bear the responsibility of participating in the destruction of our market economy and what remains of our free society. Those who understand inflation and protect themselves and their families to the best of their abilities should be complimented and not criticized; only the perpetrators of the inflationary process are deserving of our harsh condemnation.

If a balanced budget cannot achieve all that is necessary to stop the inflation, what exactly is required? Will tax reduction as proposed by the Roth-Kemp bill provide enough incentive to stimulate production, lower prices and raise government revenues? Hardly. Tax reduction is a key element in correcting our economic ills and must be done as soon as possible. Tax reduction should exceed the 30-percent proposed by the Roth-Kemp bill, but not for the purpose of providing revenue for the government. Government revenues must be reduced, not increased. A balanced budget must be achieved through reduction of government spending, not through raising its income at the taxpayer's expense. Government programs almost never achieve what is intended and usually do the opposite. Less government spending, rather than being recessionary or less stimulating to the economy, would provide a tremendous boost toward producing higher employment and lower prices. When one hears the promotion of increasing government revenues through either direct taxation or miraculously through tax reduction, it reminds me of the poem by Sir Allen Patrick Herbert:

> Well, fancy giving money to the Government
> Might as well put it down the drain.
> Fancy giving money to the Government
> Nobody will ever see the stuff again.
> Well, they've no idea what money's for
> Ten to one they'll start another war.
> I've heard a lot of silly things, but Lord,
> Fancy giving money to the Government.

My idea of taxation is to limit the maximum overall taxation for everyone to 10 percent of his income. The church only asks for 10 percent; why should the government demand more?

Massive tax reduction, elimination of all abusive regulations, reduction of government spending, and a balanced budget are all absolute musts if we expect to pull our economy out of its downward spiral. This needs to be done quickly and completely if we expect to avert the coming crises in the delivery of energy, medical care, food, clothing, and housing to our people.

Even if all this were achieved overnight by Congress and by some strange occurrence accepted by our President, it would not be enough. In many ways, this would help alleviate the bad effect of inflation, that is, it would tend to lower prices, but would do nothing to change the basic problem in stopping inflation. If anything, it would hide the problem because it would direct the attention away from the real cause of inflation. Just as wage and price controls divert our attention from the real cause, responsible programs that would lessen government control on the economy — and these should be encouraged — could actually delay the basic changes needed. Already, the productive capacity of our relatively free enterprise system rather astoundingly achieves lower prices and provides many bargains in spite of the inflationary world in which we live.

Basic Change Needed

The basic change needed is to provide for a commodity-backed currency. Commodity money, in contrast to the archaic, destructive, unbacked, paper currency which circulates throughout the world today, is an absolute must if the inflation is to stop and prices are to stabilize or fall.

Although the productive era of Western civilization was associated with gold backing to both the dollar and to the British pound, total refinement of a gold currency was never achieved. History has given us many more examples where money was unrelated to gold than the other way around. The 20th century free-market economists, such as Hayek, defend capably the different ways whereby a better currency can be devised. There is no reason to return to an old gold standard; we must be progressive enough to consider new and enlightened ideas about money and the age-old problem of inflation. Previous knowledge of how gold-related currencies functioned so much better than the fiat currencies must be coupled with new ideas for providing an even better currency than ever used before.

Unfortunately, it is hard for mankind to accept new ideas. Preference for the old ideas, no matter how disastrous they have been, seems to prevail. Sacrificing to the state the people's right to determine the nature of their money — through legal tender laws, and so forth, is carelessly accepted by most people today. Although there are those in authority who promote the use of paper money for their own personal benefits, the masses, the poor, and the middle class fail to demand a halt to the theft and loss of freedom that occurs through the rotten system of monetary expansion and credit creation. The little people and the honest people of the country must demand a halt to the inflation and insist on a gold-backed currency. No other alternative exists.

Milton Friedman claims that paper money will work, if government is just told to limit the monetary expansion to a fixed rate of 4 to 5 percent a year. This indicates little understanding about human nature. Even if we had such a law on the books, we would not be able to restrain the politicians from abusing this prerogative and arbitrarily increasing the number of dollars in circulation. Power is corrupting. Do not tempt anyone with a purchasing medium made of something artificial, without intrinsic value, and ask that a limited supply be allowed. It just will not work. If we found perfection in our elected officials, possibly Friedman's monetary ideas would have merit; but, believe me, there is such a scarcity of even the "good guys" in Washington, let alone any that are considered perfect, that it precludes any such dream.

I do not know whether or not a gold-backed currency provided and protected by the government is superior to the Hayek free-market money, but either one would be far superior to what we have now. I would be delighted with a serious consideration of any form of commodity-backed currency that would put brakes on the rapidly expanding money supply. Unless this happens, the real solution to the inflation problem will not be available to us; and we must face up to the fact that the consumer price index will continue to soar to ever-higher levels. Unemployment will rise; the standard of living will decrease for the majority of us; the rich will become richer, and our freedoms will be threatened. If history is of any significance to us, our preparations and our concerns should be paramount.

On the optimistic side is the fact that we are now legally permitted to practice economic self-protection by owning gold. Gold clause contracts are now permissible after 35 years of repression. Our government is now compelled by law to use a small percentage of the gold they dump into foreign markets each year to mint coins for purchase by American citizens. More citizens are becoming knowledgeable about the value of buying gold.

Only the government officials and the conventional economists deny the significance of gold. True economic protection on an individual level can be achieved with gold; however, if our total program of a free economy and a sound dollar is not achieved, the inevitable loss of freedom will wipe out any personal protection that one may achieve with the ownership of gold.

Understanding, promoting, and achieving a free society should top our list of priorities. If this is done, material abundance and economic security can be achieved by all who desire them and are willing to work for them. ∎

Five Myths of the Gold Standard

Testimony Before the Subcommittee on Mines and Mining
Committee on Interior and Insular Affairs
Congressional Record – U.S. House of Representatives
October 2, 1980

Throughout my remarks this morning when I refer to a gold standard I will be referring to a full 100 percent gold coin standard unless otherwise noted.

I would like to begin by discussing what might be called five myths about the gold standard. A few years ago, there was a book published called *Nine Lies About America*. Although I did not read the book, I felt the title was an excellent way for the author to make his point that America was being attacked by people who hated her and who were doing their best to spread discontent and disloyalty among the American people. Today we see the same thing happening with regard to the gold standard. What are these five myths? Let me list them briefly and discuss each one. The first myth is "There isn't enough gold." The second myth is "Since the Soviet Union and South Africa are the world's principal producers of gold, they could hold our economic system hostage and benefit tremendously if we were to return to a gold standard." The third myth is "The gold standard would cause a depression." The fourth myth is, "The gold standard will cause inflation." And the fifth myth is "The gold standard is subject to undesirable speculative influences." Let me discuss each of these myths about the gold standard in turn.

The first myth: "There isn't enough gold." I find it amazing that economists can make statements like this, for it is an elementary principle of economics that if one raises the price of a commodity one will always have enough of that commodity. What we are seeing in the run up of gold prices in the past few months is in fact the raising of the price of gold to match the depreciation of the dollar that has occurred and still is occurring.

Simply put, there will always be enough gold so long as no one interferes with the free market mechanism.

At $700 an ounce the United States government has enough gold reserves to more than cover all the Federal Reserve notes outstanding. If we were to return to a gold standard by the procedure I have outlined in my bill H.R. 7874, then the world would be fully informed of the gold holdings of the United States government, and the price of gold could adjust accordingly, so that when redemption of our greenbacks—our Federal Reserve notes—began, the price would be the market-clearing price. Quite simply, the statement that there is not enough gold is false. It is a scare tactic used by opponents of the gold standard, and it deserves to be laid to rest as soon as possible.

The second myth that should be challenged is that "The Soviet Union and South Africa could hold us hostage" were we to return to the gold standard. It is true that the Soviet Union and South Africa, because they have vast gold deposits, have reaped a windfall in the past decade. We are not today on a gold standard in any sense of the word, and the Soviet Union and South Africa are reaping windfalls because of the climbing price of gold on world markets. It is the present inflationary policies of governments the world over that are creating these windfalls. Rather than giving them windfalls, we should institute the gold standard.

I think stabilization of our monetary system—and perhaps the world monetary system, if the world emulated our practices—would remove any speculative premium that the Soviet Union and South Africa presently receive. We would see a stabilization of the world price of gold and an end to inflation throughout the world. In such a condition, the Soviet Union and South Africa would no longer be in positions to reap enormous windfall benefits as they presently are.

During the first several months of this year the Soviet Union has withheld gold from the international gold markets. It has recently been rumored that they have sold several hundred tons to Saudi Arabia at a premium price. Whether or not that is the case, it is easy to see that the current inflationary problems that beset us and the rest of the world create the conditions in which it is easy for Russia and South Africa to reap vast economic benefit. The present inflation causes fear and panic among the world's peoples.

Were we to return to a sound money system—that is a full 100 percent gold coin standard—the fear and the panic would be eliminated. There would be no premium to be reaped by the Soviet Union and South Africa, and they would not receive any windfall from the sale of their gold and their coins. Nor would Russia and South Africa be able to hold us hostage.

The gold reserves of the United States are immense, but no matter their size, it would be extremely difficult to see how Russia and South Africa, either by restraining their production or by dumping gold, could seriously affect us here in the United States.

When we reach a full gold coin standard and our unit of account is a weight of gold, as I have indicated in my bill, H.R. 7874, the world's entire production for one year will not influence significantly the value of that weight of gold.

I would point out, however, that the activities of the Soviet Union and South Africa might affect a proposal such as the one Dr. Laffer has made. As I understand it, his proposal is not a gold coin standard, but rather is a hybrid between our present system and a gold bullion standard. In that system, the activities of the Soviet Union and South Africa could affect our domestic monetary system to our detriment, but if we were to disengage government from money entirely, then there would be no such effect felt. It is only the continuing linkage between politically-printed paper money and a fractional gold reserve that allows the threat posed by the Soviet Union and South Africa to have any force. If we eliminate that politically-printed paper altogether, then no threat would remain, for our government would be under no pressure to maintain a link between paper and our gold reserves. We would simply have a weight of gold as our unit of account and nothing else.

Dr. Laffer has proposed a novel mechanism for instituting a fractional reserve system that has complex ties to gold. His intricate proposal provides for a fractional gold reserve together with gold holidays, when there would be no link between paper currency and gold. I do not believe Dr. Laffer's proposal is a genuine gold standard, nor has anything like it been attempted in our history, to my knowledge.

Let me turn to the third myth about the gold standard. The third myth is that "A return to the gold standard will cause a depression." Now this statement is a half-truth, for if we improperly return to a gold standard, then we might in fact have a depression. Following World War I, the government of Great Britain attempted to return to a gold standard, but it did so in such a fashion that it caused deflation. It did so by trying to reestablish the link that existed between the pound and gold prior to World War I, not taking into the account the increase in the number of pounds that had occurred during World War I when Great Britain was off the gold standard. The result was a depression, because the political experts completely ignored the damage that had been done by their policies during the war.

Were we to return to the gold standard, we must pursue a course that would not result in deflation and would not cause a depression. We must redeem at the market price for a period of one year the greenbacks we have printed, and then cease redemption, allowing the gold coins we have put into circulation to function as our money of account.

We must not attempt to return to a gold standard at $35 an ounce or even at $42.22 an ounce or any other figure besides the market price for gold. Should we attempt to return to the gold standard based upon an arbitrarily fixed price, such as $42 an ounce, we will cause a depression, and that is certainly not what I propose.

If we proceed to a gold standard in an orderly fashion, such as I have proposed in my bill H.R. 7874, then there will be no depression. I must also tell the Subcommittee that it's imperative, because I believe that a return to a gold standard cannot be achieved if we do not end our budget deficits. It must be accompanied by tax cuts, an end to the printing of paper money, and significant reduction of federal regulations if we expect a restoration of a sound economy.

Unless we are committed to all these things, even the establishment of a 100 percent gold coin standard cannot stop our descent into economic chaos. We must cut the federal government down to constitutional size, and the establishment of a full gold standard is part of that process. After all, the Constitution does forbid any state government from making anything except gold or silver coin a legal tender in payment of debt.

The fourth myth about the gold standard that "It will cause inflation." Opponents of the gold standard point out that the world supply of gold increases by about 2 or 3 percent per year, and such an increase in supply would result in inflation in any country that adopts a gold standard.

I do not wish to challenge the proposition that the world gold supply increases by 2 to 3 percent per year. For the sake of argument, I will accept that as given. The result of such an increase is that prices might stay stable rather than falling. It is useful in this regard to point out the behavior of prices during our past history. For most of the 19th century we had an imperfect gold coin standard. In the 67 years prior to the beginning of the Federal Reserve System in 1913 the consumer price index in this country increased by 10 percent, and in the 67 years subsequent to 1913 the CPI increased 625 percent. This growth has accelerated since 1971 when President Nixon cut our last link to gold by closing the gold window.

In 1833 the index of wholesale commodity prices in the U.S. was 75.3. In 1933, just prior to our going off the gold coin standard, the index of wholesale commodity prices in the U.S. was 76.2. A change in 100 years of 9/10ths of 1 percent. The index of wholesale commodity prices in 1976 was 410.2. Today, the index is 612.3. For 100 years on the gold standard wholesale prices rose only 9/10ths of 1 percent. In the last 45 years of paper money they have gone up 537 percent.

At this point, Mr. Chairman I would like a table showing the index of wholesale commodity prices in the United States from 1800 to 1976 to be entered into the record of this hearing. This table is taken from the book called *The Golden Constant*, by Professor Roy Jastram [the table was not recorded — Ed.].

As you can see, the indices emphasize the stability of wholesale commodity prices during the entire 19th century. This stability was first overturned during the Civil War — the Greenback period — then in World War I and once again in World War II and the inflation that has persisted since that war.

I think you'll find these figures extraordinary and enlightening, for they show that the gold standard does promise a way out of our current inflationary impasse. Rather than causing inflation, the gold standard has historically been a bulwark against inflation. It is politically-manipulated money such as we have had since 1934 that causes our inflation.

People today have come to expect that the prices will continue to rise and we see the beginnings of a hyperinflationary psychology setting in.

If we are to avoid the horrendous consequences such a psychology will lead to, we must take dramatic action and return this country to a historically proven system, a full gold coin standard.

The last myth about the gold coin standard that I would like to address is the assertion that such a standard would be subject to undesirable speculative influences.

This assertion was most recently made in a letter sent by the Federal Reserve to Chairman William Proxmire of the Senate Banking Committee. The letter argued that because gold is a commodity used in jewelry and in industry it is subject to speculative influences that are undesirable in setting up a stable monetary system.

I find such an argument amazing, for it is precisely because it is a commodity and not subject to the manipulation of a bureaucracy in Washington or London that it is desirable. If one wishes to speak of undesirable speculative influences, one need only look at the speculation that occurs daily in the U.S. dollar.

A gold standard would eliminate all speculation about the political motivations of the monetary authorities in governing the supply of money. The great virtue of the gold standard is that it removes discretionary power over the money supply from any one agency, thus ending the most fertile source of speculation. A gold standard puts the power of the monetary system into the hands of its people and takes it away from the politicians and the bankers, thus removing a potential vehicle for establishing a tyranny.

Gold cannot be mined as cheaply as Federal Reserve notes can be printed. Nor can its supply be manipulated on a daily basis. There is a great dispersion of power in a gold standard system. That is the strength of the system, for it allows the people to check any monetary excesses of their governors and does not allow the governors to exploit the people by debasing the money.

The letter from the Federal Reserve System to Chairman Proxmire closed with a call for more faith in the System and its good intentions. For over 60 years the American people have been exercising such faith and they have suffered the worst depression and the worst inflations in their history. Let us hear no more of faith in men, but bind them down with the chains of an honest monetary system—the full gold coin standard.

It is interesting that in the Coinage Act of 1792 the founders provided the penalty of death for any government employee who debased the money. One wonders that if such a penalty were enforced today how many members of the Federal Open Market Committee would survive the month.

In his *Tract on Monetary Reform* published in 1923 the father of the age of inflation, John Maynard Keynes, wrote: "The individualistic capitalism of today . . . presumes a stable measuring rod of value. It cannot be efficient—perhaps cannot survive—without one."

Lord Keynes was correct. Unless we have a stable measuring rod of value, a rod such as a gold coin standard, capitalism and freedom as we have known them cannot survive. If not vigilant we will evolve into the sort of fascism that resulted from the great German inflation following World War I.

The choice before us is quite simple: Shall we have gold and political freedom or shall we have paper and political tyranny?

I thank you very much for holding this hearing, and I'm glad that I could testify.

You are performing a great service for the American people. Thank you. ∎

Audit of the Federal Reserve

Congressional Record — U.S. House of Representatives
March 4, 1981

Mr. Speaker, today I am introducing a bill to require the General Accounting Office to conduct a complete and thorough audit of the Federal Reserve System and banks. This is not just any bill, for it was last introduced in 1915 by Representative Wright Patman of Texas, who fought for years to have the Fed audited.

This bill provides that

> the Comptroller General . . . shall make . . . an audit for each fiscal year of the Federal Reserve Board, the Federal Advisory Council, the Federal Open Market Committee, and all Federal Reserve banks and their branches, including transactions of the system open market account conducted through recognized dealers.

The bill further provides that the General Accounting Office shall have access to all books and records of the Federal Reserve.

The audit of the Federal Reserve is necessary. In considering a bill to audit the Federal Reserve in 1978, the Senate Committee on Governmental Affairs declared that:

> The three federal banking regulatory agencies are at the present time the only exceptions to audit by the GAO. Yet they are empowered to carry out functions crucial to our system of government and to our nation's economy. Last year the three agencies incurred operating expenses exceeding $920 million. None of these expenditures were subjected to an audit by the GAO which, as the investigative arm of the Congress, serves to insure the effectiveness of governmental programs as well as appropriate and legal expenditure of funds.

Amazingly, despite this declaration that the Federal Reserve, the FDIC, and the Office of the Comptroller of the Currency "are empowered to carry out functions crucial to our system of government and to our nation's economy," the Congress went on to enact a law that prevents the GAO from auditing those functions, functions which are "crucial to our system of government and our nation's economy." I quote from the 1978 Act:

> An audit made under paragraph (1)(A) shall not include—
>
> (A) transactions conducted on behalf of or with: foreign central banks, foreign governments, and nonprivate international financing organizations;
>
> (B) deliberations, decisions, and actions on monetary policy matters, including discount window operations,

reserves of members banks, securities, credit, interest on deposits, and open market operations;

(C) transactions made under the direction of the Federal Open Market Committee including transactions of the Federal Reserve System Open Market Account; and

(D) those portions of oral, written, telegraphic, or telephonic discussions and communications among or between Members, of the Board of Governors, and officers and employees of the Federal Reserve System which deal with topics listed in subparagraphs (A) (B) and (C) of this paragraph.

As the law now stands, the GAO is forbidden to look into those functions of the Federal Reserve which are "crucial to our system of government and our nation's economy." The reasons stated by the Senate committee for auditing the Fed are sound ones, but the present law explicitly forbids any investigation of the functions of the Fed which are so important in our economy.

Auditing the expenditures of the Fed is, of course, an important function. It would be nice to know how they spend the billion dollars per year that are not returned to the Treasury. I have seen their marble palace uptown and heard about their caches of cash out in Virginia, and as important as these things are, it is far more important that the Congress and the American people be provided with the results of an investigation of the essential operations of the Fed.

This is especially so since the passage last year of the Monetary Control Act, which empowered the Fed to purchase the paper obligations of foreign governments and use them as collateral for Federal Reserve notes. This extraordinary provision of the law was not debated in the House nor the Senate, nor was testimony taken on it. Yet it is just one example of the sort of power that the Federal Reserve has, and which remains beyond the reach of the investigatory arm of the Congress.

In stating a reason for excluding these "crucial functions" from the purview of the GAO audit, the Senate Committee on Governmental Affairs wrote: ". . . the Federal Reserve Board must be able to independently conduct the nation's monetary policy. . . ."

The independence of the Fed has long been used as a device to shield the Fed from congressional investigation. It is time that we recognized that the independence of the Fed is a legal fiction. One can trace the policies of the Federal Reserve merely by tracing the histories of Presidential elections. I will use the most recent campaign as an example, but one could just as easily select the earlier campaigns of Ford, or Nixon, or Johnson for illustrations of the fact that the Fed takes its cues from the White House.

Last May, when the Presidential campaign was beginning in earnest, and it was becoming increasingly clear that Ronald Reagan would be the nominee of the Republican Party, the Federal Reserve Board began a six-month expansion of the money supply that was almost unprecedented in our history. During the last six months of the year, M1B increased $25.8 billion, or 13.4 percent. Actually the increase prior to the election was greater: The Fed took the money supply up almost $29 billion before scaling back in December, after the Presidential election was over. If one excludes the decrease in December, M1B grew at a 16.4-percent rate in the five months prior to the election.

Why? Simply because restraint in the growth of the money supply during a Presidential campaign might lead to the defeat of the incumbent. The Fed knows that it can give the economy a temporary "high" by jacking up the money supply, and it does so, even though the long-run consequences of such an opportunistic policy will be severe.

But it is not only the long-run consequences that will be severe. The ups and downs in interest rates in 1980 followed the ups and downs in the Fed's manipulation of the money supply. Easy money causes high interest rates, and no better illustration of this can be found than the prime rate peaking at 21.5 percent last December, and now falling off as the Fed ceases to expand the growth in the money supply.

Yet it is decisions such as these, decisions which drive interest rates to record levels that are fatal to many businesses, decisions that increase prices at record rates in double-digit inflation, and decisions which will soon affect the unemployment rate by driving it up, that are not permitted to be included in the GAO audit.

I think it is time that the Congress and the American people found out exactly what the Fed is up to. Is there any insider dealing based on the decisions the Fed makes in its secret meetings? What is the relationship between the Fed and foreign governments and international banks? The sooner we find out the better off we will be. The system deserves no more blind faith and support from the American people. ■

High Interest Rates

Congressional Record – U.S. House of Representatives
February 25, 1982

Mr. Speaker, everyone decries the high interest rates that have stifled the economy. Many are perplexed that although prices are rising less rapidly than a year ago, interest rates have not had a corresponding drop. For decades now interest rates have generally followed the rate of price inflation. As prices rose during boom periods, interest rates also rose. As the recession set in, as a reaction to monetary policy, interest rates dropped. Many economic projections were in error because it was assumed that this relationship would persist.

However, the economists who understand the nature of money anticipated the dilemma we now face. Interest, the cost of using another's capital for a period of time, is not set by computers, or measurements of some mysterious M. It is determined by the subjective interpretations of all borrowers and lenders.

When money has no precise definition, as is the case with the dollar today, anticipated future value is predictably going to be less. Without convertibility to something of real value like gold, the inflation premium will dominate in setting interest rates. Increasing the supply of money and credit may lower the rates temporarily, but will only serve to fuel the fires of inflation and raise interest rates even further. Lowering interest rates by credit allocation will only lead to a controlled and a further collapse of the economy.

Only with money of real value, where there is no inflation premium, will we solve this problem, Until we have a gold standard, we can expect interest rates to go even higher. ∎

At the Brink

Congressional Record — U.S. House of Representatives
September 22, 1982

Mr. Speaker, the International Monetary Fund (IMF) recently finished its annual meeting in Toronto, Canada. The IMF was originally designed to smooth out the balance-of-payments problems among its members, but today it serves essentially as a social welfare agency lending to nations whose economies have been crippled by socialist and fascist central planning.

As should be expected, the United States contributes more funds than any other nation. In Toronto the international banking crisis could not be ignored, yet attempts to downplay it were made. The collapse of the Mexican peso and the threat of an Argentinean default dramatize the urgency of the situation and are omens of things to come. Mexico owes $81 billion and Argentina $39 billion, but this is only a small fraction of the total debt owed to Western governments and Western banks. Eastern bloc Communist nations and Third World nations owe over $850 billion, and reasonable people do not expect that this sum will be repaid.

The race going on now is to finance all this debt through governments—principally the United States—and bail out the international banking system. The default which many pretend can be avoided is inevitable; the only question that remains is who the victims are to be. The question is, shall it be the bankers or the innocent uninformed American citizens?

The elite attending the international conference minimized the crisis only by admitting that yes, indeed, a problem did exist, but it is manageable. We cannot manage nor ever pay our own debt let alone the world's debt, yet we continue to play the game and pretend a calamitous banking crisis does not really exist and that we will work our way out of it. That is impossible. The big default will come. Mexico has been insolvent for years but it was only recently that a panic occurred and the peso collapsed. It took a lot of years, a lot of borrowing, a lot of money creation by the Mexican central bank, to set the stage that allowed the crisis to occur.

Mexico's banking problems make the dollar look strong — compared to the peso — but compared to its former purchasing power the dollar is weak and hanging precariously on the brink of collapse. The dollar collapse which now stares us in the face brings shudders to those knowledgeable and honest about currency matters. The dollar is the most vital currency of the world, and its failure will wreak havoc on Western civilization. We can no longer ignore the threat.

It is estimated that the contingent liabilities of the U.S. government are now over $11 trillion. Fulfilling this commitment is not possible. The Social Security system alone exists only by robbing young Peter to pay elderly Paul. It is insolvent and we ought to admit it. The national debt is now over $1.1 trillion, our annual interest payment on this debt is more than $115 billion, and both are growing rapidly even under an administration which has been declared the most fiscally conservative of the 20th century. The reason for this inconsistency — whether it is deception, inept management, or the impossibility of controlling the runaway system — is economically unimportant. The fact that the floodgates of spending, taxing, and inflating are open and that debt repudiation has begun must be accepted before plans can be laid for reforming our banking institutions and preserving a free society.

In the old days, an event such as a dollar devaluation made big news. A jump of gold prices from $35 to $38 required surprise weekend announcements that only the insiders knew about. Today the price of gold — the barometer of monetary distrust as it has been for 5,000 years — can increase by one-third in a few weeks with no specific announcement and with the authorities pretending that this has little to do with devaluation and lost trust in the dollar. Fear is building, debt repudiation is occurring daily through dollar depreciation, and nominal dollar debt is expanding rapidly. As all this occurs, inflation and patching the system together at the expense of the innocent proceed.

The mountain of debt can be repudiated by default; that is, declared bankruptcies and subsequent liquidation of debt, but every effort conceivable will be made to prevent this from occurring on a massive scale. If this did occur it would be an old-fashioned 1929 deflation and everyone knows the politicians and the bankers will not let this happen, which is understandable, yet the alternative method of debt liquidation offers little benefit or reassurance.

The other method of defaulting on the debt is a 1923-style German inflation. Pay the debt with rapidly depreciating newly created dollars. When the dollar is worthless, or approaching worthlessness, real debt disappears and the holder of debt instruments have their assets liquidated even though someone may still owe them many dollars. As new money appears out of thin air, real assets of the savers and the debt denominated dollars evaporate into thin air. Both forms of debt liquidation are terribly dangerous. Economic law demands the debt be paid, the pyramiding of debt cannot last forever — the drinking binge always comes to an end. In the end the patient must sober up or face an alcoholic's death.

It is similar with an economy, and we must either give up depending on new money creation — inflation — in our efforts to achieve a false sense of well being, or face the consequences. It appears to me that we are determined to follow the course of history, failing to learn from it, and commit the errors that have brought many nations to their knees. That error is the policy of currency destruction through the inflationary process. The task of limiting government size and its expenditures far outweighs the superficial expression of sympathy for a balanced budget here in Washington. Many do not have courage for it. Those Americans who care and are still struggling to make some sense out of our political and economic system must give backbone to the public officials who have the authority to legislate wisely and constitutionally and stop the monetary catastrophe that is occurring.

In 1980, radical changes were made in the Federal Reserve Act—the Monetary Control Act of 1980—allowing a massive increase in the power of the Federal Reserve System. Among those powers was the authority of the Fed to use the debt of foreign nations as collateral for the printing of Federal Reserve notes. This is of the greatest significance in light of the $850 billion Third World and Communist nations' debt to the West. To begin with, the foreign bonds that the Fed purchases are purchased with paper money backed by our own debt—bonds and Treasury bills. Then we turn around and use the newly purchased foreign bonds as collateral to print up more Federal Reserve notes. This system of money creation is unbelievable to rational human beings. It cannot but lead to a disastrous end for the American dollar.

Under current law the recently purchased Mexican pesos could be used to back the printing of more Federal Reserve notes. The fact that the debt structure is so large and the banks holding the debt so influential causes me to predict that government will do a lot more inflating to bail out the private holders of foreign debt through this mechanism. We sent money to Poland when they were unable to meet their interest payments to the large banks; we did it with Mexico; and there is no reason we should not expect it to be done for Brazil, Argentina, Zaire, or whomever. The banks will get their payments, the socialist dictators will get our dollars, and the American middle class will get the bill. The bill will not be paid by raising taxes further, for there is a limit to how high taxes can be pushed, but it will be paid through inflation and dollar depreciation.

As so often occurs with economic problems originating in mismanaged centrally planned economies built on paper money, the seeds of economic isolationism have been planted. The decade of the 1930s certainly was a period when isolationism, nationalism, and militarism followed on the heels of depression, inflation, deflation, and disruption to the normally smooth functioning of a market economy. Today, we hear strong demands daily to take away the American consumers' right to purchase foreign goods, claiming this will somehow miraculously rectify the ills created by government intervention and inflation. Nothing could be further from the truth. It will only make the economy worse, international relationships tense, and all at the expense of the individual's right to negotiate unmolested in the purchase of a particular product. The scapegoat is not Japanese efficiency and competitiveness; they serve us economically in providing for our needs. The unfairness of course is the fact that American taxpayers are forced to subsidize our competitors. Not only do we subsidize countries who need a bailout and others who just want a grant through the international banking system — all causing more inflation since we create money to fund these international development banks — we help our rich allies like Germany and Japan by providing large sums for their defense. We literally supply all Japan's defense, allowing the Japanese to have lower taxes on their car and steel companies and other subsidies. Our free gifts to them should all be stopped. It is suicidal to continue the process. It is no longer 1945, it is 1982, and a new generation of Americans are now demanding a new relationship with our allies and our enemies.

We all want a strong defense, and we want to live in peace. Free trade with potential enemies when they pay for the goods they buy cannot make war more certain than it would be otherwise. Trade barriers create ill will, new enemies, and arouse feelings of nationalism and militarism. Economic isolationism, a consequence of inflation and central planning, is to be feared and rejected as a viable policy for any freedom-loving nation.

The American people, whenever they have had the chance, have spoken out for peace and free trade, balanced budgets, and sound money. And they are today as well. Yet our policies do not reflect this. On August 16, the Chinese communiqué was signed with the Chinese Communist dictators and our administration. On August 30, an Export-Import Bank loan of $68.5 million was authorized by the President because it was "in our national interest" to help build a steel plant for them. What for? So they can sell cheap steel to the United States? Just what we need. American steel plants are closing down, unemployment is sky high, and we subsidize Communist steel plants. It is absurd. Instead of helping the steel industry by stopping inflation and lowering taxes, we make inflation worse by more credit creation to help our competition and in this case our political enemies. The wisdom of this policy I fail to see. I venture to guess most Americans fail to see the wisdom of self-sacrifice and economic suicide as well.

The current policies of inflation, taxation, central planning, protectionism, and economic isolationism are certainly bad in that Americans and the people of the world are going to suffer from the inevitable lowering of everyone's standard of living. But a much greater threat hangs over our head. The loss of personal liberty in an age of rampant inflation, money destruction, and economic turmoil is well known. Liberty, based on a belief that it is a gift of the Creator, requires our constant and utmost vigilance. This responsibility should motivate us in all that we do, and the threat of any loss of liberty must concern us all. The material benefits of a free society are obvious, and their loss that comes with a rise in statism cannot be ignored, but the concern for the rights of each citizen must become the principal motivating force in our political actions.

Closely paralleling the loss of liberty and the economic stagnation that is also a consequence of inflation and central planning is the great danger that attempts at compensating for all previous errors of government intervention will be made with more inflation and more government programs. If this continues and economic isolationism and international resentment develop, nations are driven to producing massive armaments—and not necessarily defensive armaments—out of fear and confusion as well as economic justifications. History shows that great danger of war rises out of the very conditions we are experiencing today.

How is it that the people cry out for less taxes and they get more? How is it that the people cry out for balanced budgets and they get greater deficits? How is it that the people cry out for sound money and they get more inflation and higher interest rates? They cry out for peace and they get war. This need not be; war and famine are not inevitable. Freedom and sound money bring peace and prosperity. But if freedom is lost and honest money relegated to the underground economy, war and famine will follow even for the United States. Although the United States has been exempt from famine for most of its history, if we pursue foolish policies based on the immoral use of government force, we will reap the economic whirlwind of hunger and poverty and suffer the rattle of machine guns, the blast of bombs, and the cry of human suffering.

If we accept the notion that government should not exert unjust force on any person, that no one should be made a slave to another, and that the fraud of paper money must be outlawed, this tragedy will be averted.

A bold step is required, for a timid response with more of the same, more inflation and more government intervention, will prove disastrous. The opportunity for positive change is available to us in this decade, and if we fail to respond in a positive way, it could be years or decades before the damage can be undone and a free society restored. It is literally up to us. ∎

The Folly of Current Monetary Policy

Congressional Record – U.S. House of Representatives
December 1, 1982

Mr. Speaker, the stock market is soaring and so is the money supply. In the last three months, checking account and cash money (M1) rose at a rate of 17.6 percent. The Federal Reserve has assured the market that its restrictive money policy of the past three years is a thing of the past. No tears should be shed over dropping the experiment with monetarism, but no joy should be expressed over the return to interest rate manipulation by massive monetary inflation. It is true the economy will feel better for a short while with more inflation, but so does the alcoholic as he returns to drinking after a short period of abstinence. This is not to say that the cure for our economic malaise is prolonged agony with monetarism, but it is important for all of us to realize that these are not the only two options available to us. We will never achieve a sound monetary system by jumping back and forth between concentrating on the money supply one year, and manipulating interest rates the next.

The ultimate solution will only come when we realize that central planning in money is no more efficient than the five-year plans in Russia for agriculture. We can talk forever about controlling the supply of money and controlling interest rates, but if we continue to ignore the fact that the quality of money is that which instills the trust in money, we will get nowhere. Manipulating monetary aggregates and interest rates is economically identical to the planner's obsession with controlling production, wage rates, prices, and profit levels. It is based on the illusion that politicians and bureaucrats somehow know what only the freely operating marketplace can determine. The monetary policy of today can create a false euphoria, but it is a guarantee that tomorrow's price inflation will return with a vengeance.

It guarantees that in the long run economic stagnation, high rates of unemployment, soaring interest rates, and the threat of runaway inflation will be with us until we admit the truth — that paper cannot serve as money, and only commodity money such as silver and gold will suffice. ∎

Back Into the Woods

Congressional Record — U.S. House of Representatives
May 26, 1983

Mr. Speaker, in the past few weeks and even today on the House floor the chorus of voices urging the convening of another international monetary conference has risen to deafening levels. The President has now announced that if the subject is raised at the Williamsburg Conference this weekend — as it most certainly will be raised by François Mitterand — he will agree to discuss it.

The only model used however for such a conference is the Bretton Woods Conference held July 1–22, 1944, in the hills of New

Hampshire. I am convinced a new international monetary conference, like the first one 39 years ago, will lead us back into the woods.

The Bretton Woods Conference established a very unstable international monetary system known as a gold exchange standard. The link to gold was rather weak, and it finally snapped in 1971, after a decade of international monetary crises. Simply put, the system established by the 1944 Conference made the dollar the foundation of the international system and all other currencies were directly fixed to the dollar, and only indirectly fixed to gold.

Even though the dollar was loosely linked to gold, only certain privileged holders of dollars—non-U.S. citizens—could get gold for their dollars. The result was predictable. During the period 1945–71, the U.S. Treasury lost over 400 million ounces of gold worth over $14,000,000,000 at the fixed price of $35 per ounce. One would have thought that this gold flight from the Treasury would have caused a few policy changes, but the only two of importance until 1968 were the establishment of the Exchange Stabilization Fund in 1961 in a futile attempt to bolster the dollar in international currency markets, and the creation of the London Gold Pool in the same year in an effort to suppress the price of gold.

In 1968 the situation became intolerable. The market price of gold exceeded $35 per ounce, and a "two-tier" price system—official and market prices—emerged. This inherently unstable rigged price system collapsed completely in 1971, and President Nixon ended the Bretton Woods experiment in a 30-minute speech one Sunday afternoon in August.

Even while it lasted, the Bretton Woods agreement did not work. Billed as a system of fixed exchange rates, there were thousands of devaluations in the 1945–71 period and dozens of devaluations even among the major currencies. What the agreement accomplished was the exporting of American inflation—the Consumer Price Index rose at roughly a 2-percent per year rate for the period—and the loss of American gold.

Now we are being told that this conference is the model for the reformation of the chaotic world financial system. But rather than leading us to a sound world financial system, it will probably lead us to a global system controlled by a world central bank. Robert Mundell, the supply-side economist, has already called for the establishment of a world central bank to administer a new Bretton Woods agreement.

Such a policy would be a catastrophe. Today conditions are even less favorable than in 1944. The gold is gone and the productivity of the United States is on the wane. Rather than government control of the world's financial system, we need less control and more reliance on the free market system and an honest gold standard.

Under fixed exchange rates, without a real standard of value such as gold linking our currencies, nothing but persistent inflationary and financial chaos can result.

We can have freedom and sound money, both nationally and internationally, by adopting a gold standard. But such a standard would be incompatible with a world central bank or an IMF, and it would unemploy thousands of international bureaucrats. To achieve freedom and sound money, we do not need another summit meeting, we need only to act. Were we to adopt a gold standard, all our major trading partners would be compelled to follow suit within a matter of months, simply to protect their own currencies from a strong dollar. The world would then be on an international gold standard—monetary stability without tears or an elitist system managed by the international bankers.

The choice is quite clear: Shall we continue in our futile attempts to control economies by force of international agreements, or shall we choose free markets and gold?

If we reenter the Woods will we ever get out? I doubt it. ∎

Conduct of Monetary Policy

Banking Committee Hearing on Conduct of Monetary Policy
Congressional Record — U. S. House of Representatives
March 5, 1997

Mr. Chairman, I want to bring up the subject again about the CPI. We have talked a lot about the CPI and an effort to calculate our cost-of-living in this country, and specifically here, to measure how much we are going to increase the benefits that we are responsible for. But in reality, is not this attempt to measure a CPI or a cost-of-living nothing more than an indirect method or an effort to measure the depreciation of a currency? And that we are looking at prices, but we are also dealing with a currency problem.

When we debase or depreciate a currency we do get higher prices, but we also have malinvestment. We have distorted interest rates. We contribute to deficits. And also, we might not always be looking at the right prices. We have commodity prices, which is the usual conceded figure that everybody talks about as far as measuring inflation. But we might at times have inflated prices in the financial instruments.

So to say that inflation is under control and we are doing very well, I would suggest that we look at these other areas too, if indeed we recognize that we are talking about the depreciation of a currency.

One other thing that I would like to suggest, and it might be of interest to my colleagues, is that one of the characteristics of a currency of a country that depreciates its currency systematically is that the victims are not always equal. Some suffer more than others. Some benefit from inflation of the currency and the debasement of the currency. So indeed, I would expect the complaints that I hear. I would suggest that maybe this is related to monetary policy in a very serious manner.

The consensus now in Washington, all the important people have conceded that we should have a commission. But when we designate a commission, this usually means everybody knows what the results are. I mean, nobody complains that the CPI might undercalculate inflation or the cost-of-living for some individuals, which might be the case. So we have this commission.

But is it conceivable that this is nothing more than a vehicle to raise taxes? The *New York Times* just this week editorialized in favor of this because it raised taxes, and also it cuts benefits, and they are concerned about cutting benefits. But would it not be much more honest for Congress to deal with tax increases in an above-board fashion, especially if we think the CPI is not calculable? I think it is very difficult.

Also, I think that if it is a currency problem as well, we cannot concentrate only on prices. There have been some famous economists in our history who say, look to the people who talk about prices because they do not want to discuss the root cause of our problem, and that has to do with the inflation of the monetary system or the depreciation of the currency.

Mr. GREENSPAN. Dr. Paul, the concept of price increase is conceptually identical, but the inverse of the depreciation of the value of the currency. The best way to get a judgment of the value of the currency as such, if one could literally do it, is to separate the two components of long-term nominal interest rates into an inflation premium component and a real interest rate component. The former would be the true measure of the expected depreciation in the value of the currency.

We endeavor to capture that in these new index bonds that have been issued in which the Consumer Price Index, for good or ill, is used to approximate that. It does not exactly, and I think that is what I have been arguing with respect to the commission is to take the statistical bias out of the CPI and get a true cost-of-living index.

It is certainly the case that that is a measure of inflation. There are lots of different measures of inflation. I would argue that commodities, *per se*, steel, copper, aluminum, hides, whatever, used to be a very good indicator of overall inflation in the economy when we were heavily industrialized. Now they represent a very small part of the economy and services are far more relevant to the purchasing power of the currency than at any time, so that broader measures of price, in my judgment, are more relevant to determining what the true rate of inflation is.

Dr. PAUL. Can the inflated prices in the financial instruments not be a reflection of this same problem?

Mr. GREENSPAN. They are. This is a very important question and one which I was implicitly raising: do asset price changes affect the economy? And the answer is clearly, "yes." What you call it, whether it is inflation or not inflation, that is a nomenclature question. But the economics of it clearly means that if one is evaluating the stability of the system, you have to look at product prices, that is, prices of goods and services, and asset prices, meaning prices on items generally which have rates of return associated with them. . . .

Dr. PAUL. Mr. Chairman, much has been said about your statements regarding the stock market and I wanted to address that for just one minute. In December when you stated this, of course, the market went down and this past week there was a sudden drop. The implication being that if you are unhappy with it, they assume that you will purposefully push up interest rates. But really since the first time you made that statement it seems that almost the opposite has occurred. M3 actually has accelerated, to my best estimate in the last two months it has gone up at a 10 percent rate. The base actually has perked up a little bit. Prior to this time it was rising at less than a 5 percent rate and now it is rising a little over 8 percent.

But then too we have another factor which is not easy to calculate, and that is what our friends in the foreign central banks do. During this short period of time they bought $23 billion worth of our debt. We do know that Secretary Rubin talks to them and that maybe there is an agreement that they help you out; they buy some of these Treasury bills so you do not have to buy quite so many.

Mr. GREENSPAN. There is no such agreement, Dr. Paul. . . .

Dr. PAUL. You read about that though.

Mr. GREENSPAN. Sometimes what you read is not true.

Dr. PAUL. OK, we will get your comments on that. But anyway, they are accommodating us, whether it is policy or not. Their rate of increase on holding our bills are rising at over 20 percent, and even these two months at maybe 22 percent.

My suggestion here and the question is, instead of the sudden policy change where you may increase interest rates, it seems like to me that you may be working to maintain interest rates from not rising. Certainly, you would have a bigger job if we had a perfect balance of trade. I mean, they are accumulating a lot of our dollars and they are helping us out. So if we had a perfect balance of trade or if their policies change, all of a sudden would this not put a tremendous pressure on interest rates?

Mr. GREENSPAN. We have examined the issue to some extent on the question of what foreign holdings of U.S. Treasuries have done to U.S. interest rates. I think the best way of describing it is that you probably have got some small effect in the short run when very large changes in purchases occur. There is no evidence over a long run that interest rates are in any material way affected by purchases.

The reason, incidentally, is that they usually reflect shifts—in other words, some people buy, some people sell. Interest rates will only change if one party or the other is pressuring the market. There is no evidence which we can find which suggests that that is any consistent issue, so that the accumulation of U.S. Treasury assets, for example, is also reflected in the decumulation by other parties. We apparently cannot find any relationship which suggests to us that that particular process is significantly affecting. . . .

Dr. PAUL. For the past two years, the accumulation has been much greater.

Mr. GREENSPAN. That is correct, it has been.

Dr. PAUL. Thank you. ∎

Federal Reserve has Monopoly over Money and Credit in United States

Congressional Record – U.S. House of Representatives
April 28, 1997

Mr. Speaker, today I would like to talk about the subject of monopolies. The American people historically have been very much opposed to all monopolies. The one thing that generally is not known is that monopolies only occur with government support. There is no such thing as a free market monopoly. As long as there is free entry into the market, a true monopoly cannot exist.

The particular monopoly I am interested in talking about today is the monopoly over money and credit, and that is our Federal Reserve System.

The Federal Reserve System did not evolve out of the market, it evolved out of many, many pieces of legislation that were passed over the many years by this Congress. Our Founders debated the issue of a central bank and they were opposed to a central bank, but immediately after the Constitutional Convention there was an attempt to have a central bank, and the First Bank of the United States was established. This was repealed as soon as Jefferson was able to do it.

Not too long thereafter the Second National Bank of the United States was established, another attempt at centralized banking, and it was Jackson, who abhorred the powers given to a single bank, that abolished the Second National Bank.

Throughout the 19th century there were attempts made to reestablish the principle of central banking, but it was not until 1913 that our current Federal Reserve System was established. Since that time it has evolved tremendously, to the point now where it is literally a dictatorship over money and credit.

It works in collaboration with the banking system, where not only can the Federal Reserve create money and credit out of thin air and manipulate interest rates, it also works closely with the banks through the fractional reserve banking system that allows the money supply to expand. This is the source of a lot of mischief and a lot of problems, and if we in the Congress could ever get around to understanding this issue, we might be able to do something about the lowering standard of living which many Americans are now suffering from. If we are concerned about repealing the business cycle, we would have to finally understand the Federal Reserve and how they contribute to the business cycle.

Recently it has been in the news that Alan Greenspan had raised interest rates, and he has received a lot of criticism. There were some recent letters written to Greenspan saying that he should not be raising interest rates. That may well be true, but I think the more important thing is, why does he have the power? Why does he have the authority to even be able to manipulate interest rates? That is something that should be left to the market.

Not only is this a monopoly control over money and credit, unfortunately it is a very secret monopoly. Mr. Speaker, I serve on the Committee on Banking and Financial Services and I am on the Subcommittee on Domestic and International Monetary Policy, and I myself cannot attend the open market committee meetings. I have no access to what really goes on. I have no authority to do any oversight. There is no appropriation made for the Federal Reserve.

The recent news revealed that the chief of the janitorial services over at the Federal Reserve makes $163,000 a year, and yet we have no authority over the Federal Reserve because it is a quasi-private organization that is not responding to anything the Congress says. Yes, they come and give us some reports about what they are doing, but because Congress has reneged, they no longer have much to say about what the Federal Reserve does.

This, to me, is pretty important when we think how important money is. If they have the authority to manipulate interest rates, which is the cost of borrowing, which is the price as well as the supply of money, this is an ominous power because we use the money in every single transaction.

It is 50 percent of every transaction. Whether it is the purchase of a good or whether it is the selling of our labor, it is denominated in terms of what we call the dollar, which does not have much of a definition anymore, and yet we have reneged on our responsibility to monitor the Fed to determine whether or not this dollar will maintain value.

Things have not always been this bad, and it did not happen automatically in 1913 when the Federal Reserve was established. It took a while. But it is worse now than it has ever been. Matter of fact, a well-known former Chairman of the Federal Reserve, William McChesney Martin, had interesting comments to make about this very issue in 1953. Mr. Martin said this: "Dictated money rates breeds dictated prices all across the board."

Well, it is abhorrent to those who believe in free enterprise and the marketplace. He goes on to say, "This is characteristic of dictatorship. It is regimentation. It is not compatible with our institutions."

So here we have a former Chairman of the Federal Reserve System coming down very hard on the concept of control of money and credit, and yet today it is assumed that the Federal Reserve has this authority. And so often it gravitates into the hands of one individual.

So those who are levying criticism toward the Federal Reserve today are justified, but if it is only to modify policy and not go to the source of the problem, which means why do they have the power in the first place, it is not going to do much good. So we will have to someday restore the integrity of the monetary system, and we have to have more respect for the free market if we ever expect to undertake a reform of a monetary system which has given us a great deal of trouble, and it is bound to give us a lot more trouble as time goes on.

How will this be done? Some argue that the Federal Reserve is private and out of our control. That is not exactly true. It is secret, but it is a creature of Congress. Congress created the Federal Reserve System and Congress has the authority to do oversight, but it refuses and has ignored the responsibility of really monitoring the value of our currency and monitoring this very, very powerful central bank.

There is no doubt in my mind and in the minds of many others that this has to be done. To say that we must just badger a little bit to the Fed and to Mr. Greenspan, and say that interest rates should be lowered or raised or whatever, and tinker with policy, I think that would fall quite short of what needs to be done.

What is the motivation behind a Federal Reserve System and a central bank? Indeed, there is some very interesting motivation because it does not happen accidentally. There is a good reason to have a central bank that has this power to just with a computer create billions of dollars. It is not an accident that Congress more or less closes their eyes to it.

Between 1913 and 1971 there were a lot more restrictions on the Federal Reserve to do what they are doing today, because at that time we were still making a feeble attempt to follow the Constitution. The dollar was defined as the weight of gold. There were restrictions in the amount of new money and credit one could create because of the gold backing of the currency.

Although Americans were not allowed to own gold from the 1930s to 1971, foreigners could. Foreigners could come in and deliver their dollars back into the United States and say, "Give us $35 an ounce." But that was a fiction, too, because by that time we had created so many new dollars that the market knew that it took more dollars to get one ounce of gold. In the process, we gave up a large portion of our gold that was present in our Treasury.

Why would the Congress allow this and why would they permit it? I think the reason is Congress likes to spend money, and many here like to tax, and they have been taxing. But currently, today, the average American works more than half the time for the government. If we add up the cost of all the taxes and the cost of regulations, we all work into July just to support our government, and most Americans are not that satisfied with what they are getting from the government.

The taxes cannot be raised much more, so they can go out and borrow money. The Congress will spend too much because there is tremendous pressure to spend on all these good things we do; all the welfare programs, and all the military expenditures to police the world and build bases around the world. It takes a lot of money and there is a lot of interest behind that to spend this money.

So, then, they go and spend the money and, lo and behold, there is not enough money to borrow and not enough tax money to go around, so they have to have one more vehicle, and that is the creation of money out of thin air, and this is what they do. They send the Treasury bills or the bonds to the Federal Reserve, and with a computer they can turn a switch and create a billion or $10 billion in a single day and that debases the currency. It diminishes the value of the money and alters interest rates and causes so much mischief that, if people are concerned about the economy or their standard of living or rising costs of living, this is the source of the problem.

So it is not only with the Federal Reserve manipulating the money and the interest rates, but the responsibility falls on the Congress as well because the Federal Reserve serves the interests of the Congress in accommodating the Congress as we here in the Congress spend more than we should.

Before 1971, when there were still restraints on the Federal Reserve, there was not as much deficit spending. Since that time, since the breakdown of the final vestiges of the gold standard in 1971, we have not balanced the budget one single time. So there is definitely a relationship. Now we have a national debt built up to $5.3 trillion, and we keep borrowing more and more.

We have a future obligation to future generations of $17 trillion, and this obligation is developed in conjunction with this idea that money is something we can create out of thin air. Now, if it were only the accommodation for the excess spending that was the problem, and we just had to pay interest to the Federal Reserve, that would be a problem in itself but it would not be the entire problem that we face today and that we face in the future.

As the Federal Reserve manipulates the economy by first lowering interest rates below what they should be and then raising interest rates above what they think they should be, this causes the business cycle. This is the source of the business cycle. So anybody who is concerned about unemployment and downturns in the economy and rising costs of living must eventually address the subject of monetary policy.

As a member of the Committee on Banking and Financial Services, I am determined that we will once again have a serious discussion about what money is all about and why it is so important and why we in the Congress here cannot continue to ignore it and believe that we can endlessly accommodate deficits with the creation of new money. There is no doubt that it hurts the working man more so than the wealthy man. The working man who has a more difficult time adjusting to the rising cost of living is now suffering from a diminished standard of living because real wages are going down.

There are many, many statistics now available to show that the real wage is down. Between 1973 and 1997, the wages of the working-man have gone down approximately 20 percent. This has to do with the changes in the economy, but it also has to do with changes in the value of the currency and the wages do not keep up with the cost of living.

The increase in the supply of money is called inflation, even though there are not very many people in the news world or here in the Congress who would accept that as a definition, because everybody wants to say that inflation is that which we measure by the Consumer Price Index.

The Consumer Price Index is merely a technique or a vehicle in a feeble attempt to measure the depreciation of our money.

It is impossible to measure the money's value by some index like the Consumer Price Index. There are way too many variables because the individual who is in a $20,000 tax bracket buys different things than the individual who is in a $200,000 tax bracket. Wages are variable and the amount of money we borrow, the amount of money we spend on education as well as medicine varies from one individual to another. So this Consumer Price Index which we hang so much on is nothing more than a fiction about what we are trying to do in evaluating and accommodating and adjusting to the depreciating value of the dollar.

The critics of the Fed are numerous, as I said. The recent criticism has erupted because a few weeks ago, after warning of about three or four months by the Chairman of the Federal Reserve that interest rates were going to go up and, lo and behold, he did. The overnight interest rates that banks pay to borrow money just to adjust their books went up one-fourth of 1 percent. This is very disturbing to the markets. But Alan Greenspan mentioned this for three or four months. He started talking about the threat to the marketplace and the threat to the stock market back in December. But instead of him being entirely in control as he would pretend to be, actually market interest rates were already rising. Because if we look carefully at the monetary statistics from December up until the time he raised interest rates, he actually was doubling the growth of the money supply.

What does this mean? This means that there were pressures already on rising interest rates, and the way to keep interest rates down is to create more and more money. It is the supply-and-demand effect. So if you have more money, make it more available, interest rates come down. So this was his attempt to keep interest rates down rather than him saying, today we have to have higher interest rates.

But the real problem is why does the Federal Reserve have this much power over interest rates? In a free market, interest rates would be determined by savings. People would be encouraged to work, spend what they want, save the rest. If savings are high, interest rates go down, people then are encouraged to borrow and invest and build businesses. But today we have created an environment that there is no encouragement for savings, for tax reasons, and for psychological reasons, very, very little savings is occurring in this country. Our country saves less money than probably any country in the world. But that does not eliminate the access to credit. Because if the banks and the businesses need money, the Federal Reserve comes along and they crank out the credit and they lower the interest rates artificially, which then encourages business people and consumers to do things that they would not otherwise do.

This is the expansion or the bubble part of the business cycle, which then sets the stage for the next recession. So people can talk about how to get out of the next recession when the next recession hits and they can talk about what caused it, but the next recession has already been scheduled. It has been scheduled by the expansion of the money supply and the spending and the borrowing and the deficits that we have accumulated here over the last six to eight years. And so, therefore, we can anticipate, and we in the Congress will have to deal with it, we anticipate for the next recession.

But unfortunately, because we do not look at the fundamentals of what we have done and the spending and the deficits, the next stage will be what we have done before. That is, if unemployment is going up, the government has to spend more money, there has to be more unemployment insurance. We cannot let people suffer. So the deficits will go up, revenues will go down and as we spend more money to try to bail ourselves out of the next recession, we will obviously just compound the problems because that is what we have been doing for the past 50 years. We have not solved these problems.

As a matter of fact, what has happened, because we eventually get the economy going again, what we do is we continue to build this huge financial bubble which exists today. It is a much bigger bubble than ever existed in the 1920s, it is international in scope and it is something never experienced in the history of mankind. Yet we have to face up to this, because when that time comes, we have to do the right things.

The 64 Members of Congress recently that signed the letter to Alan Greenspan said, Mr. Greenspan, you should not raise interest rates. Of course I just mentioned that maybe interest rates were rising, anyway, maybe he was accommodating the market pressures. But when 64 Members of Congress write to Greenspan and say do not let interest rates rise, or lower interest rates, what they are really saying is crank out more money, because if there is a greater supply of money, then interest rates will be lower and everybody is going to be happy. That is true, for the short run. On the long run, it causes very serious problems.

Stiglitz, who used to be the chairman of the Council of Economic Advisers, is a very strong critic of Alan Greenspan right now. He said that there are no problems, there is no cliff we are about to go over, do not worry about the future. I do not fault Mr. Greenspan's concern, believe me. I think he knows what is coming and why adjustments have to be made. But his critics are saying, when they talk about do not raise interest rates, what we have to remember is what they are saying to him is make sure there is more inflation, more money, lower interest rates and, of course, that will add to our problems in the future.

Not only do we have Members of Congress telling the Fed what to do, and the former Chairman of the Council of Economic Advisers telling them, many others all have an opinion on what to do, but nobody really asks the question, why are they doing all this in secret and where did they get all this power and why do we tolerate this system of money?

Even the IMF, something I am very much concerned about is the internationalization of our credit system, the IMF now has issued a recent report, but they do not agree with the 64 Members of Congress and they do not agree with the critics who say lower interest rates, create more money. They are saying to our Federal Reserve, you are creating too much money and you are having too much growth. Who ever heard of anything like too much growth? What is wrong with too much growth? Some people think that too much growth causes inflation, which is an absolute fallacy. If there is a lot of growth and a lot of production, prices would come down. Prices go up when the value of the money goes down. But the IMF is saying that should not even be involved in our domestic policy, and they are more involved than ever before, they are telling our Fed, this is good, what you are doing is good, keep raising your interest rates, turn off the economy, have a little slump here.

We do not need that kind of advice from somebody. We have enough problems taking advice from our own people and our own Congress about what has to happen, but we certainly do not need the advice from the IMF telling us that we ought to have more inflation, that we should involve overheating and that for some reason growth is bad. In a free market, sound monetary system, growth is good. If you have sound money and you have economic growth of 6 or 7 or 8 percent a year, you do not have inflation. That does not cause the inflation. It is only the debasement of the money that causes prices to rise.

Why do we hear so much concern about interest rates and price? Well, there is a specific reason for this according to some very sound economic thinkers, and that is they would like for us here in the Congress to think only about prices, either the price of money, which is the interest rate, or other prices, because so often it leads to the conclusion that, well, maybe what we ought to do is have price controls, which they tried in the early 1970s and it was a total disaster, but this is essentially what we have in medicine today.

We create new credit, the money goes in certain areas, the government takes this money and channels it into education and medicine, so you have more price inflation. So what do you do? You have price controls. That is what is going on. That is what we are having today in medicine, rationing of health care. That is what managed care is all about. Patients suffer from this because they have less choice, and they do not have as much decision making on what care they are going to get. This is a consequence of government manipulation of money and credit.

Those who want to perpetuate this system do not want us to think of the real cause, and that is, the real cause is the monetary system. They would like us to think about the symptoms and not the cause, because it is not in the interest of a lot of people, not only not in the interest of the big spenders here in the Congress who love the idea that the Federal Reserve is able to accommodate them on deficits, but there are business and banking interests and international interests and even some military production interests who like the idea that the credit is readily available and that they will be accommodated. The little guy never benefits. The little guy pays the taxes, he suffers from the inflation, he suffers from the unemployment, but there is a special group of people in an inflationary environment that benefits. Today of course there are a lot of people on Wall Street benefiting from this environment.

If this type of system were really good, we would all be very, very prosperous, and if we listened to the government statistics, we would say there are no problems in this country. But I know differently. A lot of people I talk to, they tell me they are having a lot of problems making ends meet. Sometimes they work two and three jobs to get their bills paid. It is not all feminism that makes women go to work. A lot of women go to work because they have to do it to make ends meet and take care of their families. So there are a lot of problems.

But one key point that I think is important is economic growth. If we have no economic growth and there is no productivity growth, we cannot maintain the standard of living, we cannot have increasing wages. If you do not produce more, you cannot have wages going up.

Unfortunately, that is where we are really hurting in this country. We are living prosperously because we borrow a lot of money, by individuals, by corporations, and our government borrows a lot from overseas. But we are not producing. Productivity growth in the last five years has averaged 0.3 percent. This is very, very low. It is equivalent to what happened before the Industrial Revolution, and it is going to lead to major problems in this country unless we understand why we are not producing as we had in the past. We need to address this if we have any concern about the people who suffer from these consequences.

The economic growth is slow. Predictions are that they, according to the government statistics, are going to slow even more in time, whether it is the end of this year or next. We will have a recession. Even by some government statistics now, we are seeing signs that there is a rising price level in some of our commodities. There is belief that these prices will go up and we will be suffering more so, even measured by the Consumer Price Index. This story that is being passed out here in the halls of Congress and in other places in Washington that we do not have to worry about the Consumer Price Index, it overstates inflation, therefore we can make the adjustment, I do not think that is correct at all. I think the Consumer Price Index probably way underestimates inflation. If you have private sources, there are many people who suffer the cost of living much higher than the 3 or 4 percent that the government reports. But there are some commodity indices that in the past two years have gone up over 50 percent. This is a sign of the consequence of the inflating of the money supply and it is starting to hit, or will hit some of our consumer products, because it is already hitting our commodities.

This idea that if there is a sign that prices are increasing, what we have to do is take it under control and we have to suppress economic growth and raise interest rates, this says something about our policy that shows the lack of understanding. Because if we look at all the recessions that we have had since World War II, in spite of the seriousness of many of these recessions, prices still go up.

The one that we remember most clearly is in the 1970s, where they even coined the word "stagflation." This is not an unheard of economic phenomenon. It is very frequent in many other nations, where you have a lot of inflation and poor economic growth. We have not had a serious problem with that, but it is very likely that that is eventually what we will get, because we have absolutely no backing and no restraint on our monetary system.

When we have an economic and monetary system as we have today, I mention how it encourages Congress to spend beyond its means. It spends too much, it borrows too much, it inflates too much, and it leads to serious long-term problems, that as long as you can borrow again and borrow again, you sort of hide the problems, delay the consequences of the problem and prevent the major correction that eventually comes.

But what have the American people been doing? Well, they have been encouraged by this. They see the credit is available out there. They keep borrowing, living beyond their means. Government lives beyond its means, and individuals live way beyond their means.

But some of the statistics are not very good about what is happening with our consumers, the American citizens. In 1996 personal bankruptcies were up 27 percent. It is at a record high; well over a million bankruptcies were filed in 1996. This is a reflection of loose credit policies, but it also is a reflection of a moral attitude.

There was a time in our history where bankruptcy was looked down upon, that we had a moral obligation to do our very best. If we had a bad turn in our businesses, what we did was we notified everybody, we went back to work, and we systematically did our very best to pay off all our debts. There is no incentive for that today. So it is very easy today to see the bankruptcies filed, and they are increasing rapidly. I suspect that they are going to continue to increase even more dramatically.

Credit card delinquencies are at an all time high. They were at 3.72 percent in 1996, and those who have late payments, they are also at a historic high, well over 5 percent. So the credit conditions of this country are not very good.

Now what do we see as the signs of things changing to sort of take care of this problem? So far, not too many good things happening. In 1995, the latest year we have measurements for, we find out that credit card issuers, credit card companies, issued 2.7 billion credit cards, pre-approved. Pre-approved credit cards, 2.7 billion, and it was equivalent to sending every single American between the ages of 18 and 64, 17 pre-approved credit cards. Nothing like throwing out the temptation there, and many Americans fall into the temptations. Congress does it. They keep borrowing, and they exist. So the individual keeps borrowing, takes another credit card, rolls them over.

Eventually, though, the banker will call. The banker will call the individual. Who calls the Congress? Who calls a country when it spends beyond its means and it is way past the time when they should be cutting back? The problem that develops then is not so much that the government, our government, quits taxing and quits paying the bills. We will always do that. We have control over that because we now have this authority by the Federal Reserve to create the money. The checks will always come.

The one thing that we do not have in the Congress and we do not have in the Federal Reserve, and the President does not have, is to guarantee the value of the money, and that is the problem. Today all we hear about is the strength of the dollar, but if you look at the dollar from 1945 on, the dollar is on a downward spiral, and we are on a slight upward blip right now. Ultimately the dollar will be attacked by the marketplace, and it will be more powerful than any of the policy changes that our Federal Reserve might institute.

There are a couple other things that have happened in our financial system that are different than in the other ones. Some would argue with me and say you are concerned about the supply of money and credit. Well, I can show you a statistic measured by M1, M2, and M3, and the money supply is not going up all that rapidly. And this is the case compared to other times, that money supply as measured by the more conventional methods are not — those measurements are not going up as rapidly as they have in the past. But there are other things that can accommodate the lack of expansion of money as measured by, say, M2 and M3.

First, if an individual has an incentive not to hold the money and save the money, but spend their money the day they get it, that is called the velocity or the propensity to spend the money, and if you use it more often, it is like having more dollars, and that is one statistic that has gone up dramatically. Between 1993 and 1996 it has gone up 45 percent, so there is more desire to take the money and spend it, and it acts as if there is a lot more money, and we will also put pressure on the marketplace and cause the distortions that can be harmful.

The other thing that we have going that is different than ever before is that because there is no definition of the money, the dollars, no definition of the dollar, we have introduced the notion of all kinds of hedges and all kinds of speculation, and some serve financial and economic interests to do hedging, but because there is no soundness to the currency there is a greater need all the time to hedge and to try to protect against sudden changes. Some of that would be economically driven, but other activity of that sort is driven by speculation.

So in an age when you have tremendous excessive credit, money and credit, you have more speculation. Consumers speculate they spend too much money, a businessman speculates, invests in things he probably should not, but also governments do the same thing. They spend money that they should not have.

But in this area of derivatives, we have things like swaps, futures, and options, repos, and the foreign currency market. Right now there is $20, $21 trillion worth of these derivatives floating around out there outside of the measurement by our conventional money supply, which means that this participates in this huge financial bubble that exists around the world.

There is also a measurement that we make on a daily basis which is called through the clearinghouse interbank payment system, and this is all the electronic money that is traded throughout the world every single day, and this again reflects how quickly we are spending our money and how fast we are circulating and how quickly it moves among and through our computers. Today it is estimated that $1.4 trillion is transferred over the wire service.

Now, if there were a sound dollar and it was created only with a proper procedure rather than out of thin air, this would not be as bad, but the fact that this is contributing toward a financial bubble I think is a very, very dangerous condition.

We live in an age called the Information Age; we live in a computer age, and this technology is all very, very helpful to us. As a matter of fact, it has served us in many ways to accommodate this age of the paper money systems of the world. No money is sound today in the entire world. So there is what we call the fluctuating currency rates. Every single day, every single minute, the value of the dollar versus the yen, versus the mark, versus the pound is changing instantly.

Now in the old days each currency was defined by a weight of gold. There was less speculation even though under those conditions of government manipulation there were periodic times when certain countries would have to devalue. But now the computer system has really been a free market answer to those individuals who like the system, and it does work, it does work to a large degree for a time. But it also allows the system to last longer, and it allows us to create more of this financial bubble.

This is why we have been able to go along with the system of government where we have made commitments to our future generations of $17 trillion; otherwise we could not have made these commitments that would have had to be a correction. We would have had to cut back and live within our means, just as individuals do; they have to live within their means, and they have to live probably less high than they were when they were borrowing all the money. A country will have to do that, too, that has lived way beyond its means, and this is why what we are doing is so dangerous.

The fact that we had these floating exchange rates for years has permitted many of our paper currencies to last a lot longer than they otherwise would have. We in the United States have a dollar which is considered the reserve currency in the world which lends itself to even more problems because the dollar is held in higher esteem and it is considered the reserve that other countries are more willing to hold, and this came out of World War II because we had essentially all the gold, the dollar was strong, our economy was strong, so the dollar was good as gold. So people took dollars and they would hold them, and they still do that to a large degree today.

So what does that encourage us to do? It encourages here in the Congress and elsewhere to create this debt, and then as the money circulates, we go and we say, oh, we have a lot of credit, we can borrow this money, we will buy foreign products, and that is what we do. We buy a lot of foreign products, and everybody is decrying, you know, this foreign deficit. We owe more money to foreigners and we have a greater foreign deficit than any other country in the world, and it is encouraged because they are willing to take our dollars, and we are willing to spend the money and we are willing to run up these deficits and not worry about the future.

But where do these dollars go? They go into the central banks, they buy our Treasury bills, and they are quite satisfied at the moment. But when they get unsatisfied and dissatisfied with it, they are going to dump these dollars, and they will come back. But the trade deficit is running more than $100 billion a year, which means we buy more products from overseas than we sell to the tune of $100 billion.

This in many ways has allowed our Federal Reserve to get off the hook a bit because if we had $100 billion that nobody wants to loan us and they had to create that new money, that would be very, very damaging to the psychology of our market, and it would be very, very inflationary. So it is still inflationary, but it is delayed. So as long as foreigners will take our dollars and let us buy their goods and we live beyond our means and hold our dollars and we keep creating new money and paying the interest, this thing could go on for a while. But eventually though in all monetary systems which are based on fiat, the creation of money out of thin air, eventually comes to an end, and when it comes to an end, there is the rejection of the dollar, and then the dollars come home, interest rates will go up, inflation will be back with a vengeance, and there will come a time, and nobody knows when that time will come, it will not be because of us in the Congress being very deliberate and very wise to all of a sudden live within our means, but we will be forced to live within our means because those who want to loan the money to us and the value of the money will change, that there will just not be enough wealth.

What promotes all this? Well, what is the grand illusion that allows us to get ourselves into such a situation? Well, the grand illusion of the 20th century, especially in the latter half of the 20th century, has been that prosperity can come from the creation of credit. Now if you think about it, it does not make any sense if you take a Monopoly game and you create more Monopoly money and pass it out, everybody knows it has no value. But we have literally endorsed the concept that if we just print money and pass it out, everybody is going to be wealthy, and because it is government and because it was related to a gold standard and because foreigners will take money, this system continues to work because there is still trust in the money.

But eventually this trust will be lost. The wealth cannot be created by creating new money. Yes, if the Federal Reserve prints more money today and hands it to me, I can go spend it and I can feel wealthier. But in the grand scheme of things, you do not create wealth that way, and that is also the reason why productivity growth is down. We do not create it. We have to have incentives, we have to encourage work and effort. That is the only place you can get wealth.

So our taxes are too high, the regulations are too high, we borrow too much money, interest rates are too high, and we discourage savings all because of this monetary system. So eventually we are going to be required to do something about that to restore trust in the money so we do save money so we work harder. But we have to lower taxes, we have to get rid of regulations, we have to get rid of taxes on capital gains and get rid of taxes on savings and interest and get rid of taxes on inheritance. Then people will have more of an incentive to work rather than just to borrow. So the illusion of wealth today is that which comes from a fiat or paper monetary system.

We need today a very serious debate on what the monetary system ought to be all about. It cannot be a debate which is isolated from the role of government. If we have a role of government which is to run the welfare state, to give anything to anybody who needs something or wants something or claims it is an entitlement or claims it is a right, if that is a system of government that we want to perpetuate, it is going to be very difficult to have any reform. If we continue to believe that this country is the policeman of the world, that we must police the world and build bases overseas at the same time we neglect our own national defense, our own borders, our own bases here at home, but we continue to spend money on places, on Bosnia and Africa, and pay for the defense of Japan and Europe; as long as we accept those ideas, there is no way we can restore any sanity to our budget.

So I am suggesting to my colleagues here in the Congress that what we must do is address the subject of what the role of government ought to be. There should be a precise role for government. That is what the whole idea and issue was of the Constitutional Convention as well as our Revolution. We did not like the role of government that the English and the British had given us, and we here in the United States decided that the role of government ought to be there for the preservation of liberty.

The role of government ought not to be to redistribute wealth, it ought not to be the counterfeiter of the world, to create money out of thin air. It is illegal for you or I to counterfeit money. Why do we allow the government to counterfeit the money and make it worthless all the time?

As long as we accept that, we are going to have big problems. But there will be a time coming, and I suggest to all of my colleagues that we be ready for it, because it is so serious. Not only is it a serious threat to our physical and economic well-being, the greater threat is the threat to our individual liberty. As conditions worsen, and when we have to face up to our problems, so often the response is, all we need is another government program. And that is still an attitude that I see all the time around here: if we just have a little more tax money.

Already in this very early Congress, we have had tax increases in spite of the rhetoric against taxes. We have been raising taxes. We have increased the amount of regulations. We have done nothing to really address the subject.

That comes from the fact that we never really ask the right questions. What should the role of government be? The Founders, as they concluded after the Revolution, as they wrote the Constitution, it very clearly was stated that the role of government, especially at the federal level, ought to be there to protect the individual liberties of all individuals, no matter what. But today, we have lost that as a goal and as a target. We concentrate, whether it is a businessman or the person that is receiving welfare benefits, the concentration is on the material benefits that usually come from a free society in a voluntary way. But today, if anybody wants something or they need something or they think they have a right to it, what do they do? They order a political action committee and come to Washington.

I was gone for a few years. I was here in the Congress in 1976, and, after returning, there is one dramatic difference. There are more lobbyists than ever, more commands, more people coming and more people wanting things. I have more demand from the business community than I do from those who are from the poor end of the spectrum. There is a vicious maldistribution of wealth in a society that destroys its money. Inevitably, if a country destroys its money, it destroys its middle class.

This is what is happening in this country already. The poor, middle class individual who is still proud enough not to go on the dole and not to take welfare, that is the individual who suffers the very most; and he is the one that is most threatened by the loss of a job in the next downturn.

Currently right now, Wall Street, are they suffering from this financial bubble that I see? No. If you are in the stock market or the bond market or borrowing overseas, they are doing quite well. People say: You worry too much. There is no inflation. No matter what you say about the money supply and all of these things you talk about, there is no inflation, do not worry about it. Inflation deals with money, not prices.

So as I said earlier, I believe prices are going up much faster than people will admit; but at the same time, the supply of money and credit continues to expand. So we will have to eventually address these problems. I think it will be up to us as Members of Congress to at least make some plans. Because if we do not, if we do not make the plans, I see this as a serious, serious threat to our personal liberties.

Mr. Speaker, it will not be a simple reform that we need. We have to do something more than that. We have to start thinking about what do we need to do to really change the course. Is there anything wrong with addressing the subject of individual liberty? Is there anything wrong with talking about the value and the importance of sound money? I claim there is nothing wrong with that, but there is very little debate. There is very little debate among our committee members and in our committees to address this. It is usually, how do we tide ourselves over? How do we modify this so slight a degree?

But the time will come, the time will come, because we will go bankrupt, because no country has ever done this before. No country can live beyond its means endlessly. No country can spend and inflate and destroy its money. There will be this transfer of wealth. It happened in many, many countries in this century. Of course, one example of the 20th century was the German inflation, and then there has to always be a scapegoat. The middle class suffers the most. Somebody has to be blamed.

Currently today, I see a trend toward those of us who advocate limited government, those who detest big government as becoming the scapegoat saying, oh, you individuals who are against big government, you are the people who cause trouble, you cause unhappiness. That is not the case. People are unhappy. I meet them all the time because they are having a difficult time making it in this day and age. Who knows who the next scapegoat will be, but there will be one.

Mr. Speaker, the middle class in America will have to eventually join in the reforms that we need. The reforms can be all positive. There is nothing wrong with advocating limited government. There is nothing wrong in the American spirit to advocate the Constitution. There is nothing wrong with the American tradition that says work is good. And there is something wrong with a system that endorses and encourages and pushes the idea that we have the right to somebody else's life and somebody else's earnings. I do not believe that is the case. I think that is morally wrong. I do not believe it has been permitted under the Constitution, and it also leads to trouble. If it led to prosperity, it would be a harder argument for me. But if it leads to trouble and it leads to people being undermined in their financial security and in their economic security, then we have to do something else.

I would like to invite those who expressed deep concern about the poor and those who advocate more programs, more welfare programs, I would like to suggest they need to look at monetary policy. They need to look at deficits, and they need to realize that wealth has to be created. And if we truly do care about the poor people in this country, and if we do care about the people trying to build homes, public housing obviously has not worked. We have been doing public houses now and spent nearly $600 billion, and there is no sign that we have done much for the people that we have given public housing to.

We have spent $5 trillion on welfare. There are more homeless than ever. The educational system is worse than ever. Yet we do not really say, well, what should we do differently? Sometimes we will say, well, let us take the management and change the management. Let us take the bureaucrats from Washington and put them in the States. Let us do block grants. Let us make a few minor adjustments and everything is going to be OK, and it will not be.

We will not make it OK until we address the subject of what kind of a society we want to live in. I want to live in a free society. Fortunately for me, as a Member of Congress, and as one who has sworn to uphold the Constitution, this is an easy argument. It should be an easy argument for all of my colleagues who would say, yes, I have sworn to uphold the Constitution, I believe in America, I believe in hard work. But why do you vote for all of these other programs? Why do you vote for all of the deficits? Why are we getting ready to vote for more taxes soon? Why are we voting a supplemental appropriation? Why are we doing these things if we really are serious? I have not yet seen any serious attempt to cut back on spending and cut back on taxes.

Mr. Speaker, someday we will have to do it. The sooner, the better. If we do it in a graceful manner, there is no pain and suffering. The American people will not suffer if we cut their taxes. The American people will not suffer if we lower the amount of regulations. The American people will not suffer if we get out of their lives and not give them 100,000 regulations to follow day in and day out. The American people will not suffer if the federal government gets out of the management of education and medicine. That is the day I am waiting for and the day I am working for. Hopefully, I will get other Members of Congress here to join me in this effort to support the concepts and the principles of individual freedom. ■

Conduct of Monetary Policy

Banking Committee Hearing on Conduct of Monetary Policy
Congressional Record – U.S. House of Representatives
July 22, 1997

I would like to start off by saying that I have a slightly different approach to inflation and monetary policy, and I will make a few statements now so that my questions later on might make a little more sense. But it has already been referred to here and commonly so in all the media is that as soon as the CPI goes up and there is price inflation, price rising, then we have inflation. And I look at this slightly differently because there are many of us who believe that inflation is first and foremost a monetary policy. The inflation starts with the increase in the supply of money and credit and then we subsequently have different things happen.

One of those things possibly can be rising prices in consumer and in producer prices. But more importantly and what I want to concentrate on is that the other things that can occur with monetary inflation is that we get malinvestment, we get the encouragement of excessive debt, and we get speculative markets. And the reassurance that we hear continuously day in and day out in the media or here in the Congress that there is no inflation is not that reassuring to me, and I will pursue that later on, because if we are missing this and there are speculative markets out there and excessive debt and malinvestment, what we really need to be concerned about is the correction that inevitably comes after a period of inflation.

We were reassured in the 1920s do not worry about anything, there was no inflation, because they looked only at prices. Japan did the same thing in the 1980s. Do not worry, we have no inflation. Yet Japan has been suffering a bit since 1989. So the reassurance does not come across too strong as far as I am concerned.

I am not totally reassured that we have no inflation. Quite possibly the rules have changed in measuring money supply. Of course we know that M1 means nothing anymore. It is actually going down, so we do not call that deflation. In the past ten years a significant point in monetary history we have found out that the Fed has increased total Federal Reserve credit two times, but during this same period of time, something new has crept in, and that is the "monetization" of our debt by foreign central banks. They have increased their holdings by more than four times. During these past ten years we have increased M3 by $1.5 trillion. So the question is, "How has this been discounted?"

We say there is no problem because there are no price increases, but we have also had the advantage of technology. That keeps prices down. We have cheap imports. That keeps prices down. We have world labor markets now. That keeps prices down and takes the pressure off wages. We have the privilege of being the reserve currency of the world. Foreigners are still willing to take our dollars. So we inflate. Not only do they take our dollars in the form of credit and buy our Treasury bills, but they are quite willing to hold two-thirds of our cash overseas, which again leads us to believe that there is no monetary inflation.

We also know that the measurement of price inflation comes from the government measuring the CPI, and we do know that the calculation of the CPI is ongoing, as reported in the last minutes of FOMC, and therefore the CPI is reflecting something lower. Now, a lot of people in this country generally do not trust what the government tells them, and when I talk to the people in my district, they just sort of roll their eyes and laugh if they are told that there is no inflation and that prices are rising at 1 or 2 percent. And yet, if you look at a private organization that measures the cost-of-living index, Al Sindlinger of Sindlinger & Co., from Wallingford, Pennsylvania, he claims that consumer prices are rising by 5.8 percent.

So, I think that I am going to emphasize in my questioning the importance of looking at the right targets, and not being deceived and saying that "there is no inflation, there is no concern." Maybe we should have some concern about some exuberance someplace in the economy. . . .

Mr. FRANK. Open is not skeptical. I am glad you are open, but not skeptical. I did not say you were an "old fogey."

Mr. GREENSPAN. Skepticism has very significant roots in philosophy, and these are good roots. You look for real evidence to determine whether something is true or false.

Mr. FRANK. I just want to say with regard to "old fogey," far from calling you an "old fogey," when you talked about people retiring in 2009 and 2010, indeed I thought you were talking about yourself. . . .

Dr. PAUL. Mr. Chairman, I think the Banking Committee must be making progress, because even others now bring up the subject of gold, so I guess conditions are changing. But I might just suggest that the price of gold between 1945 and 1971 being held at $35 an ounce was not much reassurance to many that the future did not bode poorly for inflation. So the price of gold being $325 or $350, ten times what it was a few years back, should not necessarily be reassurance about what the future holds. Unlike my colleague from the other side accusing you of searching for gloom, I might wonder whether or not we might be hiding from some of it? So I thought that the last thing I would suggest is that we lack monetary stimulus and all we need is a little more monetary stimulus, and all of a sudden we are going to take care of the problems. And by the way, the problems that are described are the problems that I am very much concerned about, but I come up with a different conclusion on why we are having those problems.

Earlier, I made the case in my opening statement that quite possibly we are using the wrong definitions and we are looking at the wrong things, and we continue to concentrate and to reassure ourselves that the Consumer Price Index is held in check, and therefore things are OK and there is no inflation. Real interest rates and the long bond remain rather high, so there is a little bit of inflationary expectation still built into the long-term bond. But the consumer prices might be inaccurate, as Sindlinger points out, and they may become less important right now because of the various technical things going on.

And also I made the suggestion that the money-supply calculations that we use today might not be as appropriate as they were in the past, because I do not think there is any doubt that we have all the reserves and all the credit and all the liquidity we need. I mean, it is out there. It might not be doing what we want it to do, but there is evidence that it is there. The marginal debt today was reported at $113 billion, just on our stocks. So there is no problem with getting the liquidity. My argument is that what if we looked at the prices of stocks as your indicator as you would look at the CRB? I mean, we would have a rapidly rising CRB—or any commodity index. It would be going up quite rapidly. For instance, in the past three months, we had a stock price rise of 25 percent. If it continued at that rate, we would increase the stock prices 100 percent in one year. If that was occurring in the commodities or Consumer Price Index, I know you would be doing something.

My question and suggestion is maybe we ought to be doing something now, because there is a lot of credit out there doing something else, causing malinvestment, causing deficits and debt to build up, and that there will be a correction. We have not repealed the business cycle. So we have to expect something from this.

I think there are some interesting figures about what has happened to the stock market. In 1989, Japan's stock market had a greater value than our stock market does. Our market now is three times more valuable in terms of dollars than Japan. We have 48 percent of the value of all the stocks in the world, and we put out 27 percent of the output. So, there is a tremendous amount of marking up of prices, a tremendous amount of credit. So, instead of lacking any credit, I think we have maybe an excess amount. I would like to know if you can reassure us that we have no concerns about this malinvestment, that we do not have excess credit and that these stock prices are not an indicator that might be similar to a Consumer Price Index?

Mr. KENNEDY. What?

Mr. GREENSPAN. Let me first say, Dr. Paul, it is certainly the case that if you look at the structure of long-term nominal government interest rates, there is still a significant inflation premium left. In the 1950s and the 1960s, we had much lower nominal rates, and the reason was that the inflation premium was clearly quite significantly less. I think we will eventually get back there if we can maintain a stable noninflationary environment. I do not think we can remove the inflation premium immediately, because it takes a number of years for people to have confidence that they are dealing with a monetary policy which is not periodically inflationary.

To follow on the conversation I was having with Congressman Frank, the type of conversation we have at the Federal Open Market Committee is indeed the type of conversation that is coming from both of you. In other words, we are trying to look at all of these various forces and recognize where the stable relationships are and those which tell us about what is very likely to occur in the months, the quarters, and hopefully, in the years ahead.

It is a very intensive evaluation process, especially during a period when there seem to be changes in the longer-term structure which we do not yet know are significant or overwhelming. But we are experiencing changes which lead us to spend a considerable amount of time trying to evaluate what is going on. But we would be foolish to assume that all of history has somehow been wiped from the slate and that all of the old relationships, all of the problems that we have had in the past, have somehow in a period of a relatively few years, disappeared. The truth of the matter is that we suspect that there are things that are going on. We do not know yet how important they are. But we are keeping a very close evaluation of the types of events that are occurring, so that we can create what we believe to be the most appropriate monetary policy to keep this economic expansion going in a noninflationary way, because that is what is required to keep growth going.

Dr. PAUL. So, you are saying the stock price index is of a lot less value than the commodity price index or the Consumer Price Index?

Mr. GREENSPAN. I would say our fundamental purpose is to keep inflation, meaning basically the underlying general price index, stable, because that is the most likely factor which will create financial stability overall. As I have said in previous commentary and discussions before this subcommittee, we of necessity look at the whole financial system, but it has always been our conclusion that the central focus is on the stability of product prices as the crucial determinant in the system, which if you solve that one, you are likely to solve the others as well. . . .

Mr. FRANK. I appreciate that. And I have only one last sentence. And here, for once, I think lawyers may have something to tell economists. They usually don't.

I agree that is the appropriate question. I just hope that you will decide it by a preponderance of the evidence, and not say that the good news has to prove itself beyond a reasonable doubt.

Mr. GREENSPAN. I couldn't agree with you more. It is not a good news/bad news; it is a preponderance of the evidence and the facts which I hope determine what we do. I can certainly tell you that is our purpose. . . .

Dr. PAUL. Mr. Chairman, earlier on, several Members on that side made the point that ordinary people and poor people are having a tough time, and I think they are correct about this. I don't, of course, agree with some of the solutions they might propose, but I do not believe for a minute that adjustments, or an explanation of the CPI or price deflator will satisfy these people. There are a lot of people out there suffering. I think it is very real.

I think what we must remember is that the standard of living for many of these people has gone down in the period of time since we closed down the last monetary system in 1971. Fiat money — by its very nature, a characteristic of fiat money is that the middle class eventually gets wiped out if you have runaway inflation. If you have insidious inflation, you will have the poor people nibbled away with. The early users of credit benefit, the late users have difficulty. So, the people who borrow, the bankers, the big business, and governments are going to have advantages that the little guy won't have. So, I really agree with the concerns that they express and I think that we should continue to think about this and try to solve that problem.

I have a specific question dealing with central bank purchases of U.S. debt. On June 23, Hashimoto, Prime Minister of Japan, made a comment that made the news and stirred up the markets for approximately 24 hours and then it passed. He threatened, of course, that he would sell Treasury bills if we didn't fix the dollar/yen ratio to something more to his liking. But even before that statement, I noticed that there has been a significant change in what central banks have been doing.

Up until approximately three months ago, central banks have been accumulating our debt at sometimes up to 20 percent annualized rate and yet, in the last three months, we have seen a change where it has gone to a point where it is decreasing. Not only are they not buying as many, they have actually unloaded some of this debt. It may be way too early to tell, but it could be a trend.

At the same time the foreign central banks were holding a lot less of our debt, the Federal Reserve, our Federal Reserve, has increased its purchase and Federal Reserve credit has subsequently gone up 10 to 11 percent in that same period.

So my question is, how serious is this? Is this a major part to your policy, and what happens if, in the next year, the foreign central banks don't dump just $10 or $15 billion, or $20 billion, what if they dump a whole $100 billion? What kind of pressure does this put on you and what kind of pressure does it put on the interest rates, and do they — or could they — hold us hostage?

Mr. GREENSPAN. Let me just respond to the general question. If central banks decided to sell U.S. Treasury debt, somebody else is obviously buying it. So really, what it is, is a swap in which the central bank switches out of government debt into other securities and some other party is doing the opposite. So, somebody will be holding our debt. The question really is, would it significantly affect the price of the debt in the process of that exchange? In other words, would long-term interest rates in the United States go up as a consequence?

It is conceivable in a very short-term sense that, for technical reasons, if you try to sell a lot of U.S. Treasury debt, the price of the bonds would go down and the interest rate would go up in part. But, over the longer run—and that is probably a more modest shorter run, as you pointed out earlier Congressman—the determination of the level of interest rates is essentially the real interest rate plus the inflation premium. Ultimately, that is what will prevail. The mere sale of the U.S. Treasury debt would not, in and of itself, alter either the inflation premium or the real interest rate. So that, over the longer run, that should not have a significant effect. . . .

Dr. PAUL. OK. My concern, though, is what if there were not enough other parties to buy? It seems that the pressure would be put on you to buy, and it looks like you may have already done this, because what you have done in the last three months is more active than you did in the previous three months. The net sales on foreign central bank holdings have certainly changed. There has been a definite change in the last three months.

Mr. GREENSPAN. No, our policy has been directed strictly at the issue of maintaining a portfolio which is consistent with our announced federal funds rate. So what we do is we equilibrate the system of federal funds, the supply and demand within the banking system, and adjust our portfolio in a manner to maintain something close—relatively close—to that rate.

Our open market operations are not related to this particular phenomenon but net, effectively, directed toward the federal funds rate target. ∎

East Asian Economic Conditions

Banking Committee Hearing on East Asian Economic Conditions
Congressional Record – U.S. House of Representatives
January 30, 1998

Dr. PAUL. Mr. Chairman, I think I can do this in less than a minute. I would like to make two points.

It has been continuously argued that there is no cost. You wouldn't be here if there wasn't a cost. You want an $18 billion authorization. The American people don't buy that argument. You are not going to convince very many in the Congress and you are not going to convince the American people there is not a cost, or we wouldn't be going through this process.

The other thing is, we should think about the cause, rather than propping up a bad system. Credit expansion in the Far East caused this problem. Our dollar participated in it. We have a reserve currency of the world. They buy our debt, they use our dollars as a reserve currency, they have expanded it, it is inevitable that you have to have these crises, so unless we address the basic currency problems, we cannot solve this for the future or protect our dollar. . . .

Secretary RUBIN. Congressman, we are extremely sympathetic and very strongly identify with the objective. There is somebody at Treasury, an exceedingly capable member of our staff, who has that very job. We would be delighted to do that. . . .

Dr. PAUL. Mr. Chairman, I have several questions. I would like to go ahead and ask the three questions and then listen for the answers. First off, I would like to remind Mr. Summers that last time you were here, I think in November, I did ask a question in writing about the real cost, whether or not the IMF funding would appear in the national debt. That is not one of my questions, but I would like a follow-up on that. We have not yet heard from you on that. I cited a CRS report that says that it is truly part of the national debt and that interest is paid on it. Most Americans realize there is a cost to it. Most American taxpayers aren't calling us. That is one of the reasons why this funding is in trouble. I mean, nobody is calling up here and saying, "Hey, please spend the money, please refund the IMF." They are more concerned about inner city jobs and other problems. So the politics of this is very difficult for you.

Recently Henry Kissinger was visiting over in Thailand. He was interviewed over there. In his interview in the newspaper it was reported that he attacked right-wing extremists that were protectionists and not supportive of this bailout. I know it has been made mention that people on the far right and far left may make strange bedfellows. I would like to make it very clear that—and thank goodness that strange bedfellows are still legal in the political process. I do not happen to belong to either right wing or left wing, so I am glad to participate in this endeavor. I do have great concern about this. I think that the solutions that have been presented are nothing more than the same old stuff that caused the trouble in the first place; that is, credit expansion. But, for instance, I think actually you are overreacting, in the sense that you are wanting this, having the Secretary of Defense come, declaring this horrible emergency coming, people like me who speak out, say, what are you going to do if a depression comes, it is going to be blamed on me. This is getting carried away. If you look at the most important way to find out how this is being discounted, look to the markets. The markets are saying: the funding is in great trouble, and the markets are doing quite well. So I think it is hard to convince everybody that we are in big trouble if the markets are saying, "hey, forget it."

There was an agreement with the Korean government; $24 billion of loans were rolled over with the banks. The banks get a high rate of interest. The banks get a special deal because they can go down to zero reserve requirement because they belong to the OECD and do the Fed regulations, and today's paper said this is a plum for the banks, this is a sweet deal for the banks. There is a lot of reassurance there. So a lot of people are asking, why do you need additional support? Why do you need even taxpayer support to back up these loans that have already been renegotiated? One question I have for Treasury is, in this $24 billion renegotiation, I would like to know whether or not the 14 merchant banks that have already been declared bankrupt, whether or not they are going to be bailed out as well. Has the Korean government assumed those loans and indirectly are we going to assume it?

I would like to go ahead and finish my questions. The other question I have for Chairman Greenspan is in 1980 there was a significant change in the Federal Reserve Act. It permitted much more leeway in the Federal Reserve in purchasing foreign debt. Does this mean—are you allowed under today's law to buy a Korean bond in your transactions and have you or would you consider it? And also for the Exchange Stabilization Fund, in the legislation giving us the Exchange Stabilization Fund, you have the right to deal in gold. It is very explicit that you have the legal authority. Do you, have you, or would you?

Secretary RUBIN. Let me take a shot at a few of those if I may. Why don't we start with the one you addressed to Chairman Greenspan actually. He was looking too comfortable.

Mr. GREENSPAN. We hold at this stage foreign obligations in marks and yen as part of a general reserve position. We do not buy any other foreign assets. The rules which we abide by are internal rules of the Federal Open Market Committee. Those rules have been fairly restrictive with respect to what it is we can buy. The answer to your question is we don't have authority now to buy Korean bonds. My impression is that if we brought the issue up we would not achieve such authority. . . .

Secretary RUBIN. Very briefly on the other issues if I may, Dr. Paul, on the question of the markets not reflecting the issues in Asia, markets can change and change very quickly. Having lived in markets for 26 years and having done well sometimes and less well other times and horrendously still other times, I wouldn't look to markets myself—and this is my view, one person's view—I would not look to markets as a barometer of the possible risks to our interest. I think the risks are the risks that we have identified here. On the question of whether or not the bank deal in Korea is what you called a sweet deal.

Dr. PAUL. The paper called it that. I am quoting the paper.

Secretary RUBIN. The paper says a lot of things, including some things about me even sometimes, which I don't necessarily agree with. The short-term debt that is now outstanding I believe is 5 percent over the London interbank rate and that is short-term debt. The new debt which go out one year, two years, or three years is on average I believe 2 1/4 percent over the London interbank rate. So they have actually had a substantial reduction in the interest rate and a substantial extension in maturity assuming that the banks sign up for this. At the present time all you actually have is a proposal. In addition, the banks in credit extension to the corporate sectors in Korea and throughout the rest of Asia in many cases have been taking substantial losses, thus the reference today to the $777 million reserve that Deutsche Bank set aside for its losses in Asia.

Mr. GREENSPAN. $773.

Secretary RUBIN. $773. I apologize. Well, I am not so sure. I bet you a nickel.

Mr. GREENSPAN. You are on.

Secretary RUBIN. We have got a nickel-even odds. It is either $773, but in the neighborhood of three-quarters of a billion dollars. There is a slight side bet between the Chairman and me which he will probably win.

Secretary RUBIN. And then as to the merchant banks, the healthy merchant banks — when it is determined who is healthy — will be eligible to swap; the unhealthy merchant banks will not.

Dr. PAUL. The ones that have failed will not get any benefits. The Korean government hasn't assumed any risks from the field merchant banks.

Secretary RUBIN. Now that is a different question. Larry, do you want to address that? I am sorry; that's a different question, I apologize.

Mr. SUMMERS. The Korean government, in August, had offered a guarantee to bank deposits, so that government guarantee obliges the Korean government to guarantee deposits, including merchant banks that fail. The stretch-out arrangement that was just described. ∎

Conduct of Monetary Policy

Banking Committee Hearing on Conduct of Monetary Policy
Congressional Record – U.S. House of Representatives
February 24, 1998

Dr. PAUL. Second of all, picking up on a point that Mr. Frank made a moment ago of the IMF, some of us think in fact that the IMF by and large has been a failure, that in Africa and Latin America, after years of IMF structural adjustment programs, what has happened is there has been a significant increase in poverty; major cutbacks in health, in education; increases in unemployment.

In fact, in Africa what we are seeing is a dismal situation and in recent years has been made even more dismal. In Latin America, I think with the exception of Chile, every country there has seen an increase in poverty. Also, as you know, the IMF told us a year ago how splendidly the Asian economies were doing in Indonesia, in Korea, and so forth, and now they are in the middle of a meltdown.

Given the very poor record of the IMF, and given the fact that a number of economists think that the major role of the IMF is to help multinational banks and corporations rather than the poor people of Third World countries, perhaps you can elaborate on why you think the taxpayers of this country should put up $18 billion in order to replenish the IMF? So I hope you will address some of those issues. . . .

Dr. PAUL. It seems like the most appropriate subject for now would be the interrelation of the crisis in Asia with our own domestic monetary policy. And if I am not mistaken, it seems like there has already been an effect on the foreign holdings of debt, our debt now has been decreased by approximately $50 billion. It seems like it has changed our domestic monetary policy because we are expanding our Federal Reserve holdings, as well as M3 is rising now.

In the old-fashioned definition of "inflation," we are well into it, we are inflating a lot. If we do not rely on the erroneous messages that we get from the CPI — during the 1920s certainly the CPI was rather stable, and yet we had inflation that ended up with a lot of problems.

I must remind everyone that when we debase a currency, which means we inflate a currency, it inevitably leads to trade deficits which we suffer from, it inevitably leads to uneven distribution of income which we suffer from, and it always gives interest rates that are higher than the people want. But to argue for lower interest rates to me seems to compound our problem, because it requires more inflation of the money supply.

At the same time, if we want to rescue the Southeast Asian currencies by an IMF bailout, we only do that by inflating our own currency and setting the stage for a dollar crisis. . . .

Dr. PAUL. I have two brief points to make, then I have a couple of questions.

First, your comment about the deficit is very important in keeping interest rates high. It seems to me that the level of government spending has to be even more important, because if you have a $2 trillion budget, and you tax that money out of the system, that is very detrimental, just as detrimental as if you borrowed out of the economy. So I think the level of spending is probably more important.

And as a follow-up to the question from the gentleman from Washington on the currency, we certainly do export a lot of our currency. More than 60 percent ends up in foreign hands. And it serves a great benefit to us because it is like a free loan. It is not in our own country, it does not bid up prices, so we get to export our inflation. At the same time, they are willing to hold our debt; central banks are holding $600 billion worth of our debt. So again, we get to export our inflation, and the detriment is the consequence of what we are seeing in Southeast Asia.

But the real problem, though, is not the benefits that we receive temporarily, but the problem is when those dollars come home, like in 1979 and 1980, and then we have to deal with it because it is out of your hands, this money has been created. So I think we should not ignore that.

But my first question has to do with Mexico. It is bragged that we had this wonderful bailout of Mexico three years ago, and yet Mexico still has some of its same problems. They have tremendous bank loans occurring right now. The peso has weakened. Last month it went down 5 percent. Since the conditions are essentially the same, my question to you is when do you anticipate the next currency crisis in the Mexican peso?

And then another question that I would like to get in as well has to do with a follow-up with the gentleman from Massachusetts dealing with the inequity in the distribution of income. And in your statement you come across almost hostile or fearful that wages might go up. And I understand why you might be concerned about that, because you may eventually see the consequence of monetary inflation, and it will be reflected in higher wages. But where has the concern been about the escalation of value of stocks? People are expecting them to go up 30 percent a year. They are benefiting, but labor comes along and they want to get a little benefit. They want to raise their salaries 5 or 10 percent. Unlike the other side, I think the worst thing to do is interfere in the voluntary contract and mandate an increase in wages and give them minimum wage rates. That is not the answer.

But to understand the problem I think is very important. This is a natural consequence. They want to share as well, and this is a natural consequence of monetary inflation is that there is an equal distribution of income.

I would like you to address that and tell me if there is any merit to this argument and why you seem to have much greater concern about somebody making a few bucks more per hour versus the lack of concern of a stock market that is soaring at 30 percent increases per year. . . .

Mr. GREENSPAN. Let me say that when I believe that there are trends within the financial system or in the economy generally which look to me and to my colleagues to be unsustainable and potentially destructive of the economic growth, we get concerned.

I am not aware of the fact that if I see things which I perceive to be running out of line, that I have not expressed myself. At least some people have asserted that I have expressed myself more often than I should. And I have commented on innumerable occasions, as

I have, in fact, done today, that there are certain values in the system which by historical standards, are going to be difficult to sustain. And I am concerned about that, because it potentially is an issue which relates to the long-term values within the economy.

I have no concern whatever about the issue of wages going up. On the contrary, the more the better. It is only when they are real wages, whether they are wages which are tied to productivity or related to productivity gains. But wages which are moving up more than the rate of inflation, for example, I think are highly undesirable, and indeed to the extent that we do not get real wage increases, we do not get increases in standards of living. So I am strongly in favor of any increase in real wages and not strongly in favor at all of wages that go up and are wiped out by inflation.

Dr. PAUL. But the real wage is down compared to 1971. You have a little flip here or so, but since 1971 it is down.

Mr. GREENSPAN. Part of that issue, Congressman, is a statistical problem. I do not believe the real wage is truly down since 1971. . . .

Dr. PAUL. But we cannot convince our workers of that. At least in my district they are not convinced by some statistic.

Mr. GREENSPAN. Let me put it this way: Productivity after the early 1970s flattened out fairly dramatically, and that slowed real wage increases very dramatically as well. And to the extent that the sense in which earlier generations experienced significant increases in standards of living during the 1950s and 1960s and the early post-World War II period, of course productivity was advancing rapidly. That came to a dramatic end in the early 1970s and persisted until very recently. And if people were concerned about that, they should be, and they should have been, and we should have been, as I think we were.

Dr. PAUL. Do you have a comment on when the next Mexico crisis is going to occur?

Mr. GREENSPAN. Yes. I am not concerned about a crisis in Mexico at this particular stage. I think they are doing reasonably well. The peso at this particular stage is floating appropriately. I do not see any immediate crisis at the moment. And while I do not deny that, as in any country, things can go askew, they have come out of the 1995 crisis frankly, somewhat better than I expected they would. ∎

The Bubble

Congressional Record – U.S. House of Representatives
April 28, 1998

Mr. Speaker, the big question is how history will play the current financial situation if all the great wealth accumulated in the last ten years dissipates in a financial collapse.

According to an article in *The New Republic*, Greenspan is not only held in high esteem on Wall Street, he is seen as Godlike. One trader is quoted as saying, "When things go well, I hold Greenspan's picture between my hands and say, thank you. When things go poorly, I also take the photo in my hands and pray." And he is not alone on Wall Street in heaping praise on Greenspan. This comes as close to idolatry as one can get.

Alan Greenspan took over the Fed a few months before the stock market crash of October, 1987. In the ten years that Greenspan has headed the Fed, $2 trillion of new credit has been created as measured by M3. Banks threatened by bankruptcy in the early 1990s received generous assistance from the Fed policy of low interest rates and rapid credit expansion as a response to the recession of 1991. Fed fund rates were held at 3 percent for well over a year. This generous dose of Fed credit has fueled the five-year superboom on Wall Street.

We are endlessly told no inflation exists. But inflation is strictly and always a monetary phenomenon and not something that can be measured by a government consumer or producer price index.

Even so, there currently is significant price inflation for the fancy homes throughout the country, especially in the New York and Connecticut areas influenced by the New York financial center. CEO compensation is astronomically high, while wages for the common man have been held in check. The cost of all entertainment is not cheap and rises constantly. Art prices are soaring, as is the price of tickets to athletic events. Buying stocks with a 1.8 percent dividend yield is not cheap. These prices are inflated. The cost of education, medicine, and general services are expensive and rising.

In spite of government reports showing food prices are not rising, many constituents I talk to tell me food prices are always going up. It seems every family has difficulty compensating for the high cost of living and taxes are always inflating.

There is no doubt that many Americans know the salaries of the CEOs, athletes, and entertainers are astronomically high. The wages of the average working man, though, have not kept up. Workers feel poorer and resentment grows.

Even with all of Wall Street's euphoria, Main Street still harbors deep concern for their financial condition and the future of the country. Many families continue to find it difficult to pay their bills, and personal bankruptcies are at a record high at 1,400,000 per year. Downsizing of our large corporations continues as many manufacturing jobs are sent overseas.

This current financial bubble started in mid-1982. At that time, the money supply, as measured by M3, was $2.4 trillion. Today it is over $5.5 trillion. That is a lot of inflation, and money supply growth is currently accelerating.

Although the money supply has been significantly increased in the past 16 years and financial prices as well as other prices have gone up, government officials continue to try to reassure the American people that there is no inflation to worry about because price increases, as measured by the government's CPI and PPI, are not significantly rising.

Stock prices, though, are greatly inflated. If we had an average valuation of the Dow Jones Industrials for the past 87 years, as measured by the PE ratios, the Dow would be a mere 4,100 today, not over 9,000. And the Dow would be much lower yet if we took the average price-to-dividend ratio or the price-to-book ratio.

The NASDAQ is now selling at 85 times earnings. There is no doubt that most stock prices are grossly inflated and probably represent the greatest financial bubble known in history.

A lot of foreign money has been used to buy our stocks, one of the consequences of computer-age financial technology and innovations. Our negative trade balance allows foreign governments to accumulate large amounts of our Treasury debt. This serves to dampen the bad effect of our monetary inflation on domestic prices, while providing reserves for foreign central banks to further expand their own credit.

Think of this: Money can be borrowed in Japan at Depression-era rates of 1 percent and then reinvested here in the United States either in more Treasury debt earning 5 or 6 percent, or reinvested in our stock market, which is currently climbing at a 20 percent annualized rate. This sounds like a perfect deal for today's speculators, but there is nothing that guarantees this process will continue for much longer. Perfect situations never last forever.

Some of the euphoria that adds to the financial bubble on Wall Street and internationally is based on optimistic comments made by our government officials. Political leaders remind us time and again that our budget is balanced and the concern now is how to spend the excess. Nothing could be further from the truth, because all the money that is being used to offset the deficit comes from our trust funds.

In other words, it's comparable to a corporation stealing from its pension fund in order to show a better bottom line in its day-to-day operations. Government spending and deficits are not being brought under control. Tax rates are at historic highs, and all government taxation now consumes 50 percent of the gross national income.

It is now commonly believed that the East Asian financial crisis is having no impact on our economy. But it's too early to make that kind of an assessment. Our president remains popular, according to the polls, but what will it be like if there's any sign of economic weakness? There could then be a lot of "piling on" and finger pointing.

Problems and Victims

The basic cause of any financial bubble is the artificial creation of credit by a central bank (in this case our Federal Reserve). Artificially creating credit causes the currency to depreciate in value over time. It is important to understand the predictable economic problems that result from a depreciating currency:

1. In the early stages it is difficult to forecast exactly who will suffer and when.

2. Inflated currency and artificially low interest rates result in malinvestment that produces over capacity in one area or another.

3. Wealth generally transfers from the hands of the middle-class into the hands of the very wealthy. (The very poor receiving welfare gain a degree of protection, short of a total destruction of the currency.)

4. Prices indeed do go up, although which prices will go up is unpredictable, and the CPI and PPI can never be a dependable measurement of a monetary policy driven by loose credit.

5. The group that suffers the very most is the low-middle-income group (those willing to stay off welfare, yet unable to benefit from any transfer of wealth as stagnant wages fail to protect them from the ravages of the rising cost of living).

There are probably several reasons why this current economic boom has lasted longer than most others. The elimination of the Soviet threat has allowed a feeling of optimism not felt in many decades, and there has subsequently been tremendous optimism placed on potential economic development of many world markets in this age of relative peace.

There is also very poor understanding regarding economic interventionism, the system most nations of the world accept today. Today's interventionism is not close to a free market. The great Austrian economist Ludwig von Mises consistently pointed out that interventionism always leads to a form of socialism, which then eliminates the apparent benefits of interventionism.

A good example of how interventionism leads to the destruction of a market can be seen in the recent tobacco fiasco. First, the tobacco industry accepted subsidies and protectionism to build a powerful and wealthy industry. Then, having conceded this "nanny" role to the government, Big Tobacco had no defense when it was held liable for illnesses that befell some of the willing users of tobacco products. Now, the current plan of super taxation on tobacco users will allow the politicians to bail out the individual farmers who may be injured by reduced use of tobacco products (destruction of the market). This half-trillion-dollar tax proposal hardly solves the problem.

Just as in the 1920s, today's productivity has fooled some economists by keeping prices down on certain items. Certainly computer prices are down because the price of computer-power has dropped drastically, yet this should not be interpreted as an "absence" of inflation. Innovation has kept prices down in the computer industry, but it fails to do so when government becomes overly involved as it has in other technological areas, such as medical technology, where prices have gone up for services such as MRIs and CAT scans, not down.

Learn from Japan

The most important thing to remember is that perceptions and economic conditions here can change rapidly, just as they did last summer in the East Asian countries with the bursting of their financial bubble. They are now in deep recession.

Even though Japan first recognized signs of difficulty nine years ago, their problems linger because they have not allowed the liquidation of debt, or the elimination of over capacity, or the adjustment for real estate prices that would occur if the market were permitted to operate free of government intervention. The U.S. did the same thing in the 1930s, and I suspect we will do exactly what Japan is doing once our problems become more pressing. With our own problems from the inflation of the last 15 years now becoming apparent, their only answer so far is to inflate even more.

In its effort to reenergize the economy, the Bank of Japan is increasing its reserves at a 51 percent rate. This may be the greatest effort to "inflate" an economy back to health in all of history. Japan has inflated over the years and will not permit a full correction of their malinvestment. The Bank of Japan is doing everything possible to inflate again, but even with interest rates below 1 percent there are few takers.

OECD measurements, the M1 and quasi-money have been increasing at greater than 20 percent per year in East Asia. In the

United States, M3 has been increasing at 10 percent a year. It is estimated that this year the U.S. will have a $250 billion current account deficit—continued evidence of our ability to export our inflation.

We are now the world's greatest debtor, with an approximately $1 trillion debt to foreign nations. Although accumulation of our debt by foreign holders has leveled off, it has not dropped significantly. The peak occurred in mid-1997—today these holding are slightly lower.

The Cruelest Tax of All

This process of deliberately depreciating a currency over time (inflation) causes a loss in purchasing power and is especially harmful to those individuals who save. AIER (American Institute for Economic Research) calculates that 100 million households since 1945 have lost $11.2 trillion in purchasing power. This comes out to $112,000 per household, or put another way, over five decades each one of these households lost $2,200 every year.

Although many households are feeling very wealthy today because their stock portfolios are more valuable, this can change rather rapidly in a crash. The big question is what does the future hold for the purchasing power of the dollar over the next ten or twenty years?

The End in Sight?

Reassurance that all is well is a strategy found at the end of a boom cycle. Government revenues are higher than anticipated, and many are feeling richer than they are. The more inflated the stock market is as a consequence of credit creation, the less reliable these markets are at predicting future economic events. Stock markets can be good predictors of the future, but the more speculative they become, the less likely it is the markets will reveal what the world will be like next year.

The business cycle—the boom-bust cycle of history—has not been repealed. The psychological element of trust in the money, politicians, and central bankers can permit financial bubbles to last longer, but policies can vary as well as perceptions, both being unpredictable.

Central Bankers

The goal of central bankers has always been to gain "benefit" from the inflation they create, while preventing deflation and prolonging the boom as long as possible—a formidable task indeed. The more sophisticated and successful the central bankers are as technicians, the larger the bubble they create.

In recent years, central bankers have had greater "success" for several reasons. First, due to the age in which we live, internationalizing labor costs has been a great deal more convenient. It is much easier for companies to either shift labor from one country to another, or for the company itself to go to the area of the world that provides the cheapest labor. This has occurred with increased rapidity and ease over the past two decades.

Central bankers have also become more sophisticated in the balancing act between inflation and deflation. They are great technicians and are quite capable of interpreting events and striking a balance between these two horrors. This does not cancel out the basic flaw of a fiat currency; central bankers cannot replace the marketplace for determining interest rates and the proper amount of credit the economy needs.

Central bankers have also had the advantage of technological changes that increase productivity and also serve to keep down certain prices. It is true that we live in an information age, an age in which travel is done with ease and communication improvements are astounding. All of these events allow for a bigger bubble and a higher standard of living. Unfortunately this will not prove to be as sustainable as many hope.

The Price of Gold

Another reason for the central bankers' greater recent success is that they have been quite willing to cooperate with each other in propping up selected currency values and driving down others. They have cooperated vigorously in dumping or threatening to dump gold in order to keep the dollar price of gold in check. They are all very much aware that a soaring gold price would be a vote of no confidence for central-bank policy.

Washington goes along because it is furtively, but definitely, acknowledged there that a free-market, high gold price would send a bad signal worldwide about the world financial system. Therefore, every effort is made to keep the price of gold low for as long as possible. It's true the supply-siders have some interest in gold, but they are not talking about a gold standard, merely a price rule that encourages central bank fixing of the price of gold. Most defenders of the free-enterprise system in Washington are Keynesians at heart and will not challenge interventionism on principle.

Instead of making sure that policy is correct, central bankers are much more interested in seeing that the gold-price message reflects confidence in the paper money. Thus gold has remained in the doldrums despite significant rising prices for silver, platinum, and palladium. However, be assured that even central banks cannot "fix" the price of gold forever. They tried this in the 1960s with the dumping of hundreds of millions of ounces of American gold in order to artificially prop up the dollar by keeping the gold price at $35 an ounce, but in August 1971 this effort was abandoned.

The Solution

The solution to all of this is not complex. But no effort is going to be made to correct the problems that have allowed our financial bubble to develop, because Alan Greenspan has been practically declared a god by more than one Wall Street guru. Because Alan Greenspan himself understands Austrian free-market economics and the gold standard, it is stunning to see him participate in the bubble when he, deep down inside, knows big problems lurk around the corner. Without the motivation to do something, not much is likely to happen to our monetary system in the near future.

It must be understood that politicians and the pressure of the special interests in Washington demand that the current policies of spending, deficits, artificially low interest rates and easy credit will not change. It took the complete demise of the Soviet Communist system before change came there. But be forewarned: change came with a big economic bang not a whimper. Fortunately, that event occurred without an armed revolution . . . so far. The amazingly sudden economic events occurring in East Asia could still lead to some serious social and military disturbances in that region.

The key element to the financial system under which we are now living is the dollar. If confidence is lost in the dollar and a subsequent free-market price for gold develops, the whole financial system is threatened. Next year, with the European currency unit (ECU) coming on line, there could be some serious adjustments for the dollar. The success of the ECU is unpredictable, but now that they are indicating some gold will be held in reserve, it is possible that this currency will get off the ground.

Nationalism

However, I continue to have serious reservations regarding the ECU's long-term success, believing that the renewed nationalism within Europe will not permit the monetary unification of countries that have generally not trusted each other over the centuries. In Germany, 70 percent of the people oppose entering into this new monetary agreement. If economic problems worsen in Europe—currently the unemployment rate in Germany and France is 12 percent—the European Union may well get blamed.

The issue of nationalism is something that cannot be ignored. Immediately after the collapse in East Asia, Malaysia began shipping out hundreds of immigrants from Indonesia as a reaction to their economic problems. Resentment in Germany, France, and England is growing toward workers from other countries.

The same sentiment exists here in the United States, but it's not quite as bad at this particular time because our economy is doing better. But in the midst of a deep recession, the scapegoats will be found and alien workers will always be a target.

The greatest danger in a collapsing financial bubble is that the economic disruptions that follow might lead to political turmoil. Once serious economic problems develop, willingness to sacrifice political liberty is more likely, and the need for a more militant government is too often accepted by the majority.

No one has firmly assessed the Y2K problem, but it cannot bode well if a financial crisis comes near that time. Certainly a giant company like Citicorp and Travelers, who have recently merged, could really be hurt if the Y2K problem is real. Since the markets seem to be discounting this, I have yet to make up my own mind on how serious this problem is going to be.

Washington Mentality

Every politician I know in Washington is awestruck by Greenspan. The article in *The New Republic* reflects the way many Members of Congress feel about the "success" of Greenspan over the last ten years. Add to this the fact that there is no significant understanding of the Austrian business cycle in Washington, and the likelihood of adopting a solution to the pending crisis, based on such an understanding, is remote.

Liberals are heedless of the significance of monetary policy and its ill effects on the poor. They have no idea that the transfer of wealth from the poor to the rich occurs as a result of monetary policy and serves to hurt the very people they claim to represent. Liberals stick to the old cliché that all that's needed are more welfare benefits. They are, I'm sure, influenced by the fact that if more welfare benefits are handed out, they can count on the Federal Reserve to accommodate them. Unfortunately this will continue to motivate them to argue for a loose monetary policy.

The debate so often seems only to be who should get the expanded credit, the business-banking community or the welfare recipients who will receive it indirectly through the monetization of an ever-expanding government deficit. In Washington there is a craving for power and influence, and this motivates some a lot more than their public display of concern for helping the poor.

Whether it's Japan that tries to inflate their currency to get out of an economic problem, or the East Asian countries facing their crisis, or our willingness to bail out the IMF, resorting to monetary inflation is the only option being considered. We can rest assured that inflation is here to stay.

With daily pronouncements that inflation is dead, the stage is set for unlimited credit expansion whenever it becomes necessary. Just as deficit spending and massive budgets will continue, we can expect the falling value of the dollar, long term, to further undermine the economic and political stability of this country and the world.

Until we accept the free market principle that governments cannot create money out of thin air and that money must represent something of real value, we can anticipate a lot more confiscation of wealth through inflation. ■

International Economic Turmoil

Banking Committee Hearing on International Economic Turmoil
Congressional Record – U.S. House of Representatives
September 15, 1998

Mr. HINCHEY. I would forgo it except to say I want to congratulate you and thank you for the focus of attention you brought to this particular subject. It is a dire one indeed. It requires the focus of the Congress. There is even some question as to whether or not we will be capable in dealing with it completely. Nevertheless, it is a very, very serious situation and needs to be addressed.

And the way to address it is not by weakening the IMF, even though they have made some very serious mistakes in the course of their recent actions unquestionably. But our purpose here should be not to weaken the IMF, but to strengthen other international means by which the situation ought to be dealt with.

And I thank you very much, and I look forward to hearing Mr. Soros's testimony.

Chairman LEACH. Thank you.

Before turning to Mrs. Kelly—I would like to end with you—I am told Mr. Paul has an opening statement. Would you like to make—we are trying to hold it to three minutes. We made a prior agreement—prior to you coming, Ron.

Mr. PAUL. Thank you, Mr. Chairman. I will make it brief.

I would like to congratulate the Chairman for holding the hearings. Obviously, this is a very serious problem. I would like to make the point that we should not blame capitalism for this. We should direct our attention to the fiat currencies of the world, the easy credit we have been living with for decades. When we talk about lowering rates and when we talk about having liquidity, we are asking for more inflation and more debasement of the currency.

It isn't a lack of international agencies that is our problem. We lack sound money. We lack the marketplace. And the sooner we think about that and talk about the real problem, the problems brought about by the currencies of the world being a fiat currency that are created endlessly by all the central banks, we cannot get to the bottom of this problem.

More inflation, although it may help, just like it will help a drug addict, will make the problem that much worse. So, eventually, we will have to talk about the currencies of the world, and some day we should have a sound currency. . . .

So a little bit of the same thing is happening in places like Korea, but not so badly.

Mr. BENTSEN. Although we are advocating that the Japanese — and granted the Japanese are not at the IMF window at this point in time, but we are advocating that the Japanese step in and publicly fund the bad debt of the Japanese banking system, as we have done in this country. Now, maybe it is a different situation.

Mr. SOROS. Yes. You see, I think in the end, since the country does need a functioning banking system and since the banks are broke, they will have to be rescued. The discussion is on what terms. Should the banks be closed down and the Bank of Japan accept responsibility for the obligations of that bank? Or should the bank be bailed out and allowed to continue functioning? That is the debate at the moment.

Mr. BENTSEN. Thank you, Mr. Chairman.

Chairman LEACH. Well, thank you Mr. Bentsen.

A fellow Texan, Dr. Paul.

Dr. PAUL. Thank you, Mr. Chairman.

Mr. Soros, I am a physician, and I agree with you that we ought to have the right to use medical marijuana. But it is very controversial. But on the IMF, I disagree with you.

I would like to concentrate on a term, though, that we should deal with, and that is the word "capitalism." Mr. Bentsen brought it up, but I want to talk about that a little bit more. The reason being, I think we all agree that we have a major crisis going on and that we may see a lot more problems before it is resolved, but if we casually say it was capitalism that was bad, we have to do away with it, that free markets do not work, that would not make some of us very happy, because we have a great deal of faith and confidence in free choices and capitalism.

So when you talk about capitalism, I think it is casually used. Because I see that we have a system that many of us refer to as "interventionism," you know, governments are intervening continuously. We do not have a commodity standard for money, but we have an inflationism system, fiat money, along with we have a lot of welfare throughout the world. I mean, our system is based on welfarism, and we have a system inclined to favor corporations called corporatism. So it is a long distance from the classical notion of capitalism.

I agree with you entirely that there is a lot of disequilibrium in the system, and it seems that you conclude that it is the fault of capitalism. And it is almost like saying, well, we must absolutely throw out the invisible hand, that that concept was absolutely wrong, and yet I think we have the absence of the invisible hand, because we have had so much government involvement.

I want to concentrate also on the currencies. I see so much that the problem that we have is as a result of the way we have managed our currencies. We have all countries of the world working with fiat currencies and everybody inflates at a different rate and this causes by nature, and in a predictable fashion, a disequilibrium that I see.

The notion being that once governments inflate, create new credit for the purpose of driving down interest rates, the low interest rates send bad signals, confusing signals, to business people, who do dumb things. They overinvest, there is overcapacity, they have malinvestment, and they tend to accumulate a lot more debt. Banks loan out more money. But this is a consequence of the central banks' error of creating too much credit. And then, again, this leads to the speculations and to the derivatives markets that you mentioned.

And if we ignore that and just say what we need is more inflation, we need now not only to inflate through our Federal Reserve Board by driving down interest rates. And when people say we need more liquidity, that, to me, means we need more money, we need more credit, and that is inflation.

At the same time, you suggest that internationally we create SDRs, which is international inflation. I see this may be temporarily helping the cause and may tide us over. But what about long term? Have you ever considered or do you consider the necessity for maybe sitting down and thinking seriously about revamping the international monetary system, something of the equivalency of the Bretton Woods Agreement, even considering commodities once again? The European Union are talking now of a 20 percent reserve in gold. Are those ideas that you have given any consideration to?

Mr. SOROS. Well, first of all, I am very glad you agree with me on medical marijuana; and it is very nice to hear actually a legislator having the courage to say that. . . .

Dr. PAUL. Especially if you are a Republican.

Mr. SOROS. Because most legislators, they talk about the third rail, that if you touch it you are dead. So I hope that, as a doctor, you will take care of yourself.

But, actually, there is some relation between the drug problem and this capitalism thing that you talk about. Because, you see, just because I think that the War on Drugs is wrong or it has bad effects, it does not mean that I am a legalizer. And the same way, just because I think that capitalism has its defects, you see, does not mean that I am opposed to capitalism or we ought to abolish capitalism.

All our constructs are flawed, and so we have to always be aware of where those deficiencies are, and we have to look to correct it. And it so happens that financial markets are inherently unstable, and I can give you a theory for it, and I think, therefore, we have to make stability an objective of public policy, not abolish markets. We want to keep markets, because they are a much more efficient allocation than bureaucrats. But we have to recognize that instability can do tremendous damage.

Now, you talk about having a stable money, presumably gold; and I think your argument would be, let's say, stronger if you did not have booms and busts during the gold standard. Because we did have the gold standard in the 19th century, and we had similar booms and busts as we have now. So the booms and busts are actually inherent with the wave that has come in the future. Our understanding is inherently biased, and you have self-reinforcing processes. So, actually, going to the gold standard would not solve that problem.

The problem actually is with credit, not with money. You see, it is when you come to the use of credit that you have these imbalances. We do not like to admit it, so we talk of monetarism. And since there is some relationship between money and credit, money is something that you can measure so you can try to control the money supply. But, actually, underneath it you see, there is this willingness to extend credit, which is a reflexive process, self-reinforcing, and it can be self-reinforcing or self-defeating in both directions. So that is where the excess has come in.

Incidentally, you cannot eliminate it. In other words, to try to devise a system that does not reaffirm equilibrium would be an impossibility. It is just a question of trying to keep the excesses from being excessive. So that is the task. And that is why we need some institutions, which we have. We have the Federal Reserve. But we now have this global economy, and we do not have the global institutions.

Dr. PAUL. I have more challenging questions, but I am out of time.

Chairman LEACH. Well, thank you. And just so there is no misunderstanding, as a Libertarian, you are for the decriminalization for the nonpayment of income taxes; is that a fair description?

Dr. PAUL. I am not sure I figured that out. But I know we are against the income tax and almost all taxes. ∎

Revamping the Monetary System

Congressional Record – U.S. House of Representatives
September 24, 1998

Mr. Speaker, I would like to call the attention of fellow colleagues to the issue of three things that have happened in the last couple of days.

Today it was recorded in our newspapers and it was a consequence of a meeting held last night having to do with a company that went bankrupt, Long-Term Capital Management. I believe this has a lot of significance and is something that we in the Congress should not ignore.

This is a hedge fund. Their capitalization is less than $100 billion, but, through the derivatives markets, they were able to buy and speculate in over $1 trillion worth of securities, part of the financial bubble that I have expressed concern about over the past several months.

But last night an emergency meeting was called by the Federal Reserve Bank of New York. It was not called by the banks and the security firms that were standing to lose the money, but the Federal Reserve Bank of New York called an emergency meeting late last night. Some of the members of this meeting, the attendees, came back from Europe just to attend this meeting because it was of such a serious nature. They put together a package of $3.5 billion to bail out this company.

Yesterday also Greenspan announced that he would lower interest rates. I do not think this was an accident or coincidental. It was coincidental that at this very same time they were meeting this crisis, Greenspan had to announce that, yes indeed, he would inflate our currency, he would expand the money supply, he would increase the credit, he would lower interest rates. At least that is what the markets interpreted his statement to mean. And the stock market responded favorably by going up 257 points.

On September 18th, the *New York Times*, and this is the third time that that has come about in the last several weeks, the *New York Times* editorialized about why we needed a worldwide Federal Reserve System to bail out the countries involved in this financial crisis.

Yesterday, on the very same day, there was another op-ed piece in the *New York Times* by Jeffrey Garten, calling again for a worldwide central bank, that is, a worldwide Federal Reserve System to bail out the ailing economies of the world.

The argument might go, yes, indeed, the financial condition of the world is rather severe and we should do something. But the financial condition of the world is in trouble because we have allowed our Federal Reserve System, in deep secrecy, to create credit out of thin air and contribute to the bubble that exists. Where else could the credit come from for a company like Long-Term Capital Management? Where could they get this credit, other than having it created and encouraged by a monetary system engineered by our own Federal Reserve System?

We will have to do something about what is happening in the world today, but the danger that I see is that the movement is toward this worldwide Federal Reserve System or worldwide central bank. It is more of the same problem. If we have a fiat monetary system, not only in the United States but throughout the world, which has created the financial bubble, what makes anybody think that creating more credit out of thin air will solve these problems? It will make the problems much worse.

We need to have a revamping of the monetary system, but certainly it cannot be saved, it cannot be improved, by more paper money out of thin air, and that is what the Federal Reserve System is doing.

I would like to remind my colleagues that when the Federal Reserve talks about lowering interest rates, like Mr. Greenspan announced yesterday, or alluded to, this means that the Federal Reserve will create new credit. Where do they get new credit and new money? They get it out of thin air. This, of course, will lower interest rates in the short run and this will give a boost to a few people in trouble and it will bail out certain individuals.

When we create credit to bail out other currencies or other economies, yes, this tends to help. But the burden eventually falls on the American taxpayer, and it will fall on the value of the dollar. Already we have seen some signs that the dollar is not quite as strong as it should be if we are the haven of last resort as foreign capital comes into the United States. The dollar in relationship to the Swiss franc has been down 10 percent in the last two months. In a basket of currencies, 15 currencies by J.P. Morgan, it is down 5 percent in one month.

So when we go this next step of saying, yes, we must bail out the system by creating new dollars, it means that we are attacking the value of the money. When we do this, we steal the value of the money from the people who already hold dollars.

If we have an international Federal Reserve System that is permitted to do this without legislation and out of the realms of the legislative bodies around the world, it means that they can steal the value of the strong currencies. So literally an international central bank could undermine the value of the dollar without permission by the U.S. Congress, without an appropriation, but the penalty will fall on the American people by having a devalued dollar.

This is a very dangerous way to go, but the movement is on. As I mentioned, it has already been written up in the *New York Times*. George Soros not too long ago, last week, came before the Committee on Banking and Financial Services making the same argument. What does he happen to be? A hedge fund operator, the same business as Long-Term Capital Management, coming to us and saying, "Oh, what you better do is protect the system."

Well, I do not think the American people can afford it. We do have a financial bubble, but financial bubbles are caused by the creation of new credit from central banks. Under a sound monetary system you have a commodity standard of money where politicians lose total control. Politicians do not have control and they do not instill trust into the paper money system.

But we go one step further. The Congress has reneged on its responsibility and has not maintained the responsibility of maintaining value in the dollar. It has turned it over to a very secretive body, the Federal Reserve System, that has no responsibility to the U.S. Congress. So I argue for the case of watching out for the dollar and argue for sound money, and not to allow this to progress any further. ■

Congress Ignores its Constitutional Responsibility Regarding Monetary Policy

Congressional Record – U.S. House of Representatives
October 11, 2000

Mr. Speaker, at a frantic pace we anxiously rush to close down this Congress with excessive legislation while totally ignoring the all-important issue of monetary policy.

Congress has certainly reneged on its responsibility in this area. We continue to grant authority to a central bank that designs monetary policy in complete secrecy, inflating the currency at will, thus stealing value from the already existing currency through a dilution effect.

The Federal Reserve clings to the silly notion that economic growth causes inflation, thus trying to avoid the blame it deserves. The Federal Reserve then concludes that an economic slowdown is the solution to the problem it created. Those who argue to continue the inflationary process are equally in error. As if the economy were an airplane, the monetary authorities talk about a soft landing with the false hope of painlessly paying for the excesses enjoyed for a decade.

It should surprise no one that our financial markets are getting more volatile every day. Inflating a currency and causing artificially low interest rates always leads to malinvestment, overcapacity, excessive debt, speculation, and dangerous trade imbalances. We now live in a world awash in a sea of fiat currencies, with the dollar, the yen, and the Euro leading the way. The inevitable unwinding of the wild speculation, as reflected in the derivatives market, is now beginning.

And what do we do here in the Congress? We continue to ignore our constitutional responsibility to maintain a sound dollar. Our monetary policy of the last ten years has produced the largest financial bubble in all of history, with the good times paid for by borrowing and an illusion of wealth created in a speculative stock market. Our current account deficit, now running over $400 billion per year, and our $1.5 trillion foreign debt, has been instrumental in financing our extravagance. Be assured, the piper will be paid. The markets are clearly reflecting the excesses of the 1990s.

Already we hear the pundits arguing over who is to be blamed if the markets crash or a recession hits. Some have given the current President credit for the good times we have enjoyed. If the crash comes before January, some will place the blame on him as well. If problems hit later, the next President will get the blame. But the truth is our Presidents deserve neither the credit for the good times or the blame for the bad times.

The Federal Reserve, which maintains a monopoly control over the money supply, credit, and interest rates, is indeed the culprit and should be held accountable. But the real responsibility falls on the Congress, for it is Congress's neglect that permits the central bank to debase the dollar at will.

Destroying the value of a currency is immoral and remains unconstitutional. It should be illegal. And only a responsible Congress can accomplish that.

In preparation for the time when we are forced to reform the monetary system, we must immediately begin to consider the problems that befall a nation that permits systematic currency depreciation as a tool to gain short-term economic benefits while ignoring the very dangerous long-term consequences to our liberty and prosperity. ■

Warning about Foreign Policy and Monetary Policy

Congressional Record – U.S. House of Representatives
October 12, 2000

Mr. Speaker, over the last three years to four years, I have come to the floor on numerous occasions trying to sound a warning about both our foreign policy and our monetary policy. Today our monetary policy and our foreign policy have clashed. We see now that we face serious problems, not only in the Middle East, but on our financial markets.

Yesterday, I talked a bit about what I see as a financial bubble that has developed over the past decade and made the point that a financial bubble can be financed through borrowing money, as well as inflation. A financial bubble is essentially a consequence of inflation. A lot of people talk about inflation being the mere rising of some prices, but that is not the case.

Most good economists recognize that inflation is a consequence of monetary policy; as one increases the supply of money, it inflates the currency. This distorts interest rates, and it distorts the markets. Sometimes this goes into goods and services, and other times these excessive funds will go into marketplaces and distort the value of stocks and bonds.

I believe this is what has happened for the past ten years, Mr. Speaker, so in spite of the grand prosperity that we have had for this past decade, I believe it is an illusion in many ways, because we have not paid for it. In a true capitalist society, true wealth comes from hard work and savings.

Today, the American people have a negative savings rate, which means that we get our so-called capital from a printing press, because there are no savings and no funds to invest. The Federal Reserve creates these funds to be invested. On a short-term, this seems to benefit everyone.

The poor like it because they seem to get welfare benefits from it; and certainly the rich like it, because it motivates and stimulates their businesses; and politicians like it, because it takes care of deficits and it stimulates the economy.

The only problem with this is it always ends, and it always ends badly. And this is the reason that we have to meet up with a policy that seems ridiculous. The economy seems to be doing quite well, but the Federal Reserve comes along and says there is a problem with economic growth. Economic growth might cause prices to go up; so, therefore, what we have to do is cut off the economic growth. If you have slower growth, the prices will not go up any longer.

They are talking about a symptom and not the cause. The cause is the Federal Reserve. The problem is that the Federal Reserve has been granted authority that is unconstitutional to go and counterfeit money, and until we recognize that and deal with that, we will continue to have financial problems.

We have heard that the 1990s was a different decade, it was a new era economy, exactly what we heard throughout the decade prior to the collapse of the markets in Japan. The markets have now been down more than 50 percent in Japan for more than ten years, and there is no sign of significant recovery there.

Also there were other times in our history when they talked about a new era economy.

Let me read a quote: "With growing optimism, they gave birth to a foolish idea called the New Economic Era. That notion spread over the whole country. We were assured that we were in a new period where the old laws of economics no longer applied." Herbert Hoover in his memoirs.

It is an illusion to believe that the new paradigm exists. Actually, the computer industry involves 5 percent of the economy; 95 percent is what they called the old economy. I ascribe to old economic laws, because the truth is, we cannot change economic laws. And if inflating a currency distorts the market and the boom leads to the bust, that cannot be repelled.

If we are looking toward bad times, it is not because of current policy, it is because of previous policy, the previous policy of the ten years, the time when we lived beyond our means. We say how did we live beyond our means? Where did the money come from? Are we not spending less in Washington? No, we are not spending less in Washington. Are not the deficits a lot less? They are less, but they are not gone.

Where did we borrow from? We borrowed from overseas. We have a current account deficit that requires over a billion dollars a day that we borrow from foreigners just to finance our current account deficit. We are now the greatest debtor in the world, and that is a problem. This is why the markets are shaky, and this is why the markets have been going down for six months, and this is why in a foreign policy crisis such as we are facing in the Middle East, we will accentuate these problems. Therefore, the foreign policy of military interventionism overseas is something that we should seriously question. ∎

Economic Update

Congressional Record – U.S. House of Representatives
December 4, 2000

Mr. Speaker, more and more people now are talking about an oncoming recession. I tend to agree. I think we are moving into a recession, and for good reasons. But already the question that comes up so often among politicians is, who will get blamed? Will the current President be blamed for the recession or will the next President be blamed? Will the current Congress be blamed for the recession or the next Congress?

I do not believe either should be blamed. I think we should deal with the real cause of the business cycle, and that is the Federal Reserve System. The Federal Reserve System causes and brings about a boom period in a cycle, but it also brings about the bust. Because the bust, the correction, is an inevitable consequence of the boom caused by unduly inflating the money supply.

Soon we will hear from many, we have already heard some from the financial circles as well as from politicians, to lower interest rates. This will keep the economy from turning down. It will prevent the recession from coming. And if we do have a recession, it is always said, what you do is you lower the interest rates. But dwelling on the interest rates and not talking about what it takes to lower interest rates I think is a serious mistake.

The only way the Federal Reserve can lower interest rates is by inflating the money supply, increasing the money supply, which is the cause of our problems. So if the cause of our problem is the inflation, increasing the money supply which causes a boom, we can hardly solve our problems by further inflating. And then, too, there is a period of time in the business cycle where inflating the money supply or lowering interest rates do not get the response that many people hope for.

Take, for instance, what is happening in Japan today. There is no response whatsoever. They take interest rates down below one percent, and they cannot generate economic activity to really get them out of their slump.

The other irony of all this is that when we have an economic boom, another reason given for raising interest rates to slow up the economy is to stop the inflation. This is fallacious thinking because the inflation comes from the money supply. The idea that economic growth and prosperity and productivity causes inflation, that is, the price type of inflation, is wrong. If we have good productivity, prices go down, they do not go up. So the whole notion that we have to slow up the economy in order to prevent inflation is absolutely incorrect.

The problem I see is that Congress for too long has conceded too much of their authority over control of the monetary system to the Federal Reserve System, which acts in secrecy.

It is something that is directly stated in the Constitution that the Congress shall have the responsibility over the money supply, not a Federal Reserve System. Quite frankly, the Federal Reserve System is not even authorized by the Constitution.

Now, if in the midst of a recession the Federal Reserve decides that they want to lower interest rates but the dollar is also dropping and we lower interest rates, we cause the dollar to go down and price inflation will occur because of that. So it is not quite so simple as saying, well, let us just tell the Fed what to do, lower the interest rates and it will solve our problems.

We have the problem of the international debt. We, as Americans, now owe more than any other country in the world. We owe $1.7 trillion. Our current account deficit is over $400 billion a month. We borrow well over $10 billion a day to support the international debt.

The reason we should be concerned about this more so than we are is the fact that, when we are in a recession, revenues go crashing down. The inflation that occurred over these past ten years, which was artificial, created giant revenues from capital gains from this artificially high stock market. Well that is all being reversed now, so revenues are going to go down now, and we will have to deal with this in the next Congress.

Unfortunately, there are some who are concerned about this who say there is going to be gridlock and the two sides will not get together and the government is now divided, the House and the

Senate and the Presidency is undecided and therefore there will be gridlock. Quite frankly, I do not think that will happen. I sort of would hope that we would have some gridlock.

What I think is going to happen is that once the recession sets in and there is a need for additional spending and there will be no longer a concern at all about the deficit; and that is when the Congress will spend, the Federal Reserve will inflate. And it may temporarily help, but in the long-run it does not do the trick. It is not the way we gain economic prosperity out of a printing press. We just cannot allow a Federal Reserve to believe it creates capital by creating credit out of thin air.

We will soon be hearing a lot about interest rates. There will be a loud clamor from all quarters for the Fed to lower interest rates. It will be argued that it is necessary in order to help stop the stock market slide/crash and also to stimulate a sagging economy.

What we must remember though, is that every time someone pressures the Fed to lower interest rates, they are saying to the Fed that the money supply must be inflated. The only tool the Fed has for lowering interest rates is to increase the supply of money. They are arguing the case for further systematic and deliberate debasement of the U.S. dollar. Those who chant for lower interest rates are literally attacking the dollar.

And yet, depending on many variables, a deliberate attempt by the Federal Reserve to lower interest rates may instead lead to higher interest rates and precipitate a period of accelerating price inflation. Instead of boosting the stock market, this effort can do the opposite by producing conditions that will lower the stock market and do nothing to avert the economic slump that more people are now worried about.

Congress should be prepared for some surprises in the not-too-distant future. A slumping economy or definite recession will obviously lower revenues. This will reverse the illusion of the grand surpluses that everyone has been anxious to spend. Instead of expenditures being held under control, expect them to rise rapidly.

Many are starting to talk now about a legislative stalemate with no clear majority in the House or Senate and the Presidency being uncertain. This concern about a stalemate is overblown. Not that the problem isn't serious, but I am certain that under the conditions that we are about to experience, the Congress and the President will be all too willing to deal with the deteriorating conditions with increased spending and with a concerted bipartisan effort to pressure the Federal Reserve to further inflate the currency in pursuing the fiction that the Federal Reserve can prevent a "hard landing" by merely increasing the money supply in an effort to dictate short-term Fed funds rates.

Although this will not be the impasse that many anticipate, the actual capitulation by both parties to deal with the oncoming economic slowdown will actually be more harmful than gridlock because Congress will undoubtedly do more harm than good to the economy.

For decades now the Federal Reserve has followed a policy of "fine-tuning" the economy and with the relative success of the recent boom cycle, it has been deceived into believing its ability is more than it actually is. But in this effort to fine-tune the economy the Federal Reserve, since the middle of 1999 until May of this year, has systematically raised the Fed funds rate from 4.75 percent to 6.5 percent.

The explanation was that economic growth, when not controlled, leads to price inflation and therefore the economy had to be "cooled." A healthy free market economy should never have to be cooled, it should only be encouraged.

Ironically it's argued that the deliberate raising of the cost of borrowing money for everyone will hold prices in check. Yet consumers and businesses suffer from this additional cost—pushing all prices upward. But even more ironic is the claim that they now care about "inflation" after a decade of massive monetary inflation—the real culprit. The Federal Reserve meanwhile ignores the fact that the money supply is key to monetary policy, not admitting the damage has already been done.

Signs of economic slowdown are now all around with the seriously slumping stock market being the most visible and eliciting the most concern. As the slowdown spreads and accelerates the politicians will be anxious to advise the Chairman of the Federal Reserve, Alan Greenspan. Politicians from both sides of the aisle will become deeply and especially concerned when the evidence is clear that the revenues are plummeting and the "surplus" is disappearing. Since this will challenge the ability of the politician to continue the spending spree many will become deeply and vocally concerned.

The big debate already started in the financial and political circles is when, how much, and how quickly the Federal Reserve should lower interest rates. Indeed all will clamor to lower rates to revive the economy again. With the signs of rising prices in many sectors, especially energy, and in spite of the weak economy we can expect the Federal Reserve chairman to issue precautionary statements. He will reiterate that he must watch out for the resurgence of (price) inflation. In spite of his statements about concerns for inflation, if the stock market slumps and the economic slowdown is significant enough, we can be certain of one thing, the money supply will continue to grow rapidly in an attempt to keep interest rates low. But Mr. Greenspan will never admit that inflating is exactly what he's been generously doing for the past 13 years.

A short time after Chairman Greenspan took over the reins of the Federal Reserve the stock market crash of 1987 prompted him to alleviate concerns with a heavy dose of monetary inflation. Once again, in the slump of 1991 and 1992, he again reignited the financial bubble by more monetary inflation. There was no hesitation on Mr. Greenspan's part to inflate as necessary to alleviate the conditions brought about by the Mexican financial crisis, the Asian crisis, the Russian ruble crisis, and with the Long-Term Capital Management crisis. Just one year ago the nonexistent Y2K crisis prompted huge, unprecedented monetary inflation by the Federal Reserve. All these efforts kept interest rates below the market rate and contributed to the financial bubble that is now starting to deflate. But, there is no doubt that this monetary inflation did maintain an economy that seemed like it would never quit growing. Housing markets thrived, the stock market and bond market thrived, and in turn, the great profits made in these areas, especially gains made by stock market transactions, produced profits that inflated greatly the revenues that flowed into the Treasury. The serious problem that we now face, a collapsing stock market and a rapidly weakening economy, was caused by inflating the money supply along with artificially low interest rates. More inflation and continuing the policy of artificially low interest rates can't possibly be the solution to the dilemma we face.

We should never blame economic growth as the culprit. Instead artificial growth, malinvestment, overcapacity, speculation, and excessive debt that comes from systematic monetary inflation should be blamed, since these are all a result of Federal Reserve Board policy. Let there be no doubt political and financial leaders will demand lower interest rates in order to alleviate the conditions that are developing. But just because a boom can come from generous Fed credit, it doesn't mean the bubble economy can be maintained or reinflated by easy credit once a correction sets in.

Besides, Alan Greenspan knows full well that the scenario we are now experiencing can be made worse by lowering interest rates. Under the conditions we are facing it's very likely the dollar will weaken and deliberately lowering interest rates will accelerate this trend. Price inflation, which the Fed claims it is so concerned about, will not necessarily go away even with a weak economy. And the one thing we will come to realize is that even the best of all central bankers, Alan Greenspan, will not be able to determine interest rates at all times of the business cycle. Inflation premiums, confidence, the value of the dollar, and political conditions all can affect interest rates and these are out of the control of the Federal Reserve Board.

Congress definitely should be concerned about these matters. Budgetary planning will get more difficult as the revenues spiral downward and spending does the opposite. Interest on the national debt will continue and will rise as interest rates rise. The weak dollar, lower stock markets, and inflation can affect every fixed income citizen, especially the Social Security beneficiaries. We can expect the World Trade Organization's managed trade war will actually get much worse under these conditions. Military conflict is not out of the question under the precarious conditions that are developing. Oil supplies are obviously not secure, as we have already seen the run up of prices to dangerously high levels.

The question is what should one expect the Federal Reserve Board to eventually do? We can expect it to continue to inflate as they have always chosen with every crisis. There's no evidence that Alan Greenspan would choose to do anything else regardless of his expression of concern about inflation and the value of the dollar. Greenspan still believes he can control the pain and produce a weakened economy that will not get out of control. But there's no way that he can guarantee that the United States might not slip into a prolonged lethargy, similar to what Japan is now experiencing. We can be certain that Congress will accommodate with whatever seems to be necessary by bailing out a weakened financial sector.

But all this will be done at the expense of the dollar. This is a dangerous process and makes our entire economic and financial system vulnerable.

We must someday recognize that neither Congress nor the Fed is supposed to "run" the economy. Yet we still live with the belief that the administration, our Presidents, our Congress and the Federal Reserve should run the economy. This is a dangerous concept and always leads to the painful corrections to the so-called the good times for which everyone is anxious to take credit.

Congress does have responsibility for maintaining a sound dollar and a free market and not much else. Unfortunately this responsibility that is clearly stated in the Constitution is ignored.

A major financial crisis is possible since the dollar is the reserve currency of the world, held in central banks as if it were gold itself. The current account deficit for the United States continues to deteriorate, warning us of danger ahead. Our foreign debt of $1.7 trillion continues to grow rapidly and it will eventually have to be paid.

Action by the Congress and the Federal Reserve will most likely make the correction that is now starting much worse. Also, under conditions such as these, personal liberty is always vulnerable to the advocates of big government. It is well known that during the times of military wars personal liberties are endangered. Social wars such as the war on drugs are notorious for undermining the principles of liberty. So too, under economic conditions that are difficult to understand and deal with, personal liberty comes under attack. This should concern us all. ∎

The Economy

Congressional Record – U.S. House of Representatives
February 14, 2001

Mr. Speaker, many government and Federal Reserve officials have repeatedly argued that we have no inflation to fear. Yet those who claim this, define inflation as rising consumer and producer prices. Although inflation frequently leads to price increases we must remember that the free market definition of inflation is the increase in the supply of money and credit. Monetary inflation is seductive in that it can cause great harm without significantly affecting government price indices. The excess credit may well go into stock market and real estate speculation with consumer price increases limited to such things as energy, repairs, medical care and other services. One should not conclude, as so many have in the past decade, that we have no inflation to worry about. Imbalances did develop with the 1990s monetary inflation but were ignored. They are now becoming readily apparent as sharp adjustments take place — such as we have seen in the past year in the NASDAQ.

When one is permitted to use "rising prices" as the definition for inflation it is followed by a nonsensical assumption that a robust economy is the cause for rising prices. Foolish conclusions of this sort lead our economic planners and Federal Reserve officials to attempt to "solve " the problem of price or labor-cost inflation by precipitating an economic slowdown. Such a deliberate policy is anathema to a free market economy. It's always hoped that the planned economic slowdown will never do serious harm, but this is never the case. The recession with rising prices still comes. And that's what we are seeing today.

Raising interest rates six times in 1999–2000 has had an effect and the central planners are now worried. Falsely, they believe that if only the money spigot is once again turned on, all will be well. That will prove to be a pipe dream.

It is now recognized that indeed the economy has sharply turned downward—which is what was intended. But can the downturn be controlled? Not likely! And "inflation" by even the planner's own definition is now raising its ugly head. For instance, in the fourth quarter of last year labor costs rose at an annualized rate of 6.6 percent, the biggest increase in nine years.

And what's happening to employment conditions? They're deteriorating rapidly. Economist Ed Hyman reported that 270,000 people lost their jobs in January, a 678 percent increase over a year ago. A growing number of economists are now doubtful that productivity growth will save us from the correction that many free market economists predicted would come as an inevitable consequence of the interest rate distortions that Federal Reserve policy causes.

Instead of blind faith in the Federal Reserve to run the economy, we should become more aware of Congress's responsibility for maintaining a sound dollar and removing the monopoly power of our central bank to create money and credit out of thin air and fix short-term interest rates—which is the real cause of all our economic downturns.

Between 1995 and today, the Greenspan Fed increased the money supply (as measured by MZM) by $1.9 trillion or a 65 percent increase. There is no reason to look any further for the explanation of why the economy is slipping with labor costs rising, energy costs soaring, and medical and education costs skyrocketing, while the stock market is disintegrating. Until we look at the unconstitutional monopoly power the Federal Reserve has over money and credit we can expect a continuation of our problems. Demanding lower interest rates is merely insisting the Federal Reserve deliberately create even more credit, which caused the problem in the first place. We cannot restore soundness to the dollar by debasing the dollar—which is what lowering interest rates is all about—printing more money.

When control is lost in a sharp downturn, dealing with it by massive monetary inflation may well cause something worse than the stagflation that we experienced in the 1970s; an inflationary recession or depression could result.

This need not happen and won't if we demand that our dollar not be casually and deliberately debased by our unaccountable Federal Reserve. ∎

The U.S. Dollar and the World Economy

Congressional Record – U.S. House of Representatives
September 6, 2001

Congress has a constitutional responsibility to maintain the value of the dollar by making only gold and silver legal tender and not to "emit bills of credit."

This responsibility was performed relatively well in the 19th century, despite the abuse the dollar suffered during the Civil War and despite repeated efforts to form a central bank. This policy served to maintain relatively stable prices, and the shortcomings came only when the rules of the gold standard were ignored or abused.

In the 20th century, however, we saw the systematic undermining of sound money, with the establishment of the Federal Reserve System in 1913, and the outright rejection of gold, with the collapse of the Bretton Woods Agreement in 1971.

We are now witnessing the effects of the accumulated problems of 30 years of fiat money — not only the dollar but also all the world currencies — something the world has never before experienced. Exactly how it plays out is yet unknown. Its severity will be determined by future monetary management — especially by the Federal Reserve. The likelihood of quickly resolving the deeply ingrained and worldwide imbalances built up over 30 years is remote. Yielding to the addiction of credit creation (as has been the case with every market correction over the past 30 years) remains irresistible to the central bankers of the world. Central planners, who occupy the seats of power in every central bank around the world, refuse to accept the fact that markets are more powerful and smarter than they are.

The people of the United States, including the U.S. Congress, are far too complacent about the seriousness of the current economic crisis. They remain oblivious to the significance of the U.S. dollar's fiat status. Discussions about the dollar are usually limited to the question of whether the dollar is now too strong or too weak. When money is defined as a precise weight of a precious metal, this type of discussion doesn't exist. The only thing that matters under that circumstance is whether an honest government will maintain convertibility.

Exporters always want a weak dollar, importers a strong one. But no one demands a *stable* sound dollar, as they should. Manipulation of foreign trade through competitive currency devaluations has become commonplace and is used as a form of protectionism. This has been going on ever since the worldwide acceptance of fiat money 30 years ago. Although some short-term advantage may be gained for certain manufacturers and some countries by such currency manipulation, it only adds fuel to the economic and financial instability inherent in a system of paper money.

Paper money helps the strong and hurts the weak before it self-destructs and undermines international trade. The U.S. dollar, with its reserve-currency status, provides a much greater benefit to American citizens than that which occurs in other countries that follow a similar monetary policy. It allows us to export our inflation by buying cheap goods from overseas, while our dollars are then lent back to us to finance our current account deficit. We further benefit from the confidence bestowed on the dollar by our being the economic and military powerhouse of the world, thus postponing the day of reckoning. This permits our extravagant living to last longer than would have otherwise occurred under a gold standard.

Some may argue that a good deal like that shouldn't be denied, but unfortunately the piper must eventually be paid. Inevitably the distortions, such as our current account deficit and foreign debt, will come to an end with more suffering than anyone has anticipated.

The monetary inflation of the 1990s produced welcomed profits of $145 billion for the NASDAQ companies over the five years between 1996 and 2000. Astoundingly this entire amount was lost in the past year. This doesn't even address the trillions of dollars of paper losses in stock values from its peak in early 2000. Congress has expressed concern about the staggering stock-market losses but fails to see the connection between the bubble economy and the monetary inflation generated by the Federal Reserve.

Instead, Congress chooses to blame the analysts for *misleading investors*. The analysts may not be entirely *blameless*, but their role in creating the bubble is minimal compared to the misleading information that the Federal Reserve has provided, with artificially low interest rates and a financial market made flush with generous new credit at every sign of a correction over the past ten years.

By preventing the liquidation of bad debt and the elimination of malinvestment and overcapacity, the Federal Reserve's actions have kept the financial bubble inflated. Of course it's an easy choice on the short run. Who would deliberately allow the market tendency to deflate back to stability? That would be politically unacceptable.

Talk of sound money and balanced budgets is just that. When the economy sinks, the rhetoric for sound policy and a strong dollar may continue but all actions by the Congress and the Fed will be directed toward re-inflation and a congressional spending policy oblivious to all the promises regarding a balanced budget and the preservation of the Social Security and Medicare trust funds.

But if the Fed and its chairman, Alan Greenspan, have been able to guide us out of every potential crisis all the way back to the stock market crash of 1987, why shouldn't we expect the same to happen once again? Mainly because there's a limit to how long the monetary charade can be perpetuated. Now it looks like the international financial system built on paper money is coming to an end.

Modern-day globalism, since gold's demise 30 years ago, has been based on a purely fiat U.S. dollar, with all other currencies tied to the dollar. International redistribution and management of wealth through the IMF, the World Bank, and the WTO have promoted this new version of globalism. This type of globalism depends on trusting central bankers to maintain currency values and the international institutions to manage trade equitably, while bailing out weak economies with dollar inflation. This, of course, has only been possible because the dollar strength is perceived to be greater than it really is.

Modern-day globalists would like us to believe they invented globalism. Yet all they are offering is an unprecedented plan for global power to be placed in the hands of a few powerful special interests.

Globalism has existed ever since international trade started thousands of years ago. Whether it was during the Byzantine Empire or the more recent British Empire, it worked rather well when the goal was honest trade and the currency was gold. Today, however, *world government* is the goal. Its tools are fiat money and international agencies that believe they can plan globally, just as many others over the centuries believed they could plan domestically, ignoring the fact that all efforts at socialism have failed.

The day of reckoning for all this mischief is now at hand. The dollar is weakening, in spite of all the arguments for its continued strength. Economic law is overruling political edicts. Just how long will the U.S. dollar and the U.S. taxpayer be able to bail out every failed Third World economy and pay the bills for policing the world with U.S. troops now in 140 nations around the world? The answer is *certainly* not forever and probably not much longer, since the world economies are readjusting to the dislocations of the past 30 years of mismanagement and misallocation of capital, characteristic of fiat money.

Fiat money has been around for a long time off and on throughout history. But never has the world been so enthralled with the world economy being artificially structured with paper money and with a total rejection of the anchor that gold provided for thousands of years. Let there be no doubt, we live in unprecedented times, and we are just beginning to reap what has been sown the past 30 years. Our government and Federal Reserve officials have grossly underestimated this danger.

Current concerns are expressed by worries about meeting the criteria for a government-declared recession and whether a weaker dollar would help. The first is merely academic, because if you are one of the many thousands who have been laid off, you're *already* in a recession. The second doesn't make a lot of sense unless one asks "compared to what?" The dollar has been on a steady course of devaluation for 30 years, against most major currencies and against gold. Its purchasing power in general has been steadily eroded. The fact that the dollar has been strong against Third-World currencies and against most major currencies for the past decade doesn't cancel out the fact that the Federal Reserve has systematically eroded the dollar's value by steadily expanding the money supply. Recent reports of a weakening dollar on international exchange markets have investment implications but do not reflect a new policy designed to weaken the dollar. This is merely the market adjusting to 30 years of systematic monetary inflation.

Regardless of whether the experts demand a weak dollar or a strong dollar, each inevitably demands lower interest rates, hoping to spur the economy and save the stock market from crashing. But one must remember that the only way the Federal Reserve can lower interest rates is to inflate the currency by increasing the money supply and by further debasing the currency. In the long term, the dollar is always weakened, even if the economy is occasionally stimulated on a short-run basis.

Economic growth can hide the ill effects of monetary inflation by holding some prices in check. But it can't prevent the overcapacity and malinvestment which causes the economic downturn. Of course, the central bankers cling to the belief that they can somehow prevent the ugly corrections known as recessions. Economic growth, when artificially stimulated by monetary growth and low interest rates, generates the speculation we've seen in the stock, bond, and real estate markets, along with excessive debt. Once the need for rectifying the overcapacity is recognized by the market, these imbalances are destined to be wiped out. Prolonging the correction phase with the Fed's efforts to reinflate by diligently working for a soft landing, or even to prevent a recession, only postpones the day the economy can return to sustained growth. This is a problem the United States had in the 1930s and one that Japan has experienced for more than a decade, with no end in sight.

The next recession, from which I'm sure we're already suffering, will be even more pervasive worldwide than the one in the 1930s due to the artificial nature of modern globalism, with world paper money and international agencies deeply involved in the economy of every nation. We have witnessed the current and recent bailouts in Mexico, Argentina, Brazil, Turkey, and the Far East. While resisting the market's tendency for correction, faith in government deficits and belief in paper money inflation will surely prolong the coming worldwide crisis.

Alan Greenspan made a concerted effort to stave off the 1991–1992 recession with numerous reductions in the Fed funds rate to no avail. The recession hit, and most people believe it led to

George Bush's defeat in the 1992 election. It wasn't that Greenspan didn't try, and in many ways the Bush people's criticism of Greenspan's effort is not justified. Greenspan, the politician, would have liked to please the elder Bush, but was unable to control events as he had wished. This time around, however, he's been much more aggressive with the half-point cuts along with seven cuts in just eight months, for a total of a three-point cut in the Fed funds rate. But guess what? So far it hasn't helped. Stocks continue to slide, and the economy is still in the doldrums. It is now safe to say that Greenspan is pushing on a string. In the year 2000, bank loans and commercial paper were growing at an annualized rate of 23 percent. In less than a year, in spite of this massive influx of new credit, these loans have crashed to a rate of minus 5 percent.

But where is the money going? Some of it probably has helped to prop up the staggering stock market, but that can't last forever. Plenty went into consumption and to finance extravagant living.

The special nature of the dollar, as the reserve currency of the world, has permitted the bubble to last longer and to be especially beneficial to American consumers. But in the meantime, understandable market and political forces have steadily eroded our industrial base, while our service sector has thrived. Consumers enjoyed having even more funds to spend as the dollars left manufacturing. In a little over a year, one million industrial production jobs were lost while saving rates sank to zero and capital investments plummeted. Foreigners continue to grab our dollars, permitting us to raise our standard of living, but unfortunately it's built on endless printing of fiat money and self-limiting personal debt.

The Federal Reserve credit created during the last eight months has not stimulated economic growth in technology or the industrial sector, but a lot of it ended up in the expanding real estate bubble, churned by the $3.2 trillion of debt maintained by the GSEs.

The GSEs, made up of Fannie Mae, Freddie Mac, and the Federal Home Loan Bank, have managed to keep the housing market afloat, in contrast to the more logical slowdown in hotel and office construction. This spending through the GSEs has also served as a vehicle for consumption spending. This should be no surprise, considering the special status that GSEs enjoy, since their implied line of credit to the U.S. Treasury keeps interest rates artificially low. The Clinton administration encouraged growth in housing loans that were financed through this system.

In addition, the Federal Reserve treats GSE securities with special consideration. Ever since the fall of 1999, the Fed has monetized GSE securities, just as if they were U.S. Treasury bills. This message has not been lost by foreign central banks, which took their cue from the Fed and now hold more than $130 billion of United States GSE securities. The Fed holds only $20 billion worth, but the implication is clear. Not only will the Treasury loan to the GSEs if necessary, since the line of credit is already in place, but, if necessary, Congress will surely accommodate with appropriations as well, just as it did during the Savings and Loan crisis. But the Fed has indicated to the world that the GSEs are equivalent to U.S. Treasury bills, and foreign central banks have enthusiastically accommodated, sometimes by purchasing more than $10 billion of these securities in one week alone. They are merely recycling the dollars we so generously print and spend overseas.

After the NASDAQ collapsed last year, the flow of funds into real estate accelerated. The GSEs accommodated by borrowing without restraint to subsidize new mortgages, record sales, and refinancing. It's no wonder the price of houses are rising to record levels.

Refinancing especially helped the consumers to continue spending even in a slowing economy. It isn't surprising for high credit-card debt to be frequently rolled into second mortgages, since interest on mortgage debt has the additional advantage of being tax-deductible. When financial conditions warrant it, leaving financial instruments (such as paper assets), and looking for hard assets (such as houses), is commonplace and is not a new phenomenon. Instead of the newly inflated money being directed toward the stock market, it now finds its way into the rapidly expanding real estate bubble. This, too, will burst as all bubbles do. The Fed, the Congress, or even foreign investors can't prevent the collapse of this bubble, any more than the incestuous Japanese banks were able to keep the Japanese "miracle" of the 1980s going forever.

Concerned Federal Reserve economists are struggling to understand how the wealth effect of the stock market and real estate bubble affect economic activity and consumer spending. It should be no mystery, but it would be too much to expect the Fed to look to itself and its monetary policy for an explanation and assume responsibility for engineering the entire financial mess we're in.

A major problem still remains. Ultimately the market determines all value including all currencies. With the current direction of the dollar certainly downward, the day of reckoning is fast approaching. A weak dollar will prompt dumping of GSE securities before Treasuries, despite the Treasury's and the Fed's attempt to equate them with government securities. This will threaten the whole GSE system of finance, because the challenge to the dollar and the GSEs will hit just when the housing market turns down and defaults rise. Also a major accident can occur in the derivatives markets where Fannie Mae and Freddie Mac are deeply involved in hedging their interest rate bets. Rising interest rates that are inherent with a weak currency will worsen the crisis.

The weakening dollar will usher in an age of challenge to the whole worldwide financial system. The dollar has been the linchpin of economic activity, and a severe downturn in its value will not go unnoticed and will compound the already weakening economies of the world. More monetary inflation, even if it's a concerted worldwide effort, cannot solve the approaching crisis. The coming crisis will result from fiat money and monetary inflation; therefore, more of the same cannot be the solution.

Pseudo-free trade, managed poorly and driven by fiat money, is no substitute for true free trade in a world with a stable commodity currency, such as gold. Managed trade and fiat money, historically, have led to trade wars, which the international planners pretend to abhor. Yet the trade war is already gearing up. The WTO, purported to exist to lower tariffs, is actually the agency that grants permission for tariffs to be applied when complaints of dumping are levied. We are in the midst of banana, textile, steel, lumber, and tax wars, all managed by the WTO. When cheap imports hit our markets, it's a good deal for consumers, but our manufacturers are the first to demand permission to place protective tariffs on imports. If this is already occurring in an economy that has been doing quite well, one can imagine how strong the protectionists' sentiments will be in a worldwide slowdown.

Congress is starting to realize that the budget forecast based on an overly optimistic growth rate of 3 percent is way off target, and even the pseudo-surpluses are soon to be eliminated. Remember the national debt never went down with the "surpluses." The national debt is currently rising at more than $120 billion at an annualized rate and is destined to get worse.

Our dollar problem, which affects our financial and budgetary decisions, originated at the Fed with our country's acceptance of paper money 30 years ago. Federal Reserve officials and other government leaders purposely continue to mislead the people by spouting the nonsense that there is no evidence of inflation, as measured by government-rigged price indices. Even though significant price increases need not exist for monetary inflation to place a hardship on the economy, stock prices, housing prices, costs of medical care and education, and the cost of government have all been rising at very rapid rates. But the true inflation, measured by the money supply, is rising at a rate of greater than 20 percent, as measured by MZM. This fact is ignored.

The deception regarding price increases is supposed to reassure us and may do so for a while. The Fed never admits it, and the Congress disregards it out of ignorance, but the serious harm done by artificially low interest rates—leading to malinvestment, overcapacity, excessive debt and speculation causes the distortions that always guarantee the next recession.

Serious problems lie ahead. If the Fed continues with the same monetary policy of perpetual inflation, and the Congress responds with more spending and regulations, real solutions will be indefinitely delayed.

The current problems, hopefully, will cause us as a nation and, in particular, Congress to reassess the policies that have allowed the imbalances to develop over the last 30 years.

Someday, stable money based on the gold standard must be reconsidered. Stable money is a constitutional responsibility of Congress. The Federal Reserve Board's goal of stable prices, economic growth and low interest rates, through centralized economic planning by manipulating money and credit, is a concoction of 20th century Keynesian economics. These efforts are not authorized by the Constitution, and are economically detrimental.

Economic adjustments wouldn't be so bad, as many mild recessions have proven, except that wealth is inexorably and unfairly transferred from middle class and poor to the rich. Job losses and the rising cost of living hurt some more than others. If our course is not changed, the entire middle-class prosperity can be endangered, as has happened all too often in other societies that pursued a false belief that paper money could be satisfactorily managed.

Even the serious economic problems generated by a flawed monetary system could be tolerated, except for the inevitable loss of personal liberty that accompanies government's efforts to centrally plan the economy through a paper monetary policy and ever-growing welfare state.

Likewise, an imperialistic foreign policy can only be supported by inflation and high taxation. This policy compounds the threat to liberty, because all too often our leaders get us involved in overseas military adventurism in which we should have no part. Today that danger is greater than ever before, as we send our dollars and troops hither and yon to areas of the world most Americans have no knowledge or interest in. But the driving force behind our foreign policy comes from our oil corporations, international banking interests, and the military-industrial complex, which have high-stake interests in the places our troops and foreign aid are sent.

If, heaven forbid, the economy sinks as low and for as long as many free market economists believe, what policy changes must we consider? Certainly the number one change ought to be to reject the ideas that created the crisis. But rejecting old ways that Congress and the people are addicted to is not easy. Many people believe that government programs are free. The clamor for low interest rates (more monetary inflation), by virtually all public officials and prominent business and banking leaders is endless. And, the expectation for government to *do something* for every economic malady—even if ill-advised government policy has created the problem—drives this seductive system of centralized planning that ultimately undermines prosperity. A realization that we cannot continue our old ways may well be upon us, and the inflating, taxing, regulating, and centralized planning programs of the last 30 years must come to an end.

Only reining in the welfare-warfare state will suffice. This eliminates the need for the Fed to monetize the debt that politicians depend on to please their constituents and secure their reelection. We must reject our obsession with policing the world by our endless foreign commitments and entanglements. This would reduce the need for greater expenditures while enhancing our national security. It would also remove pressure on the Federal Reserve to continue a flawed monetary policy of monetizing endless government debt.

But we must also reject the notion that one man, Alan Greenspan, or any other chairman of the Federal Reserve Board, can know what the proper money supply and interest rates ought to be—only the market can determine that. This must happen if we ever expect to avoid continuous and deeper recessions and to get the economy growing in a healthy and sustainable fashion. It also must happen if we want to preserve free-market capitalism and personal liberty.

The longer the delay in establishing a free market and a commodity currency, even with interrupted blips of growth, the more unstable the economy and the more difficult the task becomes. Instead it will result in what no one wants—more poverty and political turmoil.

There are no other options if we hope to remain a free and prosperous nation. Economic and monetary meddling undermines the principles of a free society. A free society and sound money maximize production and minimize poverty. The responsibility of Congress is clear: avoid the meddling so ingrained in our system and assume the responsibility, all but forgotten, to maintain a free society while making the dollar once again as good as gold.

In the words of James Madison in *The Federalist Papers*:

> The extension of the prohibition to bills of credit must give pleasure to every citizen in proportion to his love of justice and his knowledge of the true springs of public prosperity. The loss which America has sustained since the peace, from the pestilent effects of paper money on the necessary confidence between man and man, on the necessary confidence in the public councils, on the industry and morals of the people, and on the character of republican government, constitutes an enormous debt against the States chargeable with this unadvised measure. ∎

The Foolishness of Fiat

Congressional Record — U.S. House of Representatives
October 31, 2001

Mr. Speaker, the world's politicians, special interests, government bureaucrats, and financiers all love fiat money — because they all benefit from it. But freedom loving, hard working, ethical, and thrifty individuals suffer. Fiat money is paper money that gets its value from a government edict and compulsory legal tender laws. Honest money, something of real value, like a precious metal, gets its value from the market and through voluntary exchange.

The world today is awash in fiat money like never before. And we face a financial crisis like never before, conceived many decades before the 9/11 crisis hit.

Fiat money works as long as trust in the currency lasts. But eventually trust is always withdrawn from paper money. Fiat money evolves out of sound money, which always originates in the market. But paper money inevitably fails no matter how hard the beneficiaries try to perpetuate the fraud.

We are now witnessing the early stages of the demise of a worldwide financial system built on the fiction that wealth can come out of a printing press or a computer at our central banks.

Japan, failing to understand this, has tried for more than a decade to stimulate its economy and boost its stock market by printing money and increasing government spending — and it has not worked.

Argentina, even with the hopes placed in its currency board, is nevertheless facing default on its foreign debt and a crisis in confidence. More bailouts from the IMF and the U.S. dollar may temper the crisis for a short time, but ultimately it will only hurt the dollar and U.S. taxpayers.

We cannot expect to continually bail out others with expansion of the dollar money supply, as we have with the crises in Turkey,

Argentina, and countries of southeast Asia. This policy has its limits and confidence in the dollar is the determining factor. Even though up until now confidence has reigned, encouraged by our political and economic strength, this era is coming to an end. Our homeland has been attacked, our enemies are not easily subdued, our commitments abroad are unsustainable, and our economy is fast slipping into chaos.

Printing money is not an answer. Yet that is all that is offered.

The clamor for low interest rates by all those who benefit from fiat money has prompted the Fed to create new money out of thin air like never before. Driving the federal funds rates down from 6 percent to 2.5 percent, a level below the price inflation rate, represents nothing short of panic—and has done nothing to recharge the economy. But as one would expect, confidence in the dollar is waning. I'm sure, due to the crisis, the faith in fiat, and a failure to understand the business cycle, the Fed will continue with the only thing it knows to do—credit creation and manipulation of interest rates. This policy reflects the central bank's complete ignorance as to the cause of the problem—credit creation and manipulation of interest rates.

Since the Federal Reserve first panicked in early January, it has created $830 billion of fiat money out of thin air. The country is no richer, the economy is weaker, the stock market has continued downward, and unemployment has skyrocketed. Returning to deficit spending, as we already have, will not help us any more than it has helped Japan, which continues to sink into economic morass.

Nothing can correct the problems we face if we do not give up on the foolishness of fiat. Mr. Speaker, a dollar crisis is quickly approaching. We should prepare ourselves. ∎

Gold and the Dollar

Congressional Record – U.S. House of Representatives
June 5, 2002

Mr. Speaker, I have for several years come to the House floor to express my concern for the value of the dollar. It has been, and is, my concern that we in the Congress have not met our responsibility in this regard. The constitutional mandate for Congress should only permit silver and gold to be used as legal tender and has been ignored for decades and has caused much economic pain for many innocent Americans. Instead of maintaining a sound dollar, Congress has by both default and deliberate action promoted a policy that systematically depreciates the dollar. The financial markets are keenly aware of the minute-by-minute fluctuations of all the fiat currencies and look to these swings in value for an investment advantage. This type of anticipation and speculation does not exist in a sound monetary system.

But Congress should be interested in the dollar fluctuation not as an investment but because of our responsibility for maintaining a sound and stable currency, a requirement for sustained economic growth.

The consensus now is that the dollar is weakening and the hope is that the drop in its value will be neither too much nor occur too quickly; but no matter what the spin is, a depreciating currency, one that is losing its value against goods, services, other currencies, and gold, cannot be beneficial and may well be dangerous. A sharply dropping dollar, especially since it is the reserve currency of the world, can play havoc with the entire world economy.

Gold is history's oldest and most stable currency. Central bankers and politicians hate gold because it restrains spending and denies them the power to create money and credit out of thin air. Those who promote big government, whether to wage war and promote foreign expansionism or to finance the welfare state here at home, cherish this power.

History and economic law are on the side of the gold. Paper money always fails. Unfortunately, though, this occurs only after many innocent people have suffered the consequences of the fraud that paper money represents. Monetary inflation is a hidden tax levied more on the poor and those on fixed incomes than the wealthy, the bankers, or the corporations.

In the past two years, gold has been the strongest currency throughout the world in spite of persistent central bank selling designed to suppress the gold price in hopes of hiding the evil caused by the inflationary policies that all central bankers follow. This type of depreciation only works for short periods; economic law always rules over the astounding power and influence of central bankers.

That is what is starting to happen, and trust in the dollar is being lost. The value of the dollar this year is down 18 percent compared to gold. This drop in value should not be ignored by Congress. We should never have permitted this policy that was deliberately designed to undermine the value of the currency.

There are a lot of reasons the market is pushing down the value of the dollar at this time. But only one is foremost. Current world economic and political conditions lead to less trust in the dollar's value. Economic strength here at home is questionable and causes concerns. Our huge foreign debt is more than $2 trillion, and our current account deficit is now 4 percent of GDP and growing. Financing this debt requires borrowing $1.3 billion per day from overseas. But these problems are ancillary to the real reason that the dollar must go down in value. For nearly seven years the U.S. has had the privilege of creating unlimited amounts of dollars with foreigners only too eager to accept them to satisfy our ravenous appetite for consumer items. The markets have yet to discount most of this monetary inflation. But they are doing so now; and for us to ignore what is happening, we do so at the nation's peril. Price inflation and much higher interest rates are around the corner.

Misplaced confidence in a currency can lead money managers and investors astray, but eventually the piper must be paid. Last year's record interest rate drop by the Federal Reserve was like pouring gasoline on a fire. Now the policy of the past decade is being recognized as being weak for the dollar; and trust and confidence in it is justifiably being questioned.

Trust in paper is difficult to measure and anticipate, but long-term value in gold is dependable and more reliably assessed. Printing money and creating artificial credit may temporarily lower interest rates, but it also causes the distortions of malinvestment, overcapacity, excessive debt, and speculation. These conditions cause instability, and market forces eventually overrule the intentions of the central bankers. That is when the apparent benefits of the easy money disappear, such as we dramatically have seen with the crash of the dot-coms and the Enrons and many other stocks.

Now it is back to reality. This is serious business, and the correction that must come to adjust for the Federal Reserve's mischief of the past 30 years has only begun.

Congress must soon consider significant changes in our monetary system if we hope to preserve a system of sound growth and wealth preservation. Paper money managed by the Federal Reserve System cannot accomplish this. In fact, it does the opposite. ∎

Hard Questions for Federal Reserve Chairman Greenspan

Financial Services Committee
Congressional Record – U.S. House of Representatives
July 17, 2002

Rep. PAUL. "Welcome Chairman Greenspan. I've listened carefully to your testimony but I get the sense I may be listening to the Chairman of the Board of Central Economic Planning rather than the chairman of a board that has been entrusted with protecting the value of the dollar.

"I have for quite a few years now expressed concern about the value of the dollar which I think we neglect here in the Congress, here in the committee and I do not think that the Federal Reserve has done a good job in protecting the value of the dollar. And it seems that maybe others are coming around to this viewpoint because I see that the head of the IMF this week, Mr. Koehler has expressed a concern and made a suggestion that all the central bankers of the world need to lay plans in the near future to possibly prop up the dollar. So others have this same concern.

"You have in your testimony expressed concern about the greed factor which obviously is there. And you implied that this has come out from the excessive capitalization/excessive valuations, which may be true. But I believe where you have come up short is in failing to explain why we have financial bubbles. I think when you have fiat money and excessive credit you create financial bubbles and you also undermine the value of the dollar and now we are facing that consequence. We see the disintegration of some of these markets. At the same time we have potential real depreciation of the value of our dollar. And we have pursued rampant inflation of the money supply. Since you have been Chairman of the Federal Reserve we have literally created $4.7 trillion worth of new money in M3. Even in this last year with this tremendous burst of inflation, the money supply has gone up since last January over $1 trillion. You can't have anything but lower value of that unit of account if you keep printing and creating new money.

"Now I would like to bring us back to sound money. And I would like to quote an eminent economist by the name of Alan Greenspan who gives me some credibility on what I am interested in. A time ago you said,

> In the absence of the gold standard there is no way to protect savings from the confiscation through inflation. There is no safe store of value without gold. This is the shabby secret of the welfare statists' tirades against gold. Deficit spending is simply a scheme for the hidden confiscation of wealth. Gold stands in the way of this insidious process that stands as a protector of property rights.

[Congressman Paul then added that he strongly believed this statement by Greenspan taken from a 1966 article that was included in an article he had written titled, "Gold & Economic Freedom" was true. Congressman Paul continued,]

"But gold has always had to be undermined if fiat money is to work and there has to be an illusion of trust for paper to work. And I think this has been happening for thousands of years. At one time the kings clipped coins. Then they debased the metals. Then we learned how to print money. Even as recently as the 1960s for us to perpetuate a myth about our monetary system, we dumped 2/3 of our gold, or 500 million ounces of gold at $35 per ounce in order to try to convince people to trust the money. And even today, there is a fair amount of trading by central banks, the dumping of hundreds of tonnes of gold, loaning of gold for the sole purpose that this indicator of gold does not discredit the paper money and I think there is a definite concerted effort to do that.

"My questions are twofold relating to gold. One, I have been trying desperately to find out the total amount of gold either dumped and sold on to the markets by all the central banks of the world or loaned by the central banks of the world. And this is in hundreds and hundreds of tons. But those figures are not available to me. Maybe you can help me find this. I think it would be important to know since all central banks still deal with and hold gold whether they are dumping, or loaning, or buying for that matter.

"But along this line, I have a bill that would say that our government, our Treasury could not deal in gold and could not be involved in the gold market unless the Congress knows about it. Now that to me seems like such a reasonable approach and reasonable request. But they say they don't use it (gold) so we don't need the bill. But if they are not trading in gold, what would be the harm in the Congress knowing about handling and dealing about this asset, gold?"

Chairman GREENSPAN. "Well first of all, neither we nor the Treasury trade gold. And my impression is that were we to do so, we would announce it. It is certainly the case that others do. There are data published monthly or quarterly which shows the reported gold holdings of central banks throughout the world, so you do know who holds what. The actual trading data, ah, I don't think is available though the London gold exchange does show what its volume numbers are. And periodically, individual central banks do indicate when they are planning to sell gold. But they all report what they own. So it may well be the case that you can't find specific transactions. I think what you can find is the net result of those transactions and they are published. But so far as the United States is concerned, we don't do it." ∎

Bring Back Honest Money

Congressional Record – U.S. House of Representatives
July 25, 2003

Mr. Speaker, I rise to introduce the Honest Money Act. The Honest Money Act repeals legal tender laws, a.k.a. forced tender laws, that compel American citizens to accept fiat (arbitrary) irredeemable paper-ticket or electronic money as their unit of account.

Absent legal tender laws, individuals acting through the markets, rather than government dictates, determine what is to be used as money. Historically, the free-market choice for money has been some combination of gold and silver, whenever they were available. As Dr. Edwin Vieira, the nation's top expert on constitutional money, states: "A free market functions most efficiently and most fairly when the market determines the quality and the quantity of money that's being used."

While fiat money is widely accepted thanks to legal tender laws, it does not maintain its purchasing power. This works to the disadvantage of ordinary people who lose the purchasing power of their savings, pensions, annuities, and other promises of future payment. Most importantly, because of the subsidies our present monetary system provides to banks, which, as Federal Reserve Chairman Alan Greenspan has stated, "induces" the financial sector to increase leverage, the Federal Reserve can create additional money, in Mr. Greenspan's words, "*without limit.*" For this reason, absent legal tender laws, many citizens would refuse to accept fiat irredeemable paper-ticket or electronic money.

Legal tender laws disadvantage ordinary citizens by forcing them to use money that is vulnerable to vast depreciation. As Stephen T. Byington wrote in the September 1895 issue of the *American Federationist*: "No legal tender law is ever needed to make men take good money; its only use is to make them take bad money. Kick it out!" Similarly, the American Federation of Labor asked: "If money is good and would be preferred by the people, then why are legal tender laws necessary? And, if money is not good and would not be preferred by the people, then why in a democracy should they be forced to use it?"

The American Federation of Labor understood how the erosion of the value of money cheated working people. Further, honest money, i.e., specie, was one of the three issues that encouraged ordinary people to organize into unions when the union movement began in the U.S. circa 1830.

While harming ordinary citizens, legal tender laws help expand the scope of government beyond that authorized under the Constitution. However, the primary beneficiaries of legal tender laws are financial institutions, especially banks, which have been improperly granted the special privilege of creating fiat irredeemable electronic money out of thin air through a process commonly called fractional reserve lending. According to the Federal Reserve, since 1950 these private companies (banks) have created almost $8 trillion out of nothing. This has been enormously advantageous to them.

The advantages given banks and other financial institutions by our fiat monetary system, which is built on a foundation of legal tender laws, allow them to realize revenues that would not be available to these institutions in a free market. This represents legalized plunder of ordinary people. Legal tender laws thus enable the redistribution of wealth from those who produce it, mostly ordinary working people, to those who create and move around our irredeemable paper-ticket electronic money which is, in essence, just scrip.

The drafters of the Constitution were well aware of how a government armed with legal tender powers could ravage the people's liberty and prosperity. That is why the Constitution does not grant legal tender power to the federal government, and the states are empowered to make legal tender only out of gold and silver (see Article 1, Section 10). Instead, Congress was given the power to regulate money against a standard, i.e., the dollar. When Alexander Hamilton wrote the Coinage Act of 1792, he simply made into law the market-definition of a dollar as equaling the silver content of the Spanish milled dollar (371.25 grains of silver), which is the dollar referred to in the Constitution. This historical definition of the dollar has never been changed, and cannot be changed any more than the term "inch," as a measure of length, can be changed. It is a gross misrepresentation to equate our irredeemable paper-ticket or electronic money to "dollars."

However, during the 20th century, the legal tender power enabled politicians to fool the public into believing the dollar no longer meant a weight of gold or silver. Instead, the government told the people that the dollar now meant a piece of government-issued paper backed up by nothing except the promises of the government to maintain a stable value of currency. Of course, history shows that the word of the government (to protect the value of the dollar) is literally not worth the paper it is printed on.

Tragically, the Supreme Court has failed to protect the American people from unconstitutional legal tender laws. Salmon Chase, who served as Secretary of the Treasury in President Lincoln's administration, when he was Chief Justice of the Supreme Court, dissenting in *Knox vs. Lee*, summed up the argument against legal tender laws in twelve words: "The legal tender quality [of money] is only valuable for the purposes of *dishonesty*" [emphasis added].

Another prescient Justice was Stephen Field, the only Justice to dissent in every legal tender case to come before the Court. Justice Field accurately described the dangers to our constitutional republic posed by legal tender laws:

> The arguments in favor of the constitutionality of legal tender paper currency tend directly to break down the barriers which separate a government of limited powers from a government resting in the unrestrained will of Congress. Those limitations must be preserved, or our government will inevitably drift from the system established by our Fathers into a vast, centralized, and consolidated government.

A government with unrestrained powers is properly characterized as tyrannical.

Repeal of legal tender laws will help restore constitutional government and protect the people's right to a medium of exchange chosen by the market, thereby protecting their current purchasing power as well as their pensions, savings, and other promises of future payment. Because honest money serves the needs of ordinary people, instead of fiat irredeemable paper-ticket electronic money that improperly transfers the wealth of society to a small specially privileged financial elite along with other special interests, I urge my colleagues to cosponsor the Honest Money Act. ∎

Paper Money and Tyranny

Congressional Record – U.S. House of Representatives
September 5, 2003

All great republics throughout history cherished sound money. This meant that the monetary unit was a commodity of honest weight and purity. When money was sound, civilizations were found to be more prosperous and freedom thrived. The less free a society becomes, the greater the likelihood its money is being debased and the economic well-being of its citizens diminished.

Alan Greenspan, years before he became Federal Reserve Board Chairman in charge of flagrantly debasing the U.S. dollar, wrote about this connection between sound money, prosperity, and freedom. In his article "Gold and Economic Freedom" (*The Objectivist*, July 1966), Greenspan starts by saying: "An almost hysterical antagonism toward the gold standard is an issue that unites statists of all persuasions. They seem to sense . . . that gold and economic freedom are inseparable." Further he states that: "Under the gold standard, a free banking system stands as the protector of an economy's stability and balanced growth." Astoundingly, Mr. Greenspan's analysis of the 1929 market crash, and how the Fed precipitated the crisis, directly parallels current conditions we are experiencing under his management of the Fed. Greenspan explains: "The excess credit which the Fed pumped into the economy spilled over into the stock market—triggering a fantastic speculative boom." And, "…By 1929 the speculative imbalances had become overwhelming and unmanageable by the Fed." Greenspan concluded his article by stating: "In the absence of the gold standard, there is no way to protect savings from confiscation through inflation." He explains that the "shabby secret" of the proponents of big government and paper money is that deficit spending is simply nothing more than a "scheme for the hidden confiscation of wealth." Yet here we are today with a purely fiat monetary system, managed almost exclusively by Alan Greenspan, who once so correctly denounced the Fed's role in the Depression while recognizing the need for sound money.

The Founders of this country, and a large majority of the American people up until the 1930s, disdained paper money, respected commodity money, and disapproved of a central bank's monopoly control of money creation and interest rates. Ironically, it was the abuse of the gold standard, the Fed's credit-creating habits of the 1920s, and its subsequent mischief in the 1930s, that not only gave us the Great Depression, but also prolonged it. Yet sound money was blamed for all the suffering. That's why people hardly objected when Roosevelt and his statist friends confiscated gold and radically debased the currency, ushering in the age of worldwide fiat currencies with which the international economy struggles today.

If honest money and freedom are inseparable, as Mr. Greenspan argued, and paper money leads to tyranny, one must wonder why it's so popular with economists, the business community, bankers, and our government officials. The simplest explanation is that it's a human trait to always seek the comforts of wealth with the least amount of effort. This desire is quite positive when it inspires hard work and innovation in a capitalist society. Productivity is improved and the standard of living goes up for everyone. This process has permitted the poorest in today's capitalist countries to enjoy luxuries never available to the royalty of old.

But this human trait of seeking wealth and comfort with the least amount of effort is often abused. It leads some to believe that by certain monetary manipulations, wealth can be made more available to everyone. Those who believe in fiat money often believe wealth can be increased without a commensurate amount of hard work and innovation. They also come to believe that savings and market control of interest rates are not only unnecessary, but actually hinder a productive growing economy. Concern for liberty is replaced by the illusion that material benefits can be more

easily obtained with fiat money than through hard work and inge-
nuity. The perceived benefits soon become of greater concern for
society than the preservation of liberty. This does not mean proponents of fiat money embark on a crusade to promote tyranny,
though that is what it leads to, but rather they hope they have
found the philosopher's stone and a modern alternative to the
challenge of turning lead into gold.

Our Founders thoroughly understood this issue, and warned
us against the temptation to seek wealth and fortune without the
work and savings that real prosperity requires. James Madison
warned of "The pestilent effects of paper money," as the Founders
had vivid memories of the destructiveness of the Continental dollar. George Mason of Virginia said that he had a "Mortal hatred to
paper money." Constitutional Convention delegate Oliver
Ellsworth from Connecticut thought the convention "A favorable
moment to shut and bar the door against paper money." This
view of the evils of paper money was shared by almost all the del-
egates to the convention, and was the reason the Constitution limited congressional authority to deal with the issue and mandated
that only gold and silver could be legal tender. Paper money was
prohibited and no central bank was authorized. Over and above
the economic reasons for honest money, however, Madison
argued the moral case for such. Paper money, he explained,
destroyed "The necessary confidence between man and man, on
necessary confidence in public councils, on the industry and
morals of people and on the character of republican government."

The Founders were well aware of the biblical admonitions
against dishonest weights and measures, debased silver, and
watered-down wine. The issue of sound money throughout history
has been as much a moral issue as an economic or political issue.

Even with this history and great concern expressed by the
Founders, the barriers to paper money have been torn asunder.
The Constitution has not been changed, but is no longer applied to
the issue of money. It was once explained to me, during the debate
over going to war in Iraq, that a declaration of war was not needed
because to ask for such a declaration was "frivolous" and that the
portion of the Constitution dealing with congressional war power
was "anachronistic." So too, it seems that the power over money

given to Congress alone and limited to coinage and honest weights, is now also "anachronistic."

If indeed our generation can make the case for paper money, issued by an unauthorized central bank, it behooves us to at least have enough respect for the Constitution to amend it in a proper fashion. Ignoring the Constitution in order to perform a pernicious act is detrimental in two ways. First, debasing the currency as a deliberate policy is economically destructive beyond measure. Second, doing it without consideration for the rule of law undermines the entire fabric of our Constitutional republic.

Though the need for sound money is currently not a pressing issue for Congress, it's something that cannot be ignored because serious economic problems resulting from our paper money system are being forced upon us. As a matter of fact, we deal with the consequences on a daily basis, yet fail to see the connection between our economic problems and the mischief orchestrated by the Federal Reserve.

All the great religions teach honesty in money, and the economic shortcomings of paper money were well known when the Constitution was written, so we must try to understand why an entire generation of Americans have come to accept paper money without hesitation, without question. Most Americans are oblivious to the entire issue of the nature and importance of money. Many in authority, however, have either been misled by false notions or see that the power to create money is indeed a power they enjoy, as they promote their agenda of welfarism at home and empire abroad.

Money is a moral, economic, and political issue. Since the monetary unit measures every economic transaction, from wages to prices, taxes, and interest rates, it is vitally important that its value is honestly established in the marketplace without bankers, government, politicians, or the Federal Reserve manipulating its value to serve special interests.

Money as a Moral Issue

The moral issue regarding money should be the easiest to understand, but almost no one in Washington thinks of money in these terms. Although there is a growing and deserved distrust in government *per se*, trust in money and the Federal Reserve's ability to manage it remains strong. No one would welcome a counterfeiter to town, yet this same authority is blindly given to our central bank without any serious oversight by the Congress.

When the government can replicate the monetary unit at will without regard to cost, whether it's paper currency or a computer entry, it's morally identical to the counterfeiter who illegally prints currency. Both ways, it's fraud.

A fiat monetary system allows power and influence to fall into the hands of those who control the creation of new money, and to those who get to use the money or credit early in its circulation. The insidious and eventual cost falls on unidentified victims who are usually oblivious to the cause of their plight. This system of legalized plunder (though not constitutional) allows one group to benefit at the expense of another. An actual transfer of wealth goes from the poor and the middle class to those in privileged financial positions.

In many societies the middle class has actually been wiped out by monetary inflation, which always accompanies fiat money. The high cost of living and loss of jobs hits one segment of society, while in the early stages of inflation, the business class actually benefits from the easy credit. An astute stock investor or home builder can make millions in the boom phase of the business cycle, while the poor and those dependent on fixed incomes can't keep up with the rising cost of living.

Fiat money is also immoral because it allows government to finance special interest legislation that otherwise would have to be paid for by direct taxation or by productive enterprise. This transfer of wealth occurs without directly taking the money out of someone's pocket. Every dollar created dilutes the value of existing dollars in circulation. Those individuals who worked hard, paid their taxes, and saved some money for a rainy day are hit the hardest, with their dollars being depreciated in value while earning interest that is kept artificially low by the Federal Reserve easy-credit policy. The easy credit helps investors and consumers who have no qualms about going into debt and even declaring bankruptcy.

If one sees the welfare state and foreign militarism as improper and immoral, one understands how the license to print money permits these policies to go forward far more easily than if they had to be paid for immediately by direct taxation.

Printing money, which is literally inflation, is nothing more than a sinister and evil form of hidden taxation. It's unfair and deceptive, and accordingly strongly opposed by the authors of the Constitution. That is why there is no authority for Congress, the Federal Reserve, or the executive branch to operate the current system of money we have today.

Money as a Political Issue

Although the money issue today is of little political interest to the parties and politicians, it should not be ignored. Policy makers must contend with the consequences of the business cycle, which result from the fiat monetary system under which we operate. They may not understand the connection now, but eventually they must.

In the past, money and gold have been dominant issues in several major political campaigns. We find that when the people have had a voice in the matter, they inevitably chose gold over paper. To the common man, it just makes sense. As a matter of fact, a large number of Americans, perhaps a majority, still believe our dollar is backed by huge hoards of gold in Fort Knox.

The monetary issue, along with the desire to have free trade among the states, prompted those at the Constitutional Convention to seek solutions to problems that plagued the post-revolutionary war economy. This post-war recession was greatly aggravated by the collapse of the unsound fiat Continental dollar. The people, through their representatives, spoke loudly and clearly for gold and silver over paper.

Andrew Jackson, a strong proponent of gold and opponent of central banking (the Second Bank of the United States), was a hero to the working class and was twice elected president. This issue was fully debated in his presidential campaigns. The people voted for gold over paper.

In the 1870s, the people once again spoke out clearly against the greenback inflation of Lincoln. Notoriously, governments go to paper money while rejecting gold to promote unpopular and unaffordable wars. The return to gold in 1879 went smoothly and was welcomed by the people, putting behind them the disastrous Civil War inflationary period.

Grover Cleveland, elected twice to the presidency, was also a strong advocate of the gold standard.

Again, in the presidential race of 1896, William McKinley argued the case for gold. In spite of the great orations by William Jennings Bryant, who supported monetary inflation and made a mocking "Cross of Gold" speech, the people rallied behind McKinley's bland but correct arguments for sound money.

The 20th century was much less sympathetic to gold. Since 1913 central banking has been accepted in the United States without much debate, despite the many economic and political horrors caused or worsened by the Federal Reserve since its establishment. The ups and downs of the economy have all come as a consequence of Fed policies, from the Great Depression to the horrendous stagflation of the '70s, as well as the current ongoing economic crisis.

A central bank and fiat money enable government to maintain an easy war policy that under strict monetary rules would not be achievable. In other words, countries with sound monetary policies would rarely go to war because they could not afford to, especially if they were not attacked. The people could not be taxed enough to support wars without destroying the economy. But by printing money, the cost can be delayed and hidden, sometimes for years if not decades. To be truly opposed to preemptive and unnecessary wars one must advocate sound money to prevent the promoters of war from financing their imperialism.

Look at how the military budget is exploding, deficits are exploding, and tax revenues are going down. No problem; the Fed is there and will print whatever is needed to meet our military commitments, whether it's wise to do so or not.

The money issue should indeed be a gigantic political issue. Fiat money hurts the economy, finances wars, and allows for excessive welfarism. When these connections are realized and understood, it will once again become a major political issue, since paper money never lasts. Ultimately politicians will not have a choice of whether to address or take a position on the money issue. The people and circumstances will demand it.

We do hear some talk about monetary policy and criticism directed toward the Federal Reserve, but it falls far short of what

I'm talking about. Big-spending welfarists constantly complain about Fed policy, usually demanding lower interest rates even when rates are at historic lows. Big-government conservatives promoting grand worldwide military operations, while arguing that "deficits don't matter" as long as marginal tax rates are lowered, also constantly criticize the Fed for high interest rates and lack of liquidity. Coming from both the left and the right, these demands would not occur if money could not be created out of thin air at will. Both sides are asking for the same thing from the Fed for different reasons. They want the printing presses to run faster and create more credit, so that the economy will be healed like magic—or so they believe.

This is not the kind of interest in the Fed that we need. I'm anticipating that we should and one day will be forced to deal with the definition of the dollar and what money should consist of. The current superficial discussion about money merely shows a desire to tinker with the current system in hopes of improving the deteriorating economy. There will be a point, though, when the tinkering will no longer be of any benefit and even the best advice will be of no value. We have just gone through two-and-a-half years of tinkering with 13 rate cuts, and recovery has not yet been achieved. It's just possible that we're much closer than anyone realizes to that day when it will become absolutely necessary to deal with the monetary issue—both philosophically and strategically—and forget about the band-aid approach to the current system.

Money as an Economic Issue

For a time, the economic consequences of paper money may seem benign and even helpful, but are always disruptive to economic growth and prosperity.

Economic planners of the Keynesian-socialist type have always relished control over money creation in their efforts to regulate and plan the economy. They have no qualms with using this power to pursue their egalitarian dreams of wealth redistribution. That force and fraud are used to make the economic system supposedly fairer is of little concern to them.

There are also many conservatives who do not endorse central economic planning as those on the left do, but nevertheless concede this authority to the Federal Reserve to manipulate the economy through monetary policy. Only a small group of constitutionalists, libertarians, and Austrian free-market economists reject the notion that central planning, through interest-rate and money-supply manipulation, is a productive endeavor.

Many sincere politicians, bureaucrats, and bankers endorse the current system, not out of malice or greed, but because it's the only system they have known. The principles of sound money and free market banking are not taught in our universities. The overwhelming consensus in Washington, as well as around the world, is that commodity money without a central bank is no longer practical or necessary. Be assured, though, that certain individuals who greatly benefit from a paper money system know exactly why the restraints that a commodities standard would have are unacceptable.

Though the economic consequences of paper money in the early stage affect lower-income and middle-class citizens, history shows that when the destruction of monetary value becomes rampant, nearly everyone suffers and the economic and political structure becomes unstable. There's good reason for all of us to be concerned about our monetary system and the future of the dollar.

Nations that live beyond their means must always pay for their extravagance. It's easy to understand why future generations inherit a burden when the national debt piles up. This requires others to pay the interest and debts when they come due. The victims are never the recipients of the borrowed funds. But this is not exactly what happens when a country pays off its debt. The debt, in nominal terms, always goes up, and since it is still accepted by mainstream economists that just borrowing endlessly is not the road to permanent prosperity, real debt must be reduced. Depreciating the value of the dollar does that. If the dollar loses 10 percent of its value, the national debt of $6.5 trillion is reduced in real terms by $650 billion dollars. That's a pretty neat trick and quite helpful—to the government.

That's why the Fed screams about a coming deflation, so it can continue the devaluation of the dollar unabated. The politicians don't mind, the bankers welcome the business activity, and the recipients of the funds passed out by Congress never complain. The greater the debt, the greater the need to inflate the currency, since debt cannot be the source of long-term wealth. Individuals and corporations who borrow too much eventually must cut back and pay off debt and start anew, but governments rarely do.

But where's the hitch? This process, which seems to be a creative way of paying off debt, eventually undermines the capitalist structure of the economy, thus making it difficult to produce wealth, and that's when the whole process comes to an end. This system causes many economic problems, but most of them stem from the Fed's interference with the market rate of interest that it achieves through credit creation and printing money.

Nearly 100 years ago, Austrian economist Ludwig von Mises explained and predicted the failure of socialism. Without a pricing mechanism, the delicate balance between consumers and producers would be destroyed. Freely fluctuating prices provide vital information to the entrepreneur who is making key decisions on production. Without this information, major mistakes are made. A central planning bureaucrat cannot be a substitute for the law of supply and demand.

Though generally accepted by most modern economists and politicians, there is little hesitancy in accepting the omnipotent wisdom of the Federal Reserve to know the "price" of money — the interest rate — and its proper supply. For decades, and especially during the 1990s — when Chairman Greenspan was held in such high esteem, and no one dared question his judgment or the wisdom of the system — this process was allowed to run unimpeded by political or market restraints. Just as we must eventually pay for our perpetual deficits, continuous manipulation of interest and credit will also extract a payment.

Artificially low interest rates deceive investors into believing that rates are low because savings are high and represent funds not spent on consumption. When the Fed creates bank deposits out of thin air, making loans available at below-market rates, malinvestment and overcapacity results, setting the stage for the next recession or depression. The easy credit policy is welcomed by many: stock-market investors, home builders, home buyers, congressional spendthrifts, bankers, and many other consumers who enjoy borrowing at low rates and not worrying about repayment. However, perpetual good times cannot come from a printing press or easy credit created by a Federal Reserve computer. The piper will demand payment, and the downturn in the business cycle will see to it. The downturn is locked into place by the artificial boom that everyone enjoys, despite the dreams that we have ushered in a "new economic era." Let there be no doubt: the business cycle, the stagflation, the recessions, the depressions, and the inflations are not a result of capitalism and sound money, but rather are a direct result of paper money and a central bank that is incapable of managing it.

Our current monetary system makes it tempting for all parties, individuals, corporations, and government to go into debt. It encourages consumption over investment and production. Incentives to save are diminished by the Fed's making new credit available to everyone and keeping interest rates on saving so low that few find it advisable to save for a rainy day. This is made worse by taxing interest earned on savings. It plays havoc with those who do save and want to live off their interest. The artificial rates may be 4, 5, or even 6 percent below the market rate, and the savers — many who are elderly and on fixed incomes — suffer unfairly at the hands of Alan Greenspan, who believes that resorting to money creation will solve our problems and give us perpetual prosperity.

Lowering interest rates at times, especially early in the stages of monetary debasement, will produce the desired effects and stimulate another boom-bust cycle. But eventually the distortions and imbalances between consumption and production, and the excessive debt, prevent the monetary stimulus from doing very much to boost the economy. Just look at what's been happening in Japan for the last 12 years. When conditions get bad enough the only recourse will be to have major monetary reform to restore confidence in the system.

The two conditions that result from fiat money that are more likely to concern the people are inflation of prices and unemployment. Unfortunately, few realize these problems are directly related to our monetary system. Instead of demanding reforms, the chorus from both the right and left is for the Fed to do more of the same — only faster. If our problem stems from easy credit and interest-rate manipulation by the Fed, demanding more will not do much to help. Sadly, it will only make our problems worse.

Ironically, the more successful the money managers are at restoring growth or prolonging the boom with their monetary machinations, the greater are the distortions and imbalances in the economy. This means that when corrections are eventually forced upon us, they are much more painful and more people suffer with the correction lasting longer.

Today's Conditions

Today's economic conditions reflect a fiat monetary system held together by many tricks and luck over the past 30 years. The world has been awash in paper money since removal of the last vestige of the gold standard by Richard Nixon when he buried the Bretton Woods agreement — the gold exchange standard — on August 15, 1971. Since then we've been on a worldwide paper dollar standard. Quite possibly we are seeing the beginning of the end of that system. If so, tough times are ahead for the United States and the world economy.

A paper monetary standard means there are no restraints on the printing press or on federal deficits. In 1971, M3 was $776 billion; today it stands at $8.9 trillion, an 1,100 percent increase. Our national debt in 1971 was $408 billion; today it stands at $6.8 trillion, a 1,600 percent increase. Since that time, our dollar has lost almost 80 percent of its purchasing power. Common sense tells us that this process is not sustainable and something has to give. So far, no one in Washington seems interested.

Although dollar creation is ultimately the key to its value, many other factors play a part in its perceived value, such as: the strength of our economy, our political stability, our military power, the benefit of the dollar being the key reserve currency of the world, and the relative weakness of other nations' economies and their currencies. For these reasons, the dollar has enjoyed a special place in the world economy. Increases in productivity have also helped to bestow undeserved trust in our economy with consumer prices, to some degree, being held in check and fooling the people, at the urging of the Fed, that "inflation" is not a problem. Trust is an important factor in how the dollar is perceived. Sound money encourages trust, but trust can come from these other sources as well. But when this trust is lost, which always occurs with paper money, the delayed adjustments can hit with a vengeance.

Following the breakdown of the Bretton Woods agreement, the world essentially accepted the dollar as a replacement for gold, to be held in reserve upon which even more monetary expansion could occur. It was a great arrangement that up until now seemed to make everyone happy.

We own the printing press and create as many dollars as we please. These dollars are used to buy federal debt. This allows our debt to be monetized and the spendthrift Congress, of course, finds this a delightful convenience and never complains. As the dollars circulate through our fractional reserve banking system, they expand many times over. With our excess dollars at home, our trading partners are only too happy to accept these dollars in order to sell us their products. Because our dollar is relatively strong compared to other currencies, we can buy foreign products at a discounted price. In other words, we get to create the world's reserve currency at no cost, spend it overseas, and receive manu-factured goods in return. Our excess dollars go abroad and other countries—especially Japan and China—are only too happy to loan them right back to us by buying our government and GSE debt. Up until now both sides have been happy with this arrange-ment.

But all good things must come to an end and this arrangement is ending. The process put us into a position of being a huge debtor nation, with our current account deficit of more than $600 billion per year now exceeding 5 percent of our GDP. We now owe for-eigners more than any other nation ever owed in all of history, over $3 trillion.

A debt of this sort always ends by the currency of the debtor nation decreasing in value. And that's what has started to happen with the dollar, although it still has a long way to go. Our free lunch cannot last. Printing money, buying foreign products, and selling foreign holders of dollars our debt ends when the foreign holders of this debt become concerned with the dollar's future value.

Once this process starts, interest rates will rise. And in recent weeks, despite the frenetic effort of the Fed to keep interest rates low, they are actually rising instead. The official explanation is that this is due to an economic rebound with an increase in demand for loans. Yet a decrease in demand for our debt and reluctance to hold our dollars is a more likely cause. Only time will tell whether the economy rebounds to any significant degree, but one must be aware that rising interest rates and serious price inflation can also reflect a weak dollar and a weak economy. The stagflation of the 1970s baffled many conventional economists, but not the Austrian economists. Many other countries have in the past suffered from the extremes of inflation in an inflationary depression, and we are not immune from that happening here. Our monetary and fiscal policies are actually conducive to such a scenario.

In the short run, the current system gives us a free ride, our paper buys cheap goods from overseas, and foreigners risk all by financing our extravagance. But in the long run, we will surely pay for living beyond our means. Debt will be paid for one way or another. An inflated currency always comes back to haunt those who enjoyed the "benefits" of inflation. Although this process is extremely dangerous, many economists and politicians do not see it as a currency problem and are only too willing to find a villain to attack. Surprisingly the villain is often the foreigner who foolishly takes our paper for useful goods and accommodates us by loaning the proceeds back to us. It's true that the system encourages exportation of jobs as we buy more and more foreign goods. But nobody understands the Fed role in this, so the cries go out to punish the competition with tariffs. Protectionism is a predictable consequence of paper-money inflation, just as is the impoverishment of an entire middle class. It should surprise no one that even in the boom phase of the 1990s, there were still many people who became poorer. Yet all we hear are calls for more government mischief to correct the problems with tariffs, increased welfare for the poor, increased unemployment benefits, deficit spending, and special interest tax reduction, none of which can solve the problems ingrained in a system that operates with paper money and a central bank.

If inflation were equitable and treated all classes the same, it would be less socially divisive. But while some see their incomes going up above the rate of inflation (movie stars, CEOs, stock brokers, speculators, professional athletes), others see their incomes stagnate like lower-middle-income workers, retired people, and farmers. Likewise, the rise in the cost of living hurts the poor and middle class more than the wealthy. Because inflation treats certain groups unfairly, anger and envy are directed toward those who have benefited.

The long-term philosophic problem with this is that the central bank and the fiat monetary system are not blamed; instead free market capitalism is. This is what happened in the 1930s. The Keynesians, who grew to dominate economic thinking at the time, erroneously blamed the gold standard, balanced budgets, and capitalism instead of tax increases, tariffs, and Fed policy. This country cannot afford another attack on economic liberty similar to what followed the 1929 crash that ushered in the economic interventionism and inflationism which we have been saddled with ever since. These policies have brought us to the brink of another colossal economic downturn and we need to be prepared.

Big business and banking deserve our harsh criticism, but not because they are big or because they make a lot of money. Our criticism should come because of the special benefits they receive from a monetary system designed to assist the business class at the expense of the working class. Labor leader Samuel Gompers understood this and feared paper money and a central bank while arguing the case for gold. Since the monetary system is used to finance deficits that come from war expenditures, the military industrial complex is a strong supporter of the current monetary system.

Liberals foolishly believe that they can control the process and curtail the benefits going to corporations and banks by increasing the spending for welfare for the poor. But this never happens. Powerful financial special interests control the government spending process and throw only crumbs to the poor. The fallacy with this approach is that the advocates fail to see the harm done to the poor, with cost of living increases and job losses that are a natural consequence of monetary debasement. Therefore, even more liberal control over the spending process can never compensate for the great harm done to the economy and the poor by the Federal Reserve's effort to manage an unmanageable fiat monetary system.

Economic intervention, financed by inflation, is high-stakes government. It provides the incentive for the big money to "invest" in gaining government control. The big money comes from those who have it—corporations and banking interests.

That's why literally billions of dollars are spent on elections and lobbying. The only way to restore equity is to change the primary function of government from economic planning and militarism to protecting liberty. Without money, the poor and middle class are disenfranchised since access for the most part requires money. Obviously, this is not a partisan issue since both major parties are controlled by wealthy special interests. Only the rhetoric is different.

Our current economic problems are directly related to the monetary excesses of three decades and the more recent efforts by the Federal Reserve to thwart the correction that the market is forcing upon us. Since 1998, there has been a sustained attack on corporate profits. Before that, profits and earnings were inflated and fictitious, with WorldCom and Enron being prime examples. In spite of the 13 rate cuts since 2001, economic growth has not been restored.

Paper money encourages speculation, excessive debt, and misdirected investments. The market, however, always moves in the direction of eliminating bad investments, liquidating debt, and reducing speculative excesses. What we have seen, especially since the stock market peak of early 2000, is a knock-down, drag-out battle between the Fed's effort to avoid a recession, limit the recession, and stimulate growth with its only tool, money creation, while the market demands the elimination of bad investments and excess debt. The Fed was also motivated to save the stock market from collapsing, which in some ways they have been able to do. The market, in contrast, will insist on liquidation of unsustainable debt, removal of investment mistakes made over several decades, and a dramatic revaluation of the stock market. In this go-around, the Fed has pulled out all the stops and is more determined than ever, yet the market is saying that new and healthy growth cannot occur until a major cleansing of the system occurs. Does anyone think that tariffs and interest rates of 1 percent will encourage the rebuilding of our steel and textile industries anytime soon? Obviously, something more is needed.

The world central bankers are concerned with the lack of response to low interest rates and they have joined in a concerted effort to rescue the world economy through a policy of protecting the dollar's role in the world economy, denying that inflation exists, and justifying unlimited expansion of the dollar money supply. To maintain confidence in the dollar, gold prices must be held in check. In the 1960s our government didn't want a vote of no confidence in the dollar, and for a couple of decades, the price of gold was artificially held at $35 per ounce. That, of course, did not last.

In recent years, there has been a coordinated effort by the world central bankers to keep the gold price in check by dumping part of their large horde of gold into the market. This has worked to a degree, but just as it could not be sustained in the 1960s, until Nixon declared the Bretton Woods agreement dead in 1971, this effort will fail as well.

The market price of gold is important because it reflects the ultimate confidence in the dollar. An artificially low price for gold contributes to false confidence and when this is lost, more chaos ensues as the market adjusts for the delay.

Monetary policy today is designed to demonetize gold and guarantee for the first time that paper can serve as an adequate substitute in the hands of wise central bankers. Trust, then, has to be transferred from gold to the politicians and bureaucrats who are in charge of our monetary system. This fails to recognize the obvious reason that market participants throughout history have always preferred to deal with real assets, real money, rather than government paper. This contest between paper and honest money is of much greater significance than many realize. We should know the outcome of this struggle within the next decade.

Alan Greenspan, although once a strong advocate for the gold standard, now believes he knows what the outcome of this battle will be. Is it just wishful thinking on his part? In an answer to a question I asked before the Financial Services Committee in February 2003, Chairman Greenspan made an effort to convince me that paper money now works as well as gold:

> I have been quite surprised, and I must say pleased, by the fact that central banks have been able to effectively simulate many of the characteristics of the gold standard by constraining the degree of finance in a manner which effectively brought down the general price levels.

Earlier, in December 2002, Mr. Greenspan spoke before the Economic Club of New York and addressed the same subject:

> The record of the past 20 years appears to underscore the observation that, although pressures for excess issuance of fiat money are chronic, a prudent monetary policy maintained over a protracted period of time can contain the forces of inflation.

There are several problems with this optimistic assessment. First, efficient central bankers will never replace the *invisible hand* of a commodity monetary standard. Second, using government price indices to measure the success of a managed fiat currency should not be reassuring. These indices can be arbitrarily altered to imply a successful monetary policy. Also, price increases of consumer goods are not a litmus test for measuring the harm done by the money managers at the Fed. The development of overcapacity, excessive debt, and speculation still occur, even when prices happen to remain reasonably stable due to increases in productivity and technology. Chairman Greenspan makes his argument because he hopes he's right that sound money is no longer necessary, and also because it's an excuse to keep the inflation of the money supply going for as long as possible, hoping a miracle will restore sound growth to the economy. But that's only a dream.

We are now faced with an economy that is far from robust and may get a lot worse before rebounding. If not now, the time will soon come when the conventional wisdom of the last 90 years, since the Fed was created, will have to be challenged. If the conditions have changed and the routine of fiscal and monetary stimulation don't work, we better prepare ourselves for the aftermath of a failed dollar system, which will not be limited to the United States.

An interesting headline appeared in the *New York Times* on July 31, 2003, "Commodity Costs Soar, But Factories Don't Bustle." What is observed here is a sea change in attitude by investors shifting their investment funds and speculation into things of real value and out of financial areas, such as stocks and bonds. This shift shows that in spite of the most aggressive Fed policy in history in the past three years, the economy remains sluggish and interest rates are actually rising. What can the Fed do? If this trend continues, there's little they can do. Not only do I believe this trend will continue, I believe it's likely to accelerate. This policy plays havoc with our economy; reduces revenues, prompts increases in federal spending, increases in deficits and debt occur, and interest costs rise, compounding our budgetary woes.

The set of circumstances we face today are unique and quite different from all the other recessions the Federal Reserve has had to deal with. Generally, interest rates are raised to slow the economy and dampen price inflation. At the bottom of the cycle interest rates are lowered to stimulate the economy. But this time around, the recession came in spite of huge and significant interest rate reductions by the Fed. This aggressive policy did not prevent the recession as was hoped; so far it has not produced the desired recovery. Now we're at the bottom of the cycle and interest rates not only can't be lowered, they are rising. This is a unique and dangerous combination of events. This set of circumstances can only occur with fiat money and indicates that further manipulation of the money supply and interest rates by the Fed will have little if any effect.

The odds aren't very good that the Fed will adopt a policy of not inflating the money supply because of some very painful consequences that would result. Also there would be a need to remove the pressure on the Fed to accommodate the big spenders in Congress. Since there are essentially only two groups that have any influence on spending levels, big-government liberals and big-government conservatives, that's not about to happen. Poverty is going to worsen due to our monetary and fiscal policies, so spending on the war on poverty will accelerate. Our obsession with policing the world, nation building, and preemptive war are not likely to soon go away, since both Republican and Democratic leaders endorse them. Instead, the cost of defending the American empire is going to accelerate. A country that is getting poorer cannot pay these bills with higher taxation nor can they find enough excess funds for the people to loan to the government. The only recourse is for the Federal Reserve to accommodate and monetize the federal debt, and that, of course, is inflation.

It's now admitted that the deficit is out of control, with next year's deficit reaching over one-half trillion dollars, not counting the billions borrowed from "trust funds" like Social Security. I'm sticking to my prediction that within a few years the national debt will increase over $1 trillion in one fiscal year. So far, so good, no big market reactions, the dollar is holding its own and the administration and congressional leaders are not alarmed. But they ought to be.

I agree, it would be politically tough to bite the bullet and deal with our extravagance, both fiscal and monetary, but the repercussions here at home from a loss of confidence in the dollar throughout the world will not be a pretty sight to behold. I don't see any way we are going to avoid the crisis.

We do have some options to minimize the suffering. If we decided to, we could permit some alternatives to the current system of money and banking we have today.

Already, we took a big step in this direction. Gold was illegal to own between 1933 and 1976. Today millions of Americans do own some gold.

Gold contracts are legal, but a settlement of any dispute is always in Federal Reserve notes. This makes gold contracts of limited value.

For gold to be an alternative to Federal Reserve notes, taxes on any transactions in gold must be removed, both sales and capital gains.

Holding gold should be permitted in any pension fund, just as dollars are permitted in a checking account of these funds.

Repeal of all legal tender laws is a must. Sound money never requires the force of legal tender laws. Only paper money requires such laws.

These proposals, even if put in place tomorrow, would not solve all the problems we face. It would though, legalize freedom of choice in money, and many who worry about having their savings wiped out by a depreciating dollar would at least have another option. This option would ease some of the difficulties that are surely to come from runaway deficits in a weakening economy with skyrocketing inflation.

Curbing the scope of government and limiting its size to that prescribed in the Constitution is the goal that we should seek. But political reality makes this option available to us only after a national bankruptcy has occurred. We need not face that catastrophe. What we need to do is to strictly limit the power of government to meddle in our economy and our personal affairs, and stay out of the internal affairs of other nations.

Conclusion

It's no coincidence that during the period following the establishment of the Federal Reserve and the elimination of the gold standard, a huge growth in the size of the federal government and its debt occurred. Believers in big government, whether on the left or right, vociferously reject the constraints on government growth that gold demands. Liberty is virtually impossible to protect when the people allow their government to print money at will. Inevitably, the left will demand more economic interventionism, the right more militarism and empire building. Both sides, either inadvertently or deliberately, will foster corporatism. Those whose greatest interest is in liberty and self-reliance are lost in the shuffle. Though left and right have different goals and serve different special-interest groups, they are only too willing to compromise and support each other's programs.

If unchecked, the economic and political chaos that comes from currency destruction inevitably leads to tyranny—a consequence of which the Founders were well aware. For 90 years we have lived with a central bank, with the last 32 years absent of any restraint on money creation. The longer the process lasts, the faster the printing presses have to run in an effort to maintain stability. They are currently running at record rate. It was predictable and is understandable that our national debt is now expanding at a record rate.

The panicky effort of the Fed to stimulate economic growth does produce what it considers favorable economic reports, recently citing second quarter growth this year at 3.1 percent. But in the footnotes, we find that military spending—almost all of which is overseas—was up an astounding 46 percent. This, of course, represents deficit spending financed by the Federal Reserve's printing press. In the same quarter, after-tax corporate profits fell 3.4 percent. This is hardly a reassuring report on the health of our economy and merely reflects the bankruptcy of current economic policy.

Real economic growth won't return until confidence in the entire system is restored. And that is impossible as long as it depends on the politicians not spending too much money and the Federal Reserve limiting its propensity to inflate our way to prosperity. Only sound money and limited government can do that. ∎

Reject Taxpayer Bank Bailouts

Congressional Record – U.S. House of Representatives
May 4, 2005

Mr. Speaker, H.R. 1185, the Federal Deposit Insurance Reform Act, expands the federal government's unconstitutional control over the financial services industry and raises taxes on all financial institutions. Furthermore, this legislation increases the possibility of future bank failures. Therefore, I must oppose this bill.

I primarily object to the provisions in H.R. 1185 which may increase the premiums assessed on participating financial institutions. These "premiums," which are actually taxes, are the primary source of funds for the Deposit Insurance Fund. This fund is used to bail out banks that experience difficulties meeting commitments to their depositors. Thus, the deposit insurance system transfers liability for poor management decisions from those who made the decisions to their competitors. This system punishes those financial institutions that follow sound practices, as they are forced to absorb the losses of their competitors. This also compounds the moral hazard problem created whenever government socializes business losses.

In the event of a severe banking crisis, Congress likely will transfer funds from general revenues into the Deposit Insurance Fund, which would make all taxpayers liable for the mistakes of a few. Of course, such a bailout would require separate authorization from Congress, but can anyone imagine Congress saying no to banking lobbyists pleading for relief from the costs of bailing out their weaker competitors?

Government subsidies lead to government control, as regulations are imposed on the recipients of the subsidies in order to address the moral hazard problem. This certainly is the case in banking, which is one of the most heavily regulated industries in America. However, as George Kaufman (John Smith Professor of Banking and Finance at Loyola University in Chicago and co-chair of the Shadow Financial Regulatory Committee) pointed out in a study for the CATO Institute, the FDIC's history of poor management exacerbated the banking crisis of the eighties and nineties. Professor Kaufman properly identifies a key reason for the FDIC's poor track record in protecting individual depositors: regulators have incentives to downplay or even coverup problems in the financial system such as banking facilities. Banking failures are black marks on the regulators' records. In addition, regulators may be subject to political pressure to delay imposing sanctions on failing institutions, thus increasing the magnitude of the loss.

Immediately after a problem in the banking industry comes to light, the media and Congress inevitably blame it on regulators who were "asleep at the switch." Yet most politicians continue to believe that giving more power to the very regulators whose incompetence (or worse) either caused or contributed to the problem somehow will prevent future crises!

The presence of deposit insurance and government regulations removes incentives for individuals to act on their own to protect their deposits or even inquire as to the health of their financial institutions. After all, why should individuals be concerned when the federal government is ensuring banks following sound practices and has insured their deposits?

Finally, I would remind my colleagues that the federal deposit insurance program lacks constitutional authority. Congress's only mandate in the area of money and banking is to maintain the value of the money. Unfortunately, Congress abdicated its responsibility over monetary policy with the passage of the Federal Reserve Act of 1913, which allows the federal government to erode the value of the currency at the will of the central bank. Congress's embrace of fiat money is directly responsible for the instability in the banking system that created the justification for deposit insurance. ■

The End of Dollar Hegemony

Congressional Record — U.S. House of Representatives
February 15, 2006

A hundred years ago it was called "dollar diplomacy." After World War II, and especially after the fall of the Soviet Union in 1989, that policy evolved into "dollar hegemony." But after all these many years of great success, our dollar dominance is coming to an end.

It has been said, rightly, that he who holds the gold makes the rules. In earlier times it was readily accepted that fair and honest trade required an exchange for something of real value.

First it was simply barter of goods. Then it was discovered that gold held a universal attraction, and was a convenient substitute for more cumbersome barter transactions. Not only did gold facilitate exchange of goods and services, it served as a store of value for those who wanted to save for a rainy day.

Though money developed naturally in the marketplace, as governments grew in power they assumed monopoly control over money. Sometimes governments succeeded in guaranteeing the quality and purity of gold, but in time governments learned to outspend their revenues. New or higher taxes always incurred the disapproval of the people, so it wasn't long before Kings and Caesars learned how to inflate their currencies by reducing the amount of gold in each coin—always hoping their subjects would not discover the fraud. But the people always did, and they strenuously objected.

This helped pressure leaders to seek more gold by conquering other nations. The people became accustomed to living beyond their means, and enjoyed the circuses and bread. Financing extravagances by conquering foreign lands seemed a logical alternative to working harder and producing more. Besides, conquering nations not only brought home gold, they brought home slaves as well. Taxing the people in conquered territories also provided an incentive to build empires. This system of government worked well for a while, but the moral decline of the people led to an unwillingness to produce for themselves. There was a limit to the number of countries that could be sacked for their wealth, and this always brought empires to an end. When gold no longer could be obtained, their military might crumbled. In those days those who held the gold truly wrote the rules and lived well.

That general rule has held fast throughout the ages. When gold was used, and the rules protected honest commerce, productive nations thrived. Whenever wealthy nations—those with powerful armies and gold—strived only for empire and easy fortunes to support welfare at home, those nations failed.

Today the principles are the same, but the process is quite different. Gold no longer is the currency of the realm; paper is. The truth now is: "He who prints the money makes the rules"—at least for the time being. Although gold is not used, the goals are the same: compel foreign countries to produce and subsidize the country with military superiority and control over the monetary printing presses.

Since printing paper money is nothing short of counterfeiting, the issuer of the international currency must always be the country with the military might to guarantee control over the system. This magnificent scheme seems the perfect system for obtaining perpetual wealth for the country that issues the *de facto* world currency. The one problem, however, is that such a system destroys the character of the counterfeiting nation's people—just as was the case when gold was the currency and it was obtained by conquering other nations. And this destroys the incentive to save and produce, while encouraging debt and runaway welfare.

The pressure at home to inflate the currency comes from the corporate welfare recipients, as well as those who demand handouts as compensation for their needs and perceived injuries by others. In both cases personal responsibility for one's actions is rejected.

When paper money is rejected, or when gold runs out, wealth and political stability are lost. The country then must go from living beyond its means to living beneath its means, until the economic and political systems adjust to the new rules—rules no longer written by those who ran the now defunct printing press.

"Dollar Diplomacy," a policy instituted by William Howard Taft and his Secretary of State Philander C. Knox, was designed to enhance U.S. commercial investments in Latin America and the Far East. McKinley concocted a war against Spain in 1898, and (Teddy) Roosevelt's corollary to the Monroe Doctrine preceded Taft's aggressive approach to using the U.S. dollar and diplomatic influence to secure U.S. investments abroad. This earned the popular title of "Dollar Diplomacy." The significance of Roosevelt's change was that our intervention now could be justified by the mere "appearance" that a country of interest to us was politically or fiscally vulnerable to European control. Not only did we claim a right, but even an official U.S. government "obligation" to protect our commercial interests from Europeans.

This new policy came on the heels of the "gunboat" diplomacy of the late 19th century, and it meant we could buy influence before resorting to the threat of force. By the time the "dollar diplomacy" of William Howard Taft was clearly articulated, the seeds of American empire were planted. And they were destined to grow in the fertile political soil of a country that lost its love and respect for the republic bequeathed to us by the authors of the Constitution. And indeed they did. It wasn't too long before dollar "diplomacy" became dollar "hegemony" in the second half of the 20th century.

This transition only could have occurred with a dramatic change in monetary policy and the nature of the dollar itself.

Congress created the Federal Reserve System in 1913. Between then and 1971 the principle of sound money was systematically undermined. Between 1913 and 1971, the Federal Reserve found it much easier to expand the money supply at will for financing war or manipulating the economy with little resistance from Congress — while benefiting the special interests that influence government.

Dollar dominance got a huge boost after World War II. We were spared the destruction that so many other nations suffered, and our coffers were filled with the world's gold. But the world chose not to return to the discipline of the gold standard, and the politicians applauded. Printing money to pay the bills was a lot more popular than taxing or restraining unnecessary spending. In spite of the short-term benefits, imbalances were institutionalized for decades to come.

The 1944 Bretton Woods agreement solidified the dollar as the preeminent world reserve currency, replacing the British pound. Due to our political and military muscle, and because we had a huge amount of physical gold, the world readily accepted our dollar (defined as 1/35th of an ounce of gold) as the world's reserve currency. The dollar was said to be "as good as gold," and convertible to all foreign central banks at that rate. For American citizens, however, it remained illegal to own. This was a gold-exchange standard that from inception was doomed to fail.

The U.S. did exactly what many predicted she would do. She printed more dollars for which there was no gold backing. But the world was content to accept those dollars for more than 25 years with little question—until the French and others in the late 1960s demanded we fulfill our promise to pay one ounce of gold for each $35 they delivered to the U.S. Treasury. This resulted in a huge gold drain that brought an end to a very poorly devised pseudo-gold standard.

It all ended on August 15, 1971, when Nixon closed the gold window and refused to pay out any of our remaining 280 million ounces of gold. In essence, we declared our insolvency and everyone recognized some other monetary system had to be devised in order to bring stability to the markets.

Amazingly, a new system was devised which allowed the U.S. to operate the printing presses for the world reserve currency with no restraints placed on it—not even a pretense of gold convertibility, none whatsoever! Though the new policy was even more deeply flawed, it nevertheless opened the door for dollar hegemony to spread.

Realizing the world was embarking on something new and mind boggling, elite money managers, with especially strong support from U.S. authorities, struck an agreement with OPEC to price oil in U.S. dollars exclusively for all worldwide transactions. This gave the dollar a special place among world currencies and in essence "backed" the dollar with oil. In return, the U.S. promised to protect the various oil-rich kingdoms in the Persian Gulf against threat of invasion or domestic coup. This arrangement helped ignite the radical Islamic movement among those who resented our influence in the region. The arrangement gave the dollar artificial strength, with tremendous financial benefits for the United States. It allowed us to export our monetary inflation by buying oil and other goods at a great discount as dollar influence flourished.

This post-Bretton Woods system was much more fragile than the system that existed between 1945 and 1971. Though the dollar/oil arrangement was helpful, it was not nearly as stable as the pseudo-gold standard under Bretton Woods. It certainly was less stable than the gold standard of the late 19th century.

During the 1970s the dollar nearly collapsed, as oil prices surged and gold skyrocketed to $800 an ounce. By 1979 interest rates of 21 percent were required to rescue the system. The pressure on the dollar in the 1970s, in spite of the benefits accrued to it, reflected reckless budget deficits and monetary inflation during the 1960s. The markets were not fooled by LBJ's claim that we could afford both "guns and butter."

Once again the dollar was rescued, and this ushered in the age of true dollar hegemony lasting from the early 1980s to the present. With tremendous cooperation coming from the central banks and international commercial banks, the dollar was accepted as if it were gold.

Fed Chair Alan Greenspan, on several occasions before the House Banking Committee, answered my challenges to him about his previously held favorable views on gold by claiming that he and other central bankers had gotten paper money — i.e., the dollar system — to respond as if it were gold. Each time I strongly disagreed, and pointed out that if they had achieved such a feat they would have defied centuries of economic history regarding the need for money to be something of real value. He smugly and confidently concurred with this.

In recent years central banks and various financial institutions, all with vested interests in maintaining a workable fiat dollar standard, were not secretive about selling and loaning large amounts of gold to the market even while decreasing gold prices raised serious questions about the wisdom of such a policy. They never admitted to gold price fixing, but the evidence is abundant that they believed if the gold price fell it would convey a sense of confidence to the market, confidence that they indeed had achieved amazing success in turning paper into gold.

Increasing gold prices historically are viewed as an indicator of distrust in paper currency. This recent effort was not a whole lot different than the U.S. Treasury selling gold at $35 an ounce in the 1960s, in an attempt to convince the world the dollar was sound and as good as gold. Even during the Depression, one of Roosevelt's first acts was to remove free-market gold pricing as an indication of a flawed monetary system by making it illegal for American citizens to own gold. Economic law eventually limited that effort, as it did in the early 1970s when our Treasury and the IMF tried to fix the price of gold by dumping tons into the market to dampen the enthusiasm of those seeking a safe haven for a falling dollar after gold ownership was relegalized.

Once again the effort between 1980 and 2000 to fool the market as to the true value of the dollar proved unsuccessful. In the past five years the dollar has been devalued in terms of gold by more than 50 percent. You just can't fool all the people all the time, even with the power of the mighty printing press and money creating system of the Federal Reserve.

Even with all the shortcomings of the fiat monetary system, dollar influence thrived. The results seemed beneficial, but gross distortions built into the system remained. And true to form, Washington politicians are only too anxious to solve the problems cropping up with window dressing, while failing to understand and deal with the underlying flawed policy. Protectionism, fixing exchange rates, punitive tariffs, politically motivated sanctions, corporate subsidies, international trade management, price controls, interest rate and wage controls, supernationalist sentiments, threats of force, and even war are resorted to—all to solve the problems artificially created by deeply flawed monetary and economic systems.

In the short run, the issuer of a fiat reserve currency can accrue great economic benefits. In the long run, it poses a threat to the country issuing the world currency. In this case that's the United States. As long as foreign countries take our dollars in return for real goods, we come out ahead. This is a benefit many in Congress fail to recognize, as they bash China for maintaining a positive trade balance with us. But this leads to a loss of manufacturing jobs to overseas markets, as we become more dependent on others and less self-sufficient. Foreign countries accumulate our dollars due to their high savings rates, and graciously loan them back to us at low interest rates to finance our excessive consumption.

It sounds like a great deal for everyone, except the time will come when our dollars—due to their depreciation—will be received less enthusiastically or even be rejected by foreign countries. That could create a whole new ball game and force us to pay a price for living beyond our means and our production. The shift in sentiment regarding the dollar has already started, but the worst is yet to come.

The agreement with OPEC in the 1970s to price oil in dollars has provided tremendous artificial strength to the dollar as the preeminent reserve currency. This has created a universal demand for the dollar, and soaks up the huge number of new dollars generated each year. Last year alone M3 increased over $700 billion.

The artificial demand for our dollar, along with our military might, places us in the unique position to "rule" the world without productive work or savings, and without limits on consumer spending or deficits. The problem is, it can't last.

Price inflation is raising its ugly head, and the NASDAQ bubble—generated by easy money—has burst. The housing bubble likewise created is deflating. Gold prices have doubled, and federal spending is out of sight with zero political will to rein it in. The trade deficit last year was over $728 billion. A $2 trillion war is raging, and plans are being laid to expand the war into Iran and possibly Syria. The only restraining force will be the world's rejection of the dollar. It's bound to come and create conditions worse than 1979–1980, which required 21 percent interest rates to correct. But everything possible will be done to protect the dollar in the meantime. We have a shared interest with those who hold our dollars to keep the whole charade going.

Greenspan, in his first speech after leaving the Fed, said that gold prices were up because of concern about terrorism, and not because of monetary concerns or because he created too many dollars during his tenure. Gold has to be discredited and the dollar propped up. Even when the dollar comes under serious attack by market forces, the central banks and the IMF surely will do everything conceivable to soak up the dollars in hope of restoring stability. Eventually they will fail.

Most importantly, the dollar/oil relationship has to be maintained to keep the dollar as a preeminent currency. Any attack on this relationship will be forcefully challenged—as it already has been.

In November 2000 Saddam Hussein demanded Euros for his oil. His arrogance was a threat to the dollar; his lack of any military might was never a threat. At the first cabinet meeting with the new administration in 2001, as reported by Treasury Secretary Paul O'Neill, the major topic was how we would get rid of Saddam Hussein—though there was no evidence whatsoever he posed a threat to us. This deep concern for Saddam Hussein surprised and shocked O'Neill.

It now is common knowledge that the immediate reaction of the administration after 9/11 revolved around how they could connect Saddam Hussein to the attacks, to justify an invasion and overthrow of his government. Even with no evidence of any connection to 9/11, or evidence of weapons of mass destruction, public and congressional support was generated through distortions and flat out misrepresentation of the facts to justify overthrowing Saddam Hussein.

There was no public talk of removing Saddam Hussein because of his attack on the integrity of the dollar as a reserve currency by selling oil in Euros. Many believe this was the real reason for our obsession with Iraq. I doubt it was the only reason, but it may well have played a significant role in our motivation to wage war. Within a very short period after the military victory, all Iraqi oil sales were carried out in dollars. The Euro was abandoned.

In 2001, Venezuela's ambassador to Russia spoke of Venezuela switching to the Euro for all their oil sales. Within a year there was a coup attempt against Chavez, reportedly with assistance from our CIA.

After these attempts to nudge the Euro toward replacing the dollar as the world's reserve currency were met with resistance, the sharp fall of the dollar against the Euro was reversed. These events may well have played a significant role in maintaining dollar dominance.

It's become clear the U.S. administration was sympathetic to those who plotted the overthrow of Chavez, and was embarrassed by its failure. The fact that Chavez was democratically elected had little influence on which side we supported.

Now, a new attempt is being made against the petrodollar system. Iran, another member of the "axis of evil," has announced her plans to initiate an oil bourse in March of this year. Guess what, the oil sales will be priced in Euros, not dollars.

Most Americans forget how our policies have systematically and needlessly antagonized the Iranians over the years. In 1953 the CIA helped overthrow a democratically elected president, Mohammed Mossadeqh, and install the authoritarian Shah, who was friendly to the U.S. The Iranians were still fuming over this when the hostages were seized in 1979. Our alliance with Saddam Hussein in his invasion of Iran in the early 1980s did not help matters, and obviously did not do much for our relationship with Saddam Hussein. The administration announcement in 2001 that Iran was part of the axis of evil didn't do much to improve the diplomatic relationship between our two countries. Recent threats over nuclear power, while ignoring the fact that they are surrounded by countries with nuclear weapons, doesn't seem to register with those who continue to provoke Iran. With what most Muslims perceive as our war against Islam, and this recent history, there's little wonder why Iran might choose to harm America by undermining the dollar. Iran, like Iraq, has zero capability to attack us. But that didn't stop us from turning Saddam Hussein into a modern day Hitler ready to take over the world. Now Iran, especially since she's made plans for pricing oil in Euros, has been on the receiving end of a propaganda war not unlike that waged against Iraq before our invasion.

It's not likely that maintaining dollar supremacy was the only motivating factor for the war against Iraq, nor for agitating against Iran. Though the real reasons for going to war are complex, we now know the reasons given before the war started, like the presence of weapons of mass destruction and Saddam Hussein's connection to 9/11, were false. The dollar's importance is obvious, but this does not diminish the influence of the distinct plans laid out years ago by the neoconservatives to remake the Middle East. Israel's influence, as well as that of the Christian Zionists, likewise played a role in prosecuting this war. Protecting "our" oil supplies has influenced our Middle East policy for decades.

But the truth is that paying the bills for this aggressive intervention is impossible the old fashioned way, with more taxes, more savings, and more production by the American people. Much of the expense of the Persian Gulf War in 1991 was shouldered by many of our willing allies. That's not so today. Now, more than ever, the dollar hegemony — its dominance as the world reserve currency — is required to finance our huge war expenditures. This $2 trillion never-ending war must be paid for, one way or another. Dollar hegemony provides the vehicle to do just that.

For the most part the true victims aren't aware of how they pay the bills. The license to create money out of thin air allows the bills to be paid through price inflation. American citizens, as well as average citizens of Japan, China, and other countries suffer from price inflation, which represents the "tax" that pays the bills for our military adventures. That is until the fraud is discovered, and the foreign producers decide not to take dollars nor hold them very long in payment for their goods. Everything possible is done to prevent the fraud of the monetary system from being exposed to the masses who suffer from it. If oil markets replace dollars with Euros, it would in time curtail our ability to continue to print, without restraint, the world's reserve currency.

It is an unbelievable benefit to us to import valuable goods and export depreciating dollars. The exporting countries have become addicted to our purchases for their economic growth. This dependency makes them allies in continuing the fraud, and their participation keeps the dollar's value artificially high. If this system were workable long-term, American citizens would never have to work again. We too could enjoy "bread and circuses" just as the Romans did, but their gold finally ran out and the inability of Rome to continue to plunder conquered nations brought an end to her empire.

The same thing will happen to us if we don't change our ways. Though we don't occupy foreign countries to directly plunder, we nevertheless have spread our troops across 130 nations of the world. Our intense effort to spread our power in the oil-rich Middle East is not a coincidence. But unlike the old days, we don't declare direct ownership of the natural resources — we just insist that we can buy what we want and pay for it with our paper money. Any country that challenges our authority does so at great risk.

Once again Congress has bought into the war propaganda against Iran, just as it did against Iraq. Arguments are now made for attacking Iran economically, and militarily if necessary. These arguments are all based on the same false reasons given for the ill-fated and costly occupation of Iraq.

Our whole economic system depends on continuing the current monetary arrangement, which means recycling the dollar is crucial. Currently, we borrow over $700 billion every year from our gracious benefactors, who work hard and take our paper for their goods. Then we borrow all the money we need to secure the empire (DOD budget $450 billion) plus more. The military might we enjoy becomes the "backing" of our currency. There are no other countries that can challenge our military superiority, and therefore they have little choice but to accept the dollars we declare are today's "gold." This is why countries that challenge the system—like Iraq, Iran, and Venezuela—become targets of our plans for regime change.

Ironically, dollar superiority depends on our strong military, and our strong military depends on the dollar. As long as foreign recipients take our dollars for real goods and are willing to finance our extravagant consumption and militarism, the *status quo* will continue regardless of how huge our foreign debt and current account deficit become.

But real threats come from our political adversaries who are incapable of confronting us militarily, yet are not bashful about confronting us economically. That's why we see the new challenge from Iran being taken so seriously. The urgent arguments about Iran posing a military threat to the security of the United States are no more plausible than the false charges levied against Iraq. Yet there is no effort to resist this march to confrontation by those who grandstand for political reasons against the Iraq war.

It seems that the people and Congress are easily persuaded by the jingoism of the preemptive war promoters. It's only after the cost in human life and dollars are tallied up that the people object to unwise militarism.

The strange thing is that the failure in Iraq is now apparent to a large majority of American people, yet they and Congress are acquiescing to the call for a needless and dangerous confrontation with Iran.

But then again, our failure to find Osama bin Laden and destroy his network did not dissuade us from taking on the Iraqis in a war totally unrelated to 9/11.

Concern for pricing oil only in dollars helps explain our willingness to drop everything and teach Saddam Hussein a lesson for his defiance in demanding Euros for oil.

And once again there's this urgent call for sanctions and threats of force against Iran at the precise time Iran is opening a new oil exchange with all transactions in Euros.

Using force to compel people to accept money without real value can only work in the short run. It ultimately leads to economic dislocation, both domestic and international, and always ends with a price to be paid.

The economic law that honest exchange demands only things of real value as currency cannot be repealed. The chaos that one day will ensue from our 35-year experiment with worldwide fiat money will require a return to money of real value. We will know that day is approaching when oil-producing countries demand gold, or its equivalent, for their oil rather than dollars or Euros. The sooner the better. ■

What the Price of Gold is Telling Us

Congressional Record – U.S. House of Representatives
April 25, 2006

The financial press, and even the network news shows, have begun reporting the price of gold regularly. For 20 years, between 1980 and 2000, the price of gold was rarely mentioned. There was little interest, and the price was either falling or remaining steady.

Since 2001, however, interest in gold has soared along with its price. With the price now over $600 an ounce, a lot more people are becoming interested in gold as an investment and an economic indicator. Much can be learned by understanding what the rising dollar price of gold means.

The rise in gold prices from $250 per ounce in 2001 to over $600 today has drawn investors and speculators into the precious metals market. Though many already have made handsome profits, buying gold *per se* should not be touted as a good investment. After all, gold earns no interest and its quality never changes. It's static, and does not grow as sound investments should.

It's more accurate to say that one might invest in a gold or silver mining company, where management, labor costs, and the nature of new discoveries all play a vital role in determining the quality of the investment and the profits made.

Buying gold and holding it is somewhat analogous to converting one's savings into one hundred dollar bills and hiding them under the mattress—yet not exactly the same. Both gold and dollars are considered money, and holding money does not qualify as an investment. There's a big difference between the two however, since by holding paper money one loses purchasing power. The purchasing power of commodity money, e.g., gold, however, goes up if the government devalues the circulating fiat currency.

Holding gold is protection or insurance against government's proclivity to debase its currency. The purchasing power of gold goes up not because it's a so-called good investment; it goes up in value only because the paper currency goes down in value. In our current situation, that means the dollar.

One of the characteristics of commodity money—one that originated naturally in the marketplace—is that it must serve as a store of value. Gold and silver meet that test—paper does not. Because of this profound difference, the incentive and wisdom of holding emergency funds in the form of gold becomes attractive when the official currency is being devalued. It's more attractive than trying to save wealth in the form of a fiat currency, even when earning some nominal interest. The lack of earned interest on gold is not a problem once people realize the purchasing power of their currency is declining faster than the interest rates they might earn. The purchasing power of gold can rise even faster than increases in the cost of living.

The point is that most who buy gold do so to protect against a depreciating currency rather than as an investment in the classical sense. Americans understand this less than citizens of other countries; some nations have suffered from severe monetary inflation that literally led to the destruction of their national currency. Though our inflation — i.e., the depreciation of the U.S. dollar — has been insidious, average Americans are unaware of how this occurs. For instance, few Americans know nor seem concerned that the 1913 pre-Federal Reserve dollar is now worth only four cents. Officially, our central bankers and our politicians express no fear that the course on which we are set is fraught with great danger to our economy and our political system. The belief that money created out of thin air can work economic miracles, if only properly "managed," is pervasive in D.C.

In many ways we shouldn't be surprised about this trust in such an unsound system. For at least four generations our government-run universities have systematically preached a monetary doctrine justifying the so-called wisdom of paper money over the "foolishness" of sound money. Not only that, paper money has worked surprisingly well in the past 35 years — the years the world has accepted pure paper money as currency. Alan Greenspan bragged that central bankers in these several decades have gained the knowledge necessary to make paper money respond as if it were gold. This removes the problem of obtaining gold to back currency, and hence frees politicians from the rigid discipline a gold standard imposes.

Many central bankers in the last 15 years became so confident they had achieved this milestone that they sold off large hoards of their gold reserves. At other times they tried to prove that paper works better than gold by artificially propping up the dollar by suppressing market gold prices. This recent deception failed just as it did in the 1960s, when our government tried to hold gold artificially low at $35 an ounce. But since they could not truly repeal the economic laws regarding money, just as many central bankers sold, others bought. It's fascinating that the European central banks sold gold while Asian central banks bought it over the last several years.

Since gold has proven to be the real money of the ages, we see once again a shift in wealth from the West to the East, just as we saw a loss of our industrial base in the same direction. Though Treasury officials deny any U.S. sales or loans of our official gold holdings, no audits are permitted so no one can be certain.

The special nature of the dollar as the reserve currency of the world has allowed this game to last longer than it would have otherwise. But the fact that gold has gone from $252 per ounce to over $600 means there is concern about the future of the dollar. The higher the price for gold, the greater the concern for the dollar. Instead of dwelling on the dollar price of gold, we should be talking about the depreciation of the dollar. In 1934 a dollar was worth 1/20th of an ounce of gold; $20 bought an ounce of gold. Today a dollar is worth 1/600th of an ounce of gold, meaning it takes $600 to buy one ounce of gold.

The number of dollars created by the Federal Reserve, and through the fractional reserve banking system, is crucial in determining how the market assesses the relationship of the dollar and gold. Though there's a strong correlation, it's not instantaneous or perfectly predictable. There are many variables to consider, but in the long term the dollar price of gold represents past inflation of the money supply. Equally important, it represents the anticipation of how much new money will be created in the future. This introduces the factor of trust and confidence in our monetary authorities and our politicians. And these days the American people are casting a vote of "no confidence" in this regard, and for good reasons.

The incentive for central bankers to create new money out of thin air is twofold. One is to practice central economic planning through the manipulation of interest rates. The second is to monetize the escalating federal debt politicians create and thrive on.

Today no one in Washington believes for a minute that runaway deficits are going to be curtailed. In March alone, the federal government created a historic $85 billion deficit. The current supplemental bill going through Congress has grown from $92 billion to over $106 billion, and everyone knows it will not draw President Bush's first veto. Most knowledgeable people therefore assume that inflation of the money supply is not only going to continue, but accelerate. This anticipation, plus the fact that many new dollars have been created over the past 15 years that have not yet been fully discounted, guarantees the further depreciation of the dollar in terms of gold.

There's no single measurement that reveals what the Fed has done in the recent past or tells us exactly what it's about to do in the future. Forget about the lip service given to transparency by new Fed Chairman Bernanke. Not only is this administration one of the most secretive across the board in our history, the current Fed firmly supports denying the most important measurement of current monetary policy to Congress, the financial community, and the American public. Because of a lack of interest and poor understanding of monetary policy, Congress has expressed essentially no concern about the significant change in reporting statistics on the money supply.

Beginning in March, though planned before Bernanke arrived at the Fed, the central bank discontinued compiling and reporting the monetary aggregate known as M3. M3 is the best description of how quickly the Fed is creating new money and credit. Common sense tells us that a government central bank creating new money out of thin air depreciates the value of each dollar in circulation. Yet this report is no longer available to us and Congress makes no demands to receive it.

Though M3 is the most helpful statistic to track Fed activity, it by no means tells us everything we need to know about trends in monetary policy. Total bank credit, still available to us, gives us indirect information reflecting the Fed's inflationary policies. But ultimately the markets will figure out exactly what the Fed is up to, and then individuals, financial institutions, governments, and other central bankers will act accordingly. The fact that our money supply is rising significantly cannot be hidden from the markets.

The response in time will drive the dollar down, while driving interest rates and commodity prices up. Already we see this trend developing, which surely will accelerate in the not too distant future. Part of this reaction will be from those who seek a haven to protect their wealth—not invest—by treating gold and silver as universal and historic money. This means holding fewer dollars that are decreasing in value while holding gold as it increases in value.

A soaring gold price is a vote of "no confidence" in the central bank and the dollar. This certainly was the case in 1979 and 1980. Today, gold prices reflect a growing restlessness with the increasing money supply, our budgetary and trade deficits, our unfunded liabilities, and the inability of Congress and the administration to rein in runaway spending.

Denying us statistical information, manipulating interest rates, and artificially trying to keep gold prices in check won't help in the long run. If the markets are fooled short term, it only means the adjustments will be much more dramatic later on. And in the meantime, other market imbalances develop.

The Fed tries to keep the consumer spending spree going, not through hard work and savings, but by creating artificial wealth in stock market bubbles and housing bubbles. When these distortions run their course and are discovered, the corrections will be quite painful.

Likewise, a fiat monetary system encourages speculation and unsound borrowing. As problems develop, scapegoats are sought and frequently found in foreign nations. This prompts many to demand altering exchange rates and protectionist measures. The sentiment for this type of solution is growing each day.

Though everyone decries inflation, trade imbalances, economic downturns, and federal deficits, few attempt a closer study of our monetary system and how these events are interrelated. Even if it were recognized that a gold standard without monetary inflation would be advantageous, few in Washington would accept the political disadvantages of living with the discipline of gold—since it serves as a check on government size and power. This is a sad commentary on the politics of today. The best analogy to our affinity for government spending, borrowing, and inflating is that of a drug addict who knows if he doesn't quit he'll die; yet he can't quit because of the heavy price required to overcome the dependency. The right choice is very difficult, but remaining addicted to drugs guarantees the death of the patient, while our addiction to deficit spending, debt, and inflation guarantees the collapse of our economy.

Special interest groups, who vigorously compete for federal dollars, want to perpetuate the system rather than admit to a dangerous addiction. Those who champion welfare for the poor, entitlements for the middle class, or war contracts for the military industrial corporations, all agree on the so-called benefits bestowed by the Fed's power to counterfeit fiat money. Bankers, who benefit from our fractional reserve system, likewise never criticize the Fed, especially since it's the lender of last resort that bails out financial institutions when crises arise. And it's true, special interests and bankers do benefit from the Fed, and may well get bailed out—just as we saw with the Long-Term Capital Management fund crisis a few years ago. In the past, companies like Lockheed and Chrysler benefited as well. But what the Fed cannot do is guarantee the market will maintain trust in the worthiness of the dollar. Current policy guarantees that the integrity of the dollar will be undermined. Exactly when this will occur, and the extent of the resulting damage to the financial system, cannot be known for sure—but it is coming. There are plenty of indications already on the horizon.

Foreign policy plays a significant role in the economy and the value of the dollar. A foreign policy of militarism and empire building cannot be supported through direct taxation. The American people would never tolerate the taxes required to pay immediately for overseas wars, under the discipline of a gold standard. Borrowing and creating new money is much more politically palatable. It hides and delays the real costs of war, and the people are lulled into complacency—especially since the wars we fight are couched in terms of patriotism, spreading the ideas of freedom, and stamping out terrorism. Unnecessary wars and fiat currencies go hand-in-hand, while a gold standard encourages a sensible foreign policy.

The cost of war is enormously detrimental; it significantly contributes to the economic instability of the nation by boosting spending, deficits, and inflation. Funds used for war are funds that could have remained in the productive economy to raise the standard of living of Americans now unemployed, underemployed, or barely living on the margin.

Yet even these costs may be preferable to paying for war with huge tax increases. This is because although fiat dollars are theoretically worthless, value is imbued by the trust placed in them by the world's financial community. Subjective trust in a currency can override objective knowledge about government policies, but only for a limited time.

Economic strength and military power contribute to the trust in a currency; in today's world trust in the U.S. dollar is not earned and therefore fragile. The history of the dollar, being as good as gold up until 1971, is helpful in maintaining an artificially higher value for the dollar than deserved.

Foreign policy contributes to the crisis when the spending to maintain our worldwide military commitments becomes prohibitive, and inflationary pressures accelerate. But the real crisis hits when the world realizes the king has no clothes, in that the dollar has no backing, and we face a military setback even greater than we already are experiencing in Iraq. Our token friends may quickly transform into vocal enemies once the attack on the dollar begins.

False trust placed in the dollar once was helpful to us, but panic and rejection of the dollar will develop into a real financial crisis. Then we will have no other option but to tighten our belts, go back to work, stop borrowing, start saving, and rebuild our industrial base, while adjusting to a lower standard of living for most Americans.

Counterfeiting the nation's money is a serious offense. The founders were especially adamant about avoiding the chaos, inflation, and destruction associated with the Continental dollar. That's why the Constitution is clear that only gold and silver should be legal tender in the United States. In 1792 the Coinage Act authorized the death penalty for any private citizen who counterfeited the currency. Too bad they weren't explicit that counterfeiting by government officials is just as detrimental to the economy and the value of the dollar.

In wartime, many nations actually operated counterfeiting programs to undermine our dollar, but never to a disastrous level. The enemy knew how harmful excessive creation of new money could be to the dollar and our economy. But it seems we never learned the dangers of creating new money out of thin air. We don't need an Arab nation or the Chinese to undermine our system with a counterfeiting operation. We do it ourselves, with all the disadvantages that would occur if others did it to us. Today we hear threats from some Arab, Muslim, and far Eastern countries about undermining the dollar system—not by dishonest counterfeiting, but by initiating an alternative monetary system based on gold. Wouldn't that be ironic? Such an event theoretically could do great harm to us. This day may well come, not so much as a direct political attack on the dollar system but out of necessity to restore confidence in money once again.

Historically, paper money never has lasted for long periods of time, while gold has survived thousands of years of attacks by political interests and big government. In time, the world once again will restore trust in the monetary system by making some currency as good as gold.

Gold, or any acceptable market commodity money, is required to preserve liberty. Monopoly control by government of a system that creates fiat money out of thin air guarantees the loss of liberty. No matter how well-intended our militarism is portrayed, or how happily the promises of wonderful programs for the poor are promoted, inflating the money supply to pay these bills makes government bigger. Empires always fail, and expenses always exceed projections. Harmful unintended consequences are the rule, not the exception. Welfare for the poor is inefficient and wasteful. The beneficiaries are rarely the poor themselves, but instead the politicians, bureaucrats, or the wealthy. The same is true of all foreign aid—it's nothing more than a program that steals from the poor in a rich country and gives to the rich leaders of a poor country. Whether it's war or welfare payments, it always means higher taxes, inflation, and debt. Whether it's the extraction of wealth from the productive economy, the distortion of the market by interest rate manipulation, or spending for war and welfare, it can't happen without infringing upon personal liberty.

At home the war on poverty, terrorism, drugs, or foreign rulers provides an opportunity for authoritarians to rise to power, individuals who think nothing of violating the people's rights to privacy and freedom of speech. They believe their role is to protect the secrecy of government, rather than protect the privacy of citizens. Unfortunately, that is the atmosphere under which we live today, with essentially no respect for the Bill of Rights.

Though great economic harm comes from a government monopoly fiat monetary system, the loss of liberty associated with it is equally troubling. Just as empires are self-limiting in terms of money and manpower, so too is a monetary system based on illusion and fraud. When the end comes we will be given an opportunity to choose once again between honest money and liberty on one hand; chaos, poverty, and authoritarianism on the other.

The economic harm done by a fiat monetary system is pervasive, dangerous, and unfair. Though runaway inflation is injurious to almost everyone, it is more insidious for certain groups. Once inflation is recognized as a tax, it becomes clear the tax is regressive: penalizing the poor and middle class more than the rich and politically privileged. Price inflation, a consequence of inflating the money supply by the central bank, hits poor and marginal workers first and foremost. It especially penalizes savers, retirees, those on fixed incomes, and anyone who trusts government promises. Small businesses and individual enterprises suffer more than the financial elite, who borrow large sums before the money loses value. Those who are on the receiving end of government contracts—especially in the military industrial complex during wartime—receive undeserved benefits.

It's a mistake to blame high gasoline and oil prices on price gouging. If we impose new taxes or fix prices, while ignoring monetary inflation, corporate subsidies, and excessive regulations, shortages will result. The market is the only way to determine the best price for any commodity. The law of supply and demand cannot be repealed. The real problems arise when government planners give subsidies to energy companies and favor one form of energy over another.

Energy prices are rising for many reasons: inflation; increased demand from China and India; decreased supply resulting from our invasion of Iraq; anticipated disruption of supply as we push regime change in Iran; regulatory restrictions on gasoline production; government interference in the free market development of alternative fuels; and subsidies to big oil such as free leases and grants for research and development.

Interestingly, the cost of oil and gas is actually much higher than we pay at the retail level. Much of the DOD budget is spent protecting "our" oil supplies, and if such spending is factored in gasoline probably costs us more than $5 a gallon. The sad irony is that this military effort to secure cheap oil supplies inevitably backfires, and actually curtails supplies and boosts prices at the pump. The waste and fraud in issuing contracts to large corporations for work in Iraq only adds to price increases.

When problems arise under conditions that exist today, it's a serious error to blame the little bit of the free market that still functions. Last summer the market worked efficiently after Katrina — gas hit $3 a gallon, but soon supplies increased, usage went down, and the price returned to $2. In the 1980s, market forces took oil from $40 per barrel to $10 per barrel, and no one cried for the oil companies that went bankrupt. Today's increases are for the reasons mentioned above. It's natural for labor to seek its highest wage, and businesses to strive for the greatest profit. That's the way the market works. When the free market is allowed to work, it's the consumer who ultimately determines price and quality, with labor and business accommodating consumer choices. Once this process is distorted by government, prices rise excessively, labor costs and profits are negatively affected, and problems emerge. Instead of fixing the problem, politicians and demagogues respond by demanding windfall profits taxes and price controls, while never questioning how previous government interference caused the whole mess in the first place. Never let it be said that higher oil prices and profits cause inflation; inflation of the money supply causes higher prices!

Since keeping interest rates below market levels is synonymous with new money creation by the Fed, the resulting business cycle, higher cost of living, and job losses all can be laid at the doorstep of the Fed. This burden hits the poor the most, making Fed taxation by inflation the worst of all regressive taxes. Statistics about revenues generated by the income tax are grossly misleading; in reality much harm is done by our welfare-warfare system supposedly designed to help the poor and tax the rich. Only sound money can rectify the blatant injustice of this destructive system.

The Founders understood this great danger, and voted overwhelmingly to reject "emitting bills of credit," the term they used for paper or fiat money. It's too bad the knowledge and advice of our Founders, and their mandate in the Constitution, are ignored today at our great peril. The current surge in gold prices — which reflects our dollar's devaluation — is warning us to pay closer attention to our fiscal, monetary, entitlement, and foreign policy.

Meaning of the Gold Price – Summation

A recent headline in the financial press announced that gold prices surged over concern that confrontation with Iran will further push oil prices higher. This may well reflect the current situation, but higher gold prices mainly reflect monetary expansion by the Federal Reserve. Dwelling on current events and their effect on gold prices reflects concern for symptoms rather than an understanding of the actual cause of these price increases. Without an enormous increase in the money supply over the past 35 years and a worldwide paper monetary system, this increase in the price of gold would not have occurred.

Certainly geopolitical events in the Middle East under a gold standard would not alter its price, though they could affect the supply of oil and cause oil prices to rise. Only under conditions created by excessive paper money would one expect all or most prices to rise. This is a mere reflection of the devaluation of the dollar.

Particular things to remember:

- If one endorses small government and maximum liberty, one must support commodity money.

- One of the strongest restraints against unnecessary war is a gold standard.

- Deficit financing by government is severely restricted by sound money.

- The harmful effects of the business cycle are virtually eliminated with an honest gold standard.

- Saving and thrift are encouraged by a gold standard; and discouraged by paper money.

- Price inflation, with generally rising price levels, is characteristic of paper money. Reports that the consumer price index and the producer price index are rising are distractions: the real cause of inflation is the Fed's creation of new money.

- Interest rate manipulation by a central bank helps the rich, the banks, the government, and the politicians.

- Paper money permits the regressive inflation tax to be passed off on the poor and the middle class.

- Speculative financial bubbles are characteristic of paper money — not gold.

- Paper money encourages economic and political chaos, which subsequently causes a search for scapegoats rather than blaming the central bank.

- Dangerous protectionist measures frequently are implemented to compensate for the dislocations caused by fiat money.

- Paper money, inflation, and the conditions they create contribute to the problems of illegal immigration.

- The value of gold is remarkably stable.

- The dollar price of gold reflects dollar depreciation.

- Holding gold helps preserve and store wealth, but technically gold is not a true investment.

- Since 2001 the dollar has been devalued by 60 percent.

- In 1934 FDR devalued the dollar by 41 percent.

- In 1971 Nixon devalued the dollar by 7.9 percent.

- In 1973 Nixon devalued the dollar by 10 percent.

These were momentous monetary events, and every knowledgeable person worldwide paid close attention. Major changes were endured in 1979 and 1980 to save the dollar from disintegration. This involved a severe recession, interest rates over 21 percent, and general price inflation of 15 percent.

Today we face a 60 percent devaluation and counting, yet no one seems to care. It's of greater significance than the last three events mentioned above. And yet the one measurement that best reflects the degree of inflation, the Fed and our government deny us. Since March, M3 reporting has been discontinued. For starters, I'd like to see Congress demand that this report be resumed. I fully believe the American people and Congress are entitled to this information. Will we one day complain about false intelligence, as we have with the Iraq war? Will we complain about not having enough information to address monetary policy after it's too late?

If ever there was a time to get a handle on what sound money is and what it means, that time is today.

Inflation, as exposed by high gold prices, transfers wealth from the middle class to the rich, as real wages decline while the salaries of CEOs, movie stars, and athletes skyrocket—along with the profits of the military industrial complex, the oil industry, and other special interests.

A sharply rising gold price is a vote of "no confidence" in Congress's ability to control the budget, the Fed's ability to control the money supply, and the administration's ability to bring stability to the Middle East.

Ultimately, the gold price is a measurement of trust in the currency and the politicians who run the country. It's been that way for a long time, and is not about to change.

If we care about the financial system, the tax system, and the monumental debt we're accumulating, we must start talking about the benefits and discipline that come only with a commodity standard of money—money the government and central banks absolutely cannot create out of thin air.

Economic law dictates reform at some point. But should we wait until the dollar is 1/1,000 of an ounce of gold or 1/2,000 of an ounce of gold? The longer we wait, the more people suffer and the more difficult reforms become. Runaway inflation inevitably leads to political chaos, something numerous countries have suffered throughout the 20th century. The worst example of course was the German inflation of the 1920s that led to the rise of Hitler. Even the communist takeover of China was associated with runaway inflation brought on by Chinese Nationalists. The time for action is now, and it is up to the American people and the U.S. Congress to demand it. ■

Monetary Policy and the State of the Economy

House Financial Services Committee
Congressional Record – U.S. House of Representatives
February 15, 2007

Transparency in monetary policy is a goal we should all support. I've often wondered why Congress so willingly has given up its prerogative over monetary policy. Astonishingly, Congress in essence has ceded total control over the value of our money to a secretive central bank.

Congress created the Federal Reserve, yet it had no constitutional authority to do so. We forget that those powers not explicitly granted to Congress by the Constitution are inherently denied to Congress—and thus the authority to establish a central bank never was given. Of course Jefferson and Hamilton had that debate early on, a debate seemingly settled in 1913.

But transparency and oversight are something else, and they're worth considering. Congress, although not by law, essentially has given up all its oversight responsibility over the Federal Reserve. There are no true audits, and Congress knows nothing of the conversations, plans, and actions taken in concert with other central banks. We get less and less information regarding the money supply each year, especially now that M3 is no longer reported.

The role the Fed plays in the President's secretive Working Group on Financial Markets goes unnoticed by members of Congress. The Federal Reserve shows no willingness to inform Congress voluntarily about how often the Working Group meets, what actions it takes that affect the financial markets, or why it takes those actions.

But these actions, directed by the Federal Reserve, alter the purchasing power of our money. And that purchasing power is always reduced. The dollar today is worth only 4 cents compared to the dollar in 1913, when the Federal Reserve started. This has profound consequences for our economy and our political stability. All paper currencies are vulnerable to collapse, and history is replete with examples of great suffering caused by such collapses, especially to a nation's poor and middle class. This leads to political turmoil.

Even before a currency collapse occurs, the damage done by a fiat system is significant. Our monetary system insidiously transfers wealth from the poor and middle class to the privileged rich. Wages never keep up with the profits of Wall Street and the banks, thus sowing the seeds of class discontent. When economic trouble hits, free markets and free trade often are blamed, while the harmful effects of a fiat monetary system are ignored. We deceive ourselves that all is well with the economy, and ignore the fundamental flaws that are a source of growing discontent among those who have not shared in the abundance of recent years.

Few understand that our consumption and apparent wealth is dependent on a current account deficit of $800 billion per year. This deficit shows that much of our prosperity is based on borrowing rather than a true increase in production. Statistics show year after year that our productive manufacturing jobs continue to go overseas. This phenomenon is not seen as a consequence of the international fiat monetary system, where the United States government benefits as the issuer of the world's reserve currency.

Government officials consistently claim that inflation is in check at barely 2 percent, but middle class Americans know that their purchasing power—especially when it comes to housing, energy, medical care, and school tuition—is shrinking much faster than 2 percent each year.

Even if prices were held in check, in spite of our monetary inflation, concentrating on CPI distracts from the real issue. We must address the important consequences of Fed manipulation of interest rates. When interests rates are artificially low, below market rates, insidious malinvestment and excessive indebtedness inevitably bring about the economic downturn that everyone dreads.

We look at GDP numbers to reassure ourselves that all is well, yet a growing number of Americans still do not enjoy the higher standard of living that monetary inflation brings to the privileged few. Those few have access to the newly created money first, before its value is diluted.

For example: Before the breakdown of the Bretton Woods system, CEO income was about 30 times the average worker's pay. Today, it's closer to 500 times. It's hard to explain this simply by market forces and increases in productivity. One Wall Street firm last year gave out bonuses totaling $16.5 billion. There's little evidence that this represents free market capitalism.

In 2006 dollars, the minimum wage was $9.50 before the 1971 breakdown of Bretton Woods. Today that dollar is worth $5.15. Congress congratulates itself for raising the minimum wage by mandate, but in reality it has lowered the minimum wage by allowing the Fed to devalue the dollar. We must consider how the growing inequalities created by our monetary system will lead to social discord.

GDP purportedly is now growing at 3.5 percent, and everyone seems pleased. What we fail to understand is how much government entitlement spending contributes to the increase in the GDP. Rebuilding infrastructure destroyed by hurricanes, which simply gets us back to even, is considered part of GDP growth. Wall Street profits and salaries, pumped up by the Fed's increase in money, also contribute to GDP statistical growth. Just buying military weapons that contribute nothing to the well being of our citizens, sending money down a rat hole, contributes to GDP growth! Simple price increases caused by Fed monetary inflation contribute to nominal GDP growth. None of these factors represent any kind of real increases in economic output. So we should not carelessly cite misleading GDP figures which don't truly reflect what is happening in the economy. Bogus GDP figures explain in part why so many people are feeling squeezed despite our supposedly booming economy.

But since our fiat dollar system is not going away anytime soon, it would benefit Congress and the American people to bring more transparency to how and why Fed monetary policy functions.

For starters, the Federal Reserve should:

- *Begin publishing the M3 statistics again.* Let us see the numbers that most accurately reveal how much new money the Fed is pumping into the world economy.

- *Tell us exactly what the President's Working Group on Financial Markets does and why.*

- *Explain how interest rates are set.* Conservatives profess to support free markets, without wage and price controls. Yet the most important price of all, the price of money as determined by interest rates, is set arbitrarily in secret by the Fed rather than by markets! Why is this policy written in stone? Why is there no congressional input at least?

- *Change legal tender laws to allow constitutional legal tender (commodity money) to compete domestically with the dollar.*

How can a policy of steadily debasing our currency be defended morally, knowing what harm it causes to those who still believe in saving money and assuming responsibility for themselves in their retirement years? Is it any wonder we are a nation of debtors rather than savers?

We need more transparency in how the Federal Reserve carries out monetary policy, and we need it soon. ■

Chinese Currency

Committee on Financial Services
Congressional Record – U.S. House of Representatives
May 9, 2007

The imbalances in international trade, and in particular trade between China and the United States, have prompted many to demand a realignment of the Chinese yuan and the American dollar. Since we are running a huge trade deficit with China the call now is for a stronger yuan and a weaker dollar. This trade imbalance problem will not be solved so easily.

If a stronger yuan is implemented, increased exports to China from the U.S. may or may not result. The weaker dollar will lead to higher U.S. prices and crowd out the hoped-for benefits of a realignment of the two currencies.

One thing certain is that the immediate impact would be higher prices for consumer goods for middle class Americans. In many ways a weaker dollar would act as an import tax just as if it were a tariff. Both are considered protectionist in nature.

The fact that the Chinese keep their currency artificially weak is a benefit to American consumers and in the long term is inflationary for the Chinese.

This deep and legitimate concern for the trade imbalance between China and the U.S. will fall short if the issue of fluctuating, worldwide fiat currencies, is not addressed.

The fact that the U.S. dollar is the principal reserve currency of the world gives us a benefit that others do not enjoy. It allows us to export paper dollars and import goods manufactured in countries with cheap labor. It also allows us to finance the welfare-warfare state with cheap loans from China and Japan. It's a good deal for us but according to economic law must come to an end, and the end will be messy for the U.S. consumer and for world trade.

The current system can only last as long as the trust in the dollar is maintained and foreigners are willing to accept them as if they had real value.

Ironically, the most serious problem we face is a sharply weakening dollar, in danger of collapse, and yet many are now asking for a policy, dealing with the Chinese, that would accelerate the dollar's decline. And yet we're told that we maintain a strong dollar policy.

Financing deficits with monetary inflation is in itself a weak dollar policy in the long term. Trust in our currency due to our economic and military strength artificially props up the dollar on international exchange markets. Since these benefits come not from production or sound money policies, they only contribute to the instability and imbalances in international trade.

Neither tariffs nor forced devaluations can solve the problem.

Our current account deficit and huge foreign indebtedness is a reflection of the world monetary system of fiat money. The longer the trade imbalances last, the more difficult the adjustment will be. The market will eventually force these adjustments on us.

Eventually it will be necessary to consider commodity-based money to solve the trade imbalances that concern so many here in the Congress. ■

Financial Services Paulson Hearing

Committee on Financial Services Paulson Hearing
Congressional Record — U.S. House of Representatives
June 20, 2007

A strong case can be made that our economy is not nearly as robust as our government statistics claim.

Unemployment numbers, inflation rates, tax revenues, and GDP growth all indicate there is little to worry about.

Yet underemployment and a lower standard of living for many Americans hit with significant price inflation leave them fearful of their economic future.

The shake-up in the subprime mortgage market which is now spreading, as the housing bubble deflates, has a long way to go. The same problem exists in the high-yield corporate debt market and will surely add to the economic uncertainty we now face. It's deceptive to merely blame "abusive lending practices" for these problems.

The recent sharp rise in interest rates may well be signaling the end to the painless easy money decade that has allowed us to finance our extravagant welfare-warfare spending with minimal productive effort and no savings. Monetary inflation and foreign borrowing have allowed us to live far beyond our means — a type of monetary arrangement that always comes to a painful end.

As our problems worsen, the blame game will certainly accelerate. Claiming it is all due to China's manipulation of its currency and demanding protectionist measures will unfortunately continue to gain considerable attention. Unfortunately, there is little or no concern for how our own policies—monetary, tax, and regulatory—have contributed to the problems we face.

Too often officials ignore and even distort important economic information that could be beneficial in making market decisions.

Accurate money supply growth rates are vital in anticipating future price levels, the degree of malinvestment, and chances for financial bubbles to form. Since March of 2006 M3 reports have been discontinued. Private sources now report that M3 is increasing at a significantly high 13 percent rate.

It is said that the CPI is now increasing at the rate of 2.5 percent, yet if we use the original method of calculation we find that the CPI is growing at a rate of over 10 percent.

Since money growth statistics are key to calculating currency depreciation it is interesting to note, in this era of global financial markets, in a world engulfed with only fiat currencies, what total worldwide money supply is doing.

Since 1997 the world money supply has doubled. And money growth *is* inflation which is the enemy of the poor and the middle class but a friend to the banks and Wall Street.

Monetary depreciation is clearly a sinister tax placed on the unsuspecting poor. Too many well meaning individuals falsely believe that deficit financed assistance programs can help the poor, while instead the results are opposite.

Welfare and warfare—guns and butter philosophy always leads to harmful inflation. We had severe problems in the '60s and '70s and we are doing the same thing once again. We have only started to pay for the extravagance of financing the current war and rapidly expanding the entitlement system by foreign borrowing and creating money and credit out of thin air. There are reasons to believe that the conditions we have created will be much worse than they were in 1979 when interest rates of 21 percent were required to settle the markets and reverse the stagflation process.

Congress, and especially the Financial Services Committee, must insist on total transparency and accuracy of all government financial statistics. Any market interference by government agencies must be done in full public view.

All meetings and decisions and actions by the President's Working Group on Financial Markets must be fully open to public scrutiny. If our government is artificially propping up the dollar by directly manipulating gold prices, or colluding with other central banks, it is information that belongs in the public domain. The same is true about any interference in the stock, bond, or commodity markets.

A free market economy requires that government keeps its hands off and allows the consumers to exert their rightful control over the economy. ■

PART SIX

Free Trade: Real versus Phony

Politicians, especially my fellow Republicans, love to talk about free trade. But true free trade doesn't require complicated treaties or subsidies to favored domestic producers, it simply means eliminating taxes on U.S. consumers who want to buy foreign goods. Ironically, the same people who promote (phony) "free trade" policies also downplay the massive trade deficits that we have been running in recent years, as a consequence of the Fed's expansion of the money supply and the federal government's borrowing binge.

Our Soaring Trade Deficit Cannot Be Ignored

Congressional Record – U.S. House of Representatives
April 9, 1997

Mr. Speaker, the business cycle has not yet been repealed, but if we did the right thing in the Congress, I believe we could do a lot to alleviate the great harm done by the business cycle.

Mr. Speaker, artificially low interest rates are the culprit in the government created boom-bust cycle. Federally regulated low rates cause bad business decisions, confuse consumers and encourage debt. These distortions prompt market corrections which bring on our slumps.

In recent years the artificially low interest rates that banks pay on savings have served to reduce savings. In the 1970s savings were low because it was perceived that the money was rapidly losing its purchasing power. It was better to spend than to save. As money leaves savings accounts it frequently goes into stocks and bonds adding fuel to the financial bubble which has been developing now for over 15 years. Domestic and foreign central bank purchases of our Treasury debt further serve to distort and drive interest rates below the market level.

Our soaring trade deficit is something that cannot be ignored. In January there was a negative trade deficit in goods of more than $19 billion, the highest in our history. Our deficit has now been running over $100 billion for several years, and the artificially strong dollar has encouraged this imbalance. Temporarily a negative trade balance is a benefit to American consumers by holding down price inflation here at home and allowing foreigners to finance our extravagance. These trends will end once confidence is shattered and the dollar starts to lose value on the international exchange markets.

The tragedy is that there are very few in Congress interested in this issue. Even in the Committee on Banking and Financial Services I hear very little concern expressed about the long-term weakness of the dollar, yet economic law dictates that persistent negative trade imbalances eventually have to be corrected; it is only a matter of time.

I suspect in the next several years Congress will be truly challenged. The high level of frustration in this body comes from the fact that the large majority are not yet willing to give up the principles upon which the welfare state exists. Eventually an economic crisis will force all Americans, including Congress, to face up to the serious problems that we have generated for ourselves over the past 50 years.

I expect deficits to explode and not come down. I suspect the economy is much weaker than is currently claimed. In the not too distant future we will be in a serious recession. Under these circumstances the demand for spending will override all other concerns. In spite of current dollar euphoria, dollar weakness will become the economic event of the late 1990s. Consumers and entitlement recipients will face the problem of stagflation, probably worse than we saw in the 1970s. I expect very few in Congress to see the monetary side of this problem.

The welfare state will be threatened, and yet the consensus will remain that what is needed is more revenues to help alleviate the suffering, more Federal Reserve monetary stimulus to the economy, more price controls, which we already have in medicine, higher taxes, and protectionism.

Soon it will be realized that NAFTA and GATT were not free trade treaties, but only an international effort at trade management for the benefit of special interests. Ask any home builder how protectionist sentiment adds several thousands of dollars to the cost of a home by keeping out cheaper Canadian lumber in spite of NAFTA's pretense at free trade.

The solution to this mess is not complex. It is however politically difficult to overcome the *status quo* and the conventional wisdom of our intellectual leaders and the media. What we need is a limited government designed for the protection of liberty. We need minimal control over our nation's wealth, not the more than 50-percent of government control that we currently have. Regulatory control in minutiae, as we have today, must end. Voluntary contracts need to be honored once again. None of this will work unless we have a currency that cannot be debased and a tax system that does not tax income, savings, capital gains, estates, or success.

Although it will be difficult to go from one form of government to another, there will be much less suffering if we go rapidly in the direction of more freedom rather than a protracted effort to save the welfare state. *Perestroika* and *glasnost* did not save communism. Block grants, a line item veto and a balanced budget amendment will not save the welfare state. ∎

Ron Paul Amendment to Cut Corporate Welfare

Debate from Foreign Operations, Export Financing, and Related Programs Appropriations Act, 1997
Congressional Record – U.S. House of Representatives
July 30, 1997

"Reductions in Amounts"

"Each amount otherwise provided in this title is hereby reduced to $0."

Mr. Chairman, earlier in the debate on the previous amendment, the gentleman from California [Mr. Rohrabacher] suggested that there was one problem with the Royce amendment. He said it just does not go far enough.

I have an amendment that will go far enough to deal with this entire problem of corporate welfare. My amendment strikes all the funding from title I. This means that the $632 million that goes to the Export-Import Bank, the $32 million that goes to OPIC, and the $40 million that goes to the Trade and Development Agency would be struck. This would not close these agencies down. We have heard on numerous occasions already today that OPIC and other agencies like OPIC are obviously self-supporting. If they are self-supporting, they need no more appropriations. They can use the current funding, they can be privatized. This whole idea that they come with the argument that they are self-supporting and self-sustaining and that they make a profit, there is no purpose in being here. Why do they come to the American people and ask in this particular bill for export subsidies of $704 million? My amendment would strike the $704 million. These three agencies have liabilities of well over $100 billion and this would be eliminated.

One of the reasons the argument is made that these agencies are self-sustaining is that they hold Treasury bills, which means that they receive huge sums of money through the back door through interest payments. This money is not appropriated for the specific purpose, but as long as they hold Treasury bills they get the interest payments. For instance, I mentioned earlier that OPIC in 1996 received $166 million in this manner. Self-sustaining, it is not.

We should really ask if this is good economic policy. Quite frankly, it is not good economic policy. It encourages businesspeople to do the wrong things at the taxpayers' risk.

It is mentioned that these programs are available in the private sector but they will not go into the risky areas. Obviously not. OPIC, for instance, goes into countries, and what the American people have to assume is the risk against political risk and economic risk. So if these companies go bust, the American taxpayers have to stand behind them. We have a misdirection of the economy and the misdirection of investment because we get companies to do things more risky than they would have otherwise. If they want to go into a more risky area, the private insurance would obviously be higher, so therefore this is a subsidy to corporations.

There is no reason why we should support this type of welfare. There are several kinds of welfare. We have welfare for the poor, we have welfare for the foreigners, and we have welfare for the corporations. I do not think the correct place to try to solve our problem on welfare is to go after the poor man's welfare, but we can go after foreign welfare and we can go after corporate welfare, and this is an example of corporate and foreign welfare.

It is said that with these programs there is never any loss to the taxpayers. That is a bit of a fallacy, because the loss to the taxpayers is when we take the money from the taxpayer, so they are losing all the time. Most little people never get benefits from this. It is the large corporations that lobby us so heavily to endorse these programs. There are not that many loans that default.

But there is another reason why we do not have that many loan defaults, because they quickly renew these loans at different terms.

There is a lot of generous renewing of loans and therefore the default level is very, very low, if we see it at all. But the risk is there. The real risk to the American taxpayer is when we tax the Americans to go and encourage programs like this. The assumption is made that if we do not do it, it will not happen. Maybe not, maybe it will. If it does not happen, maybe it is too risky. But most of it still would happen; it would be insured in the private sector and many of these programs would occur.

To get up and say A, B, and C company would not have existed and could not have done this is not correct because we do not know. The other thing we do not know is who suffered from this credit allocation. When the government gets involved in credit allocation, in saying this credit is guaranteed and should go in this direction, every time there is $10 billion going in that direction, it comes out of the private sector and some little guy lost his credit. So obviously the banks are going to loan to the people that have a guarantee.

Another area that we should address here is the subject of who gets these loans. For instance, one of the biggest beneficiaries is China. Red China gets over $4 billion. That in itself is enough reason to vote for this amendment and reject corporate welfare on principle.

Mr. CALLAHAN. Mr. Chairman, I rise in opposition to the amendment.

Once again, Mr. Chairman, this amendment is intended to destroy the Eximbank which might sound good and might look good on the back of a bumper sticker, but it would be a tremendous mistake for literally tens of thousands of working American people who are working today as a result of the fact that we are doing business in some overseas countries. If indeed my colleagues believe that we are not in a global economy, then my colleagues ought to do exactly what the gentleman from Texas said: build a wall around the United States of America. Let us not let anybody in and let us not let anybody out, let us not ship any of our equipment overseas.

Let us talk about General Electric. What kind of generators do Members think they use if GE builds a plant in a foreign country? They use a GE generator built by American workers, built by American workers who take that money home and support their families and support my colleagues through their taxes that they pay.

So if my colleagues want to close down America, if they do not want to do business overseas, if they really in their heart believe that a global economy is not the future of this country, then my colleagues ought to abolish the Eximbank and they ought to abolish OPIC as well.

But unfortunately, if the gentleman will read the newspapers, watch television, look at world affairs, attend some of the committee hearings that we have, when we hear the testimony of the Eximbank and these various agencies, he will learn that we are exporting our jobs overseas by letting them work in Texas, by letting them work in Alabama, in California. They are taking that money to their homes and we are shipping our generators and our products to them overseas simply because we have provided for our businesspeople the same thing that the French, the British, the Germans, the Japanese have provided to theirs. Not as much, I grant the gentleman. They still give them much more. They subsidize theirs. We do not subsidize these.

So, yes, if the gentleman wants to shut the world down as far as the United States is concerned and abolish all these; but it would be very, very unwise to do that. I would encourage my colleagues to recognize that and to vote against the gentleman's amendment.

Mr. PAUL. Mr. Chairman, will the gentleman yield?

Mr. CALLAHAN. I yield to the gentleman from Texas.

Mr. PAUL. Japan subsidizes 32 percent of their exports and we only subsidize a small amount, only 2 percent. So I guess I would be complaining a lot more if I lived in Japan because they do so much more; but if we look at the economic growth of Japan, now it is less than 1 percent and we are doing better. We have economic growth of 4 percent.

Mr. CALLAHAN. If I may reclaim my time, that is because they are doing too much. We are not doing too much. We are trying to facilitate our businesspeople in this country the opportunity to make them competitive doing business in foreign countries. If that is wrong, then I am wrong. But I am not wrong. The gentleman is wrong in trying to abolish this agency.

Ms. PELOSI. Mr. Chairman, I move to strike the last word, and I rise in opposition to the amendment of our distinguished colleague from Texas.

Mr. Chairman, this is a most unfortunate amendment, because it strikes right to the heart of eliminating title I of our bill, which is an important part of our foreign operations legislation. Eximbank, Overseas Private Investment Corporation, Trade and Development Agency programs help create more and better-paying U.S. jobs through exports. Each of these agencies has a distinct role in the administration's effort to increase U.S. exports. Increasing U.S. exports is a major pillar of our foreign policy and these agencies help do that. Every one of our major industrial competitors have publicly supported counterparts to Exim, OPIC, and TDA. Virtually all of our competitors fund their trade and investment finance agencies at a higher level than we do. Failure to fully fund Exim, OPIC, and TDA would severely handicap our exporters as they battle for market share in the key fast-growing markets. Exports create more and higher-paying jobs, support the creation of American jobs by promoting exports. Vote against this amendment.

Mr. PAUL. Mr. Chairman, will the gentlewoman yield?

Ms. PELOSI. I yield to the gentleman from Texas.

Mr. PAUL. Could the gentlewoman cite the constitutional authority for programs like this? Where did we get this authority? When did we get involved in doing this? I am confused on that constitutional issue.

Ms. PELOSI. I would not be able to cite the constitutional authority. I know the gentleman is well known for his opposition to any spending bills, but I think the question that he asks is an appropriate one to ask every Member who speaks on the floor, because these agencies of government create jobs and return revenue to our Treasury.

I would like to address one of the points the gentleman made in his remarks. He said if they are so self-sustaining, why are they not privatized, or words to that effect.

I think it is very important that this is part of our national export program, that we be able to participate in the program level and have a control on the operating expenses so that all of the funds that are put to this end are well spent and that they promote the most exports, create the most jobs, and increase the vitality and dynamism of our own economy.

Mr. PAUL. If the gentlewoman will continue to yield, I think that is a noble gesture to mix business and government, but some people are hesitant to do that, to supervise what businesses are doing.

Ms. PELOSI. Reclaiming my time, the point was not to mix business and government. The point was to promote U.S. exports abroad and to recognize the realities of the global economy, where all of the countries, the developed countries of the world and the developing countries, are very competitive for the market share out there. It is very important for us in those particular instances where, for example, OPIC would be necessary, assessing the risk very carefully so as not to put the U.S. taxpayers' dollars at an extraordinary risk, but where the calibration is such that we need OPIC's participation, or Eximbank's participation or TDA's promotion, that we give some opportunity to U.S. business to make the playing field more level. As I have said in my remarks, we do not come close to what many countries do to help promote exports, but at least we can participate in promoting exports.

Mr. PAUL. If the gentlewoman will yield further, I think earlier she said that it would be an appropriate question to ask for constitutional authority and suggested that this is a good idea, and I would like to emphasize that we do it more often.

Mr. FOGLIETTA. Mr. Chairman, will the gentlewoman yield?

Ms. PELOSI. I yield to the gentleman from Pennsylvania.

Mr. FOGLIETTA. I think if the gentleman reads the question, he will find that the Constitution calls upon the Congress to promote the general welfare of this nation. I think by increasing trade and creating jobs, we are promoting the general welfare of our nation.

Mr. PAUL. If the gentlewoman will yield further, this is frequently cited as a constitutional authority to do almost anything. But let me be specific to point out to the gentleman that we are not dealing with the general welfare. We are dealing with the very specific welfare of General Electric and other big companies at the expense of the general welfare of the taxpayers who are paying the money.

Ms. PELOSI. Reclaiming my time, I would like to say to the gentleman, I keep a very close eye on these agencies. To the extent that I believe that they are not promoting the general welfare and that special interest is served rather than the public interest, I would be certain to join with the gentleman in criticism of those aspects.

But that is not what the point is here tonight.

I urge my colleagues to oppose the Paul amendment.

Mr. BEREUTER. Mr. Chairman, I move to strike the requisite number of words.

Mr. Chairman, I rise in strongest opposition to the gentleman's amendment, offered for ideological reasons no doubt. It is devastating. It would do draconian levels of damage to the American economy, American exporters, American business, and American workers. It needs to be rejected.

Mr. Chairman, I yield to the gentleman from Illinois [Mr. Manzullo].

Mr. MANZULLO. Mr. Chairman, I would cite with authority Article I, section 8, clause 3 of the United States Constitution that it is within the powers of this body to regulate commerce with foreign nations, and if I could make my point, then I would be glad to yield for a question from my constitutional friend.

In what we are doing here with these three bodies, Exim, OPIC, and TDA, are we regulating commerce? You bet we are. We are involved in an international global war. If the amendment offered by the gentleman from Texas [Mr. Paul] were presented somehow in an international body, and I would dread that because we would have a one-world government, then I would say let us go ahead and do what he is doing because there are 73 export credit agencies, there are 36 international equivalents of OPICs. So what that means is that if we get rid of these specialty types of credit agencies, where are we? What we have done is we have effectively thrown up our hands and we have left it to the Finns and Germans to take over.

Let me give my colleagues an example that is in my backyard, Beloit Corporation. They are one of three manufacturers of paper making machines, three worldwide manufacturers of paper making machines, engaged in trying to get a contract in Indonesia. The only other two manufacturers are in Europe. One are the Finns and the other one are the Germans, and the Finns and the Germans go through extraordinary lengths in order to, if my colleagues want to use that word, subsidize, grant favorable financing so that these sales can take place.

So what happened was Beloit Corporation applied to Exim in working with Members on both sides of the aisle, including the gentleman from Wisconsin [Mr. Barrett] over here from Milwaukee. We were able to see Exim grant a $275 million loan guarantee which has to be paid back with interest at a good premium for the purpose of making sure that Beloit Corporation was put in a level playing field to sell those machines. Those were 2 machines that cost over $150 million a piece, and there are several more in the lot. Let me finish my thought here.

Now what is going on here dynamically is this. Worldwide there is an effort, there is an effort to eliminate OPIC and Exim types of financing. For example the OECD met and said that what we will do is we will have an agreement that a nation can only subsidize the spread; that is, the actual amount of interest as charged worldwide on the open market with what a nation wants to pay to a certain extent, and they continue to narrow that gap so that nations will be involved in less core subsidizing of the loans for the exports.

Mr. PAUL. Mr. Chairman, will the gentleman yield?

Mr. BEREUTER. I yield to the gentleman from Texas.

Mr. PAUL. Let me address the subject of regulation. The Constitution does give us the authority to regulate commerce, but it never mentions that we should subsidize special interests at the expense of the average American taxpayers. Yes, we can put on tariffs and we can regulate what comes and goes across our borders, but in the wildest dreams of the Founders of this country they never intended that we would have programs like this. We have to think this is a concoction of the latter part of the 20th century, the past 20 or 30 years. This is when this stuff, when welfarism has blossomed, it has been these types of programs. It was never intended by our Constitution to do these programs.

Mr. BEREUTER. Reclaiming my time, Mr. Chairman, I would say that the authorization appropriations are funds that are very much in the American taxpayers' benefit. They come out positive as a result directly of these jobs.

Mr. MANZULLO. Mr. Chairman, will the gentleman yield?

Mr. BEREUTER. I yield to the gentleman from Illinois.

Mr. MANZULLO. Mr. Chairman, back in those days the main income for the United States was international tariffs. We have these incredible tariff barriers, and that is how we supported the economy of the nation before the income tax.

I mean nobody wants those tariffs. I know the gentleman is a libertarian and does not like the tariffs, but that is what was going on 200 some years ago when the nation was founded, and I think when this was put into the Constitution it says to regulate, meaning this body, the United States Congress, is given the power to make sure that we can operate internationally.

The CHAIRMAN. The question is on the amendment offered by the gentleman from Texas [Mr. Paul].

The question was taken; and the Chairman announced that the noes appeared to have it.

Mr. PAUL. Mr. Chairman, I demand a recorded vote. ∎

What is Free Trade?

Congressional Record — U.S. House of Representatives
May 2, 2000

Madam Speaker, I asked for this Special Order this evening to talk about trade. We are going to be dealing with permanent normal trade relations with China here soon, and there is also a privileged resolution that will be brought to the floor that I have introduced, H.J.Res. 90. The discussion in the media and around the House floor has been rather clear about the permanent normal trade status, but there has not been a whole lot of talk yet about whether or not we should even really be in the World Trade Organization.

I took this time mainly because I think there is a lot of misunderstanding about what free trade is. There are not a whole lot of people who get up and say "I am opposed to free trade," and many of those who say they are for free trade quite frankly I think they have a distorted definition of what free trade really is.

I would like to spend some time this evening talking a little bit about that, because as a strict constitutionalist and one who endorses *laissez-faire* capitalism, I do believe in free trade; and there are good reasons why countries should trade with each other.

The first reason I would like to mention is a moral reason. There is a moral element involved in trade, because when governments come in and regulate how citizens spend their money, they are telling them what they can do or cannot do. In a free society, individuals who earn money should be allowed to spend the money the way they want. So if they find that they prefer to buy a car from Japan rather than Detroit, they basically have the moral right to spend their money as they see fit and those kinds of choices should not be made by government. So there is a definite moral argument for free trade.

Patrick Henry many years ago touched on this when he said, "You are not to inquire how your trade may be increased nor how you are to become a great and powerful people but how your liberties may be secured, for liberty ought to be the direct end of your government." We have not heard much talk of liberty with regards to trade, but we do hear a lot about enhancing one's ability to make more money overseas with trading with other nations. But the argument, the moral argument, itself should be enough to convince one in a free society that we should never hamper or interfere with free trade.

When the colonies did not thrive well prior to the Constitution, two of the main reasons why the Constitutional Convention was held was, one, there was no unified currency, that provided a great deal of difficulty in trading among the States, and also trade barriers among the States.

Even our Constitution was designed to make sure that there were not trade barriers, and this was what the interstate commerce clause was all about. Unfortunately though, in this century the interstate commerce clause has been taken and twisted around and is the excuse for regulating even trade within a State. Not only interstate trade, but even activities within a State have nothing to do with interstate trade. They use the interstate commerce clause as an excuse, which is a wild distortion of the original intent of the Constitution, but free trade among the States having a unified currency and breaking down the barriers certainly was a great benefit for the development and the industrialization of the United States.

The second argument for free trade is an economic argument. There is a benefit to free trade. Free trade means that you will not have high tariffs and barriers so you cannot buy products and you cannot exert this freedom of choice by buying outside. If you have a restricted majority and you can evenly buy from within, it means you are protecting industries that may not be doing a very good job, and there is not enough competition.

It is conceded that probably it was a blessing in disguise when the automobile companies in this country were having trouble in the 1970s, because the American consumer was not buying the automobiles, the better automobiles were coming in, and it should not have been a surprise to anybody that all of a sudden the American cars got to be much better automobiles and they were able to compete.

There is a tremendous economic benefit from competition by being able to buy overseas. The other economic argument is that in order to keep a product out, you put on a tariff, a protective tariff. A tariff is a tax. We should not confuse that, we should not think tariff is something softer than a tax in doing something good. A tariff is a tax on the consumer. So those American citizens who want to buy products at lower prices are forced to be taxed.

If you have poor people in this country trying to make it on their own and they are not on welfare, but they can buy clothes, or shoes, or an automobile, or anything from overseas, they are tremendously penalized by forcing them to pay higher prices by buying domestically.

The competition is what really encourages producers to produce better products at lower costs and keep the prices down. If
one believes in free trade, they do not enter into free trade for the
benefit of somebody else. There is really no need for reciprocity.
Free trade is beneficial because it is a moral right. Free trade is beneficial because there is an economic advantage to buying products
at a certain price and the competition is beneficial.

There really are no costs in the long run. Free trade does not
require management. It is implied here in conversation on the
House floor so often that free trade is equivalent to saying we will
turn over the management of trade to the World Trade Organization, which serves special interests. Well, that is not free trade; that
is a misunderstanding of free trade.

Free trade means you can buy and sell freely without interference. You do not need international management. Certainly, if we
are not going to have our own government manage our own
affairs, we do not want an international body to manage these
international trades.

Another thing that free trade does not imply is that this opens
up the doors to subsidies. Free trade does not mean subsidies, but
inevitably as soon as we start trading with somebody, we accept
the notion of managed trade by the World Trade Organization, but
immediately we start giving subsidies to our competitors.

If our American companies and our American workers have to
compete, the last thing they should ever be required to do is pay
some of their tax money to the government, to send subsidies to
their competitors; and that is what is happening. They are forced
to subsidize their competitors on foreign aid. They support their
competitors overseas at the World Bank. They subsidize their competitors in the Export-Import Bank, the Overseas Private Investment Corporation.

We literally encourage the exportation of jobs by providing
overseas protection in insurance that cannot be bought in the private sector. Here a company in the United States goes overseas for
cheap labor, and if, for political or economic reasons, they go bust,
who bails them out? It is the American taxpayer, once again, the
people who are struggling and have to compete with the free
trade.

It is so unfair to accept this notion that free trade is synonymous with permitting these subsidies overseas, and, essentially, that is what is happening all the time. Free trade should never mean that through the management of trade that it endorses the notion of retaliation and also to stop dumping.

This whole idea that all of a sudden if somebody comes in with a product with a low price that you can immediately get it stopped and retaliate, and this is all done in the name of free trade, it could be something one endorses. They might argue that they endorse this type of managed trade and subsidized trade; but what is wrong, and I want to make this clear, what is wrong is to call it free trade, because that is not free trade.

Most individuals that I know who promote free trade around Washington, D.C., do not really either understand what free trade is or they do not really endorse it. And they are very interested in the management aspect, because some of the larger companies have a much bigger clout with the World Trade Organization than would the small farmers, small rancher, or small businessman because they do not have the same access to the World Trade Organization.

For instance, there has been a big fight in the World Trade Organization with bananas. The Europeans are fighting with the Americans over exportation of bananas. Well, bananas are not grown in Europe and they are not grown in the United States, and yet that is one of the big issues of managed trade, for the benefit of some owners of corporations that are overseas that make big donations to our political parties. That is not coincidental.

So powerful international financial individuals go to the World Trade Organization to try to get an edge on their competitor. If their competitor happens to be doing a better job and selling a little bit lower, then they come immediately to the World Trade Organization and say, Oh, you have to stop them. That is dumping. We certainly do not want to give the consumers the benefit of having a lower price.

So this to me is important, that we try to be clear on how we define free trade, and we should not do this by accepting the idea that management of trade, as well as subsidizing trade and calling it free trade is just not right. Free trade is the ability of an individual or a corporation to buy goods and spend their money as they see fit, and this provides tremendous economic benefits.

The third benefit of free trade, which has been known for many, many centuries, has been the peace effect from trade. It is known that countries that trade with each other and depend on each other for certain products and where the trade has been free and open and communications are free and open and travel is free and open, they are very less likely to fight wars. I happen to personally think this is one of the greatest benefits of free trade, that it leads us to policies that direct us away from military confrontation.

Managed trade and subsidized trade do not qualify. I will mention just a little later why I think it does exactly the opposite.

There is a little bit more to the trade issue than just the benefits of free trade, true free trade, and the disadvantages of managed trade, because we are dealing now when we have a vote on the normal trade status with China, as well as getting out of the World Trade Organization, we are dealing with the issue of sovereignty. The Constitution is very clear. Article I, section 8, gives the Congress the responsibility of dealing with international trade. It does not delegate it to the President, it does not delegate it to a judge, it does not delegate it to an international management organization like the World Trade Organization.

International trade management is to be and trade law is to be dealt with by the U.S. Congress, and yet too often the Congress has been quite willing to renege on that responsibility through fast-track legislation and deliver this authority to our President, as well as delivering through agreements, laws being passed and treaties, delivering this authority to international bodies such as the UN-IMF-World Trade Organizations, where they make decisions that affect us and our national sovereignty.

The World Trade Organization has been in existence for five years. We voted to join the World Trade Organization in the fall of 1994 in the lame duck session after the Republicans took over the control of the House and Senate, but before the new Members were sworn in. So a lame duck session was brought up and they voted, and by majority vote we joined the World Trade Organization, which, under the Constitution, clearly to anybody who has studied the Constitution, is a treaty. So we have actually even invoked a treaty by majority vote.

This is a serious blunder, in my estimation, the way we have dealt with this issue, and we have accepted the idea that we will remain a member based on this particular vote.

Fortunately, in 1994 there was a provision put in the bill that said that any member could bring up a privileged resolution that gives us a chance at least to say is this a good idea to be in the World Trade Organization, or is it not? Now, my guess is that we do not have the majority of the U.S. Congress that thinks it is a bad idea. But I am wondering about the majority of the American people, and I am wondering about the number of groups now that are growing wary of the membership in the World Trade Organization, when you look at what happened in Seattle, as well as demonstrations here in D.C. So there is a growing number of people from various aspects of the political spectrum who are now saying, what does this membership mean to us? Is it good or is it bad? A lot of them are coming down on the side of saying it is bad.

Now, it is also true that some who object to membership in the World Trade Organization happen to be conservative free enterprisers, and others who object are coming from the politics of the left. But there is agreement on both sides of this issue dealing with this aspect, and it has to do with the sovereignty issue.

There may be some labor law and there may be some environmental law that I would object to, but I more strenuously object to the World Trade Organization dictating to us what our labor law ought to be and what our environmental law ought to be. I highly resent the notion that the World Trade Organization can dictate to us tax law.

We are currently under review and the World Trade Organization has ruled against the United States because we have given a tax break to our overseas companies, and they have ruled against us and said that this tax break is a tax subsidy, language which annoys me to no end. They have given us until October 1 to get rid of that tax break for our corporations, so they are telling us, the U.S. Congress, what we have to do with tax law.

You say, oh, that cannot be. We do not have to do what they tell us. Well, technically we do not have to, but we will not be a very good member, and this is what we agreed to in the illegal agreement. Certainly it was not a legitimate treaty that we signed. But in this agreement we have come up and said that we would obey what the WTO says.

Our agreement says very clearly that any ruling by the WTO, the Congress is obligated to change the law. This is the interpretation and this is what we signed. This is a serious challenge, and we should not accept so easily this idea that we will just go one step further.

This has not just happened five years ago, there has been a gradual erosion of the concept of national sovereignty. It occurred certainly after World War II with the introduction of the United Nations, and now, under current conditions, we do not even ask the Congress to declare war, yet we still fight a lot of wars. We send troops all over the world and we are involved in combat all the time, and our presidents tell us they get the authority from a UN resolution. So we have gradually lost the concept of national sovereignty.

I want to use a quote from somebody that I consider rather typical of the establishment. We talk about the establishment, but nobody ever knows exactly who they are. But I will name this individual who I think is pretty typical of the establishment, and that is Walter Cronkite. He says, "We need not only an executive to make international law, but we need the military forces to enforce that law and the judicial system to bring the criminals to justice in an international government."

"But," he goes on to say, and this he makes very clear, and this is what we should be aware of, "the American people are going to begin to realize that perhaps they are going to have to yield some sovereignty to an international body to enforce world law, and I think that is going to come to other people as well."

So it is not like it has been hidden, it is not like it is a secret. It is something that those who disagree with me about liberty and the Constitution, they believe in internationalism and the World Trade Organization and the United Nations, and they certainly have the right to that belief, but it contradicts everything America stands for and it contradicts our Constitution, so, therefore, we should not allow this to go unchallenged.

Now, the whole idea that treaties could be passed and undermine the ability of our Congress to pass legislation or undermine our Constitution, this was thought about and talked about by the

Founders of this country. They were rather clear on the idea that a treaty, although the treaty can become the law of the land, a treaty could never be an acceptable law of the land if it amended or changed the Constitution. That would be ridiculous, and they made that very clear.

It could have the effect of the law of the land, as long as it was a legitimate constitutional agreement that we entered into. But Thomas Jefferson said if the treaty power is unlimited, then we do not have a Constitution. Surely the President and the Senate cannot do by treaty what the whole government is interdicted from doing in any way.

So that is very important. We cannot just sit back and accept the idea that the World Trade Organization, we have entered into it, it was not a treaty, it was an agreement, but we have entered into it, and the agreement says we have to do what they tell us, even if it contradicts the whole notion that it is the Congress's and people's responsibility to pass their own laws with regard to the environment, with regard to labor and with regard to tax law.

So I think this is important material. I think this is an important subject, a lot more important than just the vote to trade with China. I think we should trade with China. I think we should trade with Cuba. I think we should trade with everybody possible, unless we are at war with them. I do not think we should have sanctions against Iran, Iraq, or Libya, and it does not make much sense to me to be struggling and fighting and giving more foreign aid to a country like China, and at the same time we have sanctions on and refuse to trade and talk with Cuba. That does not make a whole lot of sense. Yet those who believe and promote trade with China are the ones who will be strongly objecting to trade with Cuba and these other countries. So I think a little bit more consistency on this might be better for all of us.

Alexander Hamilton also talked about this. He said a treaty cannot be made which alters the Constitution of the country or which infringes any expressed exception to the powers of the Constitution of the United States.

So these were the Founders talking about this, and yet we have drifted a long way. It does not happen overnight. It has been over a 50-year period. Five years ago we went one step further. First we accepted the idea that international finance would be regulated by the IMF. Then we accepted the idea that the World Bank, which was supposed to help the poor people of the world and redistribute wealth, they have redistributed a lot of wealth, but most of it ended up in the hands of wealthy individuals and wealthy politicians. But the poor people of the world never get helped by these programs. Now, five years ago we have accepted the notion that the World Trade Organization will bring about order in trade around the world.

Well, since that time we have had a peso crisis in Mexico and we had a crisis with currencies in Southeast Asia. So I would say that the management of finances with the IMF as well as the World Trade Organization has been very unsuccessful, and even if one does not accept my constitutional argument that we should not be doing this, we should at least consider the fact that what we are doing is not very successful. ■

The Dollar and Our Current Account Deficit

Congressional Record — U.S. House of Representatives
May 16, 2000

Fiat money, that is, money created out of thin air, causes numerous problems, internationally as well as domestically. It causes domestic price inflation, economic downturns, unemployment, excessive debt (corporate, personal, and government), malinvestment, and overcapacity — all very serious and poorly understood by our officials. But fluctuating values of various paper currencies cause all kinds of disruptions in international trade and finance as well.

Trade surpluses and deficits when sound money conditions exist are of little concern since they prompt changes in policy or price adjustments in a natural or smooth manner. When currencies are nonconvertible into something of real value, they can be arbitrarily increased at will, trade deficits and especially current account deficits are of much greater significance.

When trade imbalances are not corrected, sudden devaluations, higher interest rates, and domestic inflation are forced on the country that has most abused its monetary power. This was seen in 1997 in the Asian crisis, and precarious economic conditions continue in that region.

Japan has yet to recover from its monetary inflation of the '70s and '80s and has now suffered with a lethargic economy for over a decade. Even after this length of time there is no serious thought for currency reform in Japan or any other Asian nation.

Although international trade imbalances are a predictable result of fiat money, the duration and intensity of the cycles associated with it are not. A reserve currency, such as is the dollar, is treated by the market quite differently than another fiat currency.

The issuer of a reserve currency—in this case the United States—has greater latitude for inflating and can tolerate a current account deficit for much longer periods of time than other countries not enjoying the same benefit. But economic law, although at times it may seem lax, is ruthless in always demanding that economic imbalances arising from abuse of economic principles be rectified. In spite of the benefits that reserve currency countries enjoy, financial bubbles still occur and their prolongation, for whatever reason, only means the inevitable adjustment, when it comes, is more harsh.

Our current state of imbalance includes a huge U.S./foreign debt of $1.5 trillion, a record 20 percent of GDP and is a consequence of our continuously running a huge monthly current account deficit that shows no signs of soon abating. We are now the world's greatest debtor. The consequence of this deficit cannot be avoided. Our current account deficit has continued longer than many would have expected. But not knowing how long and to what extent deficits can go is not unusual. The precise event that starts the reversal in the trade balance is also unpredictable. The reversal itself is not.

Japan's lethargy, the Asian crisis, the Mexican financial crisis, Europe's weakness, the uncertainty surrounding the Euro, the demise of the Soviet system, and the ineptness of the Russian bailout, all contributed to the continued strength in the dollar and prolongation of our current account deficit. This current account deficit, which prompts foreigners to loan back dollars to us and to invest in our stock and bond markets, has contributed significantly to the financial bubble. The perception that the United States is the economic and military powerhouse of the world, helps perpetuate an illusion that the dollar is invincible and has encouraged our inflationary policies.

By inflating our currency, we can then spend our dollars overseas getting products at good prices which in the short run raises our standard of living—but, on borrowed money. All currency account deficits must be financed by borrowing from abroad.

It all ends when the world wakes up and realizes it has been had by the U.S. printing press. No country can expect to inflate its currency at will forever.

Since cartels never work, OPEC does not deserve credit for getting oil prices above $30 per barrel. Demand for equivalent purchasing power for the sale of oil can. Recent commodity and wage price increases signal accelerating price inflation is at hand. We are witnessing the early stages in a sea change regarding the dollar, inflation, the stock market as well as commodity prices.

The nervousness in the stock and bond markets, and especially in the NASDAQ, indicates that the Congress may soon be facing an entirely different set of financial numbers regarding spending, revenues, interest costs on our national debt, and the value of the U.S. dollar. Price inflation of the conventional type will surely return, even if the economy slows.

Fiscal policy and current monetary policy will not solve the crisis we will soon face. Only sound money, money that cannot be created out of thin air, can solve the many problems appearing on the horizon. The sooner we pay attention to monetary policy as the source of our international financial problems, the sooner we will come up with a sound solution. ∎

International Trade

Congressional Record – U.S. House of Representatives
May 23, 2000

Mr. Speaker, this week there will be a lot of talk on the House floor about international trade. One side will talk about pseudo-free trade, the other about fair trade. Unfortunately, true free trade will not be discussed.

Both sides generally agree to subsidies and international management of trade. The pseudo-free trader will not challenge the WTO's authority to force us to change our tax, labor, and environmental laws to conform to WTO rules, nor will they object to the WTO authorizing economic sanctions on us if we are slow in following the WTO's directives.

What is permitted is a low-level continuous trade war, not free trade. The current debate over Chinese trade status totally ignores a much bigger trade problem the world faces, an ocean of fluctuating fiat currencies.

For the past decade, with sharp adjustments in currency values such as occurred during the Asian financial crisis, the dollar and the U.S. consumers benefitted. But these benefits will prove short-lived, since the unprecedented prosperity and consumption has been achieved with money that we borrow from abroad.

Our trade imbalances and our skyrocketing current account deficit once again hit a new record in March. Our distinction as the world's greatest debtor remains unchallenged. But that will all end when foreign holders of dollars become disenchanted with financing our grand prosperity at their expense. One day, foreign holders of our dollars will realize that our chief export has been our inflation.

The Federal Reserve believes that prosperity causes high prices and rising wages, thus causing it to declare war on a symptom of its own inflationary policy, deliberately forcing an economic slowdown, a sad and silly policy, indeed. The Fed also hopes that higher interest rates will curtail the burgeoning trade deficit and prevent the serious currency crisis that usually results from currency-induced trade imbalances. And of course, the Fed hopes to do all this without a recession or depression.

That is a dream. Not only is the dollar due for a downturn, the Chinese currency is as well. When these adjustments occur and recession sets in, with rising prices in consumer and producer goods, there will be those who will argue that it happened because of, or the lack thereof, of low tariffs and free trade with China.

But instead, I suggest we look more carefully for the cause of the coming currency crisis. We should study the nature of all the world currencies and the mischief that fiat money causes, and resist the temptation to rely on the WTO, the IMF, the World Bank, and pseudo-free trade, to solve the problems that only serious currency reform can address. ∎

PNTR

Congressional Record – U.S. House of Representatives
May 24, 2000

Mr. Speaker, yesterday morning the legislation which would have implemented "permanent normal trade relations" with the People's Republic of China was three pages in length. Today, it is 66 pages in length. Close examination of this bill "gone bad" is demonstrative of how this Congress misdefines "free trade" and how, like most everything else is in Washington, this "free trade" bill is a misnomer of significant proportions.

For the past several years I have favored normal trade relations with the People's Republic of China. Because of certain misconceptions, I believe it is useful to begin with some detail as to what "normal trade relations" status is and what it is not. Previous "normal trade relations" votes meant only that U.S. tariffs imposed on

Chinese goods will be no different than tariffs imposed on other countries for similar products—period. NTR status did not mean more U.S. taxpayers dollars sent to China. It did not signify more international family planning dollars sent overseas. NTR status does not mean automatic access to the World Bank, the World Trade Organization, OPIC, or any member of other "foreign aid" vehicles by which the U.S. Congress sends foreign aid to a large number of countries. Rather, NTR status was the lowering of a United States citizen's taxes paid on voluntary exchanges entered into by citizens who happen to reside in different countries.

Of course, many of the critics of NTR status for China do not address the free trade and the necessarily negative economic consequences of their position. No one should question that individual rights are vital to liberty and that the communist government of China has an abysmal record in that department. At the same time, basic human rights must necessarily include the right to enter into voluntary exchanges with others. To burden the U.S. citizens who enter into voluntary exchanges with exorbitant taxes (tariffs) in the name of "protecting" the human rights of citizens of other countries would be internally inconsistent. Trade barriers when lowered, after all, benefit consumers who can purchase goods more cheaply than previously available. Those individuals choosing not to trade with citizens of particular foreign jurisdictions are not threatened by lowering barriers for those who do. Oftentimes, these critics focus instead on human rights deprivation by government leaders in China and see trade barriers as a means to "reform" these sometimes tyrannical leaders. However, according to Father Robert Sirico, a Paulist priest who discussed this topic in the *Wall Street Journal*, American missionaries in China favor NTR status and see this as the policy most likely to bring about positive change in China.

But all of this said, this new 66-page "free trade" bill is not about free trade at all. It is about empowering and enriching international trade regulators and quasi-governmental entities on the backs of the U.S. taxpayer. Like NAFTA before us, this bill contains provisions which continue our country down the ugly path of internationally-engineered, "managed trade" rather than that of free trade. As explained by Ph.D. economist Murray N. Rothbard:

> [G]enuine free trade doesn't require a treaty (or its deformed cousin, a "trade agreement;" NAFTA was called an agreement so it can avoid the constitutional requirement of approval by two-thirds of the Senate). If the establishment truly wants free trade, all its has to do is to repeal our numerous tariffs, import quotas, anti-dumping laws, and other American-imposed restrictions of free trade. No foreign policy or foreign maneuvering is necessary.

In truth, the bipartisan establishment's fanfare of "free trade" fosters the opposite of genuine freedom of exchange. Whereas genuine free traders examine free markets from the perspective of the consumer (each individual), the merchantilist examines trade from the perspective of the power elite; in other words, from the perspective of big business in concert with big government. Genuine free traders consider exports a means of paying for imports, in the same way that goods in general are produced in order to be sold to consumers. But the mercantilists want to privilege the government business elite at the expense of all consumers, be they domestic or foreign. This new PNTR bill, rather than lowering government-imposed barriers to trade, has become a legislative vehicle under which the United States can more quickly integrate and cartelize government in order to entrench the interventionist mixed economy.

No, Mr. Speaker and my colleagues, don't be fooled into thinking this bill is anything about free trade. In fact, those supporting it should be disgraced to learn that, among other misgivings, this bill further undermines U.S. sovereignty by empowering the World Trade Organization on the backs of American taxpayers, sends federal employees to Beijing to become lobbyists to members of their communist government to become more WTO-friendly, funds the imposition of the questionable Universal Declaration of Human Rights upon foreign governments, and authorizes the spending of nearly $100 million to expand the reach of Radio Free Asia.

Mr. Speaker, I say no to this taxpayer-financed fanfare of "free trade" which fosters the opposite of genuine freedom of exchange and urge my colleagues to do the same. ∎

The Export-Import Reauthorization Act

House Financial Services Committee
Congressional Record – U.S. House of Representatives
October 31, 2001

Mr. Chairman, the Financial Services committee should reject H.R. 2871, the Export-Import Reauthorization Act, for economic, constitutional, and moral reasons. The Export-Import Bank (Eximbank) takes money from American taxpayers to subsidize exports by American companies. Of course, it is not just any company that receives Eximbank support—rather, the majority of Eximbank funding benefits large, politically powerful corporations.

Proponents of continued American support for the Eximbank claim that the bank "creates jobs" and promotes economic growth. However, this claim rests on a version of what the great economist Henry Hazlitt called "the broken window" fallacy. When a hoodlum throws a rock through a store window, it can be said he has contributed to the economy, as the store owner will have to spend money having the window fixed. The benefits to those who repaired the window are visible for all to see, therefore it is easy to see the broken window as economically beneficial. However, the "benefits" of the broken window are revealed as an illusion when one takes into account what is not seen: the businesses and workers who would have benefited had the store owner not spent money repairing a window, but rather had been free to spend his money as he chose.

Similarly, the beneficiaries of Eximbank are visible to all; what is not seen is the products that would have been built, the businesses that would have been started, and the jobs that would have been created had the funds used for the Eximbank been left in the hands of consumers.

Some supporters of this bill equate supporting Eximbank with supporting "free trade," and claim that opponents are "protectionists" and "isolationists." Mr. Chairman, this is nonsense, Eximbank has nothing to do with free trade. True free trade involves the peaceful, voluntary exchange of goods across borders, not forcing taxpayers to subsidize the exports of politically powerful companies. Eximbank is not free trade, but rather managed trade, where winners and losers are determined by how well they please government bureaucrats instead of how well they please consumers.

Expenditures on the Eximbank distort the market by diverting resources from the private sector, where they could be put to the use most highly valued by individual consumers, into the public sector, where their use will be determined by bureaucrats and politically powerful special interests. By distorting the market and preventing resources from achieving their highest valued use, Eximbank actually costs Americans jobs and reduces America's standard of living!

The case for Eximbank is further weakened considering that small businesses receive only 12–15 percent of Eximbank funds; the vast majority of Eximbank funds benefit large corporations. These corporations can certainly afford to support their own exports without relying on the American taxpayer. It is not only bad economics to force working Americans, small business, and entrepreneurs to subsidize the exports of the large corporations: it is also immoral. In fact, this redistribution from the poor and middle class to the wealthy is the most indefensible aspect of the welfare state, yet it is the most accepted form of welfare. Mr. Chairman, it never ceases to amaze me how members who criticize welfare for the poor on moral and constitutional grounds see no problem with the even more objectionable programs that provide welfare for the rich.

The moral case against Eximbank is strengthened when one considers that the government which benefits most from Eximbank funds is communist China. In fact, Eximbank actually underwrites joint ventures with firms owned by the Chinese government! Whatever one's position on trading with China, I would hope all of us would agree that it is wrong to force taxpayers to subsidize in any way this brutal regime. Unfortunately, China is not an isolated case: Colombia, Yemen, and even the Sudan benefit from taxpayer-subsidized trade courtesy of the Eximbank!

There is simply no constitutional justification for the expenditure of funds on programs such as Eximbank. In fact, the drafters of the Constitution would be horrified to think the federal government was taking hard-earned money from the American people in order to benefit the politically powerful.

In conclusion, Mr. Chairman, Eximbank distorts the market by allowing government bureaucrats to make economic decisions in place of individual consumers. Eximbank also violates basic principles of morality, by forcing working Americans to subsidize the trade of wealthy companies that could easily afford to subsidize their own trade, as well as subsidizing brutal governments like Red China and the Sudan. Eximbank also violates the limitations on congressional power to take the property of individual citizens and use them to benefit powerful special interests. It is for these reasons that I urge my colleagues to reject H.R. 2871, the Export-Import Bank Reauthorization Act. ∎

Opposing Unconstitutional "Trade Promotion Authority"

Congressional Record — U.S. House of Representatives
December 6, 2001

Mr. Speaker, we are asked today to grant the President so-called trade promotion authority, authority that has nothing to do with free trade. Proponents of this legislation claim to support free trade, but really they support government-managed trade that serves certain interests at the expense of others. True free trade occurs only in the absence of interference by government, that's why it's called "free" — it's free of government taxes, quotas, or embargoes. The term "free-trade agreement" is an oxymoron. We don't need government agreements to have free trade; but we do need to get the federal government out of the way and unleash the tremendous energy of the American economy.

Our Founders understood the folly of trade agreements between nations; that is why they expressly granted the authority to regulate trade to Congress alone, separating it from the treaty-making power given to the President and Senate. This legislation clearly represents an unconstitutional delegation of congressional authority to the President. Simply put, the Constitution does not permit international trade agreements. Neither Congress nor the President can set trade policies in concert with foreign governments or international bodies.

The loss of national sovereignty inherent in government-managed trade cannot be overstated. If you don't like GATT, NAFTA, and the WTO, get ready for even more globalist intervention in our domestic affairs. As we enter into new international agreements, be prepared to have our labor, environmental, and tax laws increasingly dictated or at least influenced by international bodies. We've already seen this with our foreign sales corporation tax laws, which we changed solely to comply with a WTO ruling. Rest assured that TPA will accelerate the trend toward global government, with our Constitution fading into history.

Congress can promote true free trade without violating the Constitution. We can lift the trade embargo against Cuba, end Jackson-Vanik restrictions on Kazakhstan, and repeal sanctions on Iran. These markets should be opened to American exporters, especially farmers. We can reduce our tariffs unilaterally — taxing American consumers hardly punishes foreign governments. We can unilaterally end the subsidies that international agreements purportedly seek to reduce. We can simply repeal protectionist barriers to trade, so-called NTBs, that stifle economic growth.

Mr. Speaker, we are not promoting free trade today, but we are undermining our sovereignty and the constitutional separation of powers. We are avoiding the responsibilities with which our constituents have entrusted us. Remember, congressional authority we give up today will not be restored when less popular Presidents take office in the future. I strongly urge all of my colleagues to vote NO on TPA. ■

Steel Protectionism

Congressional Record – U.S. House of Representatives
March 13, 2002

Mr. Speaker, I am disheartened by the administration's recent decision to impose a 30 percent tariff on steel imports. This measure will hurt far more Americans than it will help, and it takes a step backwards toward the protectionist thinking that dominated Washington in decades past. Make no mistake about it, these tariffs represent naked protectionism at its worst, a blatant disregard of any remaining free-market principles to gain the short-term favor of certain special interests. These steel tariffs also make it quite clear that the rhetoric about free trade in Washington is abandoned and replaced with talk of "fair trade" when special interests make demands. What most Washington politicians really believe in is government-managed trade, not free trade. True free trade, by definition, takes place only in the absence of government interference of any kind, including tariffs. Government-managed trade means government, rather than competence in the marketplace, determines what industries and companies succeed or fail.

We've all heard about how these tariffs are needed to protect the jobs of American steelworkers, but we never hear about the jobs that will be lost or never created when the cost of steel rises 30 percent. We forget that tariffs are taxes, and that imposing tariffs means raising taxes. Why is the administration raising taxes on American steel consumers? Apparently no one in the administration has read Henry Hazlitt's classic book, *Economics in One Lesson*. Hazlitt's fundamental lesson was simple: We must examine economic policy by considering the long-term effects of any proposal on all groups. The administration instead chose to focus only on the immediate effects of steel tariffs on one group, the domestic steel industry. In doing so, it chose to ignore basic economics for the sake of political expediency. Now I grant you that this is hardly anything new in this town, but it's important that we see these tariffs as the political favors that they are. This has nothing to do with fairness. The free market is fair; it alone justly rewards the worthiest competitors. Tariffs reward the strongest Washington lobbies.

We should recognize that the cost of these tariffs will not only be borne by American companies that import steel, such as those in the auto industry and building trades. The cost of these import taxes will be borne by nearly all Americans, because steel is widely used in the cars we drive and the buildings in which we live and work. We will all pay, but the cost will be spread out and hidden, so no one complains. The domestic steel industry, however, has complained — and it has the corporate and union power that scares politicians in Washington. So the administration moved to protect domestic steel interests, with an eye toward the upcoming midterm elections. It moved to help members who represent steel-producing states. We hear a great deal of criticism of special interests and their stranglehold on Washington, but somehow when we prop up an entire industry that has failed to stay competitive, we're "protecting American workers." What we're really doing is taxing all Americans to keep some politically-favored corporations afloat. Sure, some rank and file jobs may also be saved, but at what cost? Do steelworkers really have a right to demand that Americans pay higher taxes to save an industry that should be required to compete on its own?

If we're going to protect the steel industry with tariffs, why not other industries? Does every industry that competes with imported goods have the same claim for protection? We've propped up the auto industry in the past, now we're doing it for steel, so who should be next in line? Virtually every American industry competes with at least some imports.

What happened to the wonderful harmony that the WTO was supposed to bring to global trade? The administration has been roundly criticized since the steel decision was announced last week, especially by our WTO "partners." The European Union is preparing to impose retaliatory sanctions to protect its own steel industry. EU trade commissioner Pascal Lamy has accused the U.S. of setting the stage for a global trade war, and several other steel producing nations such as Japan and Russia also have vowed to fight the tariffs. Even British Prime Minister Tony Blair, who has been tremendously supportive of the President since September 11th, recently stated that the new American steel tariffs were totally unjustified. Wasn't the WTO supposed to prevent all this squabbling? Those of us who opposed U.S. membership in the WTO were scolded as being out of touch, unwilling to see the promise of a new global prosperity. What we're getting instead is increased hostility from our trading partners and threats of economic sanctions from our WTO masters. This is what happens when we let government-managed trade schemes pick winners and losers in the global trading game. The truly deplorable thing about all of this is that the WTO is touted as promoting free trade!

Mr. Speaker, it's always amazing to me that Washington gives so much lip service to free trade while never adhering to true free trade principles. Free trade really means freedom — the freedom to buy and sell goods and services free from government interference. Time and time again, history proves that tariffs don't work. Even some modern Keynesian economists have grudgingly begun to admit that free markets allocate resources better than centralized planning. Yet we cling to the idea that government needs to manage trade, when it really needs to get out of the way and let the marketplace determine the cost of goods. I sincerely hope that the administration's position on steel does not signal a willingness to resort to protectionism whenever special interests make demands in the future. ■

Export-Import Bank is Corporate Welfare

Congressional Record – U.S. House of Representatives
June 5, 2002

Madam Speaker, I rise in opposition to this bill. This bill is nothing more than subsidies for big corporations. If one were to look at the Constitution and look for authority for legislation of this sort in Article I, Section 8, it would not be found. That in itself should be reason to stop and think about this, but we do not look at that particular article too often any more.

Also for moral reasons, I object to this. Even if we accepted the idea that we should interfere and be involved in this type of activity, it is unfair because the little guy gets squeezed and the big guy gets all of the money. It is not morally fair because it cannot be.

One thing that annoys me the most is when Members come to the floor and in the name of free trade say we have to support the Export-Import Bank. This is the opposite of free trade. Free trade is good. Low tariffs are good, which lead to lower prices; but subsidies to our competitors is not free trade. We should call it for what it is. We have Members who claim they are free traders, and yet support managed trade through NAFTA and WTO and all these special interest management schemes, as well as competitive devaluation of currencies with the notion that we might increase exports. This has nothing to do with free trade.

I am a strong advocate for free trade, and for that reason I think this bill should not be passed. There are good economic reasons not to support this. Because some who favor this bill argue that some of these companies are doing risky things and they do not qualify in the ordinary banking system for these loans and, therefore, they need a little bit of help. That is precisely when we should not be helping. If there is a risk, it is telling us there is something wrong and we should not do it. It is transferring the liability from the company to the taxpayer. So the risk argument does not hold water at all.

The other reason why economically it is unsound, is that this is a form of credit allocation. If a bank has money and they can get a guarantee from the Export-Import Bank, they will always choose the guarantee over the nonguarantee, so who gets squeezed? The funds are taken out of the investment pool. The little people get squeezed. They do not get the loan, but they are totally unknown. Nobody sees those who did not get a loan. All we see is the loan that benefits somebody on the short run. But really in the long run, it benefits the big corporations. Many times it doesn't even do that.

Take a look at Enron. We have mentioned Enron quite a few times already. If we add up all of the subsidies to Enron, it adds up to $1.9 billion. That is if we add up the subsidies from OPIC as well. And look at what Enron did. They ran a few risks, and then they lost it. Who was left holding the bag? The taxpayers.

Madam Speaker, I strongly urge a no vote on this bill. If Members are for free trade, they will vote against this bill, and will vote for true free trade. ∎

Don't Antagonize Our Trading Partners

Congressional Record – U.S. House of Representatives
April 1, 2003

Madam Speaker, this week we will be working on the $75 billion supplemental appropriation to pay for the war. Financing the war is not as simple as it appears. It involves more than just passing a piece of legislation labeled as support for the troops.

It has now been fashionable to bash France and Germany and other friends if they are less enthusiastic for the war than we think they should be. Yet foreign corporations provide millions of jobs for American citizens. French companies alone employ over 400,000. There is a practical reason why offending the French and others may backfire on us.

In 2002 we earned $11.9 billion less from our investments overseas than foreigners did here. This is not a sign of financial strength. A negative balance on the income account contributes to the $500 billion annual current account deficit. Since 1985 when we became a deficit nation, we have acquired a foreign debt of approximately $2.8 trillion, the world's largest. No nation can long sustain a debt that continues to expand at a rate greater than 5 percent of the GDP. This means we borrowed more than $1.4 billion every day to keep the borrowing binge going. This only can be maintained until foreigners get tired of taking and holding our dollars and buying our debt. Bashing the French and others will only hasten the day that sets off the train of economic events that will please no one.

In thinking about providing funds for the war and overall military expenditures, not only must every dollar be borrowed from overseas, but an additional $150 billion each year as well. The current account deficit is now 44 percent greater than the military budget and represents the amount we must borrow to balance the accounts. The bottom line is that our international financial condition is dire and being made worse by current international events.

It is true that military might gives a boost to a nation's currency; but this is not permanent if fiscal and monetary policies are abused. Currently, our budget deficits are exploding, as there is no restraint on spending.

No one can guarantee permanent military superiority.

The dollar has already significantly weakened this past year, and this trend will surely continue. A weaker dollar requires that we pay more for everything we buy overseas. Foreign borrowing will eventually become more difficult, and this will in time cause interest rates to rise. Be assured that domestic price inflation will accelerate. Economic law dictates that these events will cause the recession to linger and deepen.

My humble advice, consider being nicer to our friends and allies. We need them more than we can imagine to finance our war efforts. There is more to it than passing the supplemental appropriation. Besides, we need time to get our financial house in order. Antagonizing our trading partners can only make that task that much more complicated.

The day will come when true monetary reform will be required. Printing money to finance war and welfare can never be a panacea. ∎

The United States Trade Rights Enforcement Act

Congressional Record — U.S. House of Representatives
July 26, 2005

Mr. Speaker, I rise in strong opposition to this legislation. Isn't it ironic that the proponents of "free trade agreements" like CAFTA are lining up squarely behind a bill like this that threatens a trade war with China, and at the least calls for the United States to initiate protectionist measures such as punitive tariffs against "subsidized" sectors of the Chinese economy? In reality, this bill, which appeared out of the blue on the House floor as a suspension bill, is part of a deal made with several Members in return for a few votes on CAFTA. That is why it is ironic: to get to "free trade" with Central America we first need to pass protectionist legislation regarding China.

Mr. Speaker, in addition to the irony of the protectionist flavor of this bill, let me say that we should be careful what we demand of the Chinese government. Take the demand that the government "revalue" its currency, for example. First, there is sufficient precedent to suggest that doing this would have very little effect on China's trade surplus with the United States. As *Barron's* magazine pointed out recently, "the Japanese yen's value has more than tripled since the breakdown of the Bretton Woods system, yet Japan's trade surplus remains huge. Why should the unpegging of the Chinese yuan have any greater impact?"

As was pointed out in the *Wall Street Journal* recently, with the yuan tied to several foreign currencies and the value of the dollar dropping, China could be less inclined to purchase dollars as a way of keeping the yuan down. Fewer Treasury bond purchases by China, in turn, would drive bond prices down and boost yields — which, subsequently, would cause borrowing costs for residential and some corporate customers to increase. Does anyone want to guess what a sudden burst of the real estate bubble might mean for the shaky U.S. economy? This is not an argument for the *status quo*, however, but rather an observation that there are often unforeseen consequences when we demand that foreign governments manipulate their currency to U.S. "advantage."

At the very least, American consumers will immediately feel the strengthening of the yuan in the form of higher U.S. retail prices. This will disproportionately affect Americans of lower incomes and, as a consequence, slow the economy and increase the hardship of those struggling to get by. Is this why our constituents have sent us here?

In conclusion, I strongly oppose this ill-considered and potentially destructive bill, and I hope my colleagues will join me in rejecting it. ∎

PART SEVEN

International Affairs

In these selections I discuss U.S. economic relations with other countries, outside the narrow context of trade policies. History shows that the most productive and peaceful behavior would be to mind our own business, not giving taxpayer money to regimes we like or imposing punitive sanctions on those we dislike. I believe the U.S. should withdraw from organizations such as the IMF, World Bank, and United Nations, as they unconstitutionally delegate U.S. sovereignty to international bodies, which are unaccountable to the American people.

Dissenting Views on H.R. 7244

Congressional Record – U.S. House of Representatives
May 15, 1980

Mr. Speaker, once again your committee has recommended pouring billions of tax dollars down an international rat hole, bringing to approximately $16.5 billion the total amount of wealth we have taken from the American people and given to the International Monetary Fund. The approximately $5.5 billion increase in our quota is the largest single increase in history, and it occurs at a most dangerous point in the history of the international monetary system.

Bailing Out the Banks

In his appearances before the Senate and House Banking Committees on this bill, Federal Reserve Governor Henry C. Wallich had some disturbing things to say about the purposes of this massive increase in our quota. Many of these statements are allusions to the desperate condition that seems to exist and be worsening in repayments of loans by developing countries to large American, Japanese, and European banks.

> 1. In an environment of increased international financial strains and of increased sensitivity of the U.S. economy to developments abroad, the United States also benefits indirectly from the IMF's efforts to alleviate such strains. In many instances, without temporary financial assistance from the IMF, countries would be

forced to take severe adjustment actions that could have a disruptive effect on the international economy.

2. The strengthening of the financial position of the Fund resulting from the increase in Fund quotas is an essential element in preparing for the strains that may well develop on the international financial system in the next year or two.

3. Given the expected increases in demands for balance of payments financing, as well as the large external indebtedness that many countries already have with commercial banks, the IMF should be in a position to meet a larger proportion of the immediate financing needs of its members in the coming years than it has assumed recently. A strengthening of the Fund's financial position by an increase in members' quotas would increase the likelihood that more countries would come under the Fund's conditional lending umbrella.

4. The letter from the chairman of the subcommittee inviting the Board to testify has accurately pointed to the dilemma facing the international financial system: a high level of lending by banks to developing countries could lead to excessive risk concentrations at banks.

5. Between the end of 1974 and the end of 1979, outstanding claims of banks from all countries on non-oil developing countries increased on average about $20 billion per year.

6. The rapid expansion in lending by foreign banks has caused some concern among foreign regulatory authorities. The German and British authorities have begun to require banks in those countries to maintain detailed records on a consolidated basis including, as a minimum, lending by their head offices and foreign branches. Since last fall, Japanese banks have been constrained by a request from the Ministry of Finance to limit their international lending.

7. Weighing all these factors is indeed complex, but, on balance, I would conclude that the general risks are somewhat greater in 1980 and 1981 than in 1974 and 1975. The situation clearly varies greatly from country to country. Recent history has taught us that the positions of some countries can improve dramatically in a short period of time. Unfortunately, in other cases, the external situation has deteriorated rapidly over time, either as a consequence of financial mismanagement or because of external (and sometimes internal) events over which the country has little control.

These warnings and allusions to impending crises cast some light on the perceived necessity for this massive infusion of American tax dollars into the IMF. The money will apparently be needed to bail out some banks that have made risky loans to the socialist governments of developing countries.

Worldwide Inflation

Ever since World War II, the IMF has permitted and encouraged worldwide inflation. This has been done through providing reserves to facilitate international payment problems. One of the reasons given for passage of this bill is that it will enable the IMF to handle the large imbalances of payments that now exist and are expected to persist into the foreseeable future. The developing nations, like the developed nations, have to face reality. There is no free lunch. An increase of international liquidity merely serves as another source of price inflation. It is true that recipient nations can buy goods and services in the international markets at yesterday's prices, thereby gaining in relationship to those who have not yet gained access to the fiat money, but this only can be paid for by those who must restrict their purchases in the face of higher prices.

By creating added liquidity, the IMF can indeed redistribute wealth, but it cannot create new wealth. The net trade imbalances of the nations that import more than they export can be met by gifts of new liquidity of IMF reserves, at least for as long as such reserves are honored by the producing nations. But this is simply a giveaway program.

In effect, it steals resources from one group of citizens and gives them to another group.

The transfer of resources from one nation to another makes the IMF just one more foreign aid bureaucracy. The wealth of middle-class citizens of the nations of the West will wind up subsidizing the grossly inefficient programs of the elitist, socialist, envious, and bureaucratized Third World nations. The middle classes of the West will have to support the educated elite of the less-developed nations. We will rob from the middle class to finance the powerful, only we will do it across borders.

What we have seen again and again during the past 30 years is that the guilt-ridden voters of the West—unnecessarily guilt-ridden—have allowed their governments to transfer their hard-earned resources to the state planning bureaucracies of the Third World. Government-to-government aid strengthens the economics of socialism. This kind of aid is nothing less than a weapon—a weapon used by Western-educated socialist bureaucrats in the Third World to suppress economic freedom in their own countries.

Because of the testimony taken by the subcommittee two amendments were incorporated into this bill regarding the social programs of nations which borrow from the IMF. The first would encourage the IMF not to impose conditions on its loans that would adversely affect the socialist programs of the borrowing governments. It seems that the conditions that the IMF has imposed in the past have curtailed the attempts of those governments to provide material security for their subjects, and the committee feels that these welfare programs should not suffer because of the irresponsible policies of the government.

Important as this amendment is, the second amendment would encourage the World Bank to coordinate its lending activities with those of the IMF so that borrowing governments may receive funds sufficient to repay their loans to the banks and also maintain the welfare programs at home. Working in tandem, the IMF and the World Bank would become the main vehicle for the international redistribution of wealth. Much of that wealth, of course, will be redistributed from the American people to large bankers via Third World governments. It will not be the first time that poor Peter will have been robbed to pay wealthy Paul. If the IMF is successful in its proposed policies, we will see even greater disruption of international economic cooperation. The IMF may have failed in its attempt to create a world of price-controlled stability; it will not fail in its attempt to subsidize uncertainty-producing socialist regimes in the Third World and large banks in the First World.

Should anyone believe that the United States needs the IMF to achieve its supposed goals of monetary reliability, price stability, and economic growth, let him consider this fact: Switzerland has never belonged to the IMF, does not suffer from price inflation, and did not contribute its gold reserves only to see its gold sold off to finance the financial follies of the Third World socialists.

We could learn a lesson from the Swiss experience, and I hope we do. I urge my colleagues to reject this bill. ■

Big Bankers Get Their Bailout

Congressional Record – U.S. House of Representatives
March 24, 1983

Mr. Speaker, in spite of the expressed concern for the poor by the proponents of big government policies, they, nevertheless, are seeing to it that the wealthy big bankers get their bailout. The budget resolution passed yesterday contains $8.4 billion for further IMF funding. I realize the budget resolution was directed toward the benefit of welfare recipients but I really do not think the bankers who made unwise foreign loans are all that deserving.

Billions of dollars were loaned by large international banks with the intention of making big profits. Because these loans are proving to be unwise and unprofitable, it is no reason why the pain and suffering should be passed on to the American taxpayer who is now just barely getting by.

Besides it is hardly necessary since the IMF is financially able to pursue other courses. It has 103 million ounces of gold on hand

and could easily sell what is needed to keep their scheme of world-wide inflation going — for a while longer that is — without further taxing the American taxpayer. The IMF's official position is that gold is not money so they have no more reason to hold gold than diamonds.

The IMF also has authority and plans to borrow funds in the market by issuing bonds. They claim their credit is good and could easily raise whatever funds are necessary. This voluntary approach is certainly preferable to the taxpayer being stuck with the bill.

The American taxpayer should not be asked to sacrifice for foreign debtors nor the world's international bankers.

The IMF funding must be rejected for moral and economic reasons. It is unfair to American taxpayers and it is unwise to perpetuate the engine of worldwide inflation.

I am really rather shocked that the bleeding hearts who seriously care for the poor have such compassion for the banking rich who stand to lose a few dollars from the ill-advised loans they made overseas with the intention of making huge profits. ∎

The Mexican Bailout

Congressional Record — U.S. House of Representatives
February 12, 1997

President Clinton, in his State of the Union Address, smugly announced that:

> We should all be proud that America led the effort to rescue our neighbor, Mexico, from its economic crisis. And we should all be proud that . . . Mexico repaid the United States — three full years ahead of schedule — with half a billion dollar profit to us.

The reporting of this payback and the State of the Union Address was all favorable, highly praising the administration. The bailout was bipartisan so leaders of both parties were pleased with the announcement. International finance, just as it is with international military operations, is rarely hindered by inter-party fights that get so much attention. But there are several reasons why we should not be too quick to congratulate the money manipulators.

First, they merely celebrate the postponement of the day of reckoning of their financial Ponzi scheme. It took 50 billion in U.S. dollars to save creditors who had unwisely invested in Mexico prior to the crisis of two years ago. Much of this $50 billion also included U.S. credit extended through the IMF, the World Bank, and the Bank of International Settlements, much of which is yet to be repaid.

Second, foreign government welfare, and there is no better name for it, takes money out of the productive sectors of the economy — the paychecks of middle-class Americans — to reward economic mismanagement and political corruption. Such "welfare" exacerbates Mexico's suffering: social disruption, economic stagnation, debt crises, and declines in real incomes.

Third, a new fund set up under the IMF will serve to bail out the next Mexico in trouble. The plan calls for the establishment of a $25 billion credit fund with the U.S. "ponying up" $3.5 billion. This fund is in addition to the IMF funds already available for such crises. Mexico has also received help from the Inter-American Development Fund; again, indirectly supported by U.S. taxpayers. These funds indirectly guarantee the newly-issued Mexican government bonds and undermine the normal incentive for investors to police governments.

As such, more confidence is now being placed in new Mexican bonds enabling Mexico to refinance its old loans. Of course, it is at slightly lower interest rates, but they are more than doubling the time of repayment. All investments involve some risks. The rewards of such risk-taking are appropriately realized by investors as loans are repaid. American taxpayers should not, however, be forced to subsidize the Wall Street financier any time such entrepreneurial ventures are unprofitable. The true test of the professed confidence in Mexico will come from the level of private investment into the productive sectors of the economy.

Fourth, the Fed is allowed to hold Mexican bonds and use them as collateral for our own Federal Reserve Notes. It does so, even though it will not admit it, and refuses to reveal just how much it holds. It is quite possible that the newly issued Mexican bonds will find their way into the Fed's holdings. How far down the road we have traveled from constitutional money when we are backing the dollar not with gold but with Mexican bonds!

Fifth, a likely motivation for this fanfare regarding the repayment of the loans, and the so-called profits engendered, is to get the U.S. Congress to go along with using this money to pay our back dues to the United Nations. How about paying our so-called U.N. back dues with our Mexican bond holdings?!

The use of the Exchange Stabilization Fund to bail out the peso was illegal and unconstitutional, and yet now we have a precedent not only established but praised for its great success. This precedent encourages political currency manipulation over sound fiscal and monetary policies as well as establishes the U.S. as lender of last resort for all governments with bad policies.

President Clinton claims that, "We stand at another moment of change and choice—and another time to be farsighted, to bring America 50 more years of security and prosperity." He earlier told us the "era of big government is over," but calls for full burden sharing through the IMF in a multilateral way with the Mexico agreement. We need to end this shell game of masking economic mismanagement by circumventing both the Constitution and Congress.

We must stand firm in our opposition to the establishment of new extra-governmental agreements that will reward governments with irresponsible policies which, at the same time, punish their own people and erode U.S. sovereignty. Such policies take us one step further from a constitutional rule of law, and institutionalize the United States as the world's lender of last resort—all at the expense of the American taxpayer.

Political and economic factors can override, only in the short run, the subtle reality that the fiat nature of the dollar guarantees its inherent weakness and steady depreciation. This new easy credit scheme that the government creates by fiat only expands the World Dollar Base leading to U.S. dollar depreciation and reduced buying power.

In essence, the bailout of Mexico and the financing of the pay-back with interest, to the sheer delight of the politicians and their Wall Street constituents, were done on the back of the U.S. dollar and the U.S. taxpayer. The real consequence, however, will not be felt until dollar confidence is lost which will surely come and be accompanied by rapid inflation and high interest rates. ■

Reaffirming Commitment of United States to Principles of the Marshall Plan

Congressional Record – U.S. House of Representatives
May 21, 1997

Mr. Speaker, I rise to make some comments about the Marshall Plan because my interpretation is somewhat different than the conventional wisdom of the past 50 years.

I happen to believe the understanding of the Marshall Plan is probably one of the most misunderstood economic events of the 20th century. The benefits are grossly overstated. The Marshall Plan through these many years has been used as the moral justification for all additional foreign aid. And once I hear it, I assume we are on the verge of extending and expanding our foreign aid overseas.

When we look at the total amount of money that flowed into Europe following World War II, the amount that came from the American taxpayers was not large. The large amount came from corporations and investors who believed that Europe would be safe and secure, so the large number of dollars then flowed into Europe.

It was interesting that the conditions were improved in Europe not so much because of America but sometimes in spite of America, because many of our economists went to Europe at this time and advised them that the most important thing that they could do, especially in Germany, was to maintain price controls. Here in this country we did not learn, and hopefully we have finally learned the lesson, but we had not learned until at least 1971 that wage and price controls were not a good idea.

Yet Ludwig Erhard at that time defied the strong advice by the American advisers and took off wage and price controls, kept taxes low, kept regulations low, produced political conditions which were very conducive to investment, and this is what caused the real recovery in Europe.

Political assistance, funds flowing into a country through political maneuvers, are never superior to those funds that flow into a country for reasons of the political stability. Because Europe did invite capital, this was the real reason why Europe recovered.

Foreign aid is used frequently throughout the world to help people. But if we look at Zaire and Rwanda and the many countries of the world, foreign aid has really been a gross failure. As a matter of fact, it does harm because it encourages the *status quo*. The market is much smarter than we as politicians, because if the market and the political conditions are not right, that country that wants capital must improve those conditions to invite the capital. A good example might be in Vietnam at the current time. They changed their conditions to invite capital. So there must be an incentive for those countries to change their condition.

Foreign aid very often and very accurately, I believe, is a condition of taking money from the poor people in a rich country and giving it to the rich people of a poor country. I think there is a lot of truth to that, because the burden of taxation and inflation and the many things that our average citizen and our middle-class citizen suffer comes from overexpenditures and good intentions whether they are here, at home, or overseas. We believed at that time, and strongly so, I guess, still, that the government's responsibility, whether it is through government expenditures or through the inflationary machinery of the Federal Reserve, that if we stimulate an economy, if we prime the pump, so to speak, that we can stimulate the economy. This was the argument after World War II, that we would prime the pump. That is not a free-market notion, that is a Keynesian notion. There has been no proof that this is beneficial. Really what counts is a sound currency. Germany after World War II and even to this date is known to have a harder and sounder currency than any other currency in Europe. Political stability is what is necessary, not taking money from taxpayers of one country and shifting it to another one.

Foreign aid very often, not so much the foreign aid that went to Europe, and I would grant my colleagues, the other conditions compensated and did not allow the foreign aid to be damaging so much as the foreign aid, say, to a country like Rwanda. That was so destabilizing, because the politicians get hold of the money and they use it for political reasons. Money to help a country must go in because conditions are beneficial, that encourage investment, that encourage the market to work.

Mr. Speaker, I would argue that there is a different interpretation, but I know that the support for this measure is justified. ∎

Calling for the United States to Withdraw from the World Trade Organization

Congressional Record – U.S. House of Representatives
March 1, 2000

Mr. Speaker, I rise today to announce my introduction of and request cosponsors for a privileged resolution to withdraw the United States from the World Trade Organization.

Last week, the *Wall Street Journal* reported that the United States was dealt a defeat in a tax dispute with the European Union by an unelected board of international bureaucrats. It seems that, according to the WTO, $2.2 billion of United States tax reductions for American businesses violates WTO's rules and must be eliminated by October 1 of this year.

Much could be said about the WTO's mistaken Orwellian notion that allowing citizens to retain the fruits of their own labor constitutes subsidies and corporate welfare. However, we need not even reach the substance of this particular dispute prior to asking: by what authority does the World Trade Organization assume jurisdiction over the United States federal tax policy? That is the question.

At last reading, the Constitution required that all appropriation bills originate in the House, and specified that only Congress has the power to lay and collect taxes. Taxation without representation was a predominant reason for America's fight for independence during the American Revolution. Yet, now we face an unconstitutional delegation of taxing authority to an unelected body of international bureaucrats.

Let me assure Members that this nation does not need yet another bureaucratic hurdle to tax reduction. Article 1, Section 8 of the United States Constitution reserves to Congress alone the authority for regulating foreign commerce. According to Article II, Section 2, it reserves to the Senate the sole power to ratify agreements, namely, treaties, between the United States government and other governments.

We all saw the recent demonstrations at the World Trade Organization meetings in Seattle. Although many of those folks who were protesting were indeed rallying against what they see as evils of free trade and capitalist markets, the real problem when it comes to the World Trade Organization is not free trade. The World Trade Organization is the furthest thing from free trade.

Instead, it is an egregious attack upon our national sovereignty, and this is the reason why we must vigorously oppose it. No nation can maintain its sovereignty if it surrenders its authority to an international collective. Since sovereignty is linked so closely to freedom, our very notion of American liberty is at stake in this issue.

Let us face it, free trade means trade without interference from governmental or quasi-governmental agencies. The World Trade Organization is a quasi-governmental agency, and hence, it is not accurate to describe it as a vehicle of free trade. Let us call a spade a spade: the World Trade Organization is nothing other than a vehicle for managed trade whereby the politically-connected get the benefits of exercising their position as a preferred group; preferred, that is, by the Washington and international political and bureaucratic establishments.

As a representative of the people of the 14th District of Texas and a Member of the United States Congress sworn to uphold the Constitution of this country, it is not my business to tell other countries whether or not they should be in the World Trade Organization. They can toss their own sovereignty out the window if they choose. I cannot tell China or Britain or anybody else that they should or should not join the World Trade Organization. That is not my constitutional role.

I can, however, say that the United States of America ought to withdraw its membership and funding from the WTO immediately.

We need to better explain that the Founding Fathers believed that tariffs were meant to raise revenues, not to erect trade barriers. American colonists even before the war for independence understood the difference.

When our Founding Fathers drafted the Constitution, they placed the treaty-making authority with the President and the Senate, but the authority to regulate commerce with the House. The effects of this are obvious. The Founders left us with a system that made no room for agreements regarding international trade; hence, our nation was to be governed not by protection, but rather, by market principles. Trade barriers were not to be erected, period.

A revenue tariff was to be a major contributor to the U.S. Treasury, but only to fund the limited and constitutionally authorized responsibilities of the federal government. Thus, the tariff would be low.

The colonists and Founders clearly recognized that these are tariffs or taxes on American consumers, they are not truly taxes on foreign corporations. This realization was made obvious by the British government's regulation of trade with the colonies, but it is a realization that has apparently been lost by today's protectionists.

Simply, protectionists seem to fail even to realize that raising the tariff is a tax hike on the American people. ∎

U.S. Membership in the World Trade Organization

Congressional Record – U.S. House of Representatives
June 19, 2000

Mr. Speaker, I rise tonight to talk about a bill that is coming to the floor either tomorrow or the next day. It is H.J. Res. 90. This resolution, if it were to pass, would get us out of the World Trade Organization.

There are many of us here in the House and many Americans who believe very sincerely that it is not in our best interests to belong to the World Trade Organization, who believe very sincerely that international managed trade, as carried on through the World Trade Organization, does not conform with our Constitution and does not serve our interests.

It is said by those who disagree with this so often in the media that those of us who disagree with the World Trade Organization that we are paranoid, we worry too much, and that there is no loss of sovereignty in this procedure. But quite frankly, there is strong evidence to present to show that not only do we lose sovereignty as we deliver this power to the World Trade Organization, that it indeed is not a legal agreement. It does not conform with our Constitution, and, therefore, we as Members of Congress should exert this privilege that we have every five years to think about the World Trade Organization, whether it is in our best interests and whether it is technically a good agreement.

The World Trade Organization came into existence, and we joined it, in a lame duck session in 1994. It was hurried up in 1994 because of the concern that the new Members of Congress, who would have much more reflected the sentiments of the people, would oppose our membership in the WTO. So it went through in 1994; but in that bill, there was an agreement that a privileged resolution could come up to offer us this opportunity.

Mr. Speaker, let me just point out the importance of whether or not this actually attacks our sovereignty. The CRS has done a study on the WTO, and they make a statement in this regard. This comes from a report from the Congressional Research Service on August 25, 1996. It is very explicit. It says, as a member of the WTO, the United States does commit to act in accordance with the rules of the multilateral body. It is legally obligated to ensure national laws do not conflict with WTO rules. That is about as clear as one can get.

Now, more recently, on June 5, the WTO director, General Michael Moore, made this statement and makes it very clear: the dispute settlement mechanism is unique in the international architecture. WTO member governments bind themselves to the outcome from panels and, if necessary, the appellate body. That is why the WTO has attracted so much attention from all sorts of groups who wish to use this mechanism to advance their interests.

Interestingly enough, in the past, if we dealt with trade matters, they came to the U.S. Congress to change the law; they came to elected representatives to deal with this, and that is the way it should be under the Constitution. Today, though, the effort has to be directed through our world trade representative, our international trade representative, who then goes to bat for our business people at the WTO. So is it any surprise that, for instance, the company of Chiquita Banana, who has these trade wars going on in the trade fights, wants somebody in the administration to fight their battle, and just by coincidence, they have donated $1.5 million in their effort to get influence?

So I think that the American people deserve a little bit more than this.

The membership in the WTO actually is illegal, illegal any way we look at it. If we are delivering to the WTO the authority to regulate trade, we are violating the Constitution, because it is very clear that only Congress can do this. We cannot give that authority away. We cannot give it to the President, and we cannot give it to an international body that is going to manage trade in the WTO. This is not legal, it is not constitutional, and it is not in our best interests. It stirs up the interest to do things politically, and unelected bureaucrats make the decision, not elected officials. It was never intended to be that way, and yet we did this five years ago. We have become accustomed to it, and I think it is very important, it is not paranoia that makes some of us bring this up on the floor.

Mr. Speaker, we will be discussing this either tomorrow or the next day. We will make a decision, and it is not up to the World Trade Organization to decide what labor laws we have or what kind of environmental laws we have, or what tax laws. ∎

New China Policy

Congressional Record — U.S. House of Representatives
April 25, 2001

President Bush deserves much credit for the handling of the spy plane crisis. However, he has received significant criticism from some of his own political supporters for saying he was "very" sorry for the incident. This seems a "very" small price to pay for the safe return of 24 American military personnel. Trade with China though should be credited for helping to resolve this crisis. President Bush, in the diplomatic handling of this event, avoided overly strong language and military threats, which would have done nothing to save the lives of these 24 Americans.

This confrontation, however, provides an excellent opportunity for us to reevaluate our policy toward China and other nations. Although trade with China, for economic reasons, encouraged both America and China to work for a resolution of the spy plane crisis, our trading status with China should be reconsidered. What today is called free trade is not exactly that. Although we engage in trade with China, it is subsidized to the tune of many billions of dollars through the Export-Import Bank—the most of any country in the world.

We also have been careless over the last several years in allowing our military secrets to find their way into the hands of the Chinese government. At the same time we subsidize trade with China, including sensitive military technology, we also build up the Taiwanese military while continuing to patrol the Chinese border with our spy planes. It's a risky, inconsistent policy.

The question we must ask ourselves is how would we react if we had Chinese airplanes flying up and down our coast and occupying the air space of the Gulf of Mexico?? We must realize that China is a long way from the U.S. and is not capable, nor is she showing any signs, of launching an attack on any sovereign territory of the United States.

Throughout all of China's history she has never pursued military adventurism far from her own borders. That is something that we cannot say about our own policy. China traditionally has only fought for secure borders predominantly with India, Russia, Japan, and in Korea against the United States, and that was only when our troops approached the Yaloo River.

It should not go unnoticed that there was no vocal support from any of our allies for our spy missions along the Chinese coast. None of our allies bothered to condemn the action of the Chinese military aircraft, although it technically was the cause of the accident. Don't forget that when a Russian aircraft landed in Japan in 1976, it was only after many months we returned the plane to Russia — in crates.

Although there is no doubt that we technically have legal grounds for making these flights, the question really is whether or not it is wise to do so or necessary for our national security. Actually a strong case can be made that our national security is more threatened by our patrolling the Chinese coast than if we avoided such flights altogether. After a half a century it's time to reassess the need for such flights. Satellite technology today gives us the ability to watch and to listen to almost everyone on earth. If there is a precise need for this type of surveillance for the benefit of Taiwan, then the Taiwanese ought to be involved in this activity, not American military personnel. We should not feel so insecure that we need to threaten and intimidate other countries in order to achieve some vague psychological reassurance that we're still the top military power in the world. This is unnecessary and may well represent a weakness rather than strength.

The Taiwan Relations Act essentially promises that we will defend Taiwan at all costs and should be reevaluated. Morally and constitutionally a treaty cannot be used to commit us to war at some future date. One generation cannot declare war for another. Making an open-ended commitment to go to war, promising troops, money, and weapons, is not permitted by the Constitution.

It is clear that war can only be declared by a Congress currently in office. Declaring war cannot be circumvented by a treaty or agreement committing us to war at some future date. If a previous treaty can commit future generations to war, the House of Representatives, the body closest to the people, would never have a say in the most important issue of declaring war.

We must continue to believe and be confident that trading with China is beneficial to America. Trade between Taiwan and China already exists and should be encouraged. It's a fact that trade did help to resolve this current crisis without a military confrontation.

Concern about our negative trade balance with the Chinese is irrelevant. Balance of payments are always in balance. For every dollar we spend in China those dollars must come back to America. Maybe not buying American goods, as some would like, but they do come back and they serve to finance our current account deficit.

Free trade, it should be argued, is beneficial even when done unilaterally, providing a benefit to our consumers. But we should take this opportunity to point out clearly and forcefully the foolishness of providing subsidies to the Chinese through such vehicles as the Export-Import Bank. We should be adamantly opposed to sending military technology to such a nation, or to any nation for that matter.

It is interesting to note that recent reports reveal that missiles, coming from Israel and financed by American foreign aid, were seen on the fighter plane that caused the collision. It should be equally clear that arming the enemies of our trading partners does not make a whole lot of sense either. For American taxpayers to continue to finance the weaponry of Taiwan, and to maintain an open commitment to send our troops if the border dispute between Taiwan and China erupts into violence, is foolhardy and risky.

Don't forget that President Eisenhower once warned that there always seems to be a need for a "monster to slay" in order to keep the military industries busy and profitable. To continue the weapons buildup, something we are always engaged in around the world, requires excuses for such expenditures—some of these are planned, some contrived, and some accidental.

When we follow only a military approach without trading in our dealings with foreign nations, and in particular with China, we end up at war, such as we did in the Korean War. Today, we are following a policy where we have less military confrontation with the Chinese and more trade, so relations are much better. A crisis like we have just gone through is more likely to be peacefully resolved to the benefit of both sides. But what we need is even less military involvement, with no military technology going to China and no military weapons going to Taiwan. We have a precise interest in increasing true free trade; that is, trade that is not subsidized nor managed by some world government organization like the WTO. Maintaining peace would then be much easier.

We cannot deny that China still has many internal moral, economic, and political problems that should be resolved. But so do we. Their internal problems are their own. We cannot impose our views on them in dealing with these issues, but we should be confident enough that engaging in free trade with them and setting a good example are the best ways for us to influence them in coming to grips with their problems. We have enough of our own imperfections in this country in dealing with civil liberties, and we ought not to pretend that we are saintly enough to impose our will on others in dealing with their problems. Needless to say we don't have the legal authority to do so either.

During the Cuban missile crisis a resolution was achieved under very dangerous circumstances. Quietly, President Kennedy had agreed to remove the missiles from Turkey that were pointed at the Soviets, making the point that American missiles on the Soviet borders was not unlike the Soviet missiles on the American borders. A few months later, quietly, the United States removed these missiles, and no one suffered. The Cold War was eventually won by the United States, but our national security was not threatened by the removal of those missiles.

It could be argued that the fact that our missiles were in Turkey and pointed at the Soviets was more of a threat to our national security because that motivated the Soviets to put their missiles in Cuba. It would do no harm to our national security for us to quietly, in time, stop the potentially dangerous and unnecessary spy missions that we have pursued for over 50 years along the Chinese border.

James Bamford recently wrote in *The New York Times* of an episode that occurred in 1956 when Eisenhower was president. On a similar spy mission off the Chinese coast the Chinese Air Force shot down one of our planes, killing 16 American crewmen. In commenting on the incident President Eisenhower said, "We seem to be conducting something that we cannot control very well. If planes were flying 20 to 50 miles from our shores we would be very likely to shoot them down if they came in closer, whether through error or not."

We have been pursuing these missions near China for over 50 years. It's time to reconsider the wisdom and the necessity of such missions, especially since we are now engaged in trade with this nation.

Bellicose and jingoistic demands for retaliation and retribution are dangerous, and indeed are a greater threat to our national security than relying on satellite technology for gathering the information that we might need. A policy of peaceful, nonsubsidized trade with China would go a long way to promoting friendly and secure relations with the Chinese people. By not building up the military arsenal of the Taiwanese, Taiwan will be forced to pursue their trade policies and investments with China, leading to the day where the conflict between these two powers can be resolved peacefully.

Today, it looks like there's a much better chance of North and South Korea getting together and solving their dispute than was the case in the 1950s, when we sent hundreds of thousands of troops and millions of bombs to resolve the conflict, which was unsuccessful.

We should have more confidence that peaceful trade is a much stronger weapon than all the military force that we can provide. That same argument can be made for our dealings with Vietnam today. We did not win with weapons of war in the 1960s, yet we are now much more engaged in a peaceful trade with the people of Vietnam. Our willingness over the past hundred years to resort to weapons to impose our will on others has generally caused a resentment of America rather than respect.

It is now time to reassess our entire foreign policy of worldwide military intervention. Staying neutral in world conflicts while showing a willingness to trade with all nations anxious to trade with us will do more to serve the cause of world peace than all the unnecessary and provocative spy missions we pursue around the globe. ∎

Ending U.S. Membership in the IMF

Congressional Record – U.S. House of Representatives
February 27, 2002

Mr. Speaker, I rise to introduce legislation to withdraw the United States from the Bretton Woods Agreement and thus end taxpayer support for the International Monetary Fund (IMF). Rooted in a discredited economic philosophy and a complete disregard for fundamental constitutional principles, the IMF forces American taxpayers to subsidize large, multinational corporations and underwrite economic destruction around the globe. This is because the IMF often uses the $37 billion line of credit provided to it by the American taxpayers to bribe countries to follow destructive, statist policies.

For example, Mr. Speaker, the IMF played a major role in creating the Argentine economic crisis. Despite clear signs over the past several years that the Argentine economy was in serious trouble, the IMF continued pouring taxpayer-subsidized loans with an incredibly low interest rate of 2.6 percent into the country. In 2001, as Argentina's fiscal position steadily deteriorated, the IMF funneled over $8 billion to the Argentine government!

According to Congressman Jim Saxton, Chairman of the Joint Economic Committee, this

> Continued lending over many years sustained and sub-
> sidized a bankrupt Argentine economic policy, whose
> collapse is now all the more serious. The IMF's generous
> subsidized bailouts lead to moral hazard problems, and
> enable shaky governments to pressure the IMF for even
> more funding or risk disaster.

Argentina is just the latest example of the folly of IMF policies. Only four years ago the world economy was rocked by an IMF-created disaster in Asia. The IMF regularly puts the taxpayer on the hook for the mistakes of the big banks. Oftentimes, Mr. Speaker, IMF funds end up in the hands of corrupt dictators who use our taxpayer-provided largesse to prop up their regimes by rewarding their supporters and depriving their opponents of access to capital.

If not corrupt, most IMF borrowers are governments of countries with little economic productivity. Either way, most recipient nations end up with huge debts that they cannot service, which only adds to their poverty and instability. IMF money ultimately corrupts those countries it purports to help, by keeping afloat reckless political institutions that destroy their own economies.

IMF policies ultimately are based on a flawed philosophy that says the best means of creating economic prosperity is through government-to-government transfers. Such programs cannot produce growth, because they take capital out of private hands, where it can be allocated to its most productive use as determined by the choices of consumers in the market, and place it in the hands of politicians. Placing economic resources in the hands of politicians and bureaucrats inevitably results in inefficiencies, shortages, and economic crises, as even the best-intentioned politicians cannot know the most efficient use of resources.

In addition, the IMF violates basic constitutional and moral principles. The federal government has no constitutional authority to fund international institutions such as the IMF. Furthermore, Mr. Speaker, it is simply immoral to take money from hard-working Americans to support the economic schemes of politically powerful special interests and Third-World dictators.

In all my years in Congress, I have never been approached by a taxpayer asking that he or she be forced to provide more subsidies to Wall Street executives and foreign dictators. The only constituency for the IMF is the huge multinational banks and corporations. Big banks used IMF funds—taxpayer funds—to bail themselves out from billions in losses after the Asian financial crisis. Big corporations obtain lucrative contracts for a wide variety of construction projects funded with IMF loans. It's a familiar game in Washington, with corporate welfare disguised as compassion for the poor.

The Argentine debacle is yet further proof that the IMF was a bad idea from the very beginning—economically, constitutionally, and morally. The IMF is a relic of an era when power-hungry bureaucrats and deluded economists believed they could micromanage the world's economy. Withdrawal from the IMF would benefit American taxpayers, as well as workers and consumers around the globe. I hope my colleagues will join me in working to protect the American taxpayer from underwriting the destruction of countries like Argentina, by cosponsoring my legislation to end America's support for the IMF. ■

Wasteful Foreign Aid to Colombia

House International Relations Committee
Congressional Record — U.S. House of Representatives
March 6, 2002

Mr. Speaker, as a member of the House International Relations committee and the subcommittee on the Western Hemisphere, I would like to state my strong objections to the manner in which this piece of legislation was raised. I was only made aware of the existence of this legislation this morning, just a couple of hours before I was expected to vote on it. There was no committee markup of the legislation, nor was there any notice that this legislation would appear on today's suspension calendar.

This legislation represents a very serious and significant shift in United States policy toward Colombia. It sets us on a slippery slope toward unwise military intervention in a foreign civil war that has nothing to do with the United States.

Our policy toward Colombia was already ill-advised when it consisted of an expensive front in our failed "war on drugs." Plan Colombia, launched nearly two years ago, sent $1.3 billion to Colombia under the guise of this war on drugs. A majority of that went to the Colombian military; much was no doubt lost through corruption. Though this massive assistance program was supposed to put an end to the FARC and other rebel groups involved in drug trafficking, two years later we are now being told — in this legislation and elsewhere — that the FARC and rebel groups are stronger than ever. So now we are being asked to provide even more assistance in an effort that seems to have had as a result the opposite of what was intended. In effect, we are being asked to redouble failed efforts. That doesn't make sense.

At the time Plan Colombia was introduced, President Clinton promised the American people that this action would in no way drag us into the Colombian civil war. This current legislation takes a bad policy and makes it much worse. This legislation calls for the United States "to assist the government of Colombia to protect its democracy from United States-designated foreign terrorist organizations . . ." In other words, this legislation elevates a civil war in Colombia to the level of the international war on terror, and it will drag us deep into the conflict.

Mr. Speaker, there is a world of difference between a rebel group fighting a civil war in a foreign country and the kind of international terrorist organization that targeted the United States last September. As ruthless and violent as the three rebel groups in Colombia no doubt are, their struggle for power in that country is an internal one. None of the three appears to have any intention of carrying out terrorist activities in the United States. Should we become involved in a civil war against them, however, these organizations may well begin to view the United States as a legitimate target. What possible reason could there be for us to take on such a deadly risk? What possible rewards could there be for United States support for one faction or the other in this civil war?

As with much of our interventionism, if you scratch the surface of the high-sounding calls to "protect democracy" and "stop drug trafficking" you often find commercial interests driving U.S. foreign policy. This also appears to be the case in Colombia. And like Afghanistan, Kosovo, Iraq, and elsewhere, that commercial interest appears to be related to oil. The U.S. administration request for FY 2003 includes a request for an additional $98 million to help protect the Cano-Limon Pipeline—jointly owned by the Colombian government and Occidental Petroleum. Rebels have been blowing up parts of the pipeline and the resulting disruption of the flow of oil is costing Occidental Petroleum and the Colombian government more than half a billion dollars per year. Now the administration wants American taxpayers to finance the equipping and training of a security force to protect the pipeline, with much of the training coming from the U.S. military. Since when is it the responsibility of American citizens to subsidize risky investments made by private companies in foreign countries? And since when is it the duty of American servicemen and -women to lay their lives on the line for these commercial interests?

Further intervention in the internal political and military affairs of Colombia will only increase the mistrust and anger of the average Colombian citizen toward the United States, as these citizens will face the prospect of an ongoing, United States-supported war in their country. Already Plan Colombia has fueled the deep resentment of Colombian farmers toward the United States. These farmers have seen their legitimate crops destroyed, water supply polluted, and families sprayed as powerful herbicides miss their intended marks. An escalation of American involvement will only make matters worse.

Mr. Speaker, at this critical time, our precious military and financial resources must not be diverted to a conflict that has nothing to do with the United States and poses no threat to the United States. Trying to designate increased military involvement in Colombia as a new front on the "war on terror" makes no sense at all. It will only draw the United States into a quagmire much like Vietnam. The Colombian civil war is now in its fourth decade; pretending that the fighting there is somehow related to our international war on terrorism is to stretch the imagination to the breaking point. It is unwise and dangerous. ■

Opposing Taxpayer Funding of Multinational Development Banks

Congressional Record – U.S. House of Representatives
May 1, 2002

Mr. Speaker, Congress can perform a great service to the American taxpayer, as well as citizens in developing countries, by rejecting H.R. 2604, which reauthorizes two multilateral development banks, the International Fund for Agricultural Development (IFAD) and the Asian Development Fund (AsDF).

Congress has no constitutional authority to take money from American taxpayers and send that money overseas for any reason. Furthermore, foreign aid undermines the recipient countries' long-term economic progress by breeding a culture of dependency. Ironically, foreign aid also undermines long-term United States foreign policy goals by breeding resentment among recipients of the aid, which may manifest itself in a foreign policy hostile to the United States.

If Congress lacks authority to fund an international food aid program, then Congress certainly lacks authority to use taxpayer funds to promote economic development in foreign lands. Programs such as the AsDF are not only unconstitutional, but, by removing resources from the control of consumers and placing them under the control of bureaucrats and politically powerful special interests, these programs actually retard economic development in the countries receiving this "aid!" This is because funds received from programs like the AsDF are all-too-often wasted on political boondoggles which benefit the political elites in the recipient countries, but are of little benefit to the individual citizens of those countries.

In conclusion, H.R. 2604 authorizes the continued taking of taxpayer funds for unconstitutional and economically destructive programs. I therefore urge my colleagues to reject this bill, return the money to the American taxpayers, and show the world that the United States Congress is embracing the greatest means of generating prosperity: the free market. ■

Why Does the IMF Prohibit Gold-Backed Currency for its Member States?

An Open Letter to Treasury Secretary O'Neill and Federal Reserve
Chairman Alan Greenspan
Congressional Record – U.S. House of Representatives
May 31, 2002

[Congressman Ron Paul sent this letter to both the Treasury and the Federal Reserve Bank in April. Neither responded.]

Dear Sirs:

I am writing regarding Article 4, Section 2b of the International Monetary Fund (IMF)'s Articles of Agreement. As you may be aware, this language prohibits countries who are members of the IMF from linking their currency to gold. Thus, the IMF is forbidding countries suffering from an erratic monetary policy from adopting the most effective means of stabilizing their currency. This policy could delay a country's recovery from an economic crisis and retard economic growth, thus furthering economic and political instability.

I would greatly appreciate an explanation from both the Treasury and the Federal Reserve of the reasons the United States has continued to acquiesce in this misguided policy. Please contact Mr. Norman Singleton, my legislative director, if you require any further information regarding this request. Thank you for your cooperation in this matter. ∎

The Myth of War Prosperity

Congressional Record – U.S. House of Representatives
March 4, 2003

Mr. Speaker, I want to talk tonight about an economic myth. There is a longstanding myth that war benefits the economy.

The argument goes that when a country is at war, jobs are created and the economy grows. This is a myth. Many argue that World War II ended the Great Depression, which is another myth. Unemployment went down because many men were drafted, but national economic output went down during the war.

Economic growth and a true end to the Depression did not occur until after World War II. So it is wrong to think there is an economic benefit arising from war.

There are many economic shortcomings during a war. During wartime it is much more common to experience inflation because the money presses are running to fund military expenses. Also, during wartime there is a bigger challenge to the currency of the warring nation, and already we see that the dollar has dropped 20 percent in the past year. Although there are many other reasons for a weak dollar, the war certainly is contributing to the weakness in the dollar.

Also, during wartime the country can expect that taxes will go up. I know we are talking about cutting taxes, and I am all for cutting taxes; but in real terms taxes will go up during wartime. And it is inevitable that deficits increase. And right now our deficits are exploding. Our national debt is going up nearly $500 billion per year at an annualized rate.

The other shortcoming economically of wartime is that funds, once they are borrowed, inflated, or taxed, once the government spends these, so much of this expenditure is overseas, and it takes away from domestic spending. So this is a strong negative for the domestic economy. Another thing that arises during wartime so often is the sentiment for protectionism — and a weak economy in wartime will really build an incentive for protectionist measures, and we are starting to see that, which I think is a danger.

During wartime, trade is much more difficult; and so if a war comes, we can expect that even our trade balances might get much worse. There are a lot of subjective problems during wartime too. The first thing that goes is confidence. Right now there is less confidence in the stock market and literally hundreds of billions of dollars lost in the stock market in the last year or two, again, due to other reasons; but the possibility of war contributes to this negative sentiment toward the stock market.

It is hard to judge the future. Nobody can know the future because of the unintended consequences of war. We do not know how long the war will last. How much will it spread? So there are a lot of uncertainties about this. There is fear. Fear comes from the potential for war and a lot of confusion. And unfortunately, when wars are not fought for national security reasons, the popularity of the war is questioned — and this may alienate our allies. And I believe we are seeing some of that already.

There is no doubt that during wartime government expands in size and scope.

And this of course is a great danger. And after war, the government rarely shrinks to its original size.

It grows. It may shrink a little, but inevitably the size of the government grows because of war.

This is a danger because when government gets bigger, the individual has to get smaller; therefore, it diminishes personal individual liberty.

So these are the costs that we cannot ignore. We have the cost of potential loss of life, but there are also tremendous economic costs that even the best economists cannot calculate closely.

War should always be fought as the very, very last resort. It should never be done casually, but only when absolutely necessary. And when it is, I believe it should be fought to be won. It should be declared. It should not be fought under UN resolutions or for UN resolutions, but for the sovereignty and the safety and the security of this country. It is explicit in our Constitution that necessary wars be declared by the Congress. And that is something that concerns me a great deal because we have not declared war outright since 1945, and if you look carefully, we have not won very many since then.

We are lingering in Korea. What a mess! We have been there for 58 years, have spent hundreds of billions of dollars, and we still have achieved nothing — because we went there under UN resolutions and we did not fight to victory. The same was true with the first Persian Gulf War. We went into Iraq without a declaration of war. We went there under the UN, we are still there, and nobody knows how long we will be there. So there are many costs, some hidden and some overt. But the greatest threat, the greatest cost of war is the threat to individual liberty. So I caution my colleagues that we should move much more cautiously and hope and pray for peace. ∎

Opposing Trade Sanctions against Syria

Congressional Record — U.S. House of Representatives
October 16, 2003

Mr. Speaker, I would like to express my strong opposition to this ill-conceived and ill-timed legislation. This bill will impose what is effectively a trade embargo against Syria and will force the severance of diplomatic and business ties between the United States and Syria. It will also significantly impede travel between the United States and Syria. Worse yet, the bill also provides essentially an open-ended authorization for the President to send U.S. taxpayer money to Syria should that country do what we are demanding in this bill.

This bill cites Syria's alleged support for Hamas, Hizballah, Palestine Islamic Jihad, the Popular Front for the Liberation of Palestine, and other terrorist groups as evidence that Syria is posing a threat to the United States. Not since the Hizballah bombing of a U.S. Marine barracks in Lebanon in 1983 have any of these organizations attacked the United States. After that attack on our Marines, who were sent to Beirut to intervene in a conflict that had nothing to do with the United States, President Ronald Reagan wisely ordered their withdrawal from that volatile area. Despite what the interventionists constantly warn, the world did not come to an end back in 1983 when the President decided to withdraw from Beirut and leave the problems there to be worked out by those countries most closely involved.

What troubles me greatly about this bill is that although the named, admittedly bad, terrorist organizations do not target the United States at present, we are basically declaring our intention to pick a fight with them. We are declaring that we will take preemptive actions against organizations that apparently have no quarrel with us. Is this wise, particularly considering their capacity to carry out violent acts against those with whom they are in conflict? Is this not inviting trouble by stirring up a hornet's nest? Is there anything to be gained in this?

This bill imposes an embargo on Syria for, among other reasons, the Syrian government's inability to halt fighters crossing the Syrian border into Iraq. While I agree that any foreign fighters coming into Iraq to attack American troops is totally unacceptable, I wonder just how much control Syria has over its borders—particularly over the chaotic border with Iraq. If Syria has no control over its borders, is it valid to impose sanctions on the country for its inability to halt clandestine border crossings? I find it a bit ironic to be imposing a trade embargo on Syria for failing to control its borders when we do not have control of our own borders. Scores cross illegally into the United States each year—potentially including those who cross over with the intent to do us harm—yet very little is done to secure our own borders. Perhaps this is because our resources are too engaged guarding the borders of countless countries overseas. But there is no consistency in our policy. Look at the border between Pakistan and Afghanistan: while we continue to maintain friendly relations and deliver generous foreign aid to Pakistan, it is clear that Pakistan does not control its border with Afghanistan. In all likelihood, Osama bin Laden himself has crossed over the Afghan border into Pakistan. No one proposes an embargo on Pakistan. On the contrary: the supplemental budget request we are taking up this week includes another $200 million in loan guarantees to Pakistan.

I am also concerned about the timing of this bill. As we continue to pursue Al-Qaeda—most of which escaped and continues to operate—it seems to me we need all the help we can get in tracking these criminals down and holding them to account for the attack on the United States. As the AP reported recently:

> So, too, are Syria's claims, supported by U.S. intelligence, that Damascus has provided the United States with valuable assistance in countering terror.
>
> The Syrians have in custody Mohammed Haydar Zammer, believed to have recruited some of the Sept. 11 hijackers, and several high-level Iraqis who were connected to the Saddam Hussein government have turned up in U.S. custody.

Numerous other press reports detail important assistance Syria has given the U.S. after 9/11. If Syria is providing assistance to the U.S. in tracking these people down—any assistance—passing this bill can only be considered an extremely counterproductive development. Does anyone here care to guess how much assistance Syria will be providing us once this bill is passed? Can we afford to turn our back on Syria's assistance, even if it is not as complete as it could be?

That is the problem with this approach. Imposing sanctions and cutting off relations with a country is ineffective and counterproductive. It is only one-half step short of war and very often leads to war. This bill may well even completely eliminate any trade between the two countries. It will almost completely shut the door on diplomatic relations. It sends a strong message to Syria and the

Syrian people: that we no longer wish to engage you. This cannot be in our best interest.

This bill may even go further than that. In a disturbing bit of *déjà vu*, the bill makes references to "Syria's acquisition of weapons of mass destruction (WMD)" and threatens to "impede" Syrian weapons ambitions. This was the justification for our intervention in Iraq, yet after more than a thousand inspectors have spent months and some $300 million none have been found. Will this bill's unproven claims that Syria has WMD be later used to demand military action against that country?

Mr. Speaker, history is replete with examples of the futility of sanctions and embargoes and travel bans. More than 40 years of embargo against Cuba have not produced the desired change there. Sadly, embargoes and sanctions most often hurt those least responsible. A trade embargo against Syria will hurt American businesses and will cost American jobs. It will make life more difficult for the average Syrian—with whom we have no quarrel. Making life painful for the population is not the best way to win over hearts and minds. I strongly urge my colleagues to reject this counterproductive bill. ■

Reject the Millennium Challenge Act

Congressional Record – U.S. House of Representatives
May 19, 2004

Mr. Chairman, though the ill-conceived Millennium Challenge Act has already become law and therefore we are only talking about its implementation today, it is nevertheless important to again address some very fundamental problems with this new foreign aid program.

I believe that the Millennium Challenge Act (MCA) may be one of the worst foreign policy blunders yet — and among the most costly. It is advertised as a whole new kind of foreign aid — apparently an honest admission that the old system of foreign aid does not work. But rather than get rid of the old, bad system of foreign aid in favor of this "new and improved" system, we are keeping both systems and thereby doubling our foreign aid. I guess it is easy to be generous with other people's money. In reality, this "new and improved" method of sending U.S. taxpayer dollars overseas will likely work no better than the old system, and may in fact do more damage to the countries that it purports to help.

The MCA budget request for fiscal year 2005 is $2.5 billion. We have been told that somewhere between 12 and 16 countries have met the following criteria for inclusion in the program: "ruling justly, investing in people, and pursuing sound economic policies."

It is a good idea to pay close attention to these criteria, as they tell the real tale of this new program. First, what does "investing in people" mean? It is probably safe to assume that "investing in people" does not mean keeping taxes low and government interference to a minimum so that individuals can create wealth through private economic activity. So, in short, this program will reward socialist-style governance.

In fact, this program will do much more harm than good.

MCA will hurt recipient country economies. Sending U.S. aid money into countries that are pursuing sound economic policies will not help these economies. On the contrary, an external infusion of money to governments meeting the economic criteria will actually obscure areas where an economy is inefficient and unproductive. This assistance will slow down necessary reform by providing a hidden subsidy to unproductive sectors of the economy. We thus do no favors for the recipient country in the long term with this harmful approach.

MCA is a waste of taxpayer money. Countries that pursue sound economic policies will find that international financial markets provide many times the investment capital necessary for economic growth. MCA funds will not even be a drop in the bucket compared to what private capital can bring to bear in an economy with promise and potential. And this capital will be invested according to sound investment strategies—designed to make a profit—rather than allocated according to the whim of government bureaucrats.

MCA is corporate welfare for politically-connected U.S. firms. These companies will directly benefit from this purported aid to foreign countries, as the money collected from U.S. taxpayers can under the program be transferred directly to U.S. companies to complete programs in the recipient countries. As bad as it is for U.S. tax dollars to be sent overseas to help poor countries, what is worse is for it to be sent abroad to help rich and politically connected U.S. and multinational companies.

MCA encourages socialism and statism. Because it is entirely geared toward foreign governments, it will force economically devastating "public-private partnerships" in developing nations: if the private sector is to see any of the money it will have to be in partnership with government. There should be no doubt that these foreign governments will place additional requirements on the private firms in order to qualify for funding. Who knows how much of this money will be wasted on those companies with the best political connections to the foreign governments in power. The MCA invites political corruption by creating a slush fund at the control of foreign governments.

MCA encourages a socialist approach to health care in recipient countries. In rewarding a top-down government-controlled approach to health care, the program ignores the fact that this model has failed miserably wherever it has been applied. Ask anyone in the former communist countries how they liked their government healthcare system.

Finally, MCA is another tool to meddle in the internal affairs of sovereign nations. Already we see that one of the countries slated to receive funds is the Republic of Georgia, where former cronies of dictator Eduard Shevardnadze staged a coup against him last year and have since then conducted massive purges of the media and state institutions, have jailed thousands in phony "anti-corruption" campaigns, and have even adopted their own political party flag as the new flag of the country. The current government in Georgia does not deserve a dime of aid from the United States.

Though the Millennium Challenge Act is advertised as a brand new approach to foreign aid—foreign aid that really works—it is in fact expensive and counterproductive, and will be very unlikely to affect real change in the countries it purports to help. The wisest approach to international economic development is for the United States to lead by example, to re-embrace the kind of economic policies that led us to become wealthy in the first place. This means less government, less taxation, no foreign meddling. Demonstrating the effectiveness of limited government in creating wealth would be the greatest gift we could send overseas. ∎

Providing for the Establishment of a Commission in the House of Representatives to Assist Parliaments in Emerging Democracies

Statement on H. Res. 135
Congressional Record – U.S. House of Representatives
March 14, 2005

Mr. Speaker, I rise in opposition to this legislation. We have absolutely no constitutional authority to establish a commission to "assist" parliaments throughout the world. Despite all the high-sounding rhetoric surrounding this legislation, we should not fool ourselves. This is nothing more than yet another scheme to funnel United States tax dollars to foreign governments. It is an international welfare scheme and an open door to more U.S. meddling in the internal affairs of foreign countries.

How can we tell an American family struggling to pay its bills that it must pay more taxes so a foreign parliament can purchase fancy plasma screen televisions, or the latest computer equipment, or ultra-modern communications equipment? Can anyone here justify this?

Mr. Speaker, this bill will do more than just take money from Americans. This commission will enable members of Congress and congressional staff employees to travel the world meddling in the affairs of foreign governing bodies. It is counterproductive to tell other nations how they should govern themselves, as even if we come loaded with dollars to hand out, our meddling is always resented by the local population — just as we would resent a foreign government telling us how to govern ourselves. Don't we have enough of our own problems to solve without going abroad in search of foreign parliaments to aid?

I urge my colleagues to reject this wasteful and counterproductive scheme. ∎

Opposing Statement to Committee on Financial Services World Bank Hearing

Congressional Record — U.S. House of Representatives
May 22, 2007

Of all the elements of the Bretton Woods system, perhaps the most enduring has been the World Bank and its associated institutions. Although highly regarded in some circles, the Bank has been a significant failure in helping the residents of poor and developing nations.

Like many bureaucracies, the World Bank has constantly attempted to reinvent itself and redefine its mission. Some critics have referred to this as "mission creep." It is the reaction of self-interested bureaucrats who are intent on saving their jobs at all costs. The noninstitutional elements of Bretton Woods, such as the gold-backed dollar standard, have gone by the wayside, but the World Bank and the IMF soldier on.

What is most annoying about the World Bank are the criticisms alleging that the Bank and its actions demonstrate the negative side of free-market capitalism. Nothing could be further from the truth. The World Bank is not an organization devoted to capitalism, or to the free market, but to state-run corporate capitalism. Established and managed by a multitude of national governments, the World Bank promotes managed trade, by which politically connected individuals and corporations enrich themselves at the expense of the poor and middle class.

Western governments tax their citizens to fund the World Bank, lend this money to corrupt Third World dictators who abscond with the funds, and then demand repayment which is extracted through taxation from poor Third World citizens, rather than from the government officials responsible for the embezzlement. It is in essence a global transfer of wealth from the poor to the rich. Taxpayers around the world are forced to subsidize the lavish lifestyles of Third World dictators and highly-paid World Bank bureaucrats who don't even pay income tax.

The World Bank has outlived its intended purpose. Capital markets are flush with money and well-developed enough to lend money not just to national governments but to local and regional development projects, at competitive market rates. In the aftermath of Mr. Wolfowitz's departure, much will be made of the question of his successor, when the questioning instead should be directed towards the phasing out of the organization. ∎

Darfur Accountability and Divestment Act

Congressional Record – U.S. House of Representatives
July 30, 2007

Madam Speaker, H.R. 180 is premised on the assumption that divestment, sanctions, and other punitive measures are effective in influencing repressive regimes, when in fact nothing could be further from the truth. Proponents of such methods fail to remember that where goods cannot cross borders, troops will. Sanctions against Cuba, Iraq, and numerous other countries failed to topple their governments. Rather than weakening dictators, these sanctions strengthened their hold on power and led to more suffering on the part of the Cuban and Iraqi people. To the extent that divestment effected change in South Africa, it was brought about by private individuals working through the market to influence others.

No one denies that the humanitarian situation in Darfur is dire, but the United States government has no business entangling itself in this situation, nor in forcing divestment on unwilling parties. Any further divestment action should be undertaken through voluntary means and not by government fiat.

H.R. 180 is an interventionist piece of legislation which will extend the power of the federal government over American businesses, force this country into yet another foreign policy debacle, and do nothing to alleviate the suffering of the residents of Darfur. By allowing state and local governments to label pension and retirement funds as state assets, the federal government is giving the go-ahead for state and local governments to play politics with the savings upon which millions of Americans depend for security in their old age. The safe harbor provision opens another dangerous loophole, allowing fund managers to escape responsibility for any potential financial mismanagement, and it sets a dangerous precedent. Would the Congress offer the same safe harbor provision to fund managers who wish to divest from firms offering fatty foods, growing tobacco, or doing business in Europe?

This bill would fail in its aim of influencing the government of the Sudan, and would likely result in the exact opposite of its intended effects. The regime in Khartoum would see no loss of oil revenues, and the civil conflict will eventually flare up again. The unintended consequences of this bill on American workers, investors, and companies need to be considered as well. Forcing American workers to divest from companies which may only be tangentially related to supporting the Sudanese government could have serious economic repercussions which need to be taken into account. ∎

Iran Sanctions Enabling Act

Congressional Record – U.S. House of Representatives
July 30, 2007

Madam Speaker, I strongly oppose any move to initiate further sanctions on Iran. Sanctions are acts of war, and expanding sanctions on Iran serves no purpose other than preparing the American people for an eventual attack on Iran. This is the same pattern we saw in the run up to the war on Iraq: Congress passes legislation calling for regime change, sanctions are imposed, and eventually we are told that only an attack will solve the problem. We should expect the same tragic result if we continue down this path. I urge my colleagues to reconsider.

I oppose economic sanctions for two very simple reasons. First, they don't work as effective foreign policy. Time after time, from Cuba to China to Iraq, we have failed to unseat despotic leaders or change their policies by refusing to trade with the people of those nations. If anything, the anti-American sentiment aroused by sanctions often strengthens the popularity of such leaders, who use America as a convenient scapegoat to divert attention from their own tyranny. History clearly shows that free and open trade does far more to liberalize oppressive governments than trade wars. Economic freedom and political freedom are inextricably linked – when people get a taste of goods and information from abroad, they are less likely to tolerate a closed society at home. So sanctions mostly harm innocent citizens and do nothing to displace the governments we claim as enemies.

Second, sanctions simply hurt American industries, particularly agriculture. Every market we close to our nation's farmers is a market exploited by foreign farmers. China, Russia, the Middle East, North Korea, and Cuba all represent huge markets for our farm products, yet many in Congress favor current or proposed trade restrictions that prevent our farmers from selling to the billions of people in these areas.

We must keep in mind that Iran has still not been found in violation of the Non-Proliferation Treaty. Furthermore, much of the information regarding Iran's nuclear program is coming to us via thoroughly discredited sources like the MeK, a fanatical cult that is on our State Department's terror list. Additionally, the same discredited neoconservatives who pushed us into the Iraq war are making similarly exaggerated claims against Iran. How often do these "experts" have to be proven wrong before we start to question their credibility?

It is said that we noninterventionists are somehow "isolationists" because we don't want to interfere in the affairs of foreign nations. But the real isolationists are those who demand that we isolate certain peoples overseas because we disagree with the policies of their leaders. The best way to avoid war, to promote American values, and to spread real freedom and liberty is to engage in trade and contacts with the rest of the world as broadly as possible.

I urge my colleagues to reconsider this counterproductive and dangerous move toward further sanctions on Iran. ∎

PART EIGHT

How Government Distorts the Housing Market

In 2007 the financial industry finally acknowledged what many of us had been saying for quite some time: The Federal Reserve's easy-credit policies had led to a bubble in the housing market. In this section I describe how the government perverts the American dream of home ownership.

Debate on the Housing Opportunity
and Responsibility Act of 1997

Congressional Record — U.S. House of Representatives
April 30, 1997

Mr. Speaker, I am very pleased . . . we will have a chance to debate housing. I think it is a very important debate. We have had this debate going on now for several weeks in the Subcommittee on Housing and Community Opportunity. Unfortunately, as far as I am concerned, the debate has not keyed in on the real important issue of whether or not public housing is a good idea.

This particular piece of legislation does very little more than juggle the bureaucrats in hopes that it will do some good. Public housing started in 1937 with the U.S. Housing Act, and we have been living with public housing ever since. In 1965 HUD was created, and since that time, we have spent literally hundreds of billions of dollars.

We have no evidence of any sort to show that public housing is a good idea. It causes a great deal of problems and actually takes housing away from many, many poor people. But it costs a lot of money and costs a lot of hardship to a lot of people. The principle of public housing is what needs to be debated. Hopefully, in the general debate and in the debate over the amendments, we will be able to direct a debate in that area.

One thing that I think our side, the side that I represent, that is the free market and the constitutional approach to housing, we have, I would grant you, done a very poor job in presenting the views on how poor people get houses in a free society. Since we have had 30 years of experience and there is proof now that it leads to corruption and drug-ridden public housing projects that do not last very long and cost too much money. We who present the market view have not done a good job, emphasizing lower tax, less regulation and growth economy, sound monetary policy, low interest rates; this is what will eventually give housing to the poor people.

But I think it is very important that we not construe anybody who opposes this bill as being one that has endorsed the notion or rejects the idea.

Mr. Speaker, the one other point that I would like to make is one of the arguments in favor of this bill is that it is going to be saving some money in the bureaucratic process. But if this is the case, one must look very closely at the CBO figures, because last year the HUD budget took $25-plus billion. This year, with this wonderful new program, we will be asking, according to CBO, $30.4 billion, an increase of about $5 billion. And this is not the end, it is just the beginning. So this is an expansion of the spending on public housing.

By the year 2002, it goes up to $36 billion. So the best I can tell is we were working on the fringes, we are not dealing with the real issues, we are not dealing with the principle of whether or not public housing is a good program.

I, for one, think we can do a lot more for the poor people. There are more homeless now, after spending nearly $600 billion over these last 20 years, than we had before. So I am on record for saying we must do more but we can do more by looking more carefully at the market. ∎

Fannie Mae and Freddie Mac Subsidies Distort the Housing Market

House Financial Services Committee
Congressional Record – U.S. House of Representatives
September 10, 2003

Mr. Chairman, thank you for holding this hearing on the Treasury Department's views regarding Government Sponsored Enterprises (GSEs). I would also like to thank Secretaries Snow and Martinez for taking time out of their busy schedules to appear before the committee.

I hope this committee spends some time examining the special privileges provided to GSEs by the federal government. According to the Congressional Budget Office, the housing-related GSEs received $13.6 billion worth of indirect federal subsidies in fiscal year 2000 alone. Today, I will introduce the Free Housing Market Enhancement Act, which removes government subsidies from the Federal National Mortgage Association (Fannie Mae), the Federal Home Loan Mortgage Corporation (Freddie Mac), and the National Home Loan Bank Board.

One of the major government privileges granted to GSEs is a line of credit with the United States Treasury. According to some estimates, the line of credit may be worth over $2 billion. This explicit promise by the Treasury to bail out GSEs in times of economic difficulty helps the GSEs attract investors who are willing to settle for lower yields than they would demand in the absence of the subsidy. Thus, the line of credit distorts the allocation of capital. More importantly, the line of credit is a promise on behalf of the government to engage in a huge unconstitutional and immoral income transfer from working Americans to holders of GSE debt.

The Free Housing Market Enhancement Act also repeals the explicit grant of legal authority given to the Federal Reserve to purchase GSE debt. GSEs are the only institutions besides the

United States Treasury granted explicit statutory authority to monetize their debt through the Federal Reserve. This provision gives the GSEs a source of liquidity unavailable to their competitors.

The connection between the GSEs and the government helps isolate the GSE management from market discipline. This isolation from market discipline is the root cause of the recent reports of mismanagement occurring at Fannie and Freddie. After all, if Fannie and Freddie were not underwritten by the federal government, investors would demand Fannie and Freddie provide assurance that they follow accepted management and accounting practices.

Ironically, by transferring the risk of a widespread mortgage default, the government increases the likelihood of a painful crash in the housing market. This is because the special privileges granted to Fannie and Freddie have distorted the housing market by allowing them to attract capital they could not attract under pure market conditions. As a result, capital is diverted from its most productive use into housing. This reduces the efficacy of the entire market and thus reduces the standard of living of all Americans.

Despite the long-term damage to the economy inflicted by the government's interference in the housing market, the government's policy of diverting capital to other uses creates a short-term boom in housing. Like all artificially-created bubbles, the boom in housing prices cannot last forever. When housing prices fall, homeowners will experience difficulty as their equity is wiped out. Furthermore, the holders of the mortgage debt will also have a loss. These losses will be greater than they would have otherwise been had government policy not actively encouraged overinvestment in housing.

Perhaps the Federal Reserve can stave off the day of reckoning by purchasing GSE debt and pumping liquidity into the housing market, but this cannot hold off the inevitable drop in the housing market forever. In fact, postponing the necessary but painful market corrections will only deepen the inevitable fall. The more people invested in the market, the greater the effects across the economy when the bubble bursts.

No less an authority than Federal Reserve Chairman Alan Greenspan has expressed concern that government subsidies provided to GSEs make investors underestimate the risk of investing in Fannie Mae and Freddie Mac.

Mr. Chairman, I would like to once again thank the Financial Services Committee for holding this hearing. I would also like to thank Secretaries Snow and Martinez for their presence here today. I hope today's hearing sheds light on how special privileges granted to GSEs distort the housing market and endanger American taxpayers. Congress should act to remove taxpayer support from the housing GSEs before the bubble bursts and taxpayers are once again forced to bail out investors who were misled by foolish government interference in the market. I therefore hope this committee will soon stand up for American taxpayers and investors by acting on my Free Housing Market Enhancement Act. ■

The American Dream Downpayment Act

Congressional Record – U.S. House of Representatives
October 1, 2003

Mr. Speaker, the American dream, as conceived by the nation's founders, has little in common with H.R. 1276, the so-called American Dream Downpayment Act. In the original version of the American dream, individuals earned the money to purchase a house through their own efforts, oftentimes sacrificing other goods to save for their first downpayment. According to the sponsors of H.R. 1276, that old American dream has been replaced by a new dream of having the federal government force your fellow citizens to hand you the money for a downpayment.

H.R. 1276 not only warps the true meaning of the American dream, but also exceeds Congress's constitutional boundaries and interferes with and distorts the operation of the free market. Instead of expanding unconstitutional federal power, Congress should focus its energies on dismantling the federal housing bureaucracy so the American people can control housing resources and use the free market to meet their demands for affordable housing.

As the great economist Ludwig von Mises pointed out, questions of the proper allocation of resources for housing and other goods should be determined by consumer preference in the free market. Resources removed from the market and distributed according to the preferences of government politicians and bureaucrats are not devoted to their highest-valued use. Thus, government interference in the economy results in a loss of economic efficiency and, more importantly, a lower standard of living for all citizens.

H.R. 1276 takes resources away from private citizens, through confiscatory taxation, and uses them for the politically favored cause of expanding home ownership. Government subsidization of housing leads to an excessive allocation of resources to the housing market. Thus, thanks to government policy, resources that would have been devoted to education, transportation, or some other good desired by consumers, will instead be devoted to housing. Proponents of this bill ignore the socially beneficial uses the monies devoted to housing might have been put to had those resources been left in the hands of private citizens.

Finally, while I know this argument is unlikely to have much effect on my colleagues, I must point out that Congress has no constitutional authority to take money from one American and redistribute it to another. Legislation such as H.R. 1276, which takes tax money from some Americans to give to others whom Congress has determined are worthy, is thus blatantly unconstitutional.

I hope no one confuses my opposition to this bill as opposition to any congressional actions to ensure more Americans have access to affordable housing. After all, one reason many Americans lack affordable housing is because taxes and regulations have made it impossible for builders to provide housing at a price that could be afforded by many lower-income Americans. Therefore, Congress should cut taxes and regulations. A good start would be generous housing tax credits. Congress should also consider tax credits and regulatory relief for developers who provide housing for those with low incomes.

For example, I am cosponsoring H.R. 839, the Renewing the Dream Tax Credit Act, which provides a tax credit to developers who construct or rehabilitate low-income housing.

H.R. 1276 distorts the economy and violates constitutional prohibitions on income redistribution. A better way of guaranteeing an efficient housing market where everyone could meet their own needs for housing would be for Congress to repeal taxes and programs that burden the housing industry and allow housing needs to be met by the free market.

Therefore, I urge my colleagues to reject this bill and instead develop housing policies consistent with constitutional principles, the laws of economics, and respect for individual rights. ∎

Reforming the Government Sponsored Enterprises (Fannie Mae and Freddie Mac)

House Committee on Financial Services
Congressional Record – U.S. House of Representatives
May 9, 2007

H.R. 1427 fails to address the core problems with the government Sponsored Enterprises (GSEs). Furthermore, since this legislation creates new government programs that will further artificially increase the demand for housing, H.R. 1427 increases the economic damage that will occur from the bursting of the housing bubble. The main problem with the GSEs is the special privileges the federal government gives the GSEs. According to the Congressional Budget Office, the housing-related GSEs received almost $20 billion worth of indirect federal subsidies in fiscal year 2004 alone, while Wayne Passmore of the Federal Reserve estimates the value of the GSE's federal subsidies to be between $122 and $182 billion.

One of the major privileges the federal government grants to the GSEs is a line of credit from the United States Treasury. According to some estimates, the line of credit may be worth over $2 billion. GSEs also benefit from an explicit grant of legal authority given to the Federal Reserve to purchase the debt of the GSEs. GSEs are the only institutions besides the United States Treasury granted explicit statutory authority to monetize their debt through the Federal Reserve. This provision gives the GSEs a source of liquidity unavailable to their competitors.

This implicit promise by the government to bail out the GSEs in times of economic difficulty helps the GSEs attract investors who are willing to settle for lower yields than they would demand in the absence of the subsidy. Thus, the line of credit distorts the allocation of capital. More importantly, the line of credit is a promise on behalf of the government to engage in a massive unconstitutional and immoral income transfer from working Americans to holders of GSE debt. This is why I am offering an amendment to cut off this line of credit.

The connection between the GSEs and the government helps isolate the GSEs' management from market discipline. This isolation from market discipline is the root cause of the mismanagement occurring at Fannie and Freddie. After all, if investors did not believe that the federal government would bail out Fannie and Freddie if the GSEs faced financial crises, then investors would have forced the GSEs to provide assurances that the GSEs are following accepted management and accounting practices before investors would consider Fannie and Freddie to be good investments.

Former Federal Reserve Chairman Alan Greenspan has expressed concern that the government subsidies provided to the GSEs makes investors underestimate the risk of investing in Fannie Mae and Freddie Mac. Although he has endorsed many of the regulatory "solutions" being considered here today, Chairman Greenspan has implicitly admitted the subsidies are the true source of the problems with Fannie and Freddie.

H.R. 1427 compounds these problems by further insulating the GSEs from market discipline. By creating a "world-class" regulator,

Congress would send a signal to investors that investors need not concern themselves with investigating the financial health and stability of Fannie and Freddie since a "world-class" regulator is performing that function.

However, one of the forgotten lessons of the financial scandals of a few years ago is that the market is superior at discovering and punishing fraud and other misbehavior than are government regulators. After all, the market discovered, and began to punish, the accounting irregularities of Enron before the government regulators did.

Concerns have been raised about the new regulator's independence from the Treasury Department. Although the Treasury now supports the creation of a new regulator, the compromise between Treasury and the drafters of H.R. 1427 does not address concerns that isolating the regulator from Treasury oversight may lead to regulatory capture.

Regulatory capture occurs when regulators serve the interests of the businesses they are supposed to be regulating instead of the public interest. While H.R. 1427 does have some provisions that claim to minimize the risk of regulatory capture, regulatory capture is always a threat where regulators have significant control over the operations of an industry. After all, the industry obviously has a greater incentive than any other stakeholder to influence the behavior of the regulator.

The flip side of regulatory capture is that managers and owners of highly subsidized and regulated industries are more concerned with pleasing the regulators than with pleasing consumers or investors, since the industries know that investors will believe all is well if the regulator is happy. Thus, the regulator and the regulated industry may form a symbiosis where each looks out for the other's interests while ignoring the concerns of investors.

Furthermore, my colleagues should consider the constitutionality of an "independent regulator." The Founders provided for three branches of government—an executive, a judiciary, and a legislature. Each branch was created as sovereign in its sphere, and there were to be clear lines of accountability for each branch. However, independent regulators do not fit comfortably within the three branches; nor are they totally accountable to any branch. Regulators at these independent agencies often make judicial-like decisions, but they are not part of the judiciary. They often make rules, similar to the ones regarding capital requirements, that have the force of law, but independent regulators are not legislative. And, of course, independent regulators enforce the laws in the same way, as do other parts of the executive branch; yet independent regulators lack the day-to-day accountability to the executive that provides a check on other regulators.

Thus, these independent regulators have a concentration of powers of all three branches and lack direct accountability to any of the democratically chosen branches of government. This flies in the face of the Founders' opposition to concentrations of power and government bureaucracies that lack accountability. These concerns are especially relevant considering the remarkable degree of power and autonomy this bill gives to the regulator. For example, in the scheme established by H.R. 1427 the regulator's budget is not subject to appropriations. This removes a powerful mechanism for holding the regulator accountable to Congress. While the regulator is accountable to a board of directors, this board may conduct all deliberations in private because it is not subject to the Sunshine Act.

Ironically, by transferring the risk of widespread mortgage defaults to the taxpayers through government subsidies and convincing investors that all is well because a "world-class" regulator is ensuring the GSEs' soundness, the government increases the likelihood of a painful crash in the housing market. This is because the special privileges of Fannie and Freddie have distorted the housing market by allowing Fannie and Freddie to attract capital they could not attract under pure market conditions. As a result, capital is diverted from its most productive uses into housing. This reduces the efficacy of the entire market and thus reduces the standard of living of all Americans.

Despite the long-term damage to the economy inflicted by the government's interference in the housing market, the government's policy of diverting capital into housing creates a short-term boom in housing. Like all artificially created bubbles, the boom in housing prices cannot last forever. When housing prices fall, homeowners will experience difficulty as their equity is wiped out. Furthermore, the holders of the mortgage debt will also have a loss. These losses will be greater than they would have been had government policy not actively encouraged overinvestment in housing.

H.R. 1427 further distorts the housing market by artificially inflating the demand for housing through the creation of a national housing trust fund. This fund further diverts capital to housing that, absent government intervention, would be put to use more closely matching the demands of consumers. Thus, this new housing program will reduce efficiency and create yet another unconstitutional redistribution program.

Perhaps the Federal Reserve can stave off the day of reckoning by purchasing the GSEs' debt and pumping liquidity into the housing market, but this cannot hold off the inevitable drop in the housing market forever. In fact, postponing the necessary and painful market corrections will only deepen the inevitable fall. The more people are invested in the market, the greater the effects across the economy when the bubble bursts.

Instead of addressing government policies encouraging the misallocation of resources to the housing market, H.R. 1427 further introduces distortion into the housing market by expanding the authority of federal regulators to approve the introduction of new products by the GSEs. Such regulation inevitably delays the introduction of new innovations to the market, or even prevents some potentially valuable products from making it to the market. Of course, these new regulations are justified in part by the GSEs' government subsidies. We once again see how one bad intervention in the market (the GSEs' government subsidies) leads to another (the new regulations).

In conclusion, H.R. 1427 compounds the problems with the GSEs and may increase the damage that will be inflicted by a bursting of the housing bubble. This is because this bill creates a new unaccountable regulator and introduces further distortions into the housing market via increased regulatory power. H.R. 1427 also violates the Constitution by creating yet another unaccountable regulator with quasi-executive, judicial, and legislative powers. Instead of expanding unconstitutional and market distorting government bureaucracies, Congress should act to remove taxpayer support from the housing GSEs before the bubble bursts and taxpayers are once again forced to bail out investors who were misled by foolish government interference in the market. ■

Mortgage Industry Has Its Roots in the Federal Reserve's Inflationary Monetary Policy

Statement before the Financial Services Committee
Congressional Record – U.S. House of Representatives
September 20, 2007

Mr. Chairman, the situation facing us now in the mortgage industry has its roots in the Federal Reserve's inflationary monetary policy. Without addressing the roots of the current crisis, any measures undertaken to improve the situation will be doomed to fail.

As with asset bubbles and investment manias in past history, the fuel for the current housing bubble had its origins in monetary manipulation. The housing boom was caused by the Federal Reserve's policy resulting in artificially low interest rates. Consumers, misled by low interest rates, were looking to consume, while homebuilders saw the low interest rates as a signal to build, and build they did.

One of the primary means the Federal Reserve uses to stimulate the economy is manipulation of the federal funds rate and the discount rates, which are used as benchmark rates throughout the economy. The interest rate is the price of time, as the value of a dollar today and the value of a dollar one year from now are not the same. Just like any price in the market, interest rates have an important informational signaling purpose. Government price fixing of the interest rate has the same deleterious effects as price controls in other areas.

Reduction in the interest rate has two major effects: it encourages consumption over saving; and it makes long-term, capital-intensive projects cheaper to undertake. Under Chairman Greenspan's tenure, the federal funds rate was so low that the real interest rate (that is the nominal interest rate minus inflation) was negative. With a negative real interest rate, someone who saves money will literally lose the value of that money.

The Federal Reserve continued and still continues to increase the money supply. After ceasing the publication of M3 last February, private economists have calculated that M3 has risen at an annual rate of almost 12 percent, which is faster than we have seen since the 1970s.

Millions of Americans now find themselves stuck in a financial quandary that is not their fault. The result of manipulation of the interest rate, money supply, and mortgage markets is the recently popped housing bubble.

Further regulation of the banking sector, of mortgage brokers, mortgage lenders, or credit rating agencies will fail to improve the current situation, and will do nothing to prevent future real estate bubbles. Any proposed solutions which fail to take into account the economic intervention that laid the ground for the bubble are merely window dressing, and will not ease the suffering of millions of American homeowners. I urge my colleagues to strike at the root of the problem and address the Federal Reserve's inflationary monetary policy. ■

PART NINE

Spending, Taxes, and Regulations

This final section contains sundry statements that I have made on various government interventions in the economy. Sadly, most of what the federal government currently does can be justified neither by the Constitution nor sound economics.

The Chrysler Bailout

Congressional Record – U.S. House of Representatives
November 21, 1979

Although I was not in Congress when either the Lockheed or the New York City bailouts were enacted, I would have opposed both of those actions, as well as the proposed action regarding Chrysler, for many of the same reasons. Let me explain those reasons.

In a nation that is sinking in a sea of debt, it is irresponsible for this Congress to be considering a measure that would add billions to that debt. The expansion of credit is one of the primary forms of inflation. It is not merely inflationary in its effects; it is inflation itself. If this $1.5 billion is created by the federal government, it will ripple and percolate through our banking system, and because of our fractional reserve system, the ultimate growth in the money supply will be far more than $1.5 billion. The standard multiplier is six; that means an infusion of $1.5 billion will eventually result in a $9 billion increase in the money supply. In his testimony before the House Banking Committee, the former Chairman of the Council of Economic Advisers, Alan Greenspan, stated that

> Loan guarantees, insofar as the issue of inflation is concerned, are virtually indistinguishable from on-budget financing, and that the major cause of inflation into this country has been an excessive amount of credit preemption, largely in the area of guarantees, which . . . has created excessive monetary growth and is the base of inflation in the system.

A vote for the Chrysler bailout is, simply put, a vote for further inflation.

Some may argue that the inflation is necessary in order to avoid unemployment, echoing the now repudiated idea of A.W. Phillips, that less inflation means more unemployment and *vice versa*. The past few years of our experience with inflation and unemployment should convince everyone that high inflation and high unemployment can exist side-by-side. I believe the connection is even closer: Inflation causes unemployment — perhaps not immediately, but in the longer run — and we are now in the longer run of our past inflationary policies. It follows that a vote for aid to Chrysler, because it is a vote for inflation, is also a vote for more unemployment.

Such unemployment may not be obvious, but it will nonetheless be real. One of the things that bothers me most about this entire discussion is that it centers around only what is obvious. Saving 100,000 jobs at Chrysler is obvious; losing 100,000 jobs, one by one around the country is not obvious, but they will nonetheless be lost, should aid to Chrysler pass.

Let me explain why I believe this to be so. If this aid takes the form of loan guarantees rather than direct loans (and, I add parenthetically, that over $1 billion of the New York City loan guarantees has been converted into direct federal loans by the Federal Financing Bank) it will be tantamount to an allocation of credit to Chrysler. That means that Chrysler will get capital that would have gone to other more efficient and more profitable businesses. Because this capital will be diverted by these loan guarantees to a less efficient business, it is highly probable that more jobs will be lost through invisible unemployment than would be were Chrysler to fail. I hasten to point out that this will result in all the increased costs to the government that the proponents of the bailout so loudly declare they wish to avoid. Of course, the costs will not all be centered in Michigan; unemployment checks, welfare checks, food stamp benefits will increase nationwide, in big and small towns, urban centers and rural America. Rather than a few localities suffering noticeably; many will suffer almost invisibly. Workers who have nothing to do with Chrysler will lose their jobs or pay the taxes and higher prices caused by this bailout. The average industrial worker earns half of what the average Chrysler workers earns, and under the UAW contract, the Chrysler workers will be receiving a $500 million pay and benefits rise over the next three years. I have always thought that businesses in trouble cut costs, the Chrysler workers will receive far more in wage increases alone over the next ten years than this bailout amounts to. That (and other facts) would indicate to me that the Chrysler workers have not made any sacrifices and that they hope, through federal aid, to maintain their relatively high wages at the expense of the lower paid workers in this country. We are being asked to shift the burden from the relatively well-off workers at Chrysler to the relatively worse-off workers throughout America. A Chrysler bailout will be a shifting of burdens that should be borne by those involved.

Do we in Congress have the authority, either moral or constitutional, to cause this suffering? I can find no provision in the Constitution authorizing Congress to make loans or loan guarantees to anyone, let alone to major corporations. Nor have I yet seen a valid moral argument concluding that we, as representatives of all the people, have the right to tax the American people — most of whom receive less in wages and benefits than Chrysler workers — to support a multibillion-dollar corporation. What right have we — and I pose a serious question that deserves an answer — what right have we to force the American taxpayers to risk their money in a business venture which private investors dealing in their own funds have judged to be too risky? Chrysler paper is now classified; that means that any private investor who is handling funds for his depositors, shareholders, or clients may be judged as violating his fiduciary responsibilities should he invest in Chrysler. Don't we have a trust equally important from the American people? Are we not betraying their trust by voting for a Chrysler bailout? I believe so.

Rather than supporting this patchwork and temporary "solution," we should be addressing those factors, over which we have control and for which we are responsible, that have brought Chrysler to the brink of bankruptcy. In his testimony before the House Banking Committee, President Iacocca listed three factors that caused the troubles at Chrysler: (1) government regulations; (2) inflation; and (3) the gasoline allocation system that caused last spring's gasoline shortages. Please note that all three factors are the responsibility of the Congress. We wrote the regulations or gave some bureaucrats a blank check to write the regulations. We are responsible for inflation through our mismanagement of the monetary system. And we empowered the Department of Energy to create a gasoline allocation system that brilliantly achieved what I had heretofore thought impossible: gasoline shortages in Houston, the oil capital of the United States.

It is our responsibility to diagnose the Chrysler disease accurately. Instead, we are acting like political quacks, prescribing potions to treat symptoms, while the cause of those symptoms rages on unabated. Chrysler is not unique; it is merely the prototype, the harbinger, of crises to come. Dr. Greenspan testified that the most likely sequence of events, in his view, would be federal loan guarantees followed by a Chrysler failure anyway. Unless the disease is correctly diagnosed, the potions we prescribe will kill the patient.

I would urge this Committee and the whole Senate to act with more deliberation than the House has acted. This form of welfare for corporations must end. Just because it was extended to Lockheed does not mean that it should be extended to Chrysler. Bad precedents should not be followed, and these precedents are particularly bad. Because Lockheed, a large corporation, New York City, the largest city, and now Chrysler, the tenth largest corporation in the country, are the three institutions to which aid has been or will be extended, one can conclude that there is an obvious pattern of discrimination in the action of this Congress.

Last year there were 200,000 bankruptcies in this country, according to *U.S. News & World Report.* Yet we have selected only the largest for our aid. This is discrimination of the crassest sort. We ignore the smaller victims of this government's policies simply because they are small. Only the largest, those with the most clout, the most pull, get our attention. This aristocracy of pull is morally indefensible. What answer can be given to the small businessman driven into bankruptcy by government regulations when he asks: "You bailed out Chrysler, why not me?" No justification can be given for this discrimination between the powerful and the powerless, the big and the small.

It is an axiom of our legal system that all citizens are to enjoy the equal protection of the laws. That axiom is violated daily by our tax laws, and now by this proposed corporate welfare plan for

Chrysler. Apparently some citizens are more equal than others. That is a notion I reject, and I hope you do, too. I urge you to reject this proposal for all the reasons I have stated. ■

The Balanced Budget Amendment

House Committee on the Budget
Congressional Record – U.S. House of Representatives
February 4, 1997

The social, corporate, and monetary interventionists have come forth with balanced budget language allowing them to retain power and control while, at the same time, increasing their likelihood of re-election at the hands of their constituents who, by more than 80 percent, favor passage of a balanced budget amendment.

One must wonder why anyone would take such an amendment by Congress seriously. There can be no reasonable expectation that a Congress, which flagrantly circumvents the existing limitations on governmental power contained in the first ten amendments to the very same Constitution, would adhere to provisions of any amendment purporting to balance the federal budget. In its first meeting this session, this very Congress voted to suspend the fourth amendment as it enacted a House Rule to allow drug testing of Congressional personnel.

However, even if Congress would adhere to the plain language of such an amendment, no language has yet been put forth which would genuinely prohibit various interventionist factions from moving the nation further down its current path of fiscal demise.

The monetary interventionists offer amendment language which allows circumvention of the deficit restrictions by Congress "in case of recession." This policy, based in the now-discredited Keynesian paradigm under which governments borrow and spend their way out of their own prior inflation-induced recessions, serves as no real justification for amendment circumvention.

Similarly, the social interventionists propose language which "herds" socially-sacred cows to the off-budget "pasture." Rather than acknowledge the irrefutable notion that subsidization of non-productivity begets more nonproductivity, new "social experiments" changing only a minor variable or two, are implemented which do little more than increase the number of recipients ever more dependent upon programs ultimately destined to fail.

Lastly, the corporate interventionists proffer language to excuse Congress from a balanced budget not only during periods of "declared war" but even during periods when the United States is engaged in "military conflicts." The taxpayers' realization of the true cost of war is one of the soundest checks on government's policy to police the world. Instead, governments have historically resorted to use of the monetary printing presses and excessive borrowing to sidestep this vital form of political pressure.

Conspicuously absent from all proposed language are words necessary to address the real issue. The real issue is excessive growth, spending, and taxation by a Congress which has long ignored the already-existing, Constitutionally-imposed limits contained in the Bill of Rights.

Rather than adding yet another of what have become meaningless amendments to a Congressionally-diluted Constitution; an amendment which is only remotely prudent because protective provisions of the Bill of Rights have been ignored over time when politically convenient; let us instead acknowledge the limitations already placed on the federal government's power, and consequently, government's level of spending and borrowing. ■

Authorizing President to Award Congressional Gold Medal to Mother Teresa

Congressional Record – U.S. House of Representatives
May 20, 1997

Mr. Speaker, I rise today in opposition to H.R. 1650. At the same time, I rise in total support of, and with complete respect for, the work of Mother Teresa, the Missionaries of Charity organization, and each of Mother Teresa's Nobel Peace Prize-winning humanitarian efforts. I oppose the Gold Medal for Mother Teresa Act because appropriating $30,000 of taxpayer money is neither constitutional nor, in the spirit of Mother Teresa who dedicated her entire life to voluntary, charitable work, particularly humanitarian.

Because of my continuing and uncompromising opposition to appropriations not authorized within the enumerated powers of the Constitution, several of my colleagues found it amusing to question me personally as to whether, on this issue, I would maintain my resolve and commitment of the Constitution—a Constitution which, only months ago, each Member of Congress swore to uphold. In each of these instances, I offered to do a little more than uphold my constitutional oath.

In fact, as a means of demonstrating my personal regard and enthusiasm for the work of Mother Teresa, I invited each of these colleagues to match my private, personal contribution of $100 which, if accepted by the 435 Members of the House of Representatives, would more than satisfy the $30,000 cost necessary to mint and award a gold medal to the well-deserving Mother Teresa. To me, it seemed a particularly good opportunity to demonstrate one's genuine convictions by spending one's own money rather than that of the taxpayers who remain free to contribute, at their own discretion, to the work of Mother Teresa and have consistently done so. For the record, not a single Representative who solicited my support for spending taxpayers' money, was willing to contribute their own money to demonstrate the courage of their so-called convictions and generosity.

It is, of course, very easy to be generous with other people's money. ∎

The Davis-Bacon Repeal Act

Congressional Record – U.S. House of Representatives
October 23, 1997

Mr. Speaker, I rise today to introduce the Davis-Bacon Repeal Act of 1997. The Davis-Bacon Act of 1931 forces contractors on all federally-funded construction projects to pay the local prevailing wage, defined as "the wage paid to the majority of the laborers or mechanics in the classification on similar projects in the area." In practice, this usually means the wages paid by unionized contractors. For more than 60 years, this congressionally-created monstrosity has penalized taxpayers and the most efficient companies while crushing the dreams of the most willing workers. Mr. Speaker, Congress must act now to repeal this 61-year-old relic of the era during which people actually believed Congress could legislate prosperity. Americans pay a huge price in lost jobs, lost opportunities, and tax-boosting cost overruns on federal construction projects every day Congress allows Davis-Bacon to remain on the books.

Davis-Bacon artificially inflates construction costs through a series of costly work rules and requirements. For instance, under Davis-Bacon, workers who perform a variety of tasks must be paid at the highest applicable skilled journeyman rate. Thus, a general laborer who hammers a nail must now be classified as a carpenter, and paid as much as three times the company's regular rate. As a result of this, unskilled workers can be employed only if the company can afford to pay the government-determined prevailing wages and training can be provided only through a highly regulated apprenticeship program. Some experts have estimated the costs of complying with Davis-Bacon regulations at nearly $200 million a year. Of course, this doesn't measure the costs in lost job opportunities because firms could not afford to hire an inexperienced worker.

Most small construction firms cannot afford to operate under Davis-Bacon's rigid job classifications or hire the staff of lawyers and accountants needed to fill out the extensive paperwork required to bid on a federal contract. Therefore, Davis-Bacon prevents small firms from bidding on federal construction projects, which, unfortunately, constitute 20 percent of all construction projects in the United States.

Because most minority-owned construction firms are small companies, Davis-Bacon keeps minority-owned firms from competing for federal construction contracts. The resulting disparities in employment create a demand for affirmative action, another ill-suited and ill-advised big government program.

The racist effects of Davis-Bacon are no mere coincidence. In fact, many original supporters of Davis-Bacon, such as Representative Clayton Allgood, bragged about supporting Davis-Bacon as a means of keeping cheap colored labor out of the construction industry.

In addition to opening up new opportunities in the construction industry for small construction firms and their employees, repeal of Davis-Bacon would also return common sense and sound budgeting to federal contracting, which is now rife with political favoritism and cronyism. An audit conducted earlier this year by the Labor Department's Office of the Inspector General found that inaccurate data were frequently used in Davis-Bacon wage determination. Although the inspector general's report found no evidence of deliberate fraud, it did uncover material errors in five states' wage determinations, causing wages or fringe benefits for certain crafts to be overstated by as much as $1.08 per hour.

The most compelling reason to repeal Davis-Bacon is to benefit the American taxpayer. The Davis-Bacon Act drives up the cost of federal construction costs by as much as 50 percent. In fact, the Congressional Budget Office has reported that repealing Davis-Bacon would save the American taxpayer almost $3 billion in four years.

Mr. Speaker, it is time to finally end this patently unfair, wildly inefficient and grossly discriminatory system of bidding on federal construction contracts. Repealing the Davis-Bacon Act will save taxpayers billions of dollars on federal construction costs, return common sense and sound budgeting to federal contracting, and open up opportunities in the construction industry to those independent contractors, and their employees, who currently cannot bid on federal projects because they cannot afford the paperwork requirements imposed by this Act. I therefore urge all my colleagues to join me in supporting the Davis-Bacon Repeal Act of 1997. ∎

The National Right to Work Act

Congressional Record – U.S. House of Representatives
May 6, 1998

Mr. Speaker, I rise today to speak for 80 percent of Americans who support the National Right to Work Act, H.R. 59.

The National Right to Work Act repeals those sections of federal law that give union officials the power to force workers to pay union dues as a condition of employment.

Compulsory unionism violates employers' and employees' constitutional rights of freedom of contract and association. Congress has no constitutional authority to force employees to pay union dues to a labor union as a condition of getting or keeping a job.

Passage of the National Right to Work Act would be a major step forward in ending Congress's illegitimate interference in the labor markets and liberating America's economy from heavy-handed government intervention. Since Congress created this injustice, we have the moral responsibility to work to end it, Mr. Speaker.

The 80 percent of Americans who support right-to-work deserve to know which Members of Congress support worker freedom. I, therefore, urge the congressional leadership, the majority of which have promised to place a National Right to Work Act on the floor, to fulfill their promise to the American people and schedule a time certain for a vote on H.R. 59. ■

Authorizing President to Award Congressional Gold Medal to Rosa Parks

Congressional Record – U.S. House of Representatives
April 20, 1999

Mr. Speaker, I rise today in opposition to H.R. 573. At the same time, I rise in great respect for the courage and high ideals of Rosa Parks who stood steadfastly for the rights of individuals against unjust laws and oppressive governmental policies. However, I oppose the Congressional Gold Medal for Rosa Parks Act because authorizing $30,000 of taxpayer money is neither constitutional nor in the spirit of Rosa Parks who is widely recognized and admired for standing up against an overbearing government infringing on individual rights.

Because of my continuing and uncompromising opposition to appropriations not authorized within the enumerated powers of the Constitution, I must remain consistent in my defense of a limited government whose powers are explicitly delimited under the enumerated powers of the Constitution—a Constitution which, only months ago, each Member of Congress swore to uphold.

Perhaps we should begin a debate among us on more appropriate processes by which we spend other people's money. Honorary medals and commemorative coins, under the current process, are allocated from other people's money. We should look for another way.

It is, of course, easier to be generous with other people's money. ∎

OSHA Home Office Regulations

Subcommittee on Oversight and Investigations
Congressional Record – U.S. House of Representatives
January 28, 2000

Mr. Chairman, I appreciate the opportunity to express my concerns regarding the possibility that the Occupational Safety and Health Administration (OSHA) will attempt to exercise regulatory authority over home-based worksites and hold employers responsible for accidents occurring in such worksites. Although OSHA has announced that it will only hold employers liable for conditions at home-based worksites if the employee is performing "hazardous manufacturing work," this proposal still raises serious concerns. This is because any expansion of OSHA's regulatory authority in the home represents a major expansion of federal authority far beyond anything intended by Congress when it created OSHA in the 1970s. Furthermore, OSHA regulation of any type of work in the private residence opens the door to the eventual regulation of all home worksites. In order to ensure home-based workers are protected from overzealous federal bureaucrats, Congressman J.D. Hayworth (R-AZ) and myself have introduced legislation, the Home Office Protection Enhancement (HOPE) Act, amending the Occupational Safety and Health Act to clarify that OSHA has no authority over worksites located in an employee's residence.

Modern technology, such as e-mail and the Internet, allows employees to be productive members of the workforce without leaving their homes! The option of "telecommuting" is particularly valuable for women with young children or those caring for elderly parents. Using technology to work at home gives these Americans the chance to earn a living and have a fulfilling career while remaining at home with their children or elderly parents. Telecommuting also makes it easier for citizens with disabilities to become productive members of the job market. Any federal requirements holding employers liable for the conditions of a home office may well cause some employers to forbid their employees from telecommuting, thus shutting millions of mothers, persons caring for elderly parents, and disabled citizens out of the workforce!

Federal policies discouraging telecommuting will harm the environment by forcing American workers out of their home and onto America's already overcrowded roads. It is ironic that an administration, which has claimed that "protecting the environment" is one of its top priorities, would even consider policies that could undermine a market-created means of protecting the environment. Employers who continue to allow their employees to telecommute will be forced by any OSHA regulations on home offices to inspect their employees' homes to ensure they are in compliance with any and all applicable OSHA regulations. This is a massive invasion of employees' privacy. What employee would want their boss snooping around their living room, den, or bedroom to make sure their "home-based worksite" was OSHA compliant?

Mr. Chairman, the fact that OSHA would even consider exercising regulatory authority over any part of a private home shows just how little respect OSHA has for private property. Private property, of course, was considered one of the bulwarks of liberty by our nation's Founding Fathers, and has been seriously eroded in this country. While it is heartening that so many members of Congress have expressed their displeasure with OSHA over this issue, I am concerned that most of the debate has focused on the negative consequences of this regulation instead of on the question of whether OSHA has the constitutional authority to regulate any part of a private residence (or private business for that matter). The economic and social consequences of allowing federal bureaucrats to regulate home offices certainly should be debated. However, I would remind my colleagues that conceding the principle that the

only way to protect worker safety is by means of a large bureaucracy with the power to impose a "one-size fits all" model on every
workplace in America ensures that defenders of the free market
will be always on the defensive, trying to rein in the bureaucracy
from going "too far" rather than advancing a positive, pro-freedom agenda.

Furthermore, many companies are experiencing great success
at promoting worker safety by forming partnerships with their
employees to determine how best to create a safe workplace. This
approach to worker safety is both more effective, and constitutionally sound, than giving OSHA bureaucrats the power to, for
example, force landscapers to use $200 gas cans instead of $5 cans
or fining a construction company $7,000 dollars because their
employees jumped in a trench to rescue a trapped man without
first putting on their OSHA-approved hard hats; or fine a company because it failed to warn employees not to eat copier toner!

Some may argue that occasional regulatory excess is a small
price to pay for a safe workplace. However, there is no evidence
that OSHA's invasiveness promotes workplace safety! While it is
true that workplace accidents have declined since OSHA's creation, OSHA itself has had little effect on the decline. Workplace
deaths and accidents were declining before OSHA's creation,
thanks to improvements in safety technology and changes in the
occupational distribution of labor. Workplace fatalities declined
from 30 deaths per 100,000 in 1945 to 18 deaths per 100,000 in 1969,
three years before OSHA's creation. In contrast to the dramatic
drop in workplace fatalities in the 24 years before OSHA's creation, workplace fatalities only declined from 18 per 100,000 to
eight in the 21 years after OSHA's creation.

OSHA's role in this decline was negligible! According to
Richard Butler of the University of Minnesota, who studied
National Safety Council data on workplace facility rates, OSHA's
contribution to workplace fatality rates is "statistically insignificant." This is not an isolated example; the vast majority of workplace studies show an insignificant role for OSHA in reducing
workplace injuries.

This is why I have supported several legislative efforts to
encourage a more cooperative approach to workplace safety. I
hope Congress will continue to work to replace the old "command

and control" model with one that respects the constitution and does not treat Americans like children in need of the protection of "big brother" government.

In conclusion, I wish to once again thank Mr. Hoesktra for holding this hearing on this important issue and urge my colleagues to join with Mr. Hayworth and myself to protect those who work at home from further over-regulation by cosponsoring the Home Office Protection Enhancement (HOPE) Act. ■

Minimum Wage Increase Act

Congressional Record – U.S. House of Representatives
March 9, 2000

Mr. Speaker, I appreciate the opportunity to explain why I oppose H.R. 3846, a bill to raise the federally-mandated minimum wage. Raising living standards for all Americans is an admirable goal; however, to believe that Congress can raise the standard of living for working Americans by simply forcing employers to pay their employees a higher wage is equivalent to claiming that Congress can repeal gravity by passing a law saying humans shall have the ability to fly.

Economic principles dictate that when government imposes a minimum wage rate above the market wage rate, it creates a surplus "wedge" between the supply of labor and the demand for labor, leading to an increase in unemployment. Employers cannot simply begin paying more to workers whose marginal productivity does not meet or exceed the law-imposed wage. The only course of action available to the employer is to mechanize operations or employ a higher-skilled worker whose output meets or exceeds the "minimum wage." This, of course, has the advantage of giving the skilled worker an additional (and government-enforced) advantage over the unskilled worker. For example, where formerly an employer had the option of hiring three unskilled workers at $5 per hour or one skilled worker at $16 per hour, a minimum wage of $6 suddenly leaves the employer only the choice of the skilled worker at an additional cost of $1 per hour. I would ask my colleagues, if the minimum wage is the means to prosperity, why stop at $6.65 — why not $50, $75, or $100 per hour?

Those who are denied employment opportunities as a result of the minimum wage are often young people at the lower end of the income scale who are seeking entry-level employment. Their inability to find an entry-level job will limit their employment prospects for years to come. Thus, raising the minimum wage actually lowers the employment and standard of living of the very people proponents of the minimum wage claim will benefit from government intervention in the economy!

Furthermore, interfering in the voluntary transactions of employers and employees in the name of making things better for low wage earners violates citizens' rights of association and freedom of contract as if to say to citizens "you are incapable of making employment decisions for yourself in the marketplace."

Mr. Speaker, I do not wish my opposition to this bill to be misconstrued as counseling inaction. Quite the contrary, Congress must enact an ambitious program of tax cuts and regulatory reform to remove government-created obstacles to job growth. For example, I would have supported the reforms of the Fair Labor Standards Act contained in this bill had those provisions been brought before the House as separate pieces of legislation. Congress should also move to stop the Occupational Safety and Health Administration (OSHA) from implementing its misguided and unscientific "ergonomics" regulation. Congress should also pass my H.J. Res. 55, the Mailbox Privacy Protection Act, which repeals Post Office regulations on the uses of Commercial Mail Receiving Agencies (CMRAs). Many entrepreneurs have found CMRAs a useful tool to help them grow their businesses. Unless Congress repeals the Post Office's CMRA regulations, these businesses will be forced to divert millions of dollars away from creating new jobs into complying with postal regulations!

Because one of the most important factors in getting a good job is a good education, Congress should also strengthen the education system by returning control over the education dollar to the American people. A good place to start is with the Family Education Freedom Act (H.R. 935), which provides parents with a $3,000 per child tax credit for K-12 education expenses. I have also introduced the Education Improvement Tax Cut (H.R. 936), which provides a tax credit of up to $3,000 for donations to private school scholarships or for cash or in-kind contributions to public schools.

I am also cosponsoring the Make College Affordable Act (H.R. 2750), which makes college tuition tax deductible for middle-and-working class Americans, as well as several pieces of legislation to provide increased tax deductions and credits for education savings accounts for both higher education and K-12. In addition, I am cosponsoring several pieces of legislation, such as H.R. 1824 and H.R. 838, to provide tax credits for employers who provide training for their employees.

My education agenda will once again make America's education system the envy of the world by putting the American people back in control of education and letting them use more of their own resources for education at all levels. Combining education tax cuts for K-12, higher education, and job training with regulatory reform and small business tax cuts, such as those Congress passed earlier today, is the best way to help all Americans, including those currently on the lowest rung of the economic ladder, prosper.

However, Mr. Speaker, Congress should not fool itself into believing that the package of small business tax cuts will totally compensate for the damage inflicted on small businesses and their employees by the minimum wage increase. This assumes that Congress is omnipotent and thus can strike a perfect balance between tax cuts and regulations so that no firm, or worker, in the country is adversely effected by federal policies. If the 20th century taught us anything it was that any and all attempts to centrally plan an economy, especially one as large and diverse as America's, are doomed to fail.

In conclusion, I would remind my colleagues that while it may make them feel good to raise the federal minimum wage, the real life consequences of this bill will be vested upon those who can least afford to be deprived of work opportunities. Therefore, rather than pretend that Congress can repeal economic principles, I urge my colleagues to reject this legislation and instead embrace a program of tax cuts and regulatory reform to strengthen the greatest producer of jobs and prosperity in human history: the free market. ∎

Awarding Gold Medal to Former President and Mrs. Ronald Reagan in Recognition of Service to Nation

Congressional Record — U.S. House of Representatives
April 3, 2000

Mr. Speaker, I rise today in opposition to H.R. 3591. At the same time, I am very supportive of President Reagan's publicly stated view of limiting the federal government to its proper and constitutional role. In fact, I was one of only four sitting members of the United States House of Representatives who endorsed Ronald Reagan's candidacy for President in 1976. The United States enjoyed sustained economic prosperity and employment growth during Ronald Reagan's presidency.

I must, however, oppose the Gold Medal for Ronald and Nancy Reagan because appropriating $30,000 of taxpayer money is neither constitutional nor in the spirit of Ronald Reagan's notion of the proper, limited role for the federal government.

Because of my continuing and uncompromising opposition to appropriations not authorized within the enumerated powers of the Constitution, I would maintain my resolve and commitment to the Constitution — a Constitution which, only last year, each Member of Congress swore to uphold. In each of these instances, I offered to do a little more than uphold my constitutional oath.

In fact, as a means of demonstrating my personal regard and enthusiasm for Ronald Reagan's advocacy for limited government, I invited each of these colleagues to match my private, personal contribution of $100 which, if accepted by the 435 Members of the House of Representatives, would more than satisfy the $30,000 cost necessary to mint and award a gold medal to Ronald and Nancy Reagan. To me, it seemed a particularly good opportunity to demonstrate one's genuine convictions by spending one's own money rather that of the taxpayers who remain free to contribute, at their own discretion, to commemorate the work of the Reagans. For the record, not a single Representative who solicited my support for spending taxpayers' money, was willing to contribute their own money to demonstrate their generosity and allegiance to the Reagans' stated convictions.

It is, of course, very easy to be generous with the people's money. ∎

Internet Gambling Prohibition Act of 2000

Congressional Record – U.S. House of Representatives
July 19, 2000

Mr. Speaker, I rise in opposition to the Internet Gambling Prohibition Act of 2000 for several reasons. The bill threatens Internet privacy, invites federal government regulation of the Internet and tramples States's rights.

H.R. 3125 establishes a precedent for federal content regulation of the Internet. By opening this Pandora's box, supporters of the bill ignore the unintended consequences. The principle will be clearly established that the federal government should intervene in Internet expression. This principle could be argued in favor of restrictions on freedom of expression and association. Disapprove of gambling? Let the government step in and ban it on the Internet! Minority rights are obviously threatened by majority whims.

The bill calls for federal law enforcement agencies, such as the Federal Bureau of Investigation, to expand surveillance in order to enforce the proposed law. In order to enforce this bill (should it become law), law enforcement would have to obtain access to an individual's computer to know if one is gambling online. Perhaps Internet Service Providers can be enlisted as law enforcement agents in the same way that bank tellers are forced to spy on their customers under the Bank Secrecy Act? It was this sort of intrusion that caused such a popular backlash against the "Know Your Customer" proposal.

Several States have already addressed the issue, and Congress should recognize States's rights. The definition of "gambling" in the bill appears narrow but could be "reinterpreted" to include online auctions or even day trading (a different sort of gambling). Those individuals who seek out such thrills will likely soon find a good substitute which will justify the next round of federal Internet regulation. ■

The Wage Act

Congressional Record – U.S. House of Representatives
February 14, 2001

Mr. Speaker, I rise to introduce the Workers Access to Accountable Governance in Employment (WAGE) Act. This bill takes a first step toward restoring the rights of freedom of association and equal protection under the law to millions of American workers who are currently denied these rights by federal law.

The WAGE Act simply gives workers the same rights to hold decertification elections as they have to hold certification elections.

Currently, while workers in this country are given the right to organize and have union certification elections each year, provided that 30 percent or more of the workforce wish to have them, workers are not given an equal right to have a decertification election, even if the same requirements are met.

As a result of the National Labor Relations Board (NLRB) created contract-bar rule, if 30 percent or more of a bargaining unit wants to hold an election to decertify a union as their representative, they are prohibited from doing so unless the contract is in at least its third year.

In other words, it does not matter whether or not workers want to continue to have the union as their representative. It does not matter whether or not the union represents the will of the workers. It does not even matter if the majority of the current workforce voted for union representation. They must accept that representation.

Mr. Speaker, this is absurd. The lowest criminal in this country has the right to change their representative in the courtroom. Yet millions of hard-working, law-abiding citizens cannot change their representation in the workplace.

As a result of the passage of the National Labor Relations Act (NLRA) in 1935 and the action taken by the federally-funded NLRB, workers can be forced to pay union dues or fees for unwanted representation as a condition of employment. Federal law may even force workers to accept union representation against the will of the majority of workers.

Talk about taxation without representation! Mr. Speaker, the WAGE Act takes a step toward returning a freedom to workers that they never should have lost in the first place: the right to choose their own representative. I urge my colleagues to support the nonpartisan, pro-worker WAGE Act. ■

Truth in Employment Act

Congressional Record – U.S. House of Representatives
August 3, 2001

Mr. Speaker, I rise to introduce the Truth in Employment Act which protects small businesses and independent-minded workers from the destructive and coercive "top-down" organizing tactic known as salting. Salting is a technique designed by unscrupulous union officials for the purpose of harassing small businesses until the businesses compel their employees to pay union dues as a condition of employment.

"Salts" are professional union organizers who apply for jobs solely in order to compel employers into consenting to union monopoly bargaining and forced-dues contract clauses. They do this by disrupting the workplace and drumming up so-called "unfair labor practice" charges which are designed to harass and tie up the small business person in constant and costly litigation.

Thanks to unconstitutional interference in the nation's labor markets by Congress, small businesses targeted by union salts often must acquiesce to union bosses' demands that they force their workers to accept union "representation" and pay union dues. If an employer challenges a salt, the salt may file (and win) an unfair labor practice charge against the employer!

Passing the Truth in Employment Act is a good first step toward restoring the constitutional rights of property and contract to employers and employees. I therefore urge my colleagues to stand up for those workers who do not wish to be forced to pay union dues as a condition of employment by cosponsoring the Truth in Employment Act. ∎

Financial Anti-Terrorism Act of 2001

House Financial Services Committee
Congressional Record – U.S. House of Representatives
October 11, 2001

Mr. Chairman, the so-called Financial Anti-Terrorism Act of 2001 (H.R. 3004) has more to do with the ongoing war against financial privacy than with the war against international terrorism. Of course, the federal government should take all necessary and constitutional actions to enhance the ability of law enforcement to locate and seize funds flowing to known terrorists and their front groups. For example, America should consider signing more mutual legal assistance treaties with its allies so we can more easily locate the assets of terrorists and other criminals.

Unfortunately, instead of focusing on reasonable measures aimed at enhancing the ability to reach assets used to support terrorism, H.R. 3004 is a laundry list of dangerous, unconstitutional power grabs. Many of these proposals have already been rejected by the American people when presented as necessary to "fight the war on drugs" or "crack down on white-collar crime." Even a ban on Internet gambling has somehow made it into this "anti-terrorism" bill!

Among the most obnoxious provisions of this bill are: expanding the war on cash by creating a new federal crime of taking over $10,000 cash into or out of the United States; codifying the unconstitutional authority of the Financial Crimes Enforcement Network (FinCeN) to snoop into the private financial dealings of American citizens; and expanding the "suspicious activity reports" mandate to broker-dealers, even though history has shown that these reports fail to significantly aid in apprehending criminals. These measures will actually distract from the battle against terrorism by encouraging law enforcement authorities to waste time snooping through the financial records of innocent Americans who simply happen to demonstrate an "unusual" pattern in their financial dealings.

H.R. 3004 also attacks the Fourth Amendment by authorizing warrantless searches of all mail coming into or leaving the country. Allowing government officials to read mail going out of or coming into the country at whim is characteristic of totalitarian regimes, not free societies.

In conclusion, Mr. Chairman, I urge my colleagues to reject this package of unconstitutional expansions of the financial police state, most of which will prove ultimately ineffective in the war against terrorism. Instead, I hope this Committee will work to fashion a measure aimed at giving the government a greater ability to locate and seize the assets of terrorists while respecting the constitutional rights of American citizens. ■

Terrorism Reinsurance Legislation

Congressional Record – U.S. House of Representatives
November 30, 2001

Mr. Speaker, no one doubts that the government has a role to play in compensating American citizens who are victimized by terrorist attacks. However, Congress should not lose sight of fundamental economic and constitutional principles when considering how best to provide the victims of terrorist attacks just compensation. I am afraid that H.R. 3210, the Terrorism Risk Protection Act, violates several of those principles and therefore passage of this bill is not in the best interests of the American people.

Under H.R. 3210, taxpayers are responsible for paying 90 percent of the costs of a terrorist incident when the total cost of that incident exceeds a certain threshold. While insurance companies technically are responsible under the bill for paying back monies received from the Treasury, the administrator of this program may defer repayment of the majority of the subsidy in order to "avoid the likely insolvency of the commercial insurer," or avoid "unreasonable economic disruption and market instability." This language may cause administrators to defer indefinitely the repayment of the loans, thus causing taxpayers to permanently bear the loss. This scenario is especially likely when one considers that terms such as "likely insolvency," "unreasonable economic disruption," and "market instability" are highly subjective, and that any administrator who attempts to enforce a strict repayment schedule likely will come under heavy political pressure to be more "flexible" in collecting debts owed to the taxpayers.

The drafters of H.R. 3210 claim that this creates a temporary government program. However, Mr. Speaker, what happens in three years if industry lobbyists come to Capitol Hill to explain that there is still a need for this program because of the continuing threat of terrorist attacks? Does anyone seriously believe that Congress will refuse to reauthorize this "temporary" insurance program or provide some other form of taxpayer help to the insurance industry? I would like to remind my colleagues that the federal budget is full of expenditures for long-lasting programs that were originally intended to be temporary.

H.R. 3210 compounds the danger to taxpayers because of what economists call the "moral hazard" problem. A moral hazard is created when individuals have the costs incurred from a risky action subsidized by a third party. In such a case individuals may engage in unnecessary risks or fail to take steps to minimize their risks. After all, if a third party will bear the costs of negative consequences of risky behavior, why should individuals invest their resources in avoiding or minimizing risk?

While no one can plan for terrorist attacks, individuals and businesses can take steps to enhance security. For example, I think we would all agree that industrial plants in the United States enjoy reasonably good security. They are protected not by the local police, but by owners putting up barbed wire fences, hiring guards with guns, and requiring identification cards to enter. One reason private firms put these security measures in place is because insurance companies provide them with incentives, in the form of lower premiums, to adopt security measures. H.R. 3210 contains no incentives for this private activity. The bill does not even recognize

the important role insurance plays in providing incentives to minimize risks. By removing an incentive for private parties to avoid
or at least mitigate the damage from a future terrorist attack, the
government inadvertently increases the damage that will be
inflicted by future attacks!

Instead of forcing taxpayers to subsidize the costs of terrorism
insurance, Congress should consider creating a tax credit or
deduction for premiums paid for terrorism insurance, as well as a
deduction for claims and other costs borne by the insurance industry connected with offering terrorism insurance. A tax credit
approach reduces government's control over the insurance market. Furthermore, since a tax credit approach encourages people to
devote more of their own resources to terrorism insurance, the
moral hazard problems associated with federally-funded insurance are avoided.

The version of H.R. 3210 passed by the Financial Services committee took a good first step in this direction by repealing the tax
penalty which prevents insurance companies from properly
reserving funds for human-created catastrophes. I am disappointed that this sensible provision was removed from the final
bill. Instead, H.R. 3210 instructs the Treasury department to study
the benefits of allowing insurers to establish tax-free reserves to
cover losses from terrorist events. The perceived need to study the
wisdom of cutting taxes while expanding the federal government
without hesitation demonstrates much that is wrong with Washington.

In conclusion, Mr. Speaker, H.R. 3210 may reduce the risk to
insurance companies from future losses, but it increases the costs
incurred by American taxpayers. More significantly, by ignoring
the moral hazard problem this bill may have the unintended consequence of increasing the losses suffered in any future terrorist
attacks. Therefore, passage of this bill is not in the long-term interests of the American people. ∎

The Collapse of Enron

House Financial Services Committee
Congressional Record – U.S. House of Representatives
February 4, 2002

Mr. Chairman, the collapse of Enron has so far been the cause of numerous hearings, as well as calls for increased federal control over the financial markets and the accounting profession. For example, legislation has been introduced to force all publicly traded companies to submit to federal audits.

I fear that many of my well-meaning colleagues are reacting to media reports portraying Enron as a reckless company whose problems stemmed from a lack of federal oversight. It is a mistake for Congress to view the Enron collapse as a justification for more government regulation. Publicly held corporations already comply with massive amounts of SEC regulations, including the filing of quarterly reports that disclose minute details of assets and liabilities. If these disclosure rules failed to protect Enron investors, will more red tape really solve anything? The real problem with SEC rules is that they give investors a false sense of security, a sense that the government is protecting them from dangerous investments.

In truth, investing carries risk, and it is not the role of the federal government to bail out every investor who loses money. In a true free market, investors are responsible for their own decisions, good or bad. This responsibility leads them to vigorously analyze companies before they invest, using independent financial analysts. In our heavily regulated economy, however, investors and analysts equate SEC compliance with reputability. The more we look to the government to protect us from investment mistakes, the less competition there is for truly independent evaluations of investment risk.

The SEC, like all government agencies, is not immune from political influence or conflicts of interest. In fact, the new SEC chief used to represent the very accounting companies now under SEC scrutiny. If anything, the Enron failure should teach us to place less trust in the SEC. Yet many in Congress and the media characterize Enron's bankruptcy as an example of unbridled capitalism gone wrong. Few in Congress seem to understand how the Federal Reserve System artificially inflates stock prices and causes financial bubbles. Yet what other explanation can there be when a company goes from a market value of more than $75 billion to virtually nothing in just a few months? The obvious truth is that Enron was never really worth anything near $75 billion, but the media focuses only on the possibility of deceptive practices by management, ignoring the primary cause of stock overvaluation: Fed expansion of money and credit.

The Fed consistently increased the money supply (by printing dollars) throughout the 1990s, while simultaneously lowering interest rates. When dollars are plentiful, and interest rates are artificially low, the cost of borrowing becomes cheap. This is why so many Americans are more deeply in debt than ever before. This easy credit environment made it possible for Enron to secure hundreds of millions in uncollateralized loans, loans that now cannot be repaid. The cost of borrowing money, like the cost of everything else, should be established by the free market—not by government edict. Unfortunately, however, the trend toward overvaluation will continue until the Fed stops creating money out of thin air and stops keeping interest rates artificially low. Until then, every investor should understand how Fed manipulations affect the true value of any company and the level of the markets.

Therefore, if Congress wishes to avoid future bankruptcies like Enron, the best thing it can do is repeal existing regulations which give investors a false sense of security and reform the country's monetary policy to end the Fed-generated boom-and-bust cycle. Congress should also repeal those programs which provide taxpayer subsidies to large, politically-powerful corporations such as Enron.

Enron provides a perfect example of the dangers of corporate subsidies. The company was (and is) one of the biggest beneficiaries of Export-Import Bank subsidies. The Export-Import Bank, a program that Congress continues to fund with tax dollars taken from hard-working Americans, essentially makes risky loans to foreign governments and businesses for projects involving

American companies. The Bank, which purports to help developing nations, really acts as a naked subsidy for certain politically-favored American corporations—especially corporations like Enron that lobbied hard and gave huge amounts of cash to both political parties. Its reward was more that $600 million in cash via six different Eximbank financed projects.

One such project, a power plant in India, played a big part in Enron's demise. The company had trouble selling the power to local officials, adding to its huge $618 million loss for the third quarter of 2001. Former President Clinton worked hard to secure the India deal for Enron in the mid-90s; not surprisingly, his 1996 campaign received $100,000 from the company. Yet the media makes no mention of this favoritism. Clinton may claim he was "protecting" tax dollars, but those tax dollars should never have been sent to India in the first place.

Enron similarly benefited from another federal boondoggle, the Overseas Private Investment Corporation. OPIC operates much like the Eximbank, providing taxpayer-funded loan guarantees for overseas projects, often in countries with shaky governments and economies. An OPIC spokesman claims the organization paid more than $1 billion for 12 projects involving Enron, dollars that now may never be repaid. Once again, corporate welfare benefits certain interests at the expense of taxpayers. The point is that Enron was intimately involved with the federal government. While most of my colleagues are busy devising ways to "save" investors with more government, we should be viewing the Enron mess as an argument for less government. It is precisely because government is so big and so thoroughly involved in every aspect of business that Enron felt the need to seek influence through campaign money. It is precisely because corporate welfare is so extensive that Enron cozied up to D.C.-based politicians of both parties. It's a game every big corporation plays in our heavily regulated economy, because they must when the government, rather than the marketplace, distributes the spoils.

This does not mean Enron is to be excused. There seems to be little question that executives at Enron deceived employees and investors, and any fraudulent conduct should of course be fully prosecuted. However, Mr. Chairman, I hope we will not allow criminal fraud in one company, which constitutionally is a matter

for state law, to justify the imposition of burdensome new accounting and stock regulations. Instead, we should focus on repealing
those monetary and fiscal policies that distort the market and
allow the politically powerful to enrich themselves at the expense
of the American taxpayer. ∎

Television Consumer Freedom Act

Congressional Record – U.S. House of Representatives
October 2, 2002

Mr. Speaker, I rise to introduce the Television Consumer Freedom Act, legislation repealing regulations that interfere with a
consumers' ability to avail themselves of desired television programming.

My office has received numerous calls from rural satellite and
cable TV customers who are upset because their satellite or cable
service providers have informed them that they will lose access to
certain network television programs and/or cable networks. The
reason my constituents cannot obtain their desired satellite and
cable services is that the satellite and cable "marketplace" is
fraught with government interventionism at every level. Cable
companies have historically been granted franchises of monopoly
privilege at the local level. Government has previously intervened
to invalidate "exclusive dealings" contracts between private parties, namely cable service providers and program creators, and has
most recently assumed the role of price setter. The Library of Congress has even been delegated the power to determine prices at
which program suppliers must make their programs available to
cable and satellite programming service providers.

It is, of course, within the constitutionally enumerated powers
of Congress to "promote the progress of science and useful arts by

securing for limited times to authors and inventors the exclusive right to their respective writings and discoveries." However, operating a clearinghouse for the subsequent transfer of such property rights in the name of setting a just price or "instilling competition" via "central planning" seems not to be an economically prudent nor justifiable action under this enumerated power. This process is one best reserved to the competitive marketplace.

Government's attempt to set the just price for satellite programming outside the market mechanism is inherently impossible. This has resulted in competition among service providers for government privilege rather than the consumer benefits inherent to the genuine free market. Currently, while federal regulation does leave satellite programming service providers free to bypass the governmental royalty distribution scheme and negotiate directly with owners of programming for program rights, there is a federal prohibition on satellite service providers making local network affiliates' programs available to nearby satellite subscribers. This bill repeals that federal prohibition and allows satellite service providers to more freely negotiate with program owners for programming desired by satellite service subscribers. Technology is now available by which viewers will be able to view network programs via satellite as presented by their nearest network affiliate. This market-generated technology will remove a major stumbling block to negotiations that should currently be taking place between network program owners and satellite service providers.

This bill also repeals federal laws that force cable companies to carry certain programs. These federal "must carry" mandates deny cable companies the ability to provide the programming desired by their customers. Decisions about what programming to carry on a cable system should be made by consumers, not federal bureaucrats.

Mr. Speaker, the federal government should not interfere with a consumer's ability to purchase services such as satellite or cable television in the free market. I therefore urge my colleagues to take a step toward restoring freedom by cosponsoring my Television Consumer Freedom Act. ∎

The Shrimp Importation Financing Fairness Act

Congressional Record – U.S. House of Representatives
October 8, 2002

Mr. Speaker, I rise to introduce the Shrimp Importation Financing Fairness Act. This bill aids America's struggling domestic shrimping industry by placing a moratorium on restrictive regulations affecting the shrimping industry. This bill also prevents tax dollars from going to the domestic shrimping industry's major foreign competitors.

The United States' domestic shrimping industry is a vital social and economic force in many coastal communities across the United States, including several in my congressional district. A thriving shrimping industry benefits not only those who own and operate shrimp boats, but also food processors, hotels and restaurants, grocery stores, and all those who work in and service these industries. Shrimping also serves as a key source of safe domestic foods at a time when the nation is engaged in hostilities abroad.

Given the importance of a strong shrimping industry to so many Americans, it seems strange that the federal government continues to burden shrimpers with excessive regulations. For example, the federal government has imposed costly regulations on this industry dealing with usage of items such as by-catch reduction devices and turtle excluder devices (TEDS). The mandatory use of these devices results in a significant reduction in the amount of shrimp caught by domestic shrimpers, thus damaging their competitive position and market share.

Many members of Congress have let the National Marine Fisheries Service, which is the lead federal agency with responsibility to regulate the domestic shrimp industry, know of their displeasure with the unreasonable regulatory burden imposed upon the industry. In response, the agency recently held briefings with

House and Senate staffers as well as industry representatives to discuss how the agency's actions are harming shrimpers.

However, even after hearing firsthand testimony from industry representatives and representatives of communities whose economies rely on a thriving shrimping industry, the agency refuses to refrain from placing regulatory encumbrances upon the domestic shrimping industry. Therefore it is up to Congress to protect this industry from overzealous regulators. The Shrimp Importation Financing Fairness Act provides this protection by placing an indefinite moratorium on all future restrictive regulations on the shrimping industry.

Seven foreign countries (Thailand, Vietnam, India, China, Ecuador, Indonesia, and Brazil) have taken advantage of the domestic shrimping industry's government-created vulnerabilities. These countries have each exported in excess of 20 million pounds of shrimp to the United States in the first six months of this year. These seven countries account for nearly 70 percent of all shrimp consumed in the United States in the first six months of this year and nearly 80 percent of all shrimp imported to this country in the same period!

Adding insult to injury the federal government is forcing American shrimpers to subsidize their competitors! In the last three years, the United States government has provided more than $1.8 billion in financing and insurance for these foreign countries through the Overseas Private Investment Corporation (OPIC). Furthermore, the U.S. current exposure relative to these countries through the Eximbank totals some $14.8 billion. Thus, the United States taxpayer is providing a total subsidy of $16.5 billion to the home countries of the leading foreign competitors of American shrimpers! Of course, the American taxpayer could be forced to shovel more money to these countries through the International Monetary Fund (IMF).

Many of the countries in question do not have free-market economies. Thus, the participation of these countries in United States-supported international financial regimes amounts to a direct subsidy by American shrimpers to their international competitors. In any case, providing aid to any of these countries indirectly grants benefits to foreign shrimpers because of the fungibility of money.

In order to ensure that American shrimpers are not forced to subsidize their competitors, the Shrimp Importation Financing Fairness Act ends all Eximbank and OPIC subsidies to the seven countries who imported more than 20 million pounds of shrimp in the first six months of 2002. The bill also reduces America's contribution to the IMF by America's *pro rata* share of any IMF aid provided to one of those seven countries.

Mr. Speaker, it is time for Congress to rein in regulation-happy bureaucrats and stop subsidizing the domestic shrimping industry's leading competitors. Otherwise, the government-manufactured depression in the price of shrimp will decimate the domestic shrimping industry and the communities whose economies depend on this industry. I, therefore, hope all my colleagues will stand up for shrimpers by cosponsoring the Shrimp Importation Financing Fairness Act. ∎

Oppose the Federal Welfare State

Congressional Record – U.S. House of Representatives
February 13, 2003

Mr. Speaker, no one can deny that welfare programs have undermined America's moral fabric and constitutional system. Therefore, all those concerned with restoring liberty and protecting civil society from the maw of the omnipotent state should support efforts to eliminate the welfare state, or, at the very least, reduce federal control over the provision of social services. Unfortunately, the misnamed Personal Responsibility, Work, and Family Promotion Act (H.R. 4) actually increases the unconstitutional federal welfare state and thus undermines personal responsibility, the work ethic, and the family.

H.R. 4 reauthorizes the Temporary Assistance to Needy Families (TANF) block grant program, the main federal welfare program. Mr. Speaker, increasing federal funds always increases federal control, as the recipients of the funds must tailor their programs to meet federal mandates and regulations. More importantly, since federal funds represent resources taken out of the hands of private individuals, increasing federal funding leaves fewer resources available for the voluntary provision of social services, which, as I will explain in more detail later, is a more effective, moral, and constitutional means of meeting the needs of the poor.

H.R. 4 further increases federal control over welfare policy by increasing federal mandates on welfare recipients. This bill even goes so far as to dictate to states how they must spend their own funds! Many of the new mandates imposed by this legislation concern work requirements. Of course, Mr. Speaker, there is a sound argument for requiring recipients of welfare benefits to work. Among other benefits, a work requirement can help welfare recipients obtain useful job skills and thus increase the likelihood that they will find productive employment. However, forcing welfare recipients to work does raise valid concerns regarding how much control over one's life should be ceded to the government in exchange for government benefits.

In addition, Mr. Speaker, it is highly unlikely that a "one-size-fits-all" approach dictated from Washington will meet the diverse needs of every welfare recipient in every state and locality in the nation. Proponents of this bill claim to support allowing states, localities, and private charities the flexibility to design welfare-to-work programs that fit their particular circumstances. Yet, this proposal constricts the ability of the states to design welfare-to-work programs that meet the unique needs of their citizens. I also question the wisdom of imposing as much as $11 billion in unfunded mandates on the states at a time when many are facing a fiscal crisis.

As former Minnesota Governor Jesse Ventura pointed out in reference to this proposal's effects on Minnesota's welfare-to-work program, "We know what we are doing in Minnesota works. We have evidence. And our way of doing things has broad support in the state. Why should we be forced by the federal government to put our system at risk?" Why indeed, Mr. Speaker, should any state be forced to abandon its individual welfare programs because a group of self-appointed experts in Congress, the federal bureaucracy, and inside-the-beltway think tanks have decided there is only one correct way to transition people from welfare to work?

Mr. Speaker, H.R. 4 further expands the reach of the federal government by authorizing approximately $10 million dollars for new "marriage promotion" programs. I certainly recognize how the welfare state has contributed to the decline of the institution of marriage. As an OB-GYN with over 30 years of private practice. I know better than most the importance of stable, two parent families to a healthy society. However, I am skeptical, to say the least, of claims that government education programs can fix the deep-rooted cultural problems responsible for the decline of the American family.

Furthermore, Mr. Speaker, federal promotion of marriage opens the door for a level of social engineering that should worry all those concerned with preserving a free society. The federal government has no constitutional authority to promote any particular social arrangement; instead, the founders recognized that people are better off when they form their own social arrangements free from federal interference. The history of the failed experiments with welfarism and socialism shows that government can only destroy a culture; when a government tries to build a culture, it only further erodes the people's liberty.

H.R. 4 further raises serious privacy concerns by expanding the use of the "New Hires Database" to allow states to use the database to verify unemployment claims. The New Hires Database contains the name and social security number of everyone lawfully employed in the United States. Increasing the states' ability to identify fraudulent unemployment claims is a worthwhile public policy goal. However, every time Congress authorizes a new use for the New Hires Database it takes a step toward transforming it into a universal national database that can be used by government officials to monitor the lives of American citizens.

As with all proponents of welfare programs, the supporters of H.R. 4 show a remarkable lack of trust in the American people. They would have us believe that without the federal government, the lives of the poor would be "nasty, brutish and short." However, as scholar Sheldon Richman of the Future of Freedom Foundation and others have shown, voluntary charities and organizations, such as friendly societies that devoted themselves to helping those in need, flourished in the days before the welfare state turned charity into a government function.

Today, government welfare programs have supplemented the old-style private programs. One major reason for this is that the policies of high taxes and inflationary Federal Reserve money imposed on the American people in order to finance the welfare state have reduced the income available for charitable giving. Many over-taxed Americans take the attitude toward private charity that "I give at the (tax) office."

Releasing the charitable impulses of the American people by freeing them from the excessive tax burden so they can devote more of their resources to charity is a moral and constitutional means of helping the needy. By contrast, the federal welfare state is neither moral nor constitutional. Nowhere in the Constitution is the federal government given the power to level excessive taxes on one group of citizens for the benefit of another group of citizens. Many of the Founders would have been horrified to see modern politicians define compassion as giving away other people's money stolen through confiscatory taxation. In the words of the famous essay by former Congressman Davy Crockett, this money is "Not Yours to Give."

Voluntary charities also promote self-reliance, but government welfare programs foster dependency. In fact, it is in the self-interest of the bureaucrats and politicians who control the welfare state to encourage dependency. After all, when a private organization moves a person off welfare, the organization has fulfilled its mission and proved its worth to donors. In contrast, when people leave government welfare programs, they have deprived federal bureaucrats of power and of a justification for a larger amount of taxpayer funding.

In conclusion, H.R. 4 furthers federal control over welfare programs by imposing new mandates on the states, which furthers unconstitutional interference in matters best left to state and local governments, and individuals. Therefore, I urge my colleagues to oppose it. Instead, I hope my colleagues will learn the lessons of the failure of the welfare state and embrace a constitutional and compassionate agenda of returning control over the welfare programs to the American people. ▪

Oppose the Spendthrift 2005 Federal Budget Resolution

Congressional Record — U.S. House of Representatives
March 25, 2004

Mr. Speaker, I once again find myself compelled to vote against the annual budget resolution (H. Con. Res. 393) for a very simple reason: it makes government bigger. Like many of my Republican colleagues who curiously voted for today's enormous budget, I campaign on a simple promise that I will work to make government smaller. This means I cannot vote for any budget that increases spending over previous years. In fact, I would have a hard time voting for any budget that did not slash federal spending by at least 25 percent, a feat that becomes less unthinkable when we remember that the federal budget in 1990 was less than half what it is today. Did anyone really think the federal government was uncomfortably small just 14 years ago? Hardly. It once took more than 100 years for the federal budget to double, now it takes less than a decade. We need to end the phony rhetoric about "priorities" and recognize federal spending as the runaway freight train that it is. A federal government that spends $2.4 trillion in one year and consumes roughly one-third of the nation's GDP is far too large.

Neither political party wants to address the fundamental yet unspoken issue lurking beneath any budget debate: What is the proper role for government in our society? Are these ever-growing social services and defense expenditures really proper in a free country? We need to understand that the more government spends, the more freedom is lost. Instead of simply debating spending levels, we ought to be debating whether the departments, agencies, and programs funded by the budget should exist at all. My Republican colleagues especially ought to know this. Unfortunately, however, the GOP has decided to abandon principle and pander to the entitlements crowd. But this approach will backfire, because Democrats will always offer to spend even more than Republicans. When Republicans offer to spend $500 billion on Medicare, Democrats will offer $600 billion. Why not? It's all funny money anyway, and it helps them get reelected.

I object strenuously to the term "baseline budget." In Washington, this means that the previous year's spending levels represent only a baseline starting point. Both parties accept that each new budget will spend more than the last, the only issue being how much more. If Republicans offer a budget that grows federal spending by 3 percent, while Democrats seek 6 percent growth, Republicans trumpet that they are the party of smaller government! But expanding the government slower than some would like is not the same as reducing it.

Furthermore, today's budget debate further entrenches the phony concept of discretionary versus nondiscretionary spending. An increasing percentage of the annual federal budget is categorized as "nondiscretionary" entitlement spending, meaning Congress ostensibly has no choice whether to fund certain programs. In fact, roughly two-thirds of the fiscal year 2005 budget is consumed by nondiscretionary spending. When Congress has no say over how two-thirds of the federal budget is spent, the American people effectively have no say either. Why in the world should the American people be forced to spend $1.5 trillion funding programs that cannot even be reviewed at budget time? The very concept of nondiscretionary spending is a big-government statist's dream, because it assumes that we as a society simply have accepted that most of the federal leviathan must be funded as a matter of course. NO program or agency should be considered sacred, and no funding should be considered inevitable.

The assertion that this budget will reduce taxes is nonsense. Budget bills do not change the tax laws one bit. Congress can pass this budget today and raise taxes tomorrow — budget and tax bills are completely separate and originate from different committees. The budget may make revenue projections based on tax cuts, but the truth is that Congress has no idea what federal revenues will be in any future year. Similarly, the deficit reduction supposedly contained in the budget is illusory. The federal government always spends more in future years than originally projected, and always runs single-year deficits when one factors in raids on funds supposedly earmarked for Social Security. The notion that today's budget will impose fiscal restraint on Congress in the future is laughable—Congress will vote for new budgets every year without the slightest regard for what we do today.

Mr. Speaker, my colleagues have discussed the details of this budget *ad nauseam*. The increases in domestic, foreign, and military spending would not be needed if Congress stopped trying to build an empire abroad and a nanny state at home. Our interventionist foreign policy and growing entitlement society will bankrupt this nation if we do not change the way we think about the proper role of the federal government. ∎

A Token Attempt to Reduce Government Spending

Congressional Record — U.S. House of Representatives
June 24, 2004

Mr. Speaker, I support H.R. 4663, the Spending Control Act of 2004, because I believe those of us concerned about the effects of excessive government spending on American liberty and prosperity should support any effort to rein in spending. However, I hold no great expectations that this bill will result in a new dawn of fiscal responsibility. In fact, since this bill is unlikely to pass the Senate, the main effect of today's vote will be to allow members to brag to their constituents that they voted to keep a lid on spending. Many of these members will not tell their constituents that later this year they will likely vote for a budget busting, pork laden, omnibus spending bill that most members will not even have a chance to read before voting! In fact, last week, many members who I am sure will vote for H.R. 4663 voted against cutting funding for the National Endowment for the Arts (NEA). Last November, many of these same members voted for the greatest expansion of the welfare state since the Great Society. If Congress cannot even bring itself to cut the budget of the NEA or refuse to expand the welfare state, what are the odds that Congress will make the tough choices necessary to restore fiscal order, much less constitutional government?

Even if this bill becomes law, it is likely that the provision in this bill allowing spending for emergency purposes to exceed the bill's spending caps will prove to be an easily abused loophole allowing future Congresses to avoid the spending limitations in this bill. I am also concerned that, by not applying the spending caps to international or military programs, this bill invites future Congresses to misplace priorities, and ignores a major source of fiscal imprudence. Congress will not get our fiscal house in order until we seriously examine our overseas commitments, such as giving welfare to multinational corporations and subsidizing the defense of allies who are perfectly capable of defending themselves.

Congress already has made numerous attempts to restore fiscal discipline, and none of them has succeeded. Even the much-heralded "surpluses" of the nineties were due to the Federal Reserve creating an economic boom and Congress continuing to raid the social security trust fund. The surplus was not caused by a sudden outbreak of fiscal conservatism in Washington, D.C.

The only way Congress will cease excessive spending is by rejecting the idea that the federal government has the authority and the competence to solve all ills, both domestic and international. If the last century taught us anything, it was that big government cannot create utopia. Yet, too many members believe that we can solve all economic problems, eliminate all social ills, and bring about worldwide peace and prosperity by simply creating new federal programs and regulations. However, the well-intended efforts of

Congress have exacerbated America's economic and social problems. Meanwhile our international meddling has failed to create perpetual peace but rather led to perpetual war for perpetual peace.

Every member of Congress has already promised to support limited government by swearing to uphold the United States Constitution. The Constitution limits the federal government to a few, well-defined functions. A good start toward restoring Constitutional government would be debating my Liberty Amendment (H.J.Res. 15). The Liberty Amendment repeals the Sixteenth Amendment, thus eliminating the income tax, the source of much of the growth of government and loss of individual liberty. The Liberty Amendment also explicitly limits the federal government to those functions it is constitutionally authorized to perform.

If Congress were serious about reining in government, it would also eliminate the Federal Reserve Board's ability to inflate the currency. Federal Reserve policy enables excessive government spending by allowing the government to monetize the debt, and hide the cost of big government through the hidden tax of inflation.

In 1974, during debate on the Congressional Budget Reform and Impoundment Control Act, Congressman H.R. Gross, a libertarian-conservative from Iowa, eloquently addressed the flaws in thinking that budget process reform absent the political will to cut spending would reduce the size of government. Mr. Speaker, I would like to conclude my remarks by quoting Mr. Gross:

> Every Member knows that he or she cannot for long spend $75,000 a year on a salary of $42,500 and remain solvent. Every Member knows this government cannot forever spend billions beyond tax revenue and endure.
>
> Congress already has the tools to halt the headlong flight into bankruptcy. It holds the purse strings. No President can impound funds or spend unwisely unless an improvident, reckless Congress makes available the money.
>
> I repeat, neither this nor any other legislation will provide morality and responsibility on the part of Members of Congress. ■

Praising Private Space Exploration

Congressional Record — U.S. House of Representatives
June 25, 2004

Mr. Speaker, I rise to congratulate and commend the designers, builders, sponsors, and pilot of SpaceShipOne on the occasion of its successful flight out of earth's atmosphere on June 21, 2004. What is most remarkable about SpaceShipOne, of course, is that it is the first privately-financed and privately built vehicle to leave the Earth's atmosphere.

SpaceShipOne was designed and built by Burt Rutan and piloted by test pilot Michael W. Melvill. It was launched successfully from Mojave California, reaching a height of 100 km (62 miles) above the Earth's surface. Remarkably, SpaceShipOne is entirely privately-financed, chiefly by Microsoft cofounder Paul G. Allen.

According to the designers and financers of SpaceShipOne, the mission of this project is to demonstrate the viability of commercial space flight and to open the door for private space tourism. The successful completion of SpaceShipOne's maiden voyage demonstrates that relatively modest amounts of private funding can significantly increase the boundaries of commercial space technology. It constitutes a major leap toward their goal and demonstrates that private capital and private enterprise can be applied to enormous success all on its own. Those associated with this project represent the best of our American traditions, embodied in our enterprising and pioneering spirit.

Their success should also be read as a cautionary tale for all of us in government. If only the United States had a taxation policy that limited government and thereby freed up more private capital, there is no telling how many more like Burt Rutan, Paul Allen, and Michael Melvill would be able to do great things to the benefit all of mankind. This not just in space exploration, but in medical research, alternative energy research, and any number of the problems that continue to perplex mankind. Private enterprise depends on results and success and therefore private capital is always targeted much more wisely than are monies confiscated by governments.

With this successful maiden voyage, SpaceShipOne is now the leading contender for the $10 million Ansari X Prize, which is to be awarded to the first privately financed three-seat aircraft that reaches an altitude of 62 miles and repeats the feat within two weeks. I wish all those involved in this remarkable project the best of luck. ■

Government Spending—A Tax on the Middle Class

Congressional Record – U.S. House of Representatives
July 8, 2004

All government spending represents a tax. The inflation tax, while largely ignored, hurts middle-class and low-income Americans the most.

The never-ending political squabble in Congress over taxing the rich, helping the poor, "Pay-Go," deficits, and special interests, ignores the most insidious of all taxes—the inflation tax. Simply put, printing money to pay for federal spending dilutes the value of the dollar, which causes higher prices for goods and services. Inflation may be an indirect tax, but it is very real—the individuals who suffer most from cost of living increases certainly pay a "tax."

Unfortunately no one in Washington, especially those who defend the poor and the middle class, cares about this subject. Instead, all we hear is that tax cuts for the rich are the source of every economic ill in the country. Anyone truly concerned about the middle class suffering from falling real wages, underemployment, a rising cost of living, and a decreasing standard of living should pay a lot more attention to monetary policy. Federal spending, deficits, and Federal Reserve mischief hurt the poor while transferring wealth to the already rich. This is the real problem, and raising taxes on those who produce wealth will only make conditions worse.

This neglect of monetary policy may be out of ignorance, but it may well be deliberate. Fully recognizing the harm caused by printing money to cover budget deficits might create public pressure to restrain spending—something the two parties don't want.

Expanding entitlements is now an accepted prerogative of both parties. Foreign wars and nation building are accepted as foreign policy by both parties.

The Left hardly deserves credit when complaining about Republican deficits. Likewise, we've been told by the vice president that Ronald Reagan "proved deficits don't matter"—a tenet of supply-side economics. With this the prevailing wisdom in Washington, no one should be surprised that spending and deficits are skyrocketing. The vocal concerns expressed about huge deficits coming from big spenders on both sides are nothing more than political grandstanding. If Members feel so strongly about spending, Congress simply could do what it ought to do—cut spending. That, however, is never seriously considered by either side.

If those who say they want to increase taxes to reduce the deficit got their way, who would benefit? No one! There's no historic evidence to show that taxing productive Americans to support both the rich and poor welfare beneficiaries helps the middle class, produces jobs, or stimulates the economy.

Borrowing money to cut the deficit is only marginally better than raising taxes. It may delay the pain for a while, but the cost of government eventually must be paid. Federal borrowing means the cost of interest is added, shifting the burden to a different group than those who benefited and possibly even to another generation. Eventually borrowing is always paid for through taxation.

All spending ultimately must be a tax, even when direct taxes and direct borrowing are avoided. The third option is for the Federal Reserve to create credit to pay the bills Congress runs up.

Nobody objects, and most Members hope that deficits don't really matter if the Fed accommodates Congress by creating more money. Besides, interest payments to the Fed are lower than they would be if funds were borrowed from the public, and payments can be delayed indefinitely merely by creating more credit out of thin air to buy U.S. Treasuries. No need to soak the rich. A good deal, it seems, for everyone. But is it?

Paying for government spending with Federal Reserve credit, instead of taxing or borrowing from the public, is anything but a good deal for everyone. In fact it is the most sinister, seductive "tax" of them all. Initially it is unfair to some, but dangerous to everyone in the end. It is especially harmful to the middle class, including lower-income working people who are thought not to be paying taxes.

The "tax" is paid when prices rise as the result of a depreciating dollar. Savers and those living on fixed or low incomes are hardest hit as the cost of living rises. Low- and middle-income families suffer the most as they struggle to make ends meet while wealth is literally transferred from the middle class to the wealthy. Government officials stick to their claim that no significant inflation exists, even as certain necessary costs are skyrocketing and incomes are stagnating. The transfer of wealth comes as savers and fixed income families lose purchasing power, large banks benefit, and corporations receive plush contracts from the government—as is the case with military contractors. These companies use the newly printed money before it circulates, while the middle class is forced to accept it at face value later on. This becomes a huge hidden tax on the middle class, many of whom never object to government spending in hopes that the political promises will be fulfilled and they will receive some of the goodies. But surprise—it doesn't happen. The result instead is higher prices for prescription drugs, energy, and other necessities. The freebies never come.

The Fed is solely responsible for inflation by creating money out of thin air. It does so either to monetize federal debt, or in the process of economic planning through interest rate manipulation. This Fed intervention in our economy, though rarely even acknowledged by Congress, is more destructive than Members can imagine.

Not only is the Fed directly responsible for inflation and economic downturns, it causes artificially low interest rates that serve the interests of big borrowers, speculators, and banks. This unfairly steals income from frugal retirees who chose to save and place their funds in interest bearing instruments like CDs.

The Fed's great power over the money supply, interest rates, the business cycle, unemployment, and inflation is wielded with essentially no Congressional oversight or understanding. The process of inflating our currency to pay for government debt indeed imposes a tax without legislative authority.

This is no small matter. In just the first 24 weeks of this year the M3 money supply increased $428 billion, and $700 billion in the past year. M3 currently is rising at a rate of 10.5 percent. In the last seven years the money supply has increased 80 percent, as M3 has soared $4.1 trillion. This bizarre system of paper money worldwide has allowed serious international imbalances to develop. We owe just four Asian countries $1.5 trillion as a consequence of a chronic and staggering current account deficit now exceeding 5 percent of our GDP. This current account deficit means Americans must borrow $1.6 billion per day from overseas just to finance this deficit. This imbalance, which until now has permitted us to live beyond our means, eventually will give us higher consumer prices, a lower standard of living, higher interest rates, and renewed inflation.

Rest assured the middle class will suffer disproportionately from this process.

The moral of the story is that spending is always a tax. The inflation tax, though hidden, only makes things worse. Taxing, borrowing, and inflating to satisfy wealth transfers from the middle class to the rich in an effort to pay for profligate government spending, can never make a nation wealthier. But it certainly can make it poorer. ■

Raising the Debt Limit: A Disgrace

Congressional Record – U.S. House of Representatives
November 18, 2004

Mr. Speaker, Congress is once again engaging in fiscal irre-sponsibility and endangering the American economy by raising the debt ceiling, this time by $800 billion. One particularly trou-bling aspect of today's debate is how many members who won their seats in part by pledging never to raise taxes, will now vote for this tax increase on future generations without so much as a second thought. Congress has become like the drunk who prom-ises to sober up tomorrow, if only he can keep drinking today. Does anyone really believe this will be the last time, that Congress will tighten its belt if we just grant it one last loan? What a joke! There is only one approach to dealing with an incorrigible spend-thrift: cut him off.

The term "national debt" really is a misnomer. It is not the nation's debt. Instead, it is the federal government's debt. The American people did not spend the money, but they will have to pay it back.

Most Americans do not spend much time worrying about the national debt, which now totals more than $8 trillion. The number is so staggering that it hardly seems real, even when economists issue bleak warnings about how much every American owes— currently about $25,000. Of course, Congress never hands each tax-payer a bill for that amount. Instead, the federal government uses your hard-earned money to pay interest on this debt, which is like making minimum payments on a credit card. Notice that the prin-cipal never goes down. In fact, it is rising steadily.

The problem is very simple: Congress almost always spends more each year than the IRS collects in revenues. Federal spending always goes up, but revenues are not so dependable, especially since raising income taxes to sufficiently fund the government would be highly unpopular. So long as Congress spends more than the government takes via taxes, the federal government must raise taxes, print more dollars, or borrow money.

Over the last three years, we have witnessed an unprecedented explosion in federal spending. The national debt has actually increased an average of $16 billion a day since September 30, 2003!

Federal law limits the total amount of debt the Treasury can carry. Despite a historic increase in the debt limit in 2002 and another increase in 2003, the current limit of $7.38 trillion was reached last month. So Congress must once again vote to raise the limit. Hard as it may be for the American people to believe, many experts expect government spending will exceed this new limit next year!

Increasing the national debt sends a signal to investors that the government is not serious about reining in spending. This increases the risk that investors will be reluctant to buy government debt instruments. The effects on the American economy could be devastating. The only reason why we have been able to endure such large deficits without skyrocketing interest rates is the willingness of foreign nations to buy the federal government's debt instruments. However, the recent fall in the value of the dollar and rise in the price of gold indicate that investors may be unwilling to continue to prop up our debt-ridden economy. Furthermore, increasing the national debt will provide more incentive for foreign investors to stop buying federal debt instruments at the current interest rates. Mr. Speaker, what will happen to our already fragile economy if the Federal Reserve must raise interest rates to levels unseen since the 1970s to persuade foreigners to buy government debt instruments?

The whole point of the debt ceiling law was to limit borrowing by forcing Congress into an open and presumably somewhat shameful vote when it wants to borrow more than a preset amount of money. Yet, since there have been no political consequences for members who vote to raise the debt limit and support the outrageous spending bills in the first place, the debt limit has become merely another technicality on the road to bankruptcy.

The only way to control federal spending is to take away the government's credit card. Therefore, I call upon my colleagues to reject S. 2986 and, instead, to reduce government spending. It is time Congress forces the federal government to live within its constitutional means. Congress should end the immoral practice of excessive spending and passing the bill to the next generation. ∎

Repeal Sarbanes-Oxley!

Congressional Record — U.S. House of Representatives
April 14, 2005

Mr. Speaker, I rise to introduce the Due Process and Economic Competitiveness Restoration Act, which repeals Section 404 of the Sarbanes-Oxley Act. Sarbanes-Oxley was rushed into law in the hysterical atmosphere surrounding the Enron and WorldCom bankruptcies, by a Congress more concerned with doing something than doing the right thing. Today, American businesses, workers, and investors are suffering because Congress was so eager to appear "tough on corporate crime." Sarbanes-Oxley imposes costly new regulations on the financial services industry. These regulations are damaging American capital markets by providing an incentive for small U.S. firms and foreign firms to deregister from U.S. stock exchanges. According to a study by the prestigious Wharton Business School, the number of American companies deregistering from public stock exchanges nearly tripled during the year after Sarbanes-Oxley became law, while the New York Stock Exchange had only ten new foreign listings in all of 2004.

The reluctance of small businesses and foreign firms to register on American stock exchanges is easily understood when one considers the costs Sarbanes-Oxley imposes on businesses. According to a survey by Kron/Ferry International, Sarbanes-Oxley cost Fortune 500 companies an average of $5.1 million in compliance expenses in 2004, while a study by the law firm of Foley and Lardner found the Act increased costs associated with being a publicly held company by 130 percent.

Many of the major problems stem from Section 404 of Sarbanes-Oxley, which requires Chief Executive Officers to certify the accuracy of financial statements. It also requires that outside auditors "attest to" the soundness of the internal controls used in preparing the statements—an obvious sop to auditors and accounting firms. The Public Company Accounting Oversight Board defines internal controls as "controls over all significant accounts and disclosures in the financial statements." According to John Berlau, a Warren Brookes Fellow at the Competitive Enterprise Institute, the definition of internal controls is so broad that a CEO possibly could be found liable for not using the latest version of Windows! Financial analysts have identified Section 404 as the major reason why American corporations are hoarding cash instead of investing it in new ventures.

Journalist Robert Novak, in his column of April 7, said that,

> [f]or more than a year, CEOs and CFOs have been telling me that 404 is a costly nightmare [and] . . . ask nearly any business executive to name the biggest menace facing corporate America, and the answer is apt to be number 404 . . . a dagger aimed at the heart of the economy.

Compounding the damage done to the economy is the harm Sarbanes-Oxley does to constitutional liberties and due process. CEOs and CFOs can be held criminally liable, and subjected to 25 years in prison, for inadvertent errors. Laws criminalizing honest mistakes done with no intent to defraud are more typical of police states than free societies. I hope those who consider themselves civil libertarians will recognize the danger of imprisoning citizens for inadvertent mistakes, put aside any prejudice against private businesses, and join my efforts to repeal Section 404.

The U.S. Constitution does not give the federal government authority to regulate the accounting standards of private corporations. These questions should be resolved by private contracts between a company and its shareholders, and by state and local regulations. Let me remind my colleagues who are skeptical of the ability of markets and local law enforcement to protect against fraud: the market passed judgment on Enron, in the form of declining stock prices, before Congress even held the first hearing on the matter. My colleagues also should keep in mind that certain state attorneys general have been very aggressive in prosecuting financial crimes.

Section 404 of the Sarbanes-Oxley Act has raised the costs of doing business, thus causing foreign companies to withdraw from American markets and retarding economic growth. By criminalizing inadvertent mistakes and exceeding congressional authority, Section 404 also undermines the rule of law and individual liberty. I therefore urge my colleagues to cosponsor the Due Process and Economic Competitiveness Restoration Act. ∎

The Republican Congress Wastes Billions Overseas

Congressional Record – U.S. House of Representatives
July 20, 2005

Mr. Speaker, I rise in strong opposition to this foreign relations authorization bill. Something has gone terribly wrong with our foreign policy when we feel we must take almost $21 billion out of the pockets of the American taxpayer and ship it overseas. Imagine what the Founders of this country would say if they were among us to see this blatant disregard for the Constitution and for the founding principles of this country. This bill proceeds from the view that with enough money we can buy friends and influence foreign governments. But as history shows us, we cannot. The trillions of dollars we have shipped overseas as aid, and to influence and manipulate political affairs in sovereign countries, has not made life better for American citizens. It has made them much poorer without much to show for it, however.

Now we have a Republican-controlled Congress and White House, and foreign spending soars. It was not that long ago when conservatives looked at such cavalier handling of U.S. tax dollars with consternation. Now it seems that they are in a race with the Left to see who can spend more.

What is wrong with this bill? Let me just mention a few of the most egregious items. In the name of promoting "religious liberty" and "fighting anti-Semitism" this bill will funnel millions of dollars to the corrupt Organization for Security and Cooperation in Europe (OSCE) and its Office of Democratic Institutions and Human Rights (ODIHR). This unaccountable international organization is at the forefront of the manipulation and meddling in the internal affairs of other sovereign states, and has repeatedly dishonored itself through politically-biased monitoring of foreign elections. The OSCE does not deserve a penny from the American taxpayer, but this bill will make sure that the lavishly paid bureaucrats that staff the organization will be able to maintain their standard of living—at our expense. With regard to religious liberty, privately funded voluntary organizations have been shown to be much more effective in promoting tolerance. This is mainly true because these are true grassroots organizations with a stake in their countries and communities, rather than unelected international bureaucrats imposing politically correct edicts from above.

This bill spends a total of $4.5 billion on various United Nations activities, UN peacekeeping, and U.S. dues to various international organizations. Forcing the taxpayer to continue to underwrite these organizations, which do not operate in our best interests, is unconscionable.

This bill continues to fund organizations such as the National Endowment for Democracy, which as I have written before has very little to do with democracy. It is an organization that uses U.S. tax money to actually subvert democracy, by showering funding on favored political parties or movements overseas. It underwrites color-coded "people's revolutions" overseas that look more like pages out of Lenin's writings on stealing power than genuine indigenous democratic movements. The NED used American taxpayer dollars to attempt to guarantee that certain candidates overseas are winners and others are losers in the electoral processes overseas. What kind of message do we think this sends to foreign states? The National Endowment for Democracy should receive no funding at all, but this bill continues to funnel tens of millions of dollars to that unaccountable organization.

I am also very concerned about several of the amendments to this legislation. First, the extremely misleading UN "reform" act was slipped into this bill even though it was already passed on the floor as a separate bill. As I have written about this terrible legislation, "it will give the United Nations unprecedented new authority to intervene in sovereign states."

Another amendment will create a chilling "Active Response Corps," to be made up of U.S. government bureaucrats and members of "nongovernmental organizations." Its purpose will be to "stabilize" countries undergoing "democratic transition." This means that as soon as the NED-funded "people's revolutionaries" are able to seize power in the streets, U.S. funded teams will be deployed to make sure they retain power. All in the name of democracy, of course.

Mr. Speaker, this is a shameful day for the U.S. Congress. We are taking billions out of the pockets of Americans and sending the money overseas in violation of the Constitution. These are billions that will not be available for investment inside the United States: investment in infrastructure, roads, new businesses, education. These are billions that will not be available to American families, to take care of their children or senior relatives, or to give to their churches or favorite charities. We must not continue to spend money like there is no tomorrow. We are going broke, and bills like this are like a lead foot on the accelerator toward bankruptcy. ∎

So-Called "Deficit Reduction Act"

Congressional Record – U.S. House of Representatives
November 18, 2005

Mr. Speaker, as one who has long urged my colleagues to cut spending, and who has consistently voted against excessive and unconstitutional expenditures, I am sure many in this body expect me to be an enthusiastic supporter of H.R. 4241, the Deficit Reduction Act. After all, supporters of this bill are claiming it dramatically reforms federal programs and puts Congress back on the road to fiscal responsibility.

For all the passionate debate this bill has generated, its effects on the federal government and taxpayers are relatively minor. H.R. 4241 does not even reduce federal expenditures! That's right—if H.R. 4241 passes, the federal budget, including entitlement programs, will continue to grow. H.R. 4241 simply slows down the rate of growth of federal spending. The federal government may spend less in the future if this bill passes than it otherwise would, but it will still spend more than it does today. To put H.R. 4241 in perspective, consider that this bill reduces spending by less than $50 billion over ten years, while the most recent "emergency" supplemental passed by this Congress appropriated $82 billion to be spent this year.

H.R. 4241 reduces total federal entitlement expenditures by one half of 1 percent over the next five years. For all the trumpeting about how this bill gets "runaway entitlement spending" under control, H.R. 4241 fails to deal with the biggest entitlement problem facing our nation—the multibillion dollar Medicare prescription drug plan, which actually will harm many seniors by causing them to lose their private coverage, forcing them into an inferior government-run program. In fact, the Medicare prescription drug plan will cost $55 billion in fiscal year 2006 alone, while H.R. 4241 will reduce spending by only $5 billion next year. Yet some House members who voted for every expansion of the federal government considered by this Congress will vote for these small reductions in spending and then brag about their fiscal conservatism to their constituents.

As is common with bills claiming to reduce spending, the majority of spending reductions occur in the later years of the plan. Since it is impossible to bind future Congresses, this represents little more than a suggestion that spending in fiscal years 2009 and 2010 reflect the levels stated in this bill. My fiscally responsible colleagues should keep in mind that rarely, if ever, does a Congress actually follow through on spending reductions set by a previous Congress. Thus, relying on future Congresses to cut spending in the "out years" is a recipe for failure.

One provision of the bill that undeniably would have benefited the American people, the language opening up the ANWR region of Alaska and expanding offshore drilling, was removed from the bill. As my colleagues know, increased gas prices are a top concern of the American people. Expanding the supply of domestically produced oil is an obvious way to address these concerns, yet Congress refuses to take this reasonable step.

Mr. Speaker, some of the entitlement reforms in H.R. 4241 are worthwhile. For example, I am hopeful the provision allowing states to require a co-payment for Medicaid will help relieve physicians of the burden of providing uncompensated care, which is an issue of great concern to physicians in my district. Still, I am concerned that the changes in pharmaceutical reimbursement proposed by the bill may unfairly impact independent pharmacies, and I am disappointed we will not get to vote on an alternative that would have the same budgetary impact without harming independent pharmacies.

I also question the priorities of singling out programs, such as Medicaid and food stamps, that benefit the neediest Americans, while continuing to increase spending on corporate welfare and foreign aid. Just two weeks ago, Congress passed a bill sending $21 billion overseas. That is $21 billion that will be spent this fiscal year, not spread out over five years. Then, last week, Congress passed, on suspension of the rules, a bill proposing to spend $130 million on water projects—not in Texas, but in foreign nations! Meanwhile, the Financial Services Committee, on which I sit, has begun the process of reauthorizing the Export-Import Bank, which uses taxpayer money to support business projects that cannot attract capital in the market. Mr. Speaker, the Export-Import Bank's biggest beneficiaries are Boeing and communist China. I find it hard to believe that federal funding for Fortune 500 companies and China is a higher priority for most Americans than Medicaid and food stamps.

H.R. 4241 fails to address the root of the spending problem— the belief that Congress can solve any problem simply by creating a new federal program or agency. However, with the federal government's unfunded liabilities projected to reach as much as $50 trillion by the end of this year, Congress no longer can avoid serious efforts to rein in spending. Instead of the smoke-and-mirrors approach of H.R. 4241, Congress should begin the journey toward fiscal responsibility by declaring a 10 percent reduction in real spending, followed by a renewed commitment to reduce spending in a manner consistent with our obligation to uphold the Constitution and the priorities of the American people. This is the only way to make real progress on reducing spending without cutting programs for the poor while increasing funding for programs that benefit foreign governments and corporate interests. ∎

What Congress Can Do About Soaring Gas Prices

Congressional Record — U.S. House of Representatives
May 2, 2006

Gasoline prices are soaring and the people are screaming. And they want something done about it — now!

$100 rebate checks to American motorists won't cut it, nor will mandatory mileage requirements for new vehicles. Taxing oil profits will only force prices higher. But there are some very important things we can do immediately to help.

First: We must reassess our foreign policy and announce some changes. One of the reasons we went into Iraq was to secure "our" oil. Before the Iraq war oil was less than $30 per barrel; today it is over $70. The sooner we get out of Iraq and allow the Iraqis to solve their own problems the better. Since 2002 oil production in Iraq has dropped 50 percent. Pipeline sabotage and fires are routine; we have been unable to prevent them. Soaring gasoline prices are a giant unintended consequence of our invasion, pure and simple.

Second: We must end our obsession for a military confrontation with Iran. Iran does not have a nuclear weapon, and according to our own CIA is not on the verge of obtaining one for years. Iran is not in violation of the Nuclear Nonproliferation Treaty, and has a guaranteed right to enrich uranium for energy—in spite of the incessant government and media propaganda to the contrary. Iran has never been sanctioned by the UN Security Council. Yet the drumbeat grows louder for attacking certain sites in Iran, either by conventional or even nuclear means. Repeated resolutions by Congress stir up unnecessary animosity toward Iran, and create even more concern about future oil supplies from the Middle East. We must quickly announce we do not seek war with Iran, remove the economic sanctions against her, and accept her offer to negotiate a diplomatic solution to the impasse. An attack on Iran, coupled with our continued presence in Iraq, could hike gas prices to $5 or $6 per gallon here at home. By contrast, a sensible approach toward Iran could quickly lower oil prices by $20 per barrel.

Third: We must remember that prices of all things go up because of inflation. Inflation by definition is an increase in the money supply. The money supply is controlled by the Federal Reserve, and responds to the deficits Congress creates. When deficits are excessive, as they are today, the Fed creates new dollars out of thin air to buy Treasury bills and keep interest rates artificially low. But when new money is created out of nothing, the money already in circulation loses value. Once this is recognized, prices rise—some more rapidly than others. That's what we see today with the cost of energy.

Exploding deficits, due to runaway entitlement spending and the cost of dangerous militarism, create pressure for the Fed to inflate the money supply. This contributes greatly to the higher prices we all claim to oppose.

If we want to do something about gas prices, we should demand and vote for greatly reduced welfare and military spending, a balanced budget, and fewer regulations that interfere with the market development of alternative fuels. We also should demand a return to a sound commodity monetary system.

All subsidies and special benefits to energy companies should be ended. And in the meantime let's eliminate federal gas taxes at the pump.

Oil prices are at a level where consumers reduce consumption voluntarily. The market will work if we let it. But as great as the market economy is, it cannot overcome a foreign policy that is destined to disrupt oil supplies and threaten the world with an expanded and dangerous conflict in the Middle East. ■

Executive Compensation

Congressional Record — U.S. House of Representatives
April 18, 2007

Madam Speaker, H.R. 1257 gives the Securities and Exchange Commission (SEC) the power to force publicly traded corporations to conduct shareholder votes on nonbinding resolutions concerning the compensation packages of Chief Executive Officers (CEOs). Giving the SEC the power to require shareholder votes on any aspect of corporate governance — even on something as seemingly inconsequential as a nonbinding resolution — illegitimately expands federal authority into questions of private governance.

In a free market, shareholders who are concerned about CEO compensation are free to refuse to invest in corporations that do not provide sufficient information regarding how CEO salaries are set or do not allow shareholders a say in setting compensation packages.

Since shareholders are a corporation's owners, the CEO and board of directors have a great incentive to respond to shareholders' demands.

In fact, several corporations have recently moved to amend the ways they determine executive compensation in order to provide increased transparency and accountability to shareholders.

Some shareholders may not care about a CEO's compensation package; instead they may want to devote time at shareholders' meetings to reviewing corporate environmental policies or ensuring the corporation has "family-friendly" workforce policies. If H.R. 1257 becomes law, the concerns of those shareholders will take a backseat to corporations' attempts to meet the demands of Congress.

It is ironic that Congress would concern itself with high salaries in the private sector when, according to data collected by the CATO Institute, federal employees, on average, make twice as much as their private sector counterparts. One of the examples of excessive compensation cited by the supporters of the bill is the multi-million dollar package paid to the former CEO of Freddie Mac. As a government sponsored enterprise that, along with its counterpart Fannie Mae, received almost $20 billion worth of indirect federal subsidies in fiscal year 2004 alone, Freddie Mac is hardly a poster child for the free market!

Past government actions have made it more difficult for shareholders to hold CEOs and boards of directors accountable for disregarding shareholder interests by, among other things, wasting corporate resources on compensation packages and golden parachutes unrelated to performance. During the 1980s, so-called corporate raiders helped keep corporate management accountable to shareholders through devices such as "junk" bonds that made corporate takeovers easier.

The backlash against corporate raiders included the enactment of laws that made it more difficult to launch hostile takeovers. Bruce Bartlett, writing in the *Washington Times* in 2001, commented on the effects of these laws,

> Without the threat of a takeover, managers have been able to go back to ignoring shareholders, treating them like a nuisance, and giving themselves bloated salaries and perks, with little oversight from corporate boards. Now insulated from shareholders once again, managers could engage in unsound practices with little fear of punishment for failure.

The federal "crackdown" on corporate raiders, combined with provisions in Sarbanes-Oxley disqualifying the people who are the most capable of serving as shareholder watchdogs from serving on corporate boards, contributed to the disconnect between CEO salaries and creation of shareholder value that is being used to justify another expansion of the regulatory state.

In addition to repealing laws that prevent shareholders from exercising control over corporations, Congress should also examine United States monetary policy's effects on income inequality. When the Federal Reserve Board injects credit into the economy, the result is at least a temporary rise in incomes. However, those incomes do not rise equally. People who first receive the new credit — who in most instances are those already at the top of the economic pyramid — receive the most benefit from the Fed's inflationist policies.

By the time those at the lower end of the income scale experience a nominal rise in incomes, they must also contend with price inflation that has eroded their standard of living. Except for the lucky few who take advantage of the new credit first, the negative effects of inflation likely more than outweigh any temporary gains in nominal income from the Federal Reserve's expansionist policies.

For evidence of who really benefits from a system of fiat money and inflation, consider that in 1971, before President Nixon severed the last link of the American currency to gold, the typical CEO's salary was 30 times higher than the average wage of the typical employee; today it is 500 times higher.

Explosions in CEO salaries can be a sign of a federal credit bubble, which occurs when Federal Reserve Board-created credit flows into certain sectors such as the stock market or the housing market. Far from being a sign of the health of capitalism, excessive CEO salaries in these areas often signal that a bubble is about to burst. When a bubble bursts, people at the bottom of the economic ladder bear the brunt of the bust.

Instead of imposing new laws on private companies, Congress should repeal the laws that have weakened the ability of shareholders to discipline CEOs and boards of directors that do not run corporations according to the shareholders' wishes. Congress should also examine how fiat money contributes to income inequality. I therefore request that my colleagues join me in opposing H.R. 1257 and instead embrace a pro-freedom, pro-shareholder, and pro-worker agenda of free markets and sound money. ∎

Glossary of Acronyms

AIDS – acquired immune deficiency syndrome
AIER – American Institute for Economic Research
ANWR – Arctic National Wildlife Refuge
AsDF – Asian Development Fund
AWAC – Airborne Warning Control
CAFTA – Central American Free Trade Agreement
CAT – computed axial tomography scan
CBO – Congressional Budget Office
CD – certificate of deposit
CEO – chief executive officer
CFO – chief financial officer
CIA – Central Intelligence Agency
CMRA – Commercial Mail Receiving Agencies
CPI – Consumer Price index
CRB – Commodity Research Bureau
CRS – Congressional Research Service
DOD – Department of Defense
ECU – European currency unit
EU – European Union
Eximbank – Export-Import Bank
Fannie Mae – Federal National Mortgage Association
FARC – Revolutionary Armed Forces of Columbia
FDA – Food and Drug Administration
FDIC – Federal Deposit Insurance Corporation
FinCeN – Financial Crimes Enforcement Network

FOMC – Federal Open Market Committee
Freddie Mac – Federal Home Loan Mortgage Corporation
GAO – General Accounting Office
GATT – General Agreement on Tariffs and Trade
GDP – Gross Domestic Product
GOP – Republication Party
GSE – Government Sponsored Enterprise
HHS – Health and Human Services
HOPE – Home Office Protection Enhancement
HUD – Housing and Urban Development
IFAD – International Fund for Agricultural Development
IMF – International Monetary Fund
IRS – Internal Revenue Service
LBJ – President Lyndon Baines Johnson
M1 – U.S. money supply: cash and checking account deposits
M2 – U.S. money supply: M1 plus savings accounts, money
     market accounts, and small denomination time deposits
     (CDs under $100,000)
M3 – U.S. money supply: M2 + CDs, deposits of Eurodollars,
     and repurchase agreements
MCA – Millennium Challenge Account
MeK – Mujahadeen-e-Khalq, Iranian rebel group
MRI – magnetic resonance imaging
MZM – money of zero maturity
NAEP – National Assessment of Education Progress
NAFTA – North American Free Trade Association
NASDAQ – stock market
NATO – North Atlantic Treaty Organization
NEA – National Endowment for the Arts
NED – National Endowment for Democracy
NLRA – National Labor Relations Act
NLRB – National Labor Relations Board
NTB – Non-Tariff Trade Barrier
NTR – normal trade relations
OB-GYN – doctor of obstetrics and gynecology
ODIHR – Office of Democratic Institutions and Human Rights
OECD – Organization of Economic Cooperation and Development

OPEC – Organization of Petroleum Exporting Countries
OPIC – Overseas Private Investment Corporation
OSCE – Organization for Security and Cooperation in Europe
OSHA – Occupational Safety and Health Administration
PE – price to earnings
PNTR – permanent normal trade relations
PPI – Producer Price Index
SAT – Scholastic Aptitude Test
SDR – special drawing right
SEC – Securities and Exchange Commission
TANF – Temporary Assistance to Needy Families
TED – turtle excluder device
TDA – Trade and Development Agency
TPA – Trade Promotion Authority
UN – United Nations
USDA – U.S. Department of Agriculture
WAGE – Workers Access to Accountable Governance in
        Employment
WMD – weapons of mass destruction
WTO – World Trade Organization
FY – fiscal year
Y2K – the year 2000

Index